Irenaeus and Genesis

Journal of Theological Interpretation Supplements
MURRAY RAE
University of Otago, New Zealand
Editor-in-Chief

1. Thomas Holsinger-Friesen, *Irenaeus and Genesis: A Study of Competition in Early Christian Hermeneutics*
2. Douglas Earl, *Reading Joshua as Christian Scripture*

Irenaeus and Genesis
A Study of Competition in Early Christian Hermeneutics

THOMAS HOLSINGER-FRIESEN

Winona Lake, Indiana
EISENBRAUNS
2009

Copyright © 2009 Eisenbrauns
All rights reserved.

Printed in the United States of America

www.eisenbrauns.com

Library of Congress Cataloging-in-Publication Data

Holsinger-Friesen, Thomas.
   Irenaeus and Genesis : a study of competition in early Christian hermeneutics / Thomas Holsinger-Friesen.
      p. cm. — (Journal of theological interpretation supplements ; v. 1)
   Includes bibliographical references and index.
   ISBN 978-1-57506-700-1 (pbk. : alk. paper)
   1. Irenaeus, Saint, Bishop of Lyon. 2. Bible—Criticism, interpretation, etc.—History. 3. Bible. O.T. Genesis—Criticism, interpretation, etc.
   I. Title.
   BR1720.I7H65 2009
   220.6092—dc22
                                                                 2009012304

The paper used in this publication meets the minimum requirements of the American National Standard for Information Sciences—Permanence of Paper for Printed Library Materials, ANSI Z39.48-1984.♾™

To Sarah, whose constant love has been a gift more precious than words can say...

With deep gratitude to Gerald and Jean for their life-long encouragement...

Many thanks to Francis, as well as Jim and Barbara, for their valued help...

Noting my indebtedness to Bob, whose presence is dearly missed...

In appreciation of the very generous support of "A Foundation for Theological Education," the Asbury Foundation of Asbury Theological Seminary, and the Overseas Research Students Awards Scheme (UK)...

Your kindness has made this work possible.

TABLE OF CONTENTS

INTRODUCTION IX

ABBREVIATIONS XII
   1. ANCIENT TEXTS XII
   2. MODERN PERIODICALS, REFERENCE WORKS AND SERIALS XIII

1. GENESIS: RECAPITULATION AND PROTOLOGICAL PERSPECTIVE 1
   RECAPITULATION: THE KEY TO IRENAEUS' THEOLOGY? 1
      Recapitulation "speculation": Harnack's influential proposal 3
      Recapitulation "reclamation": Harnack on the defensive 7
      Recapitulation "inflation": an assessment 18
   IRENAEUS REVISITED: RECAPITULATION, HERMENEUTICS, AND GEN 1-2 26
      Recapitulation "limitation" 27
      Hermeneutics: Genesis 1-2 and Irenaeus' protological orientation 30
      Focal Texts? Mapping the road ahead 33

2. COMPETITION: GNOSTIC INTERPRETATIONS OF GENESIS 42
   INTRODUCTION AND METHODOLOGY 42
      Why rely upon Irenaeus' account of Gnostic interpretations of Genesis? 43
      Why include the Ophite interpretation of Genesis 1-3? 51
   VALENTINIANS AND OPHITES AS READERS OF GENESIS 56
      Gnostic hermeneutics in practice: Ophite readings of Genesis 1-3 57
      Gnostic hermeneutics in practice: Valentinian readings of Genesis 1-3 .. 75
   ASSESSING GNOSTIC READINGS OF GENESIS 98
      Generalizing and refiguring 99
      The Valentinians and Genesis 101

3. GENESIS 1.26 AND THE DIVINE ECONOMY 104
   INVESTIGATING IRENAEUS: CHOOSING OUR PATH 104
      Irenaeus the exegete? 106
      Methodology and theology 107
   GENESIS 1.26: HUMANITY MADE ACCORDING TO GOD'S IMAGE AND LIKENESS 109
      Using Genesis 1.26: The original human constitution 111
      Using Genesis 1.26: Human fallenness and restoration 120
      Using Genesis 1.26: Human eschatological destiny 132
   CONCLUSION 142

4. GENESIS 2.7 AND THE *HOMO VIVENS* 145

INTRODUCTION 145
   Irenaeus' "roadmap" for Christian anthropology 147
   Previewing Irenaeus' anthropological debate 155
THE FATHER AND THE *HOMO VIVENS* (*HAER*. V.3-8) 157
   Gnostic visions of creator in Genesis 2.7 158
   Irenaeus' vision of "Father" in Genesis 2.7 159
THE SPIRIT AND THE *HOMO VIVENS* (*HAER*. V.9-12) 164
   The Spirit and human potential 166
   The Triumph of the Spirit 168
CHRIST AND THE *HOMO VIVENS* (*HAER*. V.13-16) 174
   Transition: From one divine hand to another 175
   Using Genesis 2.7: Recapitulation (Haer. v.14) 178
   Using Genesis 2.7: Revelation (Haer. v.15.1-3) 191
   Christ-speech summarized (Haer. v.15.4-16.2) 210
"SUMMING UP": IRENAEUS' EXPLOITS WITH GENESIS 2.7 AND 1.26 214

CONCLUSION 218

METHODOLOGY 219
PROTOLOGICAL ORIENTATION 222
ANTHROPOLOGY 225

BIBLIOGRAPHY 230

1. TEXTS AND TRANSLATIONS: IRENAEUS 230
2. OTHER ANCIENT TEXTS AND TRANSLATIONS 231
3. GENERAL BIBLIOGRAPHY 233

AUTHOR INDEX 243

SCRIPTURE INDEX 247

INTRODUCTION

If it is reasonable to describe Irenaeus, the second-century bishop of Lyons, as "theology's founding father,"[1] we might naturally seek to isolate and assess his unique achievements. Commonly, scholars attribute Irenaeus' renown to certain landmark theological concepts and doctrines. Primary examples are his formulation of the *regula fidei* (or "rule of faith") and his doctrine of recapitulation. Arguably, recapitulation – the definitive "summing up" of human destiny in the person and work of Christ – is the "key to Irenaeus's understanding of the divine economy."[2] Unfortunately, most Irenaean scholars have treated recapitulation essentially as a concept to be probed and delimited. According to one well-respected commentator, this complex concept is best understood as the combination and permutation of "at least eleven ideas" (e.g., "unification," "repetition," "redemption").[3] Such an exclusive conceptual focus, though, tends to overshadow Irenaeus' truly innovative manner of reading sacred texts together as Christian Scripture. Robert Louis Wilken offers a wise corrective in this regard when he claims that, generally speaking, "the study of early Christian thought has been too preoccupied with ideas."[4] "Early Christian thought is biblical," he observes, "and one of the lasting accomplishments of the patristic period was to forge a way of thinking, scriptural in language and inspiration, that gave to the church and to Western civilization a unified and coherent interpretation of the Bible as a whole."[5] In the words of O'Keefe and Reno, then, we might envision a "vast ocean of biblical sensibility upon which all the particular forms of patristic thought and practice floats."[6]

Our particular attention will be on Irenaeus' interpretation and use of Genesis creation texts, given that these texts were pivotal battlegrounds in the early struggle to identify ecclesial boundaries. Both Irenaeus and his Gnostic-Christian opponents were drawn to these foundational texts and acknowledged their inherent authority. The fact that subsequent generations found Irenaeus' vision of God's activity and human destiny to be compelling owes as much to his unique hermeneutical decisions as to his distinctive ideas. Though we

---

[1] Hans Urs von Balthasar, The Scandal of the Incarnation: Irenaeus Against the Heresies (trans. John Saward; San Francisco: Ignatius Press, 1988), 8.
[2] Peter C. Bouteneff, *Beginnings* (Grand Rapids: Baker Academic, 2008), 78.
[3] Eric Osborn, *Irenaeus of Lyons* (Cambridge: Cambridge University Press, 2001), 97-98.
[4] Robert Louis Wilken, *The Spirit of Early Christian Thought* (New Haven: Yale University Press, 2003), xiv.
[5] Wilken, *The Spirit of Early Christian Thought*, xvii.
[6] John J. O'Keefe and R. R. Reno, *Sanctified Vision: An Introduction to Early Christian Interpretation of the Bible* (Baltimore: The Johns Hopkins University Press, 2005), 4.

highlight the way these biblical texts function[7] in Irenaeus' theological construction, this focus ought not to be construed as endorsing a purely utilitarian understanding of biblical interpretation. Irenaeus' avowed intent is to explicate biblical truth claims about God and humanity. If, as we imply, this activity is inseparably linked with the instrumental use of Scripture, one need not adopt a cynical view of Irenaeus. Such a realistic appraisal in no way erodes Irenaeus' credibility, for (to anticipate an argument we shall address more fully in chapter two) we may "sustain the point that the battle of truth is always at the same time a battle of or for power without reducing truth to power."[8] It is, of course, possible that Irenaeus is being disingenuous or naïve when he insists that his biblical interpretations are patently and exclusively correct. However, our goal is to listen to both Irenaeus *and* his competitors sympathetically and on their own terms. In this process, we shall try to explain why Irenaeus' biblical interpretations ultimately proved to be the ones deemed more plausible and fruitful within the mainstream of the church.

In our first chapter, we make the case that predominant ways of evaluating Irenaeus' work are, at best, incomplete. Scholarship in the wake of Adolf von Harnack has tended to inflate Irenaeus' notion of recapitulation without proper warrant. A more modest approach to recapitulation illuminates the primary context of this term: Irenaeus' predilection for matters of origin and his corresponding use of Genesis creation texts to make theological claims. To better understand the crucible of hermeneutic competition in the second-century church, our second chapter surveys his opponents. With an eye toward methods of interpretation, we detail and assess Valentinian readings of Genesis, as well as the dramatic interpretations of the "Ophites" which may have exerted a contributory influence. Chapters three and four examine Irenaeus' own theological uses of Genesis, particularly of two focal texts, Genesis 1.26 and 2.7. For Irenaeus, the *imago Dei* motif was well-suited for elaborating a comprehensive vision of God's economy because it could be used flexibly to locate humanity inside its span: from human origination, through fall and restoration, to eschatological destiny. The "breath of life" text was found conducive for exceptionally wide typological readings. By using it to paint a portrait of God, Irenaeus also aims to supply a more satisfying anthropological sketch than the Valentinians can offer. The purposeful work of the Father, through his two hands (Son and Spirit), will present the human creation as fully alive – in body no less than soul.

---

[7] For example, we shall, at times, refer to Irenaeus' use of a biblical text (e.g., Genesis 1.26 or 2.7) as a "tool."
[8] Cyril O'Regan, *Gnostic Return in Modernity* (Albany, NY: State University of New York Press, 2001), 16.

As contemporary life becomes increasingly shaped by postmodern tendencies, such as "mystery, holism, and interpreted [rather than 'brute'] fact," the church today also finds itself in a season of transition.[9] In its classical tradition, Robert Webber finds particularly relevant resources:

> The theology of the ancient church was characterized by mystery, a holism that rejected all dualistic structures of thought and the interpretation of the Christ-fact. The understanding of God and God's relationship to the world in creation, incarnation, and re-creation, was hammered out in the framework of a commitment to a God who participates in history and works out the salvation of the entire cosmos from within the created order. This holistic understanding of God and creation as the central mystery of the Christian faith holds the greatest potential for an intelligent recovery of classical Christianity in a postmodern world.[10]

We cannot simply turn the clock backward, ignoring the significant discontinuities between Irenaeus' world and ours. Modern-era scholarship has, in fact, yielded much-needed insight in the areas of biblical studies and historical theology. Yet both within and without the walls of the church, we find an increasing thirst for holism. Does the Christian faith speak credibly about "physical" issues related to, for example, bodies, politics, economics, and the environment as well as it speaks about the soul and life after death? Irenaeus' bold declaration of God's comprehensive work helps to address such questions. By exploring his hermeneutical strategies and critically weighing their results, we may be reminded of the rich resources that are available to the church as it undertakes its mission in the twenty-first century.

---

[9] Robert E. Webber, *Ancient-Future Faith: Rethinking Evangelicalism for a Postmodern World* (Grand Rapids: Baker, 1999), 22.
[10] Ibid.

ABBREVIATIONS

1. Ancient Texts

An.	Tertullian, *The Soul*
Ap. John	*Apocryphon of John*
Autol.	Theophilus, *To Autolycus*
Barn.	*Barnabas*
Cels.	Origen, *Against Celsu*
Conf.	Augustine, *Confessions*
Confusion	Philo, *On the Confusion of Tongues*
Dial.	Justin, *Dialogue with Trypho*
Diogn.	*Diognetus*
Epid.	Irenaeus, *Demonstration of the Apostolic Preaching*
Exc.	Ambrose, *De excessu fratris sui Satyri*
Flor.	Ptolemy, *Letter to Flora*
Gen. Rab.	*Genesis Rabba*
Gos. Phil.	*Gospel of Philip*
Gos. Truth	*Gospel of Truth*
Haer.	Irenaeus, *Adversus Haereses*
Hist. eccl.	Eusebius, *Ecclesiastical History*
Ign. Magn.	Ignatius, *To the Magnesians*
Ign. Smyrn.	Ignatius, *To the Smyrnaeans*

Inc.	Athanasius, *On the Incarnation*
Marc.	Tertullian, *Against Marcion*
Opif.	Philo, *On the Creation of the World*
Paed.	Clement of Alexandria, *Christ the Educator*
Pan.	Epiphanius, *Refutation of All Heresies*
QG	Philo, *Questions and Answers on Genesis*
Res.	Tertullian, *De resurrectione carnis*
Strom.	Clement of Alexandria, *Miscellanies*
Val.	Tertullian, *Against the Valentinians*

2. Modern Periodicals, Reference Works and Serials

ACW	*Ancient Christian Writers*
ANF	*Ante-Nicene Fathers*
ATR	*Anglican Theological Review*
BAGD	Bauer, W., F. W. Danker, W. F. Arndt, and F. W. Gingrich. *Greek-English Lexicon of the New Testament and Other Early Christian Literature.* 3d ed. Chicago, 1999
CCSL	Corpus Christianorum: Series latina. Turnhout, 1953-
Dom. St.	*Dominican Studies*
GOTR	*Greek Orthodox Theological Review*
HTR	*Harvard Theological Review*
IJST	*International Journal of Systematic Theology*
JECS	*Journal of Early Christian Studies*
JJS	*Journal of Jewish Studies*

JTS	*Journal of Theological Studies*
L&N	*Greek-English Lexicon of the New Testament: Based on Semantic Domains.* Edited by J. P. Louw and E. A. Nida. 2d ed. New York, 1989
LCL	Loeb Classical Library
NHC	*Nag Hammadi Codices*
NHL	*Nag Hammadi Library in English.* Edited by J. M. Robinson. Leiden, 1977.
NHS	Nag Hammadi Studies
NRTh	*Nouvelle revue théologique*
OECT	Oxford Early Christian Texts. Edited by H. Chadwick. Oxford, 1970-
PG	Patrologia graeca. Edited by J.-P. Migne. 162 vols. Paris, 1857-1886
PL	Patrologia latina. Edited by J.-P. Migne. 217 vols. Paris, 1844-1864
ProEccl	*Pro ecclesia*
RevBen	*Revue Bénédictine*
SC	Sources chrétiennes. Paris: Cerf, 1943-
SecCent	*Second Century*
StPatr	Studia patristica
SVTQ	*St. Vladimir's Theological Quarterly*
ThH	Théologie historique
TU	Texte und Untersuchungen
VC	*Vigiliae Christianae*
VetChr	*Vetera Christianorum*

ZAC *Zeitschrift für Antikes Christentum*

ZKT *Zeitschrift für katholische Theologie*

1. GENESIS: RECAPITULATION AND PROTOLOGICAL PERSPECTIVE

Recapitulation: The key to Irenaeus' theology?

Reflecting upon the historical sweep of the church's first few centuries, Adolf von Harnack does not mask his admiration for Irenaeus. The "power, vividness, and unity of [his] religious intuition," says Harnack, marks him as a second-century "Luther" of sorts.[1] Perhaps Harnack was impressed by Erasmus' glowing assessment of this "great champion of the church" whom he had just "ushered into the light of day": "Certainly [Irenaeus] did not deserve to languish in perpetual darkness, for his writings breathe the ancient power of the gospel...."[2] Yet, as is well known, Harnack was not entirely pleased with Irenaeus. He simply found his work less problematic than that of proximate contemporaries Justin Martyr and Tertullian. Not only did Harnack bemoan Irenaeus' "slavish dependence on authority,"[3] he also held Irenaeus responsible for a fateful decision that would make the "gradual hellenising of Christianity" virtually inevitable in the future.[4] In "preserving" the "letter" and "spirit" of early Christian tradition, Irenaeus had rebuffed the immediate Hellenistic threat to the Gospel.[5] But "the price of this preservation was the adoption of a series of

---

[1] Harnack, *History of Dogma* (trans. Neil Buchanan; 7 vols.; London: Williams & Norgate, 1894-99), 2:16. In Harnack's comparison, Tertullian was to Irenaeus what Calvin was to Luther.
[2] Desiderius Erasmus, letter to Bernhard von Cles, written on 27 August 1526 (*The Correspondence of Erasmus, Letters 1658 to 1801: January 1526-March 1527* [vol. 12 in *The Collected Works of Erasmus*; trans. Alexander Dalzell; Toronto: University of Toronto Press, 1974], 12:290-91).
[3] Harnack, *History of Dogma*, 2:12.
[4] Ibid., 2:247.
[5] Ibid.

'Gnostic' formulae."[6] Once smuggled in like a Trojan horse, these Hellenistic forces and the speculative theologies they spawned would eventually capture Christianity from the inside-out. By conceding to his enemies the right to dictate the terms and language of the debate, Irenaeus paradoxically won the battle but lost the war.

In this introductory chapter, we shall highlight Harnack's verdict on Irenaeus' term *recapitulation* precisely because its powerful influence upon ongoing scholarship has been overlooked. Ironically, Harnack's legacy is evident among a progression of scholars over the past century which has sought to restore Irenaeus' credibility as a theologian in part by overturning Harnack's conclusions about recapitulation. Yet because these recent efforts frequently extended the operative scope of recapitulation without questioning Harnack's basic assumptions regarding this term, they further obfuscate what is arguably Irenaeus' most significant contribution. It is in the area of hermeneutics – his innovative manner of reading biblical texts as Christian Scripture – that Irenaeus exercises a seminal influence within the emerging Christian tradition. When one examines how Irenaeus himself uses the term *recapitulatio*, it is (arguably) inappropriate to ascribe it a controlling role in his theology. Instead, one should recognize that recapitulation is embedded within the context of two more dominant features: Irenaeus' interest in origins, and his attention to the theological utility of certain texts. The former, which we shall label a "protological orientation," does not imply that Irenaeus' reputation as an eschatologically-focused theologian is unwarranted. Instead, it suggests Irenaeus' judgment that in order to understand the ultimate and crowning significance of Jesus Christ for humanity, one must start with the beginning. This protological orientation led Irenaeus to adopt two texts from the Genesis creation narratives for special roles. Accordingly, the second dominant feature to which Irenaeus' notion of recapitulation contributes is his deployment of these two focal texts for theological *uses*. Thus when Irenaeus refers to the *imago Dei* or the "breath of life" in a variety of seemingly disparate settings, he is being neither inconsistent nor enigmatic. Rather, he is adapting these creation texts for work in specialized theological tasks. In the face of an enticing Gnostic-Christian alternative, Irenaeus repeatedly draws on Genesis 1.26 and 2.7 to proclaim that God's economic act of enlivening humanity is fully comprehensive. These texts, as much as any others, function as central pillars in his effort to provide an authoritative and persuasive response to his opponents' challenge.

---

[6] Ibid.

Recapitulation "speculation": Harnack's influential proposal

To begin, however, it is necessary to recall one of Harnack's more basic suppositions, given its pertinence to our overall thesis on Irenaeus' use of Scripture. The task which Irenaeus and his contemporaries assumed (according to Harnack) was to provide an *"interpreted* baptismal confession" which could be a guide for faith:[7]

> This interpretation took its *matter* from the sacred books of *both* Testaments. It owed its guiding lines, however, on the one hand to philosophical theology, as set forth by the Apologists, and on the other to the earnest endeavor to maintain and defend against all attacks... In addition to this, certain interests, which had found expression in the speculations of the so-called Gnostics... also could not but influence the ecclesiastical teachers.[8]

In a footnote, Harnack continues: "As a matter of fact the theology of Irenaeus remains a riddle so long as we try to explain it merely from the Apologists and only consider its antithetical relations to Gnosis.... [W]e can... little understand the theology of Irenaeus without taking into account the schools of Valentinus and Marcion."[9] It would seem that Harnack was both right and wrong on this point. Contrary to the claims of many more recent scholars,[10] Harnack was indeed right to assert Irenaeus' indebtedness to his Gnostic opponents. However, he was quite wrong to identify the content of this debt as Hellenistic theological "speculation." As our studies of "Ophite" and Valentinian uses of Genesis 1-2 will suggest, Irenaeus shares the same protological predilection and textual concerns as do his opponents. The distinctiveness of his response, then, is a matter of *hermeneutics*. Neither he nor his opponents merely assumed these texts or read them casually; they put them to work. By means of his christological interpretations of Genesis 1-2, Irenaeus aims to harness the witnesses of Scripture[11] and apostolic tradition for the larger enterprise of constructive theology.

---

[7] Ibid., 2:230; emphasis is original.
[8] Ibid., 2:230-31; emphasis is original.
[9] Ibid., 2:231 n. 1.
[10] Shortly, we will examine the claims of commentators who argue, *pace* Harnack, that Gnostic influence on Irenaeus was quite marginal in comparison to, say, that exerted by the biblical texts.
[11] It is true that in the late second-century, boundaries demarcating a Christian canon had not yet been definitively drawn. Arguably, Irenaeus' writings would themselves prove influential in ensuing developments. On the question of Irenaeus' view of "Scripture," a study by Josef Hoh found that ἡ γραφή / αἱ γραφαί "occur 135 times in Irenaeus, of which 57 refer to the O.T. alone, a few to the N.T. alone, and the majority to the Old and

Furthermore (though the question lies beyond the scope of our work) we suggest that Harnack is wrong to portray Irenaeus' appropriation of – or accommodation to – the interests of his opponents as being unequivocally detrimental to the church.[12] Harnack asserts that when church leaders "proceed[ed] to put the same questions as the 'Gnostics,' they were obliged to work by their method."[13] Yet this claim surely discounts clear evidence of Irenaeus' interpretative freedom and innovation – evidence which our thesis presents. It also propagates a gross oversimplification: In following the lead of Gnostic theologians, Irenaeus is found negligent by allowing speculative ideas to obscure the textual witness. On the contrary, we propose that the fact that Irenaeus shares the same initial concerns as his opponents, namely, how christological beliefs relate to the texts of Genesis 1-2, demonstrates that Irenaeus rightly understood that the battle for these critical protological texts must be immediately joined. A coherent, satisfying interpretation of the Jesus Christ of apostolic texts, Irenaeus will insist, depends upon the interpretation and theological usage of the *Genesis* texts.[14] The apostolic church could make no concession of its claim upon them.

Given the preceding background, we turn now to the task of clarifying Harnack's understanding of Irenaeus' favored term, *recapitulation*. Broadly speaking, Harnack judges that Irenaeus (despite his stated intention to the contrary) has "contributed a great deal to the transformation of faith into a monistic speculation" by his facile notion that "theological Gnosis" was "simply

---

New Testaments combined" (Hoh, *Die Lehre des Hl. Irenäus über das Neue Testament* [Münster i. W.: Aschendorff, 1919], 62; cf. Hans von Campenhausen, *The Formation of the Christian Bible* [trans. John Austin Baker; London: A&C Black, 1972], 188). More recently, Graham Stanton observes a few occasions wherein Irenaeus does explicitly refer to the gospels as Scripture (cf. *Haer.* ii.27.2; ii.35.4). Yet, Stanton concludes, "Irenaeus remains somewhat coy..." (*Jesus and Gospel* [Cambridge: Cambridge University Press, 2004], 105). "For Irenaeus 'Scripture' is first and foremost the OT though it is quite clear that the gospels and sayings of Jesus enjoy the same level of authority as the OT" (106). Stanton's claim is well supported by *Adversus Haereses* However, for our purposes, we shall use the term Scripture loosely, denoting a body of sacred texts which, in Irenaeus' time, enjoyed a certain privileged status in the Christian tradition.

[12] To be fair, Irenaeus himself does not admit to borrowing anything from Gnostic interpreters. If he is mistaken on this point, the distinct contribution he makes to theological hermeneutics should nevertheless not be doubted.

[13] Harnack, *History of Dogma*, 2:252.

[14] After Isaiah (137 times) and Psalms (111 times), Genesis is the third-most frequently cited biblical text (103 times) in *Adversus Haereses*. (cf. Gregory T. Armstrong, *Die Genesis in der Alten Kirche: die drei Kirchenvater* [Tübingen: Mohr, 1962], 55 n. 1). Furthermore, in our upcoming chapter four we shall suggest that Irenaeus' christological interpretations of prophetic materials (which in his view included the Psalms) have their ground in his anti-Gnostic readings of Genesis 1-2.

a continuation" of faith.[15] Because Irenaeus assumed the given-ness of faith, which could be viewed as distinct from (though related to) theological knowledge, he was not on guard against metaphysical speculations drawn from Gnostic systems rather than from the gospel: "Here the speculative theories are as a matter of fact quite imbedded in the historical propositions of traditions."[16] We will see Harnack's general view particularized in his supposition that recapitulation is a foreign "theory" that has been dressed up in the clothing of biblical language.

According to Harnack, Irenaeus' notion of recapitulation is his view that Christ's redemption constitutes "the reunion of things unnaturally separated [die Wiedervereinigung des widernatürlich Getrennten]."[17] Yet whereas Harnack recognizes Irenaeus' intent to speak of recapitulation as a biblically-informed theological bridge (Christ joins the old humanity to the new in himself), he thinks that historical analysis shows recapitulation to actually have been be an ill-advised *conceptual* bridge (spanning Hellenist and "biblical" worlds). Herein lies the root of the problem. Irenaeus, says Harnack, counters a Valentinian doctrine of redemption by means of recapitulation. This one *"spekulativ Gedanke"* is the means by which he builds connections between Pauline ideas, the Apologists' theology, and christological interests in order to answer a central question: *Cur Deus homo?*[18] What is conspicuously absent from Harnack's explanation – as well as from the alternatives suggested by his inheritors – is the intrinsic connection between Irenaeus' use of the term recapitulation and his hermeneutic of Scripture, particularly that of Genesis. Besides referring to recapitulation as a "speculative thought," Harnack frequently labels it *"Recapitulationstheorie."*[19] It is not that Harnack is completely insensitive to the essential relationship between the biblical texts and Irenaeus' notion of recapitulation.[20] Rather, it is as if his determination to characterize recapitulation as a conceptual import decisively overpowers another dimension that has a much greater claim to foreground attention, that is, the hermeneutic of Scripture that gives this notion its distinctive shape. Instead of depicting recapitulation as a somewhat artificial, Gnostic-informed construct, we might find better reason (given the text of *Adversus Haereses* itself) to view it as primarily a matter of

---

[15] Ibid., 2:245-46; 246 n. 1.
[16] Ibid., 2:246.
[17] Ibid., 2:238. The original is from *Lehrbuch der Dogmengeschichte* (3d ed.; 3 vols. Freiburg I. B.: J.C.B. Mohr, 1894), 1:515.
[18] Harnack, *Lehrbuch der Dogmengeschichte*, 1:515; cf. English translation in *History of Dogma*, 2:238-39; 240. Emphasis is added.
[19] Harnack uses this term on at least six different occasions (*Lehrbuch der Dogmengeschichte*, 1:551, 558, 561, 565 [three times]). In the English translation, cf. *History of Dogma*, 2:276, 284, 288, 291.
[20] Cf. for example, *History of Dogma*, 2:284; *Haer*. iii.19.3.

texts. More precisely, we discover how a given interpreter reads and uses particular texts in light of others, being motivated primarily by hermeneutical rather than speculative interests.

Harnack may credit Irenaeus for having "worked out" the "thought" of recapitulation "by the aid of simple and essentially biblical ideas."[21] Yet what he means is that in "following the method of Valentinus," Irenaeus simply limits himself to biblical "language."[22] Indeed, Harnack portrays Irenaeus as introducing a "Gnostic and realistic doctrine of recapitulation."[23] "Here," he says, "comes in the mystical Adam-Christ speculation, in accordance with the epistles to the Ephesians and Corinthians. Everything, that is, the *longam hominum expositionem*, was recapitulated by Christ in himself...."[24] The biblical texts, then, are not constitutive, but rather provide the words with which to clothe a foreign-born metaphysical substructure. "Recapitulation" is a shorthand reference to a system that Irenaeus has in mind. Though Irenaeus' methodological starting point is Jesus Christ,[25] the end product is an argument "of an abstract, philosophico-rational kind."[26] To be more precise, Harnack concludes (following the studies of H. H. Wendt and L. Duncker) that Irenaeus actually holds "two dissimilar trains of thought... with regard to man's original state" and two "in regard to his Christology."[27] The first is an "apologetic and moralistic train of thought" centered on the famous Adam-as-infant text in *Adversus Haereses* iv.38.[28] The second is a "mystical" train of thought.[29] According to the former, Adam's disobedience interrupted God's work of enabling human growth through the proper exercise of the will. Accordingly, humanity is hindered from reaching its destination not so much by the "consequences of the fall" but by the actual disobedience itself.[30] Christ is a Savior figure in two ways. In him, the Spirit of God becomes accustomed to dwell in humanity.[31] He is also the teacher who calls humanity to follow the way of obedience and thereby be enabled to receive incorruptibility. Significantly, recapitulation does not feature in this model but only in the next: the "mystic" train of thought. In this second system, "[i]ncorruptibility is a habitus which is

---

[21] Harnack, *History of Dogma*, 2:242-43.
[22] Ibid., 2:244.
[23] Ibid., 2:272.
[24] Ibid., 2:273.
[25] Ibid., 2:262.
[26] Ibid., 2:249-50.
[27] Ibid., 2:274 n. 1.
[28] Ibid., 2:268-72.
[29] Ibid., 2:274 n. 1; cf. 2:272-81.
[30] Ibid., 2:270-71.
[31] Ibid., 2:271.

the opposite of... man's natural condition."[32] It can only be acquired if a possessor of incorruptibility were to "unit[e] himself *realiter* with human nature, in order to deify it 'by adoption.'"[33] Unlike the educative model, this view alleges that Adam actually *lost* something in the fall which Christ restores when he recapitulates the *"longam hominum expositionem."*[34] From Harnack's dispassionate vantage point, recapitulation was a "speculation" that Irenaeus had "contrived" in order to "reconcile" the Pauline "discrepancy" between two soteriological foci: the death of Christ and the "appearance of God in the flesh."[35] Recapitulation assumes that humanity is united under the "head" of Adam and Christ, in turn. Thus Adam's death and Christ's life are not matters of "hereditary transmission" but "mystical unity."[36] Accordingly, for some who followed Harnack, Irenaeus' recapitulation became primarily associated with a physical, objectivist doctrine of the atonement. In the last century, however, many commentators have blazed a different trail, finding no allure in Harnack's antipathy for alleged metaphysical enquiry and mystical religious experience. They would rediscover Irenaeus' notion of recapitulation and defend it as a potentially rich resource, particularly when revisiting the subject of atonement theology. Yet in the process of dismantling Harnack's outmoded architecture, had they been as thorough as they might have supposed?

Recapitulation "reclamation": Harnack on the defensive

It is our contention that Harnack's portrayal of Irenaeus' recapitulation has had a persistent, though subtle, influence on Irenaean scholarship throughout the past century. Often times, even when commentators self-consciously renounce Harnack's general presuppositions and agenda, they nonetheless remain captive to his gravitational force. A chronological survey of select representative and influential figures commenting on recapitulation will help to establish this claim.

In his noted work *Kyrios Christos* (first published in 1913), Wilhelm Bousset's approach to recapitulation follows Harnack's lead with a few embellishments. Irenaeus' "recapitulation theory" is said to answer the question of "how" the "κοινωνία of deity and humanity is possible and how the human nature which is taken into this unity was constituted."[37] The "beginnings reappear at the end," such as the virgin earth / virgin birth, the tree / cross, and

---

[32] Ibid., 2:241.
[33] Ibid., 2:241.
[34] Ibid., 2:273; cf. 2:242.
[35] Ibid., 2:290.
[36] Ibid., 2:274.
[37] Wilhelm Bousset, *Kyrios Christos* (trans. John E. Steely; Nashville: Abingdon, 1970), 437.

the temptation.³⁸ Apparently, Bousset suggests, Irenaeus has "inserted" the drama of Jesus' life depicting his conquest of Satan "into this context of the recapitulation theory."³⁹ As Harnack had done, Bousset postulates possible external sources standing behind Irenaeus' innovative end-product, a "mythical view" of Christ's recapitulation: "Is Irenaeus perhaps actually stimulated in his fantasies here by the myth of the Primal Man, by that speculation about a divine redeemer figure...? Much could point to this...."⁴⁰ As for textual inspiration, Bousset concludes that though Irenaeus claims to draw from Paul, a reading of *Adversus Haereses* v.9-14 (on the "flesh and blood" statement of 1 Corinthians 15.50) will reveal "how violently the ideas of Paul are twisted and distorted" by Irenaeus.⁴¹

Unlike Bousset, Emil Brunner was eager to challenge Harnack's portrayal of Irenaean soteriology, particularly its assumption of an underlying dichotomy. In *Der Mittler*, published in 1927, Brunner claims that Irenaeus' Christology "is always soteriological, and his soteriology is always christological, so that here, if anywhere, the accusation that the ecclesiastical doctrine of Christ was deflected into the paths of metaphysical speculation can be refuted."⁴² Specifically, Brunner denies that Irenaeus held to a "physical" view of salvation which functioned "mechanically" apart from the subjective human response.⁴³ Rather than a "magical objectivity," the doctrine of the incarnation affirms the love of God and the union between God and humanity that "should be received into our hearts through faith."⁴⁴ Insofar as the incarnation relates not just to Christ's birth, but to his life, death and resurrection, Irenaeus' "recapitulation *theory*" should be understood eschatologically.⁴⁵

With his thin volume, *Christus Victor* (first published in 1931), Gustaf Aulén put forth a different proposal which, in hindsight, is seen to herald a new trend in Irenaean studies.⁴⁶ Aulén's specific interest was in the development of Christian views of atonement. Rather than attributing the genesis of true atonement theories to the objectivism of Anselm or the subjectivism of Abelard,

---

³⁸ Ibid., 440.
³⁹ Ibid.
⁴⁰ Ibid., 441.
⁴¹ Ibid., 449.
⁴² Emil Brunner, *The Mediator* (trans. Olive Wyon; London: Lutterworth, 1934), 250.
⁴³ Ibid., 255. Brunner points to *Haer.* v.10.2 and iv.2.7 wherein Irenaeus describes salvation not as a bestowal applied indiscriminately, but as a gift obtained by those who respond appropriately to God.
⁴⁴ Ibid., 258-59.
⁴⁵ Ibid., 256 n. 1; 259. Emphasis is added.
⁴⁶ Even Aulén's detractors acknowledge the substantial influence of his contribution. *Christus Victor* is recognized to be a "modern classic" (cf. William Loewe, "Irenaeus' Soteriology: Christus Victor Revisited," *ATR* 67 [1985]: 1).

Aulén goes much further back. He credits Irenaeus with providing a first sketch of an atonement doctrine, here set in *dramatic* form. Where Harnack had hypothesized about recapitulation's foreign pedigree, Aulén's emphasis was on the "divine victory accomplished in Christ" which "stands in the centre of Irenaeus' thought and forms the central element in the *recapitulatio*...."[47] Because Aulén (unlike Harnack) discerned a relatively coherent and unified soteriology in Irenaeus which galvanized the conceptual notion of atonement by recapitulation, Aulén prepared the way for a subsequent period in Irenaean studies marked by "recapitulation inflation." More than other noteworthy characteristics of Irenaeus' work, recapitulation would be elevated and invited to preside over the wide-ranging vista of Irenaeus' theology.

In the mid-1930s, another Swede, Anders Nygren, deemed Irenaeus a crucial figure in the development of the "Christian idea of love."[48] Though Nygren's classifications of types of love are not directly relevant to our study, it is noteworthy that he both assumes and subverts Harnack's "two trains of thought" approach to Irenaean soteriology. Irenaeus, he avers, makes God's wholly self-giving ("agape") love the "ground of creation."[49] This is the "love [that] God's Logos has become flesh in order to 'recapitulate' in himself the fallen human race and reconcile it to God...."[50] Yet, according to Nygren, Irenaeus' "view of Agape" is "not entirely untouched by alien motifs," for "the Eros [Hellenistic-informed, human-centered love] motif affects the very centre of his thought."[51] This latter refers to "Hellenistic piety" whose drive is human deification.[52] In *Adversus Haereses* iv.38, Nygren sees that the "*strands* from the Eros and the Agape motifs are *woven together*."[53] God's work of incarnation and recapitulation enables humanity to be raised up to fellowship with him.[54] So where Harnack finds the educative, human-ascent strand of *Adversus Haereses* iv.38 to express biblical ideas whereas recapitulation bespeaks a Gnostic-Hellenistic intrusion, Nygren argues exactly the reverse.

The next work of note in our chronological survey of recapitulation and Harnack's legacy is Gustaf Wingren's *Man and the Incarnation* (1947). Irenaeus is praised for his unique ability to propound a strong anthropological emphasis

---

[47] Gustaf Aulén, *Christus Victor: An Historical Study of the Three Main Types of the Idea of the Atonement* (trans. A. G. Hebert; London: SPCK, 1970), 21.
[48] Anders Nygren, *Agape and Eros: Part II, The History of the Christian Idea of Love* (trans. Philip S. Watson; 2 vols.; London: SPCK, 1938).
[49] Ibid., 1:180.
[50] Ibid., 1:193.
[51] Ibid., 1:193.
[52] Ibid., 1:194.
[53] Ibid., 1:196; emphasis is added.
[54] Ibid., 1:196.

without setting humanity in opposition to God.⁵⁵ "Recapitulation is through Christ, but it is also achieved through men;" it is predicated not only on the incarnation, but also on Jesus' "victory over evil through the temptations and Passion."⁵⁶ When humanity is "drawn into this recapitulation," it "realize s [its] origin" and "achieves the purpose of [its] creation."⁵⁷ For Wingren, recapitulation is all-important: "The best confirmation that a particular interpretation of Irenaeus is a correct one will be whether or not we have given the terms *recapitulatio* or *anakephalaiosis* a definite and objective meaning."⁵⁸ Though admitting many ways to "analyze" this "concept," Wingren aims to show that recapitulation, nonetheless, "has only one basic meaning throughout."⁵⁹ This term is "an attempt by Irenaeus to embody the *whole* of the Biblical proclamation about the work of Christ in a single word,"⁶⁰ namely, "the accomplishment of God's plan of salvation... within history."⁶¹ Like Aulén, Wingren wishes to distance himself from the approaches of earlier "historians of dogma." He rejects the judgments of Loofs and Harnack that recapitulation was a foreign element which Irenaeus, as innovator, injected into the native contexts of Scripture and apostolic tradition. Instead, it is in the Gnostics, not Irenaeus, that Wingren finds originality.⁶² Irenaeus' recapitulation construct was merely his means of "unifying theological concepts" already at hand.⁶³ Wingren also protests against models that identify physical incarnation as the focal point of salvation in Irenaeus, to the exclusion of Christ's life and "ethical struggle" (a view which often presupposes that these aspects exemplify two different strands of thought).⁶⁴ At the other extreme, he dislikes Martin Werner's history of dogma (first edition, 1941) which attributes such a "strong anthropocentricity" to Irenaeus that the doctrine of recapitulation, now deprived of eschatological and cosmic dimensions, elicits a "largely naturalistic description."⁶⁵ Wingren

---

⁵⁵ Gustaf Wingren, *Man and the Incarnation: A Study in the Biblical Theology of Irenaeus* (trans. Ross MacKenzie; London: Oliver and Boyd, 1959), xii.
⁵⁶ Ibid., xiv-xv.
⁵⁷ Ibid., xv. Wingren's point helpfully recasts the discussion of recapitulation. Our intent is to build on this insight by focusing on the crucial biblical texts which are constitutive for a Christian view of creation.
⁵⁸ Ibid., xv.
⁵⁹ Ibid., xv.
⁶⁰ Ibid., 80; emphasis is added.
⁶¹ Ibid., 81.
⁶² Ibid., xvi.
⁶³ Ibid., xvi; cf. 81-82.
⁶⁴ Ibid., 82.
⁶⁵ Wingren, *Man and the Incarnation*, 91. Martin Werner had followed Harnack in arguing that Irenaeus' "recapitulation theory" was an innovative way of "setting forth the ancient notion of reconciliation" through Christ by drawing on a "notion of 'physical' redemption and the ancient concept of substance" (*The Formation of Christian Dogma:*

Genesis: Recapitulation and Protological Perspective 11

builds on the foundation prepared earlier by Aulén to give substance and shape to a mediating position. In this schema, recapitulation is the one concept that makes sense of the whole of Irenaeus' theology. The soteriological poles which Harnack had seen in opposition – divine and human (objective / subjective), incarnation and obedience, cosmic and ethical – find their interrelation and meaning in Irenaeus' system because of recapitulation. Our chronological survey will highlight the gathering momentum of this scholarly position from the middle twentieth to early twenty-first centuries.

In 1948, John Lawson offered his own monograph with the intention of defending Irenaeus' reputation as a genuinely biblical theologian. He thus counters critics who claim that Irenaeus' readings of Paul (to cite the most contentious issue) were flawed because of the insidious influence of Hellenist thought. According to Lawson, earlier scholars such as Harnack, Bonwetsch, Seeberg, and Bousset were not unjustified in discerning mystical Johannine connotations – cosmic collecting and restoring – in the notion of recapitulation. Yet Lawson argues that the "foundation of all would seem to be the *conception* of 'going over the ground again' rather than that of 'comprehension in unity'... [Christ] went through all the experiences of Adam, but with the opposite result."[66] Lawson subsequently describes two additional "conceptions" or "elements" in the "scheme of Irenaeus" represented by the word recapitulation.[67] He furthermore applauds Aulén's work to associate recapitulation with Christ's "championship through obedience" (*Christus Victor*), a connection which Lawson sees to be substantiated by Irenaeus' Adam / Christ analogy.[68] "One of the most valuable and pleasing things about S. Irenaeus," asserts Lawson, "is the circumstance that the Recapitulation provides a doctrinal system in which an adequate place is found for the whole human career and the human character of our Lord."[69] Irenaeus may depict salvation in a variety of ways (and Lawson is "less happy" about the theme of incorruptibility in Irenaeus' doctrine of divinization[70]), but his overarching notion of *Christus Victor* is "most essentially associated with the idea of Recapitulation" and is a "specifically *biblical* element" in Irenaean theology.[71] Despite the presence of occasional elements of Greek philosophy, the *Christus Victor* model ensures that "recapitulation has a

---

An Historical Study of its Problem [trans. S.G.F. Brandon; London: A&C Black, 1957]), 197; 211).
[66] John Lawson, *The Biblical Theology of St. Irenaeus* (London: Epworth, 1948), 143. Emphasis is added.
[67] Ibid.
[68] Ibid., 150.
[69] Ibid., 153.
[70] Ibid., 165.
[71] Ibid., 155; emphasis is added.

necessary ethical and rational connotation."[72] Lawson's analysis of Irenaeus' soteriology is quite unlike Harnack's. Yet he concedes that a "certain contrast" between the Johannine and Pauline influences is seen in Irenaeus,[73] resulting in a "two-sided expression of the doctrine of God, and of the way of salvation."[74] The Johannine strand of "biblical Hellenism"[75] evokes the "philosophical or intellectual aspect of Christian salvation" with its imagery of truth, light, and the path to eternal life.[76] On the other hand, Irenaeus draws upon Paul to describe salvation in terms of "moral will, and of love dwelling in the heart."[77] It is the central conception of *Christus Victor*,[78] "essentially represented by the *word* 'Recapitulation,'"[79] which superintends them both and establishes a sense of unity. Lawson's large chapter entitled "The Recapitulation," is actually a study of Irenaeus' soteriology in its multiple, biblically-informed expressions, primarily *Christus Victor*, divinization, and the Pauline "sacrifice metaphor."[80] That Lawson here draws material from Irenaeus' writings, whether the term *recapitulatio* is found in context or not, suggests that Lawson considers the term recapitulation to be the epitome of all that Irenaeus may say about salvation.

A brief look at a few representative examples in 1950s scholarship on Irenaeus' notion of recapitulation shows a general desire to continue in the path prepared by Brunner, Wingren and Lawson in opposition to Harnack's direction. Johannes Quasten, like Wingren, accepts Irenaeus' denial of originality or speculation.[81] Similarly, he also declares that the "theory of recapitulation" is the "heart of Irenaeus' Christology and indeed of his entire theology."[82] Roland Potter would seem to adopt the conclusions of both Harnack and his detractors.[83] He accepts the claim that Irenaeus is the first "to express clearly what has come to be called the physical or mystical theory," a theory to which "the notion of

---

[72] Ibid., 167.
[73] Ibid., 162.
[74] Ibid., 163.
[75] Lawson contrasts this with "religious Hellenism" which is to be considered "illegitimate" because it "admits into the very substance of its creed fundamentally pagan notions of God and of the religious life." Such is the Hellenism of the Gnostics (164-65).
[76] Ibid., 161.
[77] Ibid., 162-63.
[78] Lawson argues that "we catch glimpses of '*Christus Victor*'" even in "typical Johannine mystical theology," not just in the other New Testament materials (ibid., 177).
[79] Ibid., 148; emphasis is added.
[80] Cf. the discussion in Lawson, *Biblical Theology*, 178-86.
[81] "[Irenaeus'] mind was not given to theorizing nor did he make any new theological discoveries..." Johannes Quasten, *Patrology, Volume 1: The Beginnings of Patristic Literature* (4 vols.; Westminster, Md.: Newman, 1950), 294; cf. *Haer.* ii.26.1.
[82] Ibid., 1:295.
[83] Roland Potter, "Irenaeus and Recapitulation," *Dom. St.* 4 (1951): 192-200.

recapitulation easily lends."[84] Yet Potter's sympathetic reading of Irenaeus finds recapitulation to be an integrative "theory of *reciprocal finality*" encompassing "every domain" – both human history and the cosmos.[85] At the same time, Irenaeus is found wise enough to avoid a "wooden adherence to a principle of recapitulation."[86] H. E. W. Turner is persuaded by Aulén's link between *"Christus Victor* thinking" and Irenaeus' "doctrine of the recapitulation."[87] After noting the New Testament "sources" of this doctrine, he proceeds to analyze it in terms of three component parts: restoration, summation, and iteration.[88] Turner laments that whereas in Irenaeus' *"Christus Victor,"* it is the "Word in his humanity" who is the "subject of the *recapitulatio*," later theologians[89] substitute a *"Logos Victor"* model.[90] In his popular introduction, *Early Christian Doctrines* (first edition, 1958), J. N. D. Kelly considers Irenaeus and Tertullian to be "cautious and pedestrian" in contrast to the "intellectually adventurous" eastern theologians such as Clement and Origen. The former, he says, "limited the function of theology to expounding the doctrines set out in Holy Scripture."[91] As is well known, Kelly did not share Harnack's view that Gnosticism and catholic-Christianity could be located on a shared Hellenist continuum, albeit occupying different points.[92] As for recapitulation, this is deemed a "theory" or "conception" (ultimately derived from Paul) which was "taken up and deepened by Irenaeus."[93] Irenaeus *"clearly presupposes* some kind of mystical solidarity, or rather identity, between the father of the race and all his descendants."[94] In essence, recapitulation means that "if we fell through our solidarity with the first man, we can be restored through our solidarity with Christ."[95] Although Kelly dismisses the "physical theory of the atonement" as "a dangerous half-truth,"[96] he (like Harnack) sees the context in which Irenaeus'

---

[84] Ibid., 199. The unusual pairing of "physical" and "mystical" describes a soteriological view that emphasizes the salvific consequences of Christ's physical incarnation. Subsequently, believers are said to participate in Christ through mystical (as opposed to literal) union.
[85] Ibid., 194, 195; emphasis is original.
[86] Ibid., 197.
[87] H. E. W. Turner, *The Patristic Doctrine of Redemption* (London: Mowbray, 1952), 62.
[88] Ibid., 62; 63-65.
[89] I.e., a line from Apollinarius to Paul of Samosata, Diodore, Flavian, Athanasius, and Gregory of Nyssa.
[90] Ibid., 67-69. Douglas Farrow, whom we will address shortly, is a recent scholar who particularly echoes this complaint.
[91] J. N. D. Kelly, *Early Christian Doctrines* (5th ed.; London: A&C Black, 1977), 4.
[92] Cf. Kelly, *Early Christian Doctrines*, 22-29.
[93] Ibid., 170.
[94] Ibid., 172; emphasis is added.
[95] Ibid., 172.
[96] Ibid., 174.

work is set as the struggle between two opposing poles: a "traditional eschatological scheme" (i.e., "primitive" millenarianism) and a more recent Platonic / Gnostic notion of soul-ascent.[97]

Jaroslav Pelikan, another prominent mid-to-late twentieth-century scholar on the development of Christian doctrine, outlines a position on Irenaeus that roughly corresponds with Kelly's. In elaborating his "doctrine of recapitulation," Irenaeus must have been "reflecting the mind of the Christian community," since it can scarcely be imagined that the mainstream church would have tolerated and even celebrated a mere "private speculation."[98] In Pelikan's analysis, "Irenaeus's doctrine of recapitulation can be read as the most profound theological vindication in the second and third centuries of the universal Christian ideal of the imitation of Christ."[99] His doctrine served as a "corrective" to any view of salvation that discounted such a call to obedience and "assimilation" to Christ, for whereas "Adam had been the example for Christ," now Christ became the "example" for all of humanity.[100] Thus Pelikan (unlike Harnack) apparently finds recapitulation to be highly relevant to the ethical / subjectivist features of Irenaeus' soteriology, though not exclusively so. In due course, he concludes that recapitulation entails not only Christ's living example, but also his redemptive death.[101]

As the debate over Irenaeus' understanding of salvation continues on into the latter decades of the twentieth century and the early years of the twenty-first, Harnack's name continues to be invoked – even if (as more often than not) it is to challenge rather than to endorse his portrayal of Irenaeus' system. Trevor Hart, for example, agrees with Harnack that Irenaeus could not but use "Greek philosophico-religious terminology."[102] Yet he disagrees with Harnack's (and Loofs') interpretation of such language. Irenaeus does not suggest that Christ's incarnation communicates divine immortality (in a Greek sense) to humanity in a "naturalistic" or "mechanical" sense, otherwise Irenaeus' appeal for human faith is inexplicable.[103] Greater clarity is achieved when one gives attention to *how* Irenaeus uses the language he does, most importantly, how Irenaeus uses

---

[97] Cf. Kelly, *Early Christian Doctrines*, 465-67.
[98] Jaroslav Pelikan, *The Christian Tradition: A History of the Development of Doctrine. Vol. 1: The Emergence of the Catholic Tradition (100-600)* (5 vols.; Chicago: University of Chicago Press, 1971), 144.
[99] Ibid.
[100] Ibid., 145-46.
[101] Ibid., 146.
[102] Trevor Hart, "Irenaeus, Recapitulation and Physical Redemption," in *Christ in our Place: The Humanity of God in Christ for the Reconciliation of the World* (ed. Trevor A. Hart and Daniel P. Thimell; Exeter: Paternoster, 1989), 155.
[103] Ibid., 155.

Genesis: Recapitulation and Protological Perspective   15

the "language of 'recapitulation'... with reference to the humanity of Christ."[104] In this, Hart discerns two primary emphases: (1) "Christ the new man," that is, the "reiterative" quality of Christ's recapitulation, and (2) "Christ in our place," that is, its "inclusive" quality wherein all persons are "implicated in his actions."[105] T. F. Torrance, in an essay focusing on Irenaeus' *Demonstration of the Apostolic Preaching*, proposes to name three "soteriological features" of Irenaeus' "doctrine of recapitulation."[106] Recapitulation "links the virgin birth of Jesus and his bodily resurrection closely together," shows the incarnation and redemption to be "intrinsically interrelated," and points to the "central importance" of a "saving union with Christ."[107] Douglas Farrow, perhaps more emphatically than many of his peers, shares Harnack's dissatisfaction with the trajectory of early doctrinal development. Speculative cosmological and metaphysical interests (evidenced in Origen's approach) all too quickly overtook the traditional concern to ground Christian faith in the apostolic witness to the human and historical person of Jesus. Yet Farrow sees Irenaeus as a champion of the latter, and thus in his assessment of recapitulation he parts company with Harnack, Loofs, and Bousset. Recapitulation, declares Farrow, begins not with universals (as does Platonism) but with the particulars of the created order and the biblical narrative of "Jesus-history."[108] It is from this basis that recapitulation then instigates the fulfillment of these particulars as brought into communion with God through Christ. The "doctrine" of recapitulation is predicated not on a λόγος ἄσαρκος but on the *incarnate* Christ.[109] It manifests the "triumph of the particular."[110]

In a major monograph, *Irenaeus of Lyons* (2001), Eric Osborn devotes two full chapters to the "idea" of recapitulation.[111] Almost as if to warn the

---

[104] Ibid., 170. Though Hart thinks it likely that Pauline texts such as Ephesians 1.10 influenced Irenaeus, he offers a crucial caveat (with which we heartily agree): "... we must beware here of committing the fallacy of origins, and assuming any simple continuity of meaning between the biblical author and the second century bishop" (171).

[105] Ibid., 171, 175.

[106] Thomas F. Torrance, *Divine Meaning: Studies in Patristic Hermeneutics* (Edinburgh: T&T Clark, 1994).

[107] Ibid., 68-69.

[108] Cf. Douglas Farrow, *Ascension and Ecclesia* (Edinburgh: T&T Clark, 1999), 54-56. Farrow pays only limited attention to Irenaeus as an exegete of Scripture, not interacting with the texts of Genesis 1-2 as far as concerns a "doctrine of recapitulation." In an appendix, he does offer the tantalizing suggestion that the gospel of John "arguably is the Gospel of recapitulation" (298). Admittedly, it must be granted that Farrow's primary concern, the loss and recovery of the doctrine of ascension in the church, requires him to be selective in his use of Irenaeus.

[109] Ibid., 55.

[110] Ibid., 99.

[111] Cf. *Irenaeus of Lyons* (Cambridge: Cambridge University Press, 2001), 97.

unsuspecting layperson against approaching recapitulation without the proper technical expertise, Osborn declares,

> The complexity of the concept [of recapitulation] is formidable. At least eleven ideas – unification, repetition, redemption, perfection, inauguration and consummation, totality, the triumph of Christus Victor, ontology, epistemology and ethics (or being, truth and goodness) – are combined in different permutations....[112]

Osborn undertakes to examine each of these eleven "variables and their relationships." Recapitulation is an idea which can be "traced to Scripture," whose component parts are tied together by a certain "logic," the image of "Christus Victor."[113] Like other commentators we have mentioned, Osborn would seem to solve the problem of Harnack's bifurcation of two Irenaean "trains of thought" by crowning recapitulation to be the rubric that constitutes each and superintends both. Osborn asserts that Christ's union of all, "by his death on the cross," is "both physical and moral."[114] In his first two categories, recapitulation as "correction" and as "perfection," Irenaeus' Christology encompasses the tension between Pauline and Johannine influences, respectively. The latter two categories, recapitulation as "inauguration" and "consummation," address how Irenaeus related this concept to the span between the birth of the church and the eschaton.[115] Osborn boldly underscores the almost heroic nature of Irenaeus' efforts: "The idea of recapitulation is neither a piece of rhetoric nor a pretty picture, but a speculative achievement which is at the same time vibrant and poetic."[116] At times, Irenaeus is a "*doctor constructivus* who piles image on image."[117] He is said to describe Christ's work "with unrivaled intricacy."[118] Recapitulation "reflects the theme of inclusive totality" because of the "mass of detail" which Irenaeus has brought to bear.[119] Osborn's sophisticated analysis of Irenaeus' idea of recapitulation is *itself* impressive; we lack the space here to relate an adequate summary of his proposal. Nevertheless, from Osborn's perspective, if Irenaeus was a logically

---

[112] Ibid., 97-98.
[113] Ibid., 98.
[114] Ibid., 99.
[115] Cf. Osborn, *Irenaeus of Lyons*, 117. Speaking of Irenaeus' eschatology – how he "ties" recapitulation and consummation together – Osborn remarks: "Splendid as inauguration [of a new humanity] sounds, it presents the most difficult *problem* among all Irenaeus' *concepts*" (140, emphasis is added).
[116] Ibid., 195.
[117] Ibid., 102.
[118] Ibid., 110.
[119] Ibid., 115.

Genesis: Recapitulation and Protological Perspective

consistent thinker, then the best accounting of recapitulation entails systematic analysis. Constituent ideas are first separated, then related in light of what is known about Irenaeus' conceptual world and the philosophical influences upon it.

John Behr, in a recent monograph comparing the anthropologies of Irenaeus and Clement of Alexandria, also employs recapitulation to relativize, if not erase the Harnackian distinction between "physical" and pedagogical notions of atonement in Irenaeus. "As the two dimensions of the apostasy, the catastrophic and the pedagogic, are but a matter of *perspective*, so also are the two dimensions of Christ's work of salvation – liberating the weak man from the Devil [cf. *Christus Victor*] and bestowing incorruptibility [cf. pedagogical model] – a matter of *perspective*, relating to the human and the divine in the one Jesus Christ."[120] Said in another way, both the dimension of Christ's physical incarnation and that of his exemplary life (obedience, suffering, and death) are, claims Behr, "expressed in Irenaeus's use of the idea of recapitulation."[121]

We conclude our survey of post-Harnackian perspectives on Irenaeus' recapitulation with Hans Boersma. In *Violence, Hospitality, and the Cross* (2004), Boersma aims to show that the three traditional atonement models may be coordinated by means of Irenaeus' "concept" of recapitulation.[122] "Christ's work of recapitulation has a prophetic element (moral influence), a priestly element (representative punishment), and a royal element (*Christus Victor*)."[123] Ultimately, Irenaeus points to divine "hospitality" (which is not the antithesis of violence) as the overarching metaphor which we may discern in all three models. According to Boersma, the notion of recapitulation "coheres well with all three traditional models" because it is a "formal rather than a material concept."[124] That is, while it affirms *that* Christ has recapitulated Israel and Adam such that the Church "becomes the transformed beneficiary of his work of redemption," it does not specify the *way* in which he does so.[125] This question of manner is addressed differently by the three atonement models. Boersma grants that a "high regard" for the incarnation accompanies the notion of recapitulation, yet he calls Harnack's term "physical" redemption "confusing and

---

[120] John Behr, *Asceticism and Anthropology in Irenaeus and Clement* (Oxford: Oxford University Press, 2000), 61; emphasis is added.
[121] Ibid., 62.
[122] Cf. Hans Boersma, *Violence, Hospitality, and the Cross* (Grand Rapids: Baker Academic, 2004), 14; 119.
[123] Ibid., 122.
[124] Ibid., 112.
[125] Ibid., 112, 113.

unfortunate."[126] Recapitulation must be understood to encompass the life of Christ and his suffering, as well as his incarnation.[127]

Recapitulation "inflation": an assessment

Although we have only offered a much-abbreviated diachronic survey of scholarly work on Irenaeus' notion of recapitulation since Harnack, we draw our conclusions by suggesting that Harnack's legacy may be envisioned as a three-tier pyramid, with each level being built on the one below it. Harnack begins by assuming recapitulation to be a "speculative thought."[128] Easily abstracted from its basis in texts, recapitulation is conducive to *systematization* and arrangement within a particular schema. On top of that basic foundation, Harnack adds a second claim: the concept of recapitulation is essentially *alien* to Scripture and the apostolic tradition. Irenaeus certainly drew ideas[129] from Pauline and other texts, but the final conceptual form owes more to the influence of Hellenistic abstract thought as channeled unwittingly to Irenaeus from Gnostic "theologians."[130] Harnack's third and crowning piece is his *dichotomization* of Irenaean soteriology. If there are two incongruent "trains of thought," it follows that recapitulation should be found to (more or less) constitute a Hellenistic "mystical / physical" strand, which stands in opposition to a (more traditionally) biblical "moralistic" strand. What we shall suggest is that in the years since Harnack, many scholars have effectively demolished the top two tiers of his superstructure. But while it is no longer fashionable to speak of a strict dichotomy in Irenaeus' soteriology or of recapitulation as borrowed from non-biblical sources, Harnack's first level remains largely intact. Accordingly, the solutions proposed to supplant these two most visible features of Harnack's structure are found wanting precisely because they accept the hegemony of Harnack's unduly constrictive basic assumption, that recapitulation is *best* understood as a matter of theory, thought, or concept. Instead of widening the scope of enquiry to consider recapitulation as a subordinate (though certainly crucial) part of Irenaeus' larger hermeneutical project, many scholars have instead simply *inflated* the "concept" of recapitulation so as to cast it as an omnipresent, controlling "master-concept."

---

[126] Ibid., 122, 123 n. 28.
[127] Ibid., 124-25.
[128] Harnack, *History of Dogma*, 2:238-39.
[129] Ibid., 2:243.
[130] Cf. Harnack, *History of Dogma*, 2:250, 297.

RECAPITULATION AND *DICHOTOMOUS* SYSTEMS?

Predictably, the first bit of Harnack's structure to be attacked was the tenuously balanced top tier, the notion of two competing systems in *Adversus Haereses*. In disputing the "formal" and (subsequently) theological unity of *Adversus Haereses*, source critics such as Harnack and Loofs had pointed to alleged incongruities in the text of *Adversus Haereses* book four.[131] Accordingly, Harnack pronounced the rather unique developmental view in iv.38 to be evidence of Irenaeus' theological heterogeneity. Though some scholars have retained vestiges of this "two-train" view, the majority have either modified or rejected it. As noted above, Nygren's proposed dichotomy reversed Harnack's judgment on recapitulation. The recapitulation-informed strand, not the educative, is deemed closer to biblical tradition. In Potter and Kelly, we see elements of both minority and majority stances wherein recapitulation relates to a picture of mystical and physical redemption, but not exclusively so. It is, however, increasingly popular to argue that Irenaeus sketched one coherent vision of salvation whose central unifying concept is recapitulation. Brunner argues that Irenaeus brings together the Johannine and Pauline streams of thought – which are not incompatible – to yield a "third element" of faith.[132] Thus it is possible to affirm both the objectivity and subjectivity of the atonement. Irenaeus' "recapitulation theory" shows the joining of incarnation, atonement, and eschatology. Aulén essentially replaces Harnack's two competing atonement models (physical and moralist) with a third model that encloses and trumps them both. By taking recapitulation out of the "physicalist" camp and framing it in the context of his all-inclusive *Christus Victor* model, we may suspect, then, that Aulén opened the door to the subsequent totalization of recapitulation which we shall observe. Wingren takes the bold move of proclaiming that, in fact, "it is *recapitulatio* which *creates unity* in the theology of Irenaeus."[133] Wingren subsequently reiterates that recapitulation "is, to be perfectly simple, *everything* that Christ has done or is doing...."[134] Osborn concedes that even his eleven "ideas" to be found in recapitulation are an "understatement, because everything that God does is part of his economy and *every part* of his economy is defined in relation to its recapitulation."[135] In Lawson's arrangement, the heading recapitulation subsumes virtually everything that Irenaeus may state about salvation or Christ. Pelikan considers that

---

[131] Cf. Mary Ann Donovan, "Irenaeus in Recent Scholarship," *SecCent* 4 (1984): 219-41.
[132] Brunner, *The Mediator*, 254.
[133] Wingren, *Man and the Incarnation*, 81; emphasis is added.
[134] Ibid., 82; emphasis is added.
[135] Osborn, *Irenaeus of Lyons*, 98; emphasis is added. Conversely, we contend that Irenaeus seeks to relate "every part" of God's economy to the Genesis creation texts, particularly 1.26 and 2.7.

recapitulation must be related to both ethical and atonement themes in Irenaean soteriology. Boersma insists that Irenaeus "masterfully weaves together different elements from the various [atonement] theories by means of his concept of recapitulation"[136] – a concept which "encapsulates each of the three elements of the atonement."[137] Philippe Bacq musters a defense of the literary and theological unity of the much maligned *Adversus Haereses* book iv.[138] Behr proposes to soften the Harnackian distinction. Rather than revealing two separate "trains of thought," he asks, is not Irenaeus merely elaborating two "dimensions," both of which are "expressed" in the "idea of recapitulation"?[139] While arguing for a general sense of unity in Irenaeus' theology (rather than specifically about recapitulation), Donovan offers another option, maintaining that Irenaeus' credentials as a "systematician" will become visible if only we judge him by the "canons of his system" not our own.[140]

Clearly, many scholars in the last century have judged Harnack's inference of two competing views of salvation in Irenaeus to be more of a hindrance than a help. For many, the solution offered to remedy this problem is apologetic; evidence is proposed so as to resolve apparent discrepancies and manifest the single, coherent soteriology that Irenaeus must have intended. His "concept" of recapitulation is frequently invoked as the means by which doctrinal unity may be recognized. In some cases recapitulation is enlisted to actually constitute this unity. Regardless, this solution casts aside Harnack's narrow view of recapitulation as a component piece of one of two systems, and embraces a much broader vision wherein recapitulation may *be* the theological system itself. However, this approach is vulnerable to criticism on at least two fronts, both of which concern linguistics.

First, a tendency found in many of the above figures (and especially pronounced in the extensive studies of Wingren, Lawson, Osborn, and Boersma) is to appeal to recapitulation to explain or relate theological themes (i.e., of Christ, humanity or salvation) when Irenaeus does not even use the actual term recapitulation in the context cited. Without a doubt, recapitulation is a primary theme in Irenaeus' work, and inferences could be suggested where details are lacking. Yet insufficient warrant has been given for the leap from a scattered collection of the term *recapitulatio* to totalizing assertions that recapitulation means "everything" Christ does, or that it brings into alignment all of the diverse themes in Irenaeus' description of salvation. Must recapitulation necessarily be

---

[136] Boersma, *Violence, Hospitality, and the Cross*, 119.
[137] Ibid., 122.
[138] Cf. Philippe Bacq, *De l'ancienne à la nouvelle alliance selon S. Irénée: unité du livre IV de l'Adversus Haereses* (Paris: Lethielleux, 1978).
[139] Behr, *Asceticism and Anthropology*, 61.
[140] Mary Ann Donovan, "Irenaeus in Recent Scholarship," 222.

found to underlie and motivate every one of Irenaeus' theological claims? At the least, where the term is not found in particular contexts, greater reticence toward generalization is preferable. Irenaeus' freedom as a theologian ought to be respected, not overlooked in a rush to reduce his thought to the most convenient, manageable form possible.

The second weakness with the integrative "unification-by-recapitulation" approaches is that even in cases where the term recapitulation *is* used in the context of a specified theological claim, a commentator ought not to presume that an entire semantic range can be imported for this term on the basis of its meaning in other contexts. On this point, it is necessary to recall that Wingren and Lawson wrote their "biblical theologies" of Irenaeus in the heyday of the "biblical theology movement." James Barr's stinging, yet insightful rebuke of some of the assumptions of this movement included his insistence that "the real communication of religious and theological patterns is by the larger word-combinations and not by the lexical units or words."[141] Though Barr's intention was to critique theologians whom (he thought) distorted Scripture by making inordinate investment in purported word-level meanings, his message has broader applicability. Barr claimed that the scholarly discontent with the "distinctiveness" of sentences that had propelled efforts to establish the distinctive meanings of *words* may be traced backwards to a fear of the "fragmentation of the Bible."[142] Given Harnack's threat to the theological unity of Irenaeus, might we also suspect that similar fears (at least in part) motivated the scholarly drive to invest heavily in the distinctiveness of the *term* recapitulation, entrusting to it the charge of producing the desired fundamental cohesiveness?[143] Wingren and Lawson, of course, cannot be held accountable for a critique that was subsequent to their time. It is somewhat surprising, though, that over forty years after Barr's initial challenge, some Irenaean commentators might be open to the charge of seeking linguistic short-cuts to achieve certain theological outcomes. A more constructive way forward would involve greater sensitivity to the fluid semantic range of the term recapitulation. It is better to recognize that Irenaeus uses this crucial word *flexibly* in various situations precisely because he most typically does so in conjunction with the

---

[141] James Barr, *The Semantics of Biblical Language* (London: Oxford University Press, 1961), 264.
[142] Ibid., 270-71.
[143] Admittedly, such an analogy between missteps in the biblical theology movement and those in the scholarly treatment of Irenaeus is open to question. With the former, the texts of multiple biblical authors in varied cultural contexts are under consideration. With the latter, the scope is narrower: a single author and, at most, two works. Yet, from a heuristic standpoint, such a comparison is defensible given that the work of scholars such as Wingren and Lawson reflects some of the aims and assumptions of the biblical theology movement of their times.

use of *different biblical texts* (rather than underlying concepts or ideas). Irenaeus finds the word recapitulation to be much more valuable than its relative scarcity in Scripture would suggest because it enables him to use Scripture itself flexibly, adapting it for a variety of purposes. Approaches to Irenaean soteriology should find *these* uses to be of primary significance, rather than the mere presence (or assumed presence) of the word recapitulation. As we shall argue shortly, Irenaeus' uniqueness is not reducible to a preferred word or concept. What is daring is his employment of this word to construct "larger linguistic complexes,"[144] especially his christological interpretations of Genesis 1 and 2. John McHugh's approach to recapitulation is a step in the right direction. The term recapitulation, he says, ought not to be heard as a "single well-pitched note" but rather a "euphonious harmony."[145] McHugh argues that Irenaeus' use of ἀνακεφαλαιώσασθαι (*recapitulare*), like its original context in Ephesians 1.10, conveys a stronger connotation of "making everything new" than of "unifying."[146] Perhaps it is no coincidence that scholars (such as Wingren) who emphasize the term's meaning as "unification" seek to make this word do the very unifying work to Irenaeus' theology that they attribute to the word's referent, Christ. However, some might see McHugh as envisioning a diversity of concepts (notes) which then contribute to one great system (a symphony). We instead shall discover "recapitulation" to involve Irenaeus' performance of biblical *texts* rather than of concepts.[147] This proposal, which we shall test in the chapters ahead, thus leads us to examine the second tier of Harnack's architecture.

RECAPITULATION AS *ALIEN* TO SCRIPTURE?

Harnack's allegation of dichotomous soteriological systems in Irenaeus – and the relegation of recapitulation to only one of these – rested on a logically prior conclusion. Recapitulation itself was a theological concept better characterized as an alien intrusion *into* scripture than an organic growth from it. As we have noted, a number of scholars have responded to Harnack on this

---

[144] I.e., the sentence is irreducible as a conveyer of theological sense (cf. Barr, *The Semantics of Biblical Language*, 263).
[145] John McHugh, "A Reconsideration of Ephesians 1.10b in the Light of Irenaeus" in *Paul and Paulinism: Essays in Honour of C. K. Barrett* (ed. M. D. Hooker and S. G. Wilson; London: SPCK, 1982), 302-309.
[146] Cf. McHugh, "A Reconsideration of Ephesians 1.10b," 308.
[147] On the general notion of Irenaeus' biblical interpretation as a "creative performance of the repertoire involv[ing] selection, development and clarification," see the seminal monograph by Frances Young, *The Art of Performance* (London: Darton, Longman and Todd, 1990), 61; cf. 45-65. Young suggests that for Irenaeus, it is not the text itself but tradition which "provides the canons of classic performance" (46).

Genesis: Recapitulation and Protological Perspective

point, taking up the task of corroborating (for the most part) Irenaeus' modest claim to simply "bring forth proofs from Scripture."[148] Qualifying as a "biblical theologian" required more than the copious citation of scriptural texts, otherwise Irenaeus (and subsequent commentators) would have no grounds to distinguish himself from Marcion and Valentinus. Vindicating Irenaeus, particularly on the matter of recapitulation, obliged one, then, to demonstrate that Irenaeus "read" Paul the way that Paul would have intended (or at least as the "plain sense" might indicate). This is exactly what Lawson seeks to show in arguing that Irenaeus' concept of recapitulation is more biblical than Hellenistic. Unlike Loofs and Harnack who strove to isolate possible extra-biblical sources behind Irenaeus' recapitulation,[149] Wingren saw recapitulation as Irenaeus' attempt "to embody the whole of the *Biblical* proclamation about the work of Christ in a single word."[150] Having the benefit of history, the scholarship of the past hundred years has surely been more probing and thorough than ever before in assessing Irenaeus' credentials as a "biblical theologian," and comparing his notion of recapitulation to scriptural teachings. Yet there are deficiencies in the proposed solutions provided to counter Harnack's "alien origin" charge.

The extremely valuable work of Wingren and Lawson would seem to be in need of an update. Both scholars, as indicated above, reflected the general paradigms and interests of the biblical theology movement of their day. Among them is the belief that linguistic observations, such as the presence or absence of certain words in a language, can reveal the distinctive features of an underlying collective "mind" and thus provide a warrant for generalizations. For example, Wingren remarks: "We notice here how far Irenaeus is from Hellenistic thought with its tendency to define human and divine as two mutually opposed substances or natures, and how close he is to Hebraic thought...."[151] Lawson signals his approval of Irenaeus' "two hands of God" image by labeling it "Hebraic." On the other hand, Irenaeus' comments on Romans 1.28 are deemed

---

[148] *ex Scripturis inferemus ostensiones* (*Haer.* iii.preface). Unless otherwise noted, citations of *Adversus Haereses* in Latin and Greek are from the Sources chrétiennes (*SC*) editions, volumes 264, 294, 211, 100, and 153 (Paris: Cerf, 1959-1982). Unless noted, English translations of *Adversus Haereses* are loosely based on the text in the *ANF* edition (Alexander Roberts and James Donaldson, eds., *The Ante-Nicene Fathers*; 10 vols. [Edinburgh: T&T Clark, 1883-1884; repr., Grand Rapids: Eerdmans, 1986-1990], 1:315-567). However, we shall modify this translation when deemed appropriate, based on the *SC* edition.

[149] Wingren terms this task "hopeless" because of the "technical impossibility of marking *unknown* sources off from one another" (*Man and the Incarnation*, 80-81; emphasis is original). Cf. F. Loofs, *Theophilus von Antiochien Adversus Marcionem, und die anderen theologischen Quellen bei Irenaeus* (TU 46, 2; Leipzig: Hinrich, 1930), 359-64; 371.

[150] Wingren, *Man and the Incarnation*, 80; emphasis is added.

[151] Ibid., 87.

evidence that he "did not understand that Hebrew manner of thought which had no room for the conception of indirect divine causation."[152] To Lawson's credit, he adopts a more flexible view of Irenaeus' thought-life than did Harnack. Yet he continues to try to locate Irenaeus in a landscape demarcated by an intellectual, theological and linguistic polarity. In Lawson's final estimation of Irenaeus, "the scales are weighted in favor of the Hebraic interest. He is definitely Greek, but he is eminently Biblical."[153] As for the "*conception* of recapitulation," Lawson undertakes to "define" it and show how it is "connected with S. Paul's rationale."[154] In other words, this concept belongs to the "biblical" rather than the "Greek" mind.

James Barr's critique has convincingly debunked the assumption that linguistics provides easy access to a presumed mindset. Furthermore, not only is it now somewhat unfashionable to presume a strict division between a "Hebrew" (or biblical) and a "Greek" (or metaphysical) mindset, the claim that such distinct entities even exist may be greeted with skepticism. Efforts, then, to try to fit Irenaeus and his key term recapitulation into any one camp – if these camps are to be defined *conceptually* – would seem outmoded. Lawson's avowed aim was "to establish the primitive and *Biblical character* of most of the important *ideas* of S. Irenaeus in a more comprehensive, connected, and definite way than heretofore...."[155] However, the question closer to our own interests is rather: How does recapitulation attest to Irenaeus' creative hermeneutical interaction with a selection of biblical *texts*? This sort of enquiry is better aligned with twenty-first century concerns and promises to open new avenues for fruitful interaction with Irenaeus' work. Ultimately, questions of whether Irenaeus' ideas (standing behind his concepts) conform to the ideas or intentions behind Paul's writings may become moot in an age of changing assumptions about language, texts, authors, and readers. Even if theoretically possible, it would seem that we lack the tools by which to render definitive judgments about the "mind" of an author. However, judging by the tenor of recent Irenaean scholarship, critiques of the biblical theology movement, and the older related assumptions upon which Harnack relied, have not yet been fully appreciated. Despite conceding that aesthetic as well as rational features ought to be ascribed to Irenaeus' view of recapitulation, Osborn, for example, models an approach

---

[152] Lawson, *Biblical Theology*, 68; cf. *Haer*. iv.29.2.
[153] Ibid., 165.
[154] Ibid., 19; emphasis is added.
[155] Lawson does add the qualification: "... yet with such provisos as may serve to guard against over-simplification" (ibid., 18; emphasis is added).

Genesis: Recapitulation and Protological Perspective

that might be described as the dissection of recapitulation.[156] The larger "concept of recapitulation" is comprised of eleven "ideas."[157] Irenaeus shows astounding ability by integrating Hellenistic philosophical constructs such as "participation" with biblical concepts and images. Using an ingenious logic, he makes the component parts cohere.

In this portrayal, Osborn is not alone. Many other commentators pay homage to Irenaeus in pronounced tones of awe before they embark on their studies of his work. For some, the quest to penetrate the mystery shrouding this man in order to explain *him* looks immediately to an analysis of his most novel concept, recapitulation. Here, Barr's comments might suggest a parallel. Gerhard Kittel, using his trademark linguistic approach, admittedly aspired to detect an "ultimate element."[158] This, says Barr, shows Kittel's drive for a "higher level of distinctiveness" than the level of biblical "ideas." Kittel ascribed significant heft to individual words or concepts precisely because they were thought able to bypass the murky clutter of ideas and provide direct access to that elusive "ultimate element," the very "shape of Christ." Although certain scholars may eschew Harnack's attempts to understand Irenaeus' distinctiveness as a factor of a Hellenistic mindset and extra-biblical sources, might they also be seeking a similar "ultimate element," Irenaeus *himself* – or at least the contents of his head?[159] For them, recapitulation is the vehicle of choice to provide the needed transportation. They may not agree that recapitulation is a *foreign* concept, yet – more significantly – they seem to tacitly agree that it is best envisioned as a *concept*.

RECAPITULATION AS (FIRSTLY) A *CONCEPT* TO BE SYSTEMATIZED?

As we have highlighted all along in our citation of Irenaean scholarship, Harnack was not alone in branding recapitulation with such labels as "theory,"

---

[156] Although its "substance" may be "aesthetic," recapitulation "holds within it a mass of tightly woven argument, which wearies the most energetic mind" (Eric Osborn, *The Emergence of Christian Theology* [Cambridge: Cambridge University Press, 1993], 171).
[157] Osborn, *Irenaeus of Lyons*, 97-98.
[158] For the following, cf. Barr, *The Semantics of Biblical Language*, 271. Barr cites G. Kittel, *Lexicographia Sacra* (Theology Occasional Papers, no. 7, London: SPCK, 1938), 25f.
[159] J. F. Bethune-Baker's now-dated work suggests an explicit example of such a quest: "The *thought expressed* by the words *recapitulare, recapitulatio*, applied in this way to Christ, is the *chief clue to the full conception of this writer*, both as to the Incarnation and as to the Atonement" (*An Introduction to the Early History of Christian Doctrine* [3d ed.; London: Methuen, 1923]), 334 n. 2; emphasis is added. Bethune-Baker identifies passages in *Adversus Haereses* on recapitulation which "shew clearly that the *writer's thought* was as distinct as possible..." (334-35); emphasis is added.

"conception," "idea," and "speculative thought." Not only for Bousset and Werner (who somewhat intentionally followed Harnack), but also for Brunner, Quasten, and Kelly (who did not), recapitulation was primarily a "theory." Wingren, Lawson, Osborn, and Boersma opine on what they call Irenaeus' "concept" of recapitulation. The argument could be made that such labels are not used self-consciously, but are merely convenient shorthand indicators. If true, though, alternative approaches to Harnack's are being hindered by a settled sense of familiarity with recapitulation. Commentators might no longer associate recapitulation with a Greek "speculative thought," as did Harnack. Yet by adopting and repeating the language of *Recapitulationstheorie*, they reinforce, rather than challenge, the underpinnings of Harnack's legacy. A more comprehensive one-track soteriological system may be substituted for the older two-track variety. The content boxed inside the "container" of the recapitulation concept may be significantly augmented. Yet the possibility of adopting an entirely new vantage point is rarely entertained. In fact, as we have seen, many of the twentieth-century interpreters of Irenaeus have responded to Harnack not by questioning his hegemonic portrayal of recapitulation, but by extending and inflating his "recapitulation concept" so as to make it a master-concept.

Irenaeus Revisited:
Recapitulation, Hermeneutics, and Genesis 1-2

In short, our hypothesis is that Irenaeus' skilful and daring work as an interpreter of Scripture warrants more attention and appreciation than has typically been given. Studies seeking to excavate Irenaeus' philosophical roots or champion his theological heritage tend to overlook this facet. The frequent inflation of Irenaeus' "doctrine" of recapitulation only serves to illustrate this point. Our alternative approach to recapitulation, and indeed to a reading of *Adversus Haereses* as a whole, has three aspects. First, as hinted above, we advocate a more *limited* view of the role of recapitulation in Irenaeus' work. The second point (which follows from this) is that recapitulation ought to be seen as a subordinate expression of Irenaeus' broader hermeneutical endeavor, that is, illustrating how texts may be appropriately read and *used* as Christian Scripture. Third, among the many biblical passages he employs, there are two protological texts that hold uniquely pivotal roles in Irenaeus' hermeneutical work: *Genesis 1.26* and *2.7*. In our third and fourth chapters, we shall endeavor to substantiate these last two claims by examining in greater depth how Irenaeus uses these texts to undermine the doctrines of God and humanity proposed by his competitors. It seems that for Irenaeus, an understanding of God and his economic design for human salvation requires an extensive though adaptive intertextual engagement with these two Genesis passages. It is true that Genesis

3 also features in Irenaeus' account of Christ's redemptive activity. Yet, as we shall see, when Irenaeus looks to the beginning, he deems Christ's unique role in creation as having primary significance. The divine Word who first formed humanity also re-formed it after taking this formation upon himself. Thus, for Irenaeus, Genesis 1.26 and 2.7 – the two texts that vividly depict the defining features of the human creature and the process of its creation – promise more explanatory power for proclaiming God's work as a *re*-capitulation of humanity in Christ. Together, our three claims lead us to conclude that it is not so much recapitulation but the theological use of protological texts which is emblematic of Irenaeus' approach. Enquiries into Christian theology, Christology, and human soteriology are drawn backward to consider how Scriptural texts might communicate (or stimulate) a Christ-informed view of beginnings.

Recapitulation "limitation"

To summarize our critique above, the investment made by numerous post-Harnackian scholars in Irenaeus' notion of recapitulation is rather excessive and probably unwarranted – at least when measured by the standard of Irenaeus' own texts. Neither is there any pressing need to postulate any single guiding rubric by which to organize all of Irenaeus' thought. Although we have highlighted the fact that many scholars adopt Harnack's language of "concept" or "theory" to refer to recapitulation, we must now explain our concerns more specifically. Concepts themselves are not the problem; they are relatively neutral, abstract intellectual tools that may be gainfully employed in various ways. To handle recapitulation as if it were a concept is not, therefore, necessarily inappropriate. It does offer certain benefits, possibly fostering understanding through processes of analysis, generalization, extrapolation, and application. Yet such an approach enjoins certain constraints that should be acknowledged as well. For example, a concept is generally understood and appreciated according to the rules that give order to the systematic framework in which it is located. Thus if recapitulation is deemed a concept, we are not surprised to find Wingren's assertion that it must have only "one basic meaning throughout."[160] In our view, although ubiquitous references to a "concept" or "theory" of recapitulation do not constitute the problem, they do manifest one. Specifically troubling is a modern tendency to first isolate then inflate a concept of recapitulation. As a result, its contextual roots are obscured and this concept acquires disproportionate independent significance. Harnack may not have been

---

[160] Wingren, *Man and the Incarnation*, xv. However, if recapitulation is viewed in light of its basis in biblical interpretation(s), this tenet is neither necessary nor even likely. The term need not be fixed in meaning nor indeterminate, but could be multivalent in function.

convinced of or sensitized to the *textual* basis of recapitulation. Yet, ironically, many of those who wish to rehabilitate Irenaeus as a "biblical theologian" also fail to grasp this connection. To trumpet recapitulation as a master-concept is to loosen it from its roots in biblical interpretation amid efforts to construe it as the key to Irenaeus' thought. Expressly biblical theologians are certainly attuned to biblical texts as potential *sources* in order to defend the legitimacy of Irenaeus' *Recapitulationstheorie*. Yet they unintentionally extract recapitulation from its context when they do not acknowledge that this context is Scriptural *interpretation*, not just a *prima facie* reading of Scripture. If recapitulation, as Wingren says, means "*everything*" that Christ has done or is doing," it is not so by virtue of a self-evident truth or a borrowed bit of theology or philosophy (cf. Harnack). But neither is it "everything" based on a simple recitation or proof from Scripture and the apostolic tradition. Rather, recapitulation could only be "everything that Christ has done or is doing" when this is understood by means of a particular reading of Scripture that is *constituted and arranged by a guiding hermeneutic*. In fact, Wingren's claim is debatable. A careful word study of the actual occurrences of the word "recapitulation" in *Adversus Haereses* suggests it to be an overstatement. Here, Barr's caution against making ambitious theological generalizations based on limited linguistic (i.e., term) evidence ought to be heard. According to a more modest approach to recapitulation, in places where the term is not present in Irenaeus' text, its concept or theory is not easily presumed. Boersma is right to argue for greater flexibility wherein recapitulation is treated more like a "formal rather than a material concept."[161] Yet beyond this modest compromise lies even greater promise. Perhaps recapitulation is both less and more than often expressed. Recapitulation is "less" insofar as its heuristic role should be limited to those contexts where the word is actually used. At the same time, recapitulation is also "more" in that it is set in relation not just to minimalist, fixed concepts (useful though these may be), but also to larger, more fluid textual and hermeneutical constructions. A scholarly fixation on recapitulation may ignore the pioneering quality of Irenaeus' hermeneutic of Scripture, for recapitulation is but one example that illustrates Irenaeus' broader concern for biblical interpretation. Despite the vocal protests of many recent scholars, Harnack surely was right to credit Irenaeus as a true innovator. However, whereas Harnack ascribes originality to his theological and ecclesiological contributions to Christian doctrine, we find it to an even greater extent in Irenaeus' hermeneutics. Studies by Douglas Farrow and Christopher Smith help us to substantiate this claim that Irenaeus' scriptural interpretation, rather than his doctrine of recapitulation, ought to be placed in the foreground of study.

---

[161] Boersma, *Violence, Hospitality and the Cross*, 112.

Although in *Ascension and Ecclesia*, Douglas Farrow's primary interest in Irenaeus relates to the doctrine of ascension, his comments are profitable to our discussion. Whereas Osborn emphasizes the continuities between Irenaeus and his philosophical environs, Farrow stresses the differences: "Taking his cue from the ascension of Jesus and its pentecostal consequences, and building conceptually on the fruitfulness motif from Genesis... Irenaeus pushed things a step further. In doing so, he developed a worldview which completely reversed the gnostic scheme of things."[162] Indeed, Farrow brings a welcomed focus to the texts, rather than extra-biblical speculation, as catalysts for Irenaeus' thought on such notions as ascension and recapitulation.[163] As noted above, Farrow insists that recapitulation centers on the incarnate Christ and begins with the particulars of the created order and of the concrete biblical narrative of "Jesus-history." Only once this starting point has been acknowledged does recapitulation assert that the cosmic particulars are brought to their fulfillment in divine communion by Christ.[164] Farrow finds Irenaeus' doctrine remarkable in that "the tension between creation and redemption has been contained *within* christology rather than being allowed to co-opt and disintegrate christology."[165] We might wish that Farrow would elaborate further on how recapitulation might relate more specifically to Irenaeus' uses of the Genesis texts, though admittedly this is more our concern than Farrow's. Nonetheless, by returning attention to Irenaeus' readings of the particulars of Jesus-history, Farrow sheds light not only on Irenaeus' specific doctrine of recapitulation, but also on his meticulous and purposive theological interaction with the sacred texts in general.

Christopher Smith's vision of recapitulation breaks new ground, pointing to a possible bridge between traditional interests in a theological construct of recapitulation and our concern to stress Irenaeus' hermeneutics of Scripture. We have previously suggested that a common response to Harnack's notion that recapitulation was a borrowed philosophical presupposition was to insist that it is either a theological assumption or an end product (cf. Lawson, et al.). Smith, however, finds that Irenaeus' *uses* of recapitulation show it to be "not so much a dictate for him as a device, not so much a taskmaster as a tool."[166] Smith's purpose, challenging standard assessments of Irenaeus as a chiliast, is not ours. Yet his insight provides a basis for relating recapitulation to the *process* of Irenaeus' argumentation (i.e., hermeneutics and rhetoric) rather than primarily to

---

[162] Farrow, *Ascension and Ecclesia*, 49.

[163] Irenaeus' doctrine of recapitulation is predicated on his refusal (unlike the Gnostics and perhaps Origen, later) "to allow cosmology to control christology" (ibid., 53).

[164] Cf., ibid., 99.

[165] Ibid., 56; emphasis is original.

[166] Christopher R. Smith, "Chiliasm and Recapitulation in the Theology of Ireneus," *VC* 48 (1994): 321.

the content of a doctrinal construct. Recapitulation, claims Smith, is Irenaeus' premise allowing him to "posit a correspondence between first and last things."[167] It is "not the goal but rather the vehicle of argumentation for Irenaeus."[168]

Hermeneutics:
Genesis 1-2 and Irenaeus' protological orientation

Arguably, then, enquiry into the single notion of recapitulation in *Adversus Haereses* is but an entrée into a much larger issue: the methodology by which Irenaeus reads and uses Scripture theologically. Surely the need to provide a superior model for interpreting texts as Christian Scripture would have been a natural priority for Irenaeus. Without addressing this root concern, his doctrinal proposals could scarcely be expected to resist (in the long term at least) the ever-changing avant-garde teachings of his opponents. Irenaeus, therefore, is immediately concerned with how to use existing Scripture to understand and appropriate the texts that gave apostolic attestation to "Jesus-history." The limited occurrence of the term recapitulation corresponds to its limited purpose: to contribute to the realization of this larger hermeneutical goal. By framing recapitulation as a tool for this project, we seek to ensure that the concepts that will inevitably be drawn from Irenaeus are not uprooted from the context in which they are embedded. Furthermore, if *Adversus Haereses* is indeed a showcase of Irenaeus' hermeneutical efforts, providing a glimpse of the way he brings texts into relationships of meaningful interaction, it is helpful to discern the operation of two primary dynamics that need not be seen as competing. Not only do we find Irenaeus' attempts to interpret texts in fidelity to an apostolic standard (as he sees it), we also see the tell-tale signs of his own creativity and freedom as an interpreter.

CHOOSING TEXTS

If the concept of recapitulation is of subordinate importance to Irenaeus' clear interest in biblical texts, we turn to consider the question of whether some texts might be more worthy of directed study than others. Taking up Mary Ann Donovan's challenge, that there is "much scope for further work" in studies of Irenaeus "as an exegete,"[169] Mark Jeffrey Olson focuses on Irenaeus' explications of Pauline texts. 1 Corinthians 15.50, of course, is a crucial text that Irenaeus deals with at length in response to Gnostic interpreters. Olson argues

---

[167] Ibid., 322.
[168] Ibid., 326.
[169] Mary Ann Donovan, "Irenaeus in Recent Scholarship," 241.

that although Irenaeus "... occasionally engages in eisegesis, [he] does grasp the essential elements of Paul's thought and successfully presents them in a coherent fashion."[170] Broadly speaking, Irenaeus "interpreted Paul's letters in a manner congruent with the Old Testament Scripture and with the gospel accounts of Jesus' teaching."[171] These statements would seem to place Olson's work in the company of Lawson, Osborn, and others in evaluating whether Irenaeus "got" Paul right. Our task, however, is different, for we wish to show *how* Irenaeus reads texts such as Paul's in a particular manner. Our suspicion is that Irenaeus is not a mere conformer but an innovator. This methodological enquiry requires us to give primary attention not to Irenaeus' readings of Paul (such as 1 Corinthians 15.50) as Scripture but to his readings of the texts that he used to interpret Paul and the evangelists. Using this criterion, two particular texts assume paramount significance for Irenaeus' task: the Genesis accounts of the creation of humanity. Even more specifically, Irenaeus is interested in how Genesis 1.26 and 2.7 may be interpreted and effectively used as Christian Scripture. His choice of these texts was not happenstance. Possibly, they were not even chosen proactively but rather in response to the hermeneutical strategies of his Gnostic-Christian opponents.[172] Yet Irenaeus' salvo would come to depend on christological (and theological) readings of Genesis 1-2 which could shed illumination not only on Christ, but indeed on God's entire economy toward humankind. Although Irenaeus calls upon these texts to perform a remarkable variety of specific theological tasks, even commentators who are intrigued by Irenaeus the exegete (rather than as a theologian or rhetorician) tend to concentrate on his readings of Paul, John, or Matthew. Furthermore, when the theological (or philosophical) concept of, for example, the *imago Dei* is discussed at length, rarely are commentators attuned to how Genesis 1-2 functions hermeneutically as Irenaeus reads a wide range of texts (including law, prophets, gospels, and epistles) together as Christian Scripture.

Strangely, even those scholars who make heavy investments in Irenaeus' doctrine of recapitulation seldom take the opportunity to comment on the role of the Genesis texts. A basic word study shows that when he mentions "recapitulation," Irenaeus frequently depends upon citations and allusions from the creation accounts (especially Genesis 2.7) to help explain what he means.[173]

---

[170] Mark Jeffrey Olson, *Irenaeus, the Valentinian Gnostics, and the Kingdom of God* (Lewiston, New York: Edwin Mellen Press, 1992), 2.
[171] Ibid., 2.
[172] Cf. our second chapter.
[173] In the surrounding contexts of the fifty-two occurrences of *recapitulare / recapitulatio* in *Adversus Haereses*, Irenaeus makes reference to Genesis 1.26 in fourteen instances, Genesis 2.7 in twenty-seven, and Genesis 3 in twenty. (Note: the sum does not equal the total occurrences due to contexts where more than one Genesis text is found.)

Turner's omission of Genesis references is not atypical. He describes recapitulation as "the element in the doctrine which is most noticeably to the fore in the work of S. Irenaeus. Its sources, though still Pauline, are rather Romans and 1 Corinthians than Ephesians."[174] In the surrounding context, Turner mentions motifs from Genesis 1-2 such as Adam, virgin soil, and the tree of the knowledge of good and evil. So we must assume either that Turner overlooks the obvious by focusing only on Paul or that he assumes that the Genesis influence is so self-evident so as to be unworthy of comment. As we have seen in Harnack, Lawson, and Olson, the popular debate has tended toward the question of whether Irenaeus' reading of Paul was justifiable. Yet Turner and others would be mistaken if they assumed that Irenaeus' christological readings of Genesis 1-2 were a given and not a variable. Irenaeus' reading, like those of the Valentinians and Ophites (to which we shall shortly turn), was the product of an intentionally crafted hermeneutical strategy. Hart justly criticizes the "Harnack-Loofs interpretation" of Irenaeus because it attends only to the language that Irenaeus uses (i.e., the "Greek" terminology) rather than considering "the way in which he used language, and... the frame of reference within which that language is firmly set."[175] Unfortunately, this call has not been heeded by commentators who might, at best, footnote or make a passing reference to Genesis 1-2 in their topical discussions of Irenaeus' theology.

As noted above, Farrow, however, shows a greater sensitivity to the act of interpretation. He suggests that "Irenaeus allowed Jesus-history to serve as a commentary on Genesis 1 and to govern his view of the creation of man. Thinking together Jesus' baptism, his ascension to the Father, and the appearance of the ecclesial community, he developed the thesis that it is of the very essence of man to advance... through communion with God."[176] Although Farrow does not substantially engage with Irenaeus' readings of Genesis 1-2, he does provide us with the opportunity to preview our analysis of Irenaeus' hermeneutic. Instead of "commentary" (and accompanying pedestrian connotations which do not do justice to Irenaeus' use), it would seem that Irenaeus sets two texts, an apostolic (or gospel) text and a Genesis text in a relationship of dynamic interaction. The resulting re-interpretation is in fact more than a commentary; it is, in essence, a hypothetical *third* text. It is this new theological text that provides a biblical basis for Irenaeus' doctrinal constructs such as recapitulation. Widening the scope, we shall discover that Genesis 1-2 holds an integral, irreplaceable role in Irenaeus' prescriptive model for a ruled reading of Scripture as a whole. To substantiate this claim will require us to bring out specific examples from *Adversus Haereses* itself to note the functions

---

[174] Turner, *The Patristic Doctrine of Redemption*, 65.
[175] Hart, "Irenaeus, Recapitulation and Physical Redemption," 155.
[176] Farrow, *Ascension and Ecclesia*, 59.

of Genesis 1.26 and 2.7 in Irenaeus' interpretative and theological work. This we shall undertake in our third and fourth chapters.

IRENAEUS' PROTOLOGICAL ORIENTATION

If indeed the text of *Adversus Haereses* invites us to find recapitulation not as a controlling feature in itself but rather an instance and illustration of Irenaeus' interpretative strategy with respect to Scripture, and if Genesis 1-2 are texts upon which he shows a unique reliance, then we may summarize the hypothesis we aim to demonstrate: Irenaeus' *Adversus Haereses* is noteworthy for its *protological orientation*. By no means do we wish to minimize the significance of the eschatological vision that scholars have traditionally (and rightly) discerned in Irenaeus' theology. Yet a sharper attentiveness to Irenaeus' use of essential protological texts lends sparkling illumination to his portrayal of a creation fulfilled in the climax of God's economy. According to Irenaeus' protological orientation, the desire for a comprehensive understanding of what *happened* in Jesus Christ, what *is* presently happening, and what *will* happen in the future, compels a re-reading and re-appropriation of the texts which attest to the *beginning*. Because Irenaeus' notion of recapitulation is a subset of his broader protological tendency, it should be relieved of much of the burden that scholars have frequently laid upon it. Insofar as it constitutes a more fundamental and distinctive hallmark of his project, Irenaeus' hermeneutical stance toward Genesis 1-2 offers an excellent point of entry into and departure from Irenaean studies, recommending new areas in which his contribution may be valued.

Focal Texts? Mapping the road ahead

At this introductory stage, it seems appropriate to substantiate more fully our claim that Genesis 1.26 and 2.7 should be regarded as *focal texts* in Irenaeus' functional hermeneutic of Scripture. Irenaeus' *Adversus Haereses* was written as an occasional piece. In the second century, certain Valentinian teachers were, it seems, increasingly successful in persuading adherents of the rather variegated Christian community that their doctrinal system addressed the contemporary questions of the day while remaining faithful to the apostolic tradition of the past. These two imperative qualities, contemporaneity and fidelity, may correlate with Valentinian interests to speak, respectively, of anthropology and Christology, and to situate these interrelated subjects within the all-embracing context of a divine economy. As for the first quality, contemporaneity, it is likely that Valentinian teachings would have stood out as relevant or novel because they granted a certain priority to basic questions of human identity and purpose. New disciples could find a welcome sense of security and belonging in the fixed theological schema that the Valentinians proposed in order to make sense of the diverse experiences and vicissitudes of human life. Among other things, a Valentinian compositional view of humanity[177] explained the presence of evil as well as the divergence in human responses to the gospel. Their description of the way of salvation offered adherents clear direction and confidence. Yet the Valentinians had every reason to relate their anthropological concerns to Christ. After all, they insisted that they were not abandoning the Christian church but rather recovering its truest meaning. Thus the Valentinians' demonstration of fidelity to apostolic texts and traditions was important. If Christian enquiries into human identity draw attention to the question of Christ's identity, one might expect such a quest to elicit backward reflection on what sacred texts might reveal about the origins of humanity and of Christ. The Valentinians' "protological orientation" led them to reread the gospels and the Pauline letters intently. Tackling the question of Christ's identity, they found secret insights particularly in the Johannine prologue and in Ephesians 1.10. In fact, Irenaeus' proposal that a theological notion of bodily recapitulation could explain Christ's relationship to humanity may have actually been a response to Valentinian christological readings of these two texts. Based on Irenaeus' account, we surmise that the Valentinians sought to *understand Christ by understanding Christ's origin* (i.e., theogony). For those who had the right sort of "eyes" to read, the opening of John's gospel ("In the beginning…") discloses the names and ranks of divine Aeons (cf. *Haer.* i.1.1-3). Furthermore, Ephesians 1.8-10 claims to reveal a "mystery" that clarifies Christ's beginnings and his relationship to the rest of the divine realm (i.e., Pleroma): "With all wisdom and insight he has made known to us the mystery of his will, according to his good pleasure that he set forth in Christ as a plan for the fullness ($\pi\lambda\eta\rho\omega\mu\alpha$) of time, to gather up ($\dot{\alpha}\nu\alpha\kappa\epsilon\phi\alpha\lambda\alpha\iota\dot{\omega}\sigma\alpha\sigma\theta\alpha\iota$) all things ($\tau\dot{\alpha}\ \pi\dot{\alpha}\nu\tau\alpha$) in him, things in heaven and things on earth." Irenaeus recounts how the Valentinians understood Christ's "recapitulation." "With one design and desire," all of the Aeons offered contributions which, when united, produced "a being of most perfect beauty, the very star of the Pleroma, and the perfect fruit [of it], namely Jesus" (*Haer.* i.2.6). They also call him "Savior," "Christ," "Logos," and "Everything" ($\tau\dot{\alpha}\ \Pi\dot{\alpha}\nu\tau\alpha$) "because he was formed from the contributions of all" (i.2.6).[178] The Valentinians must have insisted that their

---

[177] I.e., a tri-partite, hierarchical view of humanity, extrapolated from Pauline terminology ($\pi\nu\epsilon\upsilon\mu\alpha\tau\iota\kappa\acute{o}\varsigma$, $\psi\upsilon\chi\iota\kappa\acute{o}\varsigma$, and $\dot{\upsilon}\lambda\iota\kappa\acute{o}\varsigma$).

[178] Such differentiation in terms of Jesus Christ's identity ought not necessarily be confused with polytheism. From a Platonist-informed perspective, each Aeon would have been reckoned to be a "divine partial aspect" proceeding from one supreme God (Christoph Markschies, *Gnosis: An Introduction* [trans. John Bowden; London: T&T Clark, 2003], 90-91). "In the end," says Markschies, "all the differentiations that merely

Christology (or christogony) was simply based on readings of Ephesians 1.10 together with Colossians 2.9, 3.11, and Romans 11.36.[179] Paul would seem to speak of Christ's supremacy as a matter of his recapitulation of all things divine (i.3.4). Indeed, "in him the whole fullness (πλήρωμα) of deity dwells bodily."[180] For Irenaeus' opponents, then, Christ's recapitulation was unrelated to his physical incarnation; it was (according to Paul and John) a reference to Christ's spiritual identity and origin. On the other hand, the Genesis 1-2 narrative of the creator god ("Demiurge") held cryptic clues to humanity's origin and destiny, as implied by Paul in 1 Corinthians 15. This text, beholden to the tradition of the uninformed Demiurge and his prophet Moses, does not speak of Christ – neither his relation to the creator, nor his role in the anthropological texts of Genesis 1.26 and 2.7. The Christ-events of the gospels were earthly counterparts or shadows of what had taken place previously in heavenly Pleroma (i.7.2) before the beginning of Genesis.[181] In keeping with their proclivity for protology, the intricate Valentinian doctrinal system rested on solid hermeneutical piers – the authority of Christian texts that spoke of beginnings, albeit necessarily in veiled fashion. Practically speaking, the Valentinians offered eschatological hope to their disciples. Those who grasped Christ's spiritual revelation and thus were counted among the elect could anticipate the exchange of their embodied existence in a corruption-prone world for eternal rest in Pleroma above. In effect, their system outlined the "big picture" of God's economic activity, illustrating how Christ was relevant to everyday human concerns. Crucially, though, the Valentinian distinction between the Father of Jesus Christ and the creator of the world is expressed in the hermeneutical *disconnect* between appropriating Johannine and Pauline texts for christological interpretation and appropriating Genesis texts for anthropological interpretation. Their vision of the divine economy drew from these two sources somewhat independently. The gnosis that could be recovered from each could then be mapped upon a narrative that, from a historical perspective at least, is found to borrow much from Middle-Platonism.[182]

For Irenaeus, by contrast, Genesis 1.26 and 2.7 are vital texts in that they illumine *all* aspects of God's economy – Christology and theology as much as

---

served to explain how far the one God was connected with the man Jesus of Nazareth and could be designated redeemer of humankind" (92).

[179] Colossians 3.11: "In that renewal there is no longer Greek and Jew... but Christ is all (τὰ πάντα) and in all." Romans 11.36: "For from him and through him and to him are all things (τὰ πάντα)...."

[180] Colossians 2.9.

[181] The Christ of the gospels was the second Christ patterned from the first Christ (cf. *ANF* 1:319 n. 15 and 1:325 n. 6).

[182] In our second chapter, we look at a few of the clear similarities between Irenaeus' account of Valentinian cosmology and characteristics found in Plato's *Timaeus*.

anthropology. When allowed to inform the interpretation of both older sacred writings and newer apostolic tradition, these texts project a stirring vision of God's activity as a single comprehensive and coherent narrative. To be sure, Irenaeus' rebuttal shared many of the same concerns and methodological starting points as his opponents. While he stakes his claim on fidelity to the christological teachings of the apostolic church, he must have been mindful of the need to speak about humanity in a way that addressed contemporary interests. Combating the protological viewpoint of his opponents with one of his own, Irenaeus' success would depend on his ability to offer engaging interpretations of Christian texts that satisfactorily explained how Christ's narrative intersected with and informed the human narrative. The degree to which Irenaeus was indebted to the Christian apologists and others preceding him has been a matter of debate. Yet clearly in the second century, a variety of interpreters in Jewish, Christian, and Gnostic circles were intrigued by Genesis 1-3 and creatively sought to appropriate this source in their current religious contexts. Philo had previously found these texts indispensable for his apologetic work. Later, Irenaeus' contemporary, Theophilus, suggested that the Genesis account of God creating seed-bearing plants indicates a pattern of the future resurrection of humankind.[183] He also proposed that baptism was "prefigured in [God's] production of living creatures from the waters."[184] In the Valentinian *Gospel of Truth*, the language and imagery of Genesis 2-3 aided a discerning reading of the gospels, calling attention to Christ's revelation and its soteriological significance. For Irenaeus, Valentinian interpretations of Genesis must be refuted because they epitomized an "impious"[185] doctrine of *God*, resulting in a faulty understanding of humanity and salvation.[186] Irenaeus thinks he finds rich theological resources in Genesis 1-2 to describe how Christ relates to an *embodied* humanity – resources that his opponents had overlooked because of their commitment to certain presuppositions of a Platonist worldview.

---

[183] Theophilus, *Autol.* 2.14 (OECT, *Theophilus of Antioch*, 48-51).

[184] Frances Young, *Biblical Exegesis and the Formation of Christian Culture* (Oxford: Oxford University Press, 1997), 55. Cf. Theophilus, *Autol.* 2.16.

[185] Cf. *Haer.* ii.10.2, et al.

[186] Given Irenaeus' chief concern in theology (cf. his doctrine of the Creator God in *Haer.* ii) and Valentinian preoccupation with soteriology, Rowan Greer remarks that the two sides were "talking at cross purposes" ("The Dog and the Mushrooms: Irenaeus's View of the Valentinians Assessed" in *The Rediscovery of Gnosticism: Proceedings of the International Conference on Gnosticism at Yale*, [ed. and trans. Bentley Layton; 2 vols.; Leiden: Brill, 1980], 1:171). We shall argue that Irenaeus contends with Valentinian (and Ophite) interpretations of Genesis 1-2 precisely because he finds in these biblical texts the basis for a Christian doctrine of God, which is the crucial source for derivative doctrines of humanity and salvation.

Genesis: Recapitulation and Protological Perspective

Early in *Adversus Haereses* book one, Irenaeus takes issue with a Valentinian hermeneutic that enforces a separation between the texts about Jesus and those about creation. Accusing them of "abusing"[187] texts such as John 1, he lashes out: "Learn then, you foolish men, that Jesus who suffered for us, and who dwelt among us, is himself the Word of God" (*Haer.* i.9.3). Battles over how to portray Christ as the answer to questions emerging from the human condition expressed a hermeneutical dilemma. How shall the church's various sacred texts be interpreted so as to be consonant with the new understanding of reality inaugurated by and embodied in the church's founder, Jesus Christ? Irenaeus seems to have been driven to read biblical texts protologically for the same reasons as his opponents, that is, to better explain Christ. However, if the Valentinians found their point of entry into Christology in biblical depictions of theogony, Irenaeus, by contrast, found his in anthropogony. Rather than understanding humanity in terms of Christ's origin, he sought to *understand Christ in terms of humanity's origin*. The best way to interpret the "Christ" of Paul and John was to read their texts in light of Genesis 1-2. In other words, Irenaeus thought that Jesus was best "read" in context of the beginning of the God-human relationship. From the very start, Christology is to be oriented along anthropological lines because of the significance of the Christ-Adam connection. Irenaeus' christological readings of the creation accounts, of course, depended upon his basic presupposition that the God in the gospels is the same as the God in Genesis (i.e., Irenaeus' *regula veritatis*[188]). From a Valentinian perspective, Genesis 1-2 could inform a reading of Christ in the gospels only indirectly by setting up a foil, the inferior Demiurge, and by showing his work to be reversed and superseded by Christ. But the *regula veritatis* made Genesis 1-2 potentially a direct source of revelation about Christ, and if so, then also about human salvation. Indeed, the notion of recapitulation pointed to the intersection where christological enquiry meets anthropological enquiry. The divine hands which first formed "Adam" from the dust and breathed into his nostrils the breath of life are the very hands that re-form (grant bodily healing) and re-vive (grant spiritual life) him. If Christ's recapitulation of "all things" (Ephesians 1.10) has soteriological value for humanity, it must involve his summing up of a humanity that, according to Genesis, was meant to be embodied.[189] Viewed through this hermeneutical lens, the apostles and prophets affirm a consistent witness to God's intention for the *homo vivens* he is fashioning.

---

[187] ἐπηρεάζειν / *calumniari* (*SC* 264 [136.2; 137.975]).
[188] Cf. *Haer.* i.22.1; et al.
[189] Cf. especially *Haer.* iii.21.9-10.

CREATION AND FALL

It may be asked why we do not include Genesis 3, the story of human fallenness, in our exploration of Irenaeus' hermeneutic of Scripture from a protological perspective. It is true that Irenaeus does occasionally refer to Christ's recapitulation as reversing the effects of one tree – disobedience, enmity, and death – by means of another tree. First, however, we should distinguish the approach to Genesis 1-3 that is paradigmatic of our era from that of Irenaeus'. As is well known, modern scholars typically divide Genesis 1-3 into a "priestly" source text, Genesis 1.1-2.4a, and a "Yahwist" source text, Genesis 2.4b-3.24, given compelling evidence of two distinct literary units each rooted in its own historical origin. Yet despite his awareness of textual anomalies, Irenaeus, of course, is not concerned to render a critical account of the text's history. His interests in Genesis 1-3 stem from a thematic or theological standpoint. On these grounds, it could be useful to discriminate between Genesis 1-2, the story of human origination and its underlying divine intent, and Genesis 3, the story of human regression. Thus although Irenaeus' interest in beginnings suggests that he would use both stories for christological purposes, we might expect the creation imagery of Genesis 1.26 and 2.7 to fulfill common hermeneutical functions that differ from those served by Genesis 3. The second reason that we place emphasis on the creation accounts is that a survey of *Adversus Haereses* shows Genesis 1-2 to be a more crucial christological text for Irenaeus than Genesis 3. A word study of the term "recapitulation" is instructive.[190] Whereas *nineteen of the objects*[191] of the action of recapitulation refer to humanity in some sense (whether corporately or not), only *five* refer to the evil associated with or attached to humanity. In the former category, Irenaeus connects Christology to anthropology specifically with human origination in view, as seen in his frequent use of terms such as *plasma(tio)*. The evidence indicates that Irenaeus' "recapitulation Christology" finds its primary basis in *God's* creation of humanity (with an emphasis on physical embodiment) rather than in the story of *human* calamity. The same divine Word who fashions human flesh later takes it upon himself. Irenaeus does make use of Genesis 3 to argue that Christ recapitulates the *history* of humanity,

---

[190] The eleven references to Christ's recapitulation of "all things" (τὰ πάντα / *omnia, universa*) can be seen as Irenaeus' close adherence to the sense of this term as it occurs in Ephesians 1.10. The other non-rhetorical uses represent Irenaeus' more innovative and expansive theological adaptations (though Irenaeus apparently credits Justin for using it earlier [cf. *Haer.* iv.6.2]).

[191] Where *recapitulare* occurs in verbal form (the majority), the object is simply that which, as a direct object, is acted upon by the subject, Christ. When *recapitulatio* occurs in nominal form, the object may be discerned as that which stands in a genitive or appositional relationship to the noun.

Genesis: Recapitulation and Protological Perspective

wherein Christ experiences and hallows every stage of development (even old age). By remaining obedient under temptation, Christ overturns Adam's disobedience. Yet important as is this dimension of recapitulation, it is entirely predicated on Christ's prior recapitulation of the *formation* or physicality of humanity.[192] An example from his later work, *Demonstration of the Apostolic Preaching*, further confirms that Irenaeus is most concerned to relate Christ's recapitulation to his assumption of the original human formation. The first man's "substance," Irenaeus avers, comes from God's "will and wisdom" and from "virgin earth." "From this earth, then, while it was still virgin, God took dust and fashioned the man, the beginning of humanity. So the Lord, *recapitulating* this man, reproduced the scheme of his incarnation... that he too might copy the incarnation of Adam, and man might be made... according to the image and likeness of God."[193] This linkage explains why the tradition of Jesus' virgin birth is essential for Irenaeus' Christology. Without it, the crucial parallel between Christ and Adam breaks down and thus also the precondition for humanity's salvation. Not only do Genesis 1.26 and 2.7 speak more intensively about Christ and his divine activity in God's economy than does Genesis 3, these texts also say more about humanity. A Christian reading of the tragic history of Adam and Eve helpfully locates Christ in light of humanity. However, a christological reading of the creation texts locates humanity in light of Christ; it articulates a comprehensive history spanning from origin to destiny. Although others (Augustine, for one) might disagree, Irenaeus sees the fall as more of an interlude in the economy than a catastrophic disruption. A Christian re-reading of Genesis, then, traces the effects of Christ's recapitulation not just to the beginning of human sin, but back to the very beginning of God's intent for his human creation.

PREVIEW OF CHAPTERS

In summary, we judge Genesis 1.26 and 2.7 to be Irenaeus' focal texts because his theological usage of them constitutes the most decisive variable separating his system from that of his opponents. As noted, other factors in the equation are constant, most significantly, an orientation toward protological enquiry. But Irenaeus arrives at a different answer, a unique non-Platonic depiction of humanity in God's purview, largely because of his multivalent theological readings of these creation texts. It would seem that Irenaeus found

---

[192] Cf. the order affirmed by 1 Corinthians 15.46: "the physical, and then the spiritual."

[193] *Epid.* 32. The translation, with our slight modification and addition of emphasis, is by Joseph P. Smith (*Proof of the Apostolic Preaching* [*ACW* 16; Westminster, Md.: Newman, 1952], 68).

these texts to be peerless because of two characteristic features: extraordinary *flexibility* and suitability for *wide typological readings*.

In our second chapter, we begin by investigating Gnostic interpretations of Genesis 1-3 that prompt Irenaeus' rebuke and constructive counter-proposal. The readings of the Ophite and Valentinian communities manifest their conviction that "truth" is implicitly found in the beginning, though sometimes it lies behind the text or between its lines. Though rejecting his adversaries' hermeneutics as dangerously flawed, Irenaeus follows their protological orientation in offering ruled readings of Scripture. Our third and fourth chapters provide specific evidence of how Irenaeus draws on the protological vision of Genesis in order to discern Christ's contemporary significance for human living. They also highlight, in turn, the two prized textual features listed above. For Irenaeus, a craftsman marshalling words to address practical concerns in the church, different tasks might require different hermeneutical tools. But if one tool (i.e., a text) were sufficiently reliable and adaptive to assist in a variety of tasks, it would be especially valuable. While building his case for a Christian non-Platonic anthropology, Irenaeus discovered that the "image and likeness" language of Genesis 1.26 could be effectively used to sketch the contours of God's grand oikonomia and to locate humanity's place in each crucial segment of its span: origination, fallenness, restoration, and destiny. When viewing this text in light of Christ and Christ in light of it, Genesis 1.26 functions as a hermeneutical "tool," illumining the divine economy in a general way so as to supply a cohesive, theological basis for anthropology. The result was a suitable scheme to be matched against an attractive Valentinian system. A second characteristic of these texts is their unusual ability to bring together a whole range of issues, and thus invite wide typological readings. Irenaeus, it appears, thinks he can enunciate the content of God's entire oikonomia by means of Genesis 2.7. Indeed, this text is pivotal for Irenaeus' theological understanding of Christ's work as recapitulation. If, following Paul's lead, Irenaeus invites us to draw parallels between and extrapolate from creation narratives to redemption narratives, we note that just as original formation was an activity undertaken by God, so also is *re*-capitulation. Christ's redeeming action is divine, not human. Thus whereas Genesis 1.26 places the emphasis on the human object (i.e., "who is this that is made?"), Genesis 2.7 addresses the divine activity and the process of creating (i.e., "how is this made?"). The "formed from dust" / "breath of life" language of Genesis 2.7 enables Irenaeus to paint a more detailed picture of the activities of God – Father, Spirit and Son – to bring about the goal of this economy: the *homo vivens*. In so doing, this text also facilitates christological readings of (now termed) Old and New Testament texts *as Christian Scripture*. By setting Genesis 2.7 in a dynamic relation with other texts that are seen to attest Christ (whether those of the prophets, evangelists or apostles), the divine portrait which Irenaeus discerns in Genesis 2.7 undergirds his anthropology. At the same time (as mentioned above), Irenaeus' Christology, the centerpiece of such a triune view of God, has taken its hermeneutical point of departure from the two most crucial anthropological texts. As one of God's hands, the Word establishes and then reconfirms the divine work of vivifying the humanity that is made after God's image. The resulting interlocking doctrines of Christ and humanity were commissioned to undermine the Valentinian system by purporting to make better sense of the very scriptural texts on which it claimed to be built.

Conclusion

Thus far, we have raised the possibility of looking at Irenaeus' potential contributions from a different standpoint than has commonly been used. Harnack and those responding to his school of thought were not so much unfair to Irenaeus as unduly restrictive in the scope of their enquiry. Perhaps, though, it is only natural that each generation should have in hand its own set of questions and interests when returning to this venerable second-century theologian in hopes of gaining fresh insight. Recapitulation is indeed a doctrinal treasure, of sorts, entrusted to the church. Yet we aim to demonstrate that Irenaeus' fondness for using Genesis 1-2 to speak theologically is perhaps an even more basic feature that ought not to be taken for granted. A wider focus on Irenaeus' hermeneutics, that is, the way he read and used particular texts as authoritative Scripture, points to an expansion of Irenaeus' potential relevance in our increasingly text-sensitized world. The hermeneutical (or linguistic) turn evident in philosophy and theology has engendered not only an enhanced suspicion of blunt pronouncements of "truth," but also a greater curiosity regarding the methodologies standing behind all such claims. The vital interests and insights of previous generations of Irenaean scholars ought not to be forgotten. Yet a critical appreciation of Irenaeus as an interpreter introduces new grounds for potentially fruitful dialogue that may engage both church and academy. Practically speaking, Irenaeus' early constructive model of reading the Old Testament as Christian Scripture may be found to be surprisingly progressive by those who engage in the twenty-first century versions of this ongoing ecclesial debate.

2. COMPETITION: GNOSTIC INTERPRETATIONS OF GENESIS

Introduction and Methodology

As we suggested in our previous chapter, studies that focus on theological constructs such as recapitulation risk overlooking features which undergird and power Irenaeus' theology: a protological orientation and a pioneering hermeneutical approach. However, before we shine the spotlight on Irenaeus' pivotal readings and uses of Genesis 1.26 and 2.7, our prerequisite task is to survey his competition, entertaining the supposition that "the root of the controversy was exegesis."[1] Thus, Irenaeus' success in overturning the teachings of his opponents would depend upon his ability to explain "how and why the Valentinians interpreted falsely" and how he "read the scriptures rightly."[2] Irenaeus' indebtedness to Gnostic hermeneuts is evident by his recognition that they were setting a new standard of comprehensiveness. "We should not let the bizarre language of [Gnostic] myths conceal from us the grandeur of this religious system," cautions Denis Minns.[3] "It sought to take account of *all* aspects of the human condition...."[4] Irenaeus was well aware that his interpretation of Scripture, particularly of the programmatic Genesis creation narratives, must be more persuasive and enriching than the Gnostic readings.

In our efforts to retell the stories that two Gnostic[5] groups apparently found in Genesis, we will initially be more sympathetic than was Irenaeus. Naturally

---

[1] O'Keefe and Reno, *Sanctified Vision*, 34.
[2] Ibid.
[3] Denis Minns, *Irenaeus* (London: Geoffrey Chapman, 1994), 17-18.
[4] Ibid., 18; emphasis is added.
[5] Insofar as the focus of this chapter is *Gnostic* interpretations of Genesis, a caveat is in order. From a historical standpoint, modern scholars are right to press for a more

the Gnostics brought their own theological presuppositions to these texts. However, our assumption is that the Ophites and Valentinians, to differing degrees, genuinely ascribed authority to Genesis. They looked to the Genesis texts not simply to discredit them but to learn from them – even if a radical hermeneutic of suspicion were needed to bring truth to the surface. Accordingly, in light of Irenaeus' counterproposal, we are interested in how the Genesis readings and concurrent interpretative assumptions of the Ophites and Valentinians informed (not merely confirmed) their doctrines of God and humanity. Unlike Irenaeus, these two Gnostic groups relied on Genesis 3 to fill out their characterization of divinity (whether supreme Father, creator Demiurge, or divine Jesus). Additionally, Genesis 3 also assumes a more central place in Gnostic anthropology than it does in Irenaeus' alternative, particularly as regards the role of the physical body in the divine plan. Thus in this chapter, we shall extend the bounds of our study to examine Gnostic interpretations of Genesis 1-3 and the accompanying implications for Christology. First, however, it is necessary to address some possible methodological objections toward the principal sources we shall use.

Why rely upon Irenaeus' account of Gnostic interpretations of Genesis?

It would be safe to say that of the five books comprising Irenaeus' *Adversus Haereses*, the first does not normally garner the appreciation ascribed to others. Even Erasmus, who proudly reintroduced Irenaeus to the world, is quite candid. In his letter dedicating the first edition of *Adversus Haereses* to Bishop Bernard von Cles, he writes, "The first and second books, since they consist mainly of a survey of the strange language and ideas of the heretics, caused me from time to time a lot of pain. No one, unless possessed of uncommon patience, will be able

---

critically reflective view of the religious groups of Irenaeus' day, particularly as this relates to categorization and labeling. As for the terms "Gnostics" or "Gnosticism," Michael Allen Williams warns: "Irenaeus is not really trying to show us what 'gnosticism' is, but what heresy is.... It is modern scholarship that has singled out a portion of that family tree [of heresies] to form the basis for a typological grouping" (*Rethinking "Gnosticism": An Argument for Dismantling a Dubious Category* [Princeton: Princeton University Press, 1996], 45). Yet despite the shortcomings associated with imprecise (and potentially misleading) labels, we shall refer to particular groups as Valentinians, Ophites, and even Gnostics because we address them primarily as literary constructs in *Adversus Haereses* rather than as historical referents. With this in mind, the quotation marks around these terms will be omitted purely as a matter of style. For the sake of convenience, we will use the term Ophite to describe the group discussed by Irenaeus in *Haer*. i.30. Even though this descriptor was only added later by editors (likely in view of Origen's related comments), it seems preferable to other options.

to read these books without boredom."[6] Erasmus' comments aside, such pain and boredom should be braved, for the theologically-rich latter three books of *Adversus Haereses* make much more sense after struggling with the first two books. Our decision to focus chiefly on Irenaeus' second-hand Gnostic interpretations of Genesis 1-3 in *Adversus Haereses* book one, rather than on more primary sources (such as the Nag Hammadi codices), requires a defense. It may be claimed that such a methodology is ill-advised because Irenaeus was either *unwilling* or *unable* to supply an account that accurately corresponds to his opponents' positions. Some recent scholars judge that since Irenaeus obviously had a polemic intention, his depiction of the teachings of his opponents cannot be trusted. Certainly at the very outset Irenaeus announces his motivation for writing: to "set forth" (*ostendere* / ἀπαγγέλλειν) the teaching of Ptolemy and his followers "with brevity and clearness," and "to furnish the means of overthrowing them (*evertere* / ἀνατρέπειν) by showing how absurd and inconsistent with the truth are their statements."[7] On the one hand, contemporary commentators who are particularly sensitized to the oft-unacknowledged role of political and social influences may view Irenaeus' former task ("setting forth") with great suspicion given his latter task (refutation). Others may argue that Irenaeus was not intentionally deceptive, but simply lacked the requisite skills and / or knowledge to provide a fair account. To these significant objections we now turn.

OBJECTION ONE: IRENAEUS WAS *UNWILLING* TO PROVIDE A FAIR ACCOUNTING OF HIS OPPONENTS

According to the first type of critique (a sort of "hermeneutic of suspicion") Irenaeus' avowed motivation for writing implies that significant distortions – perhaps even fabrications – may be expected in his textual accounts of Gnostic teaching. Catherine Keller, for example, accuses church fathers (particularly Irenaeus, Tertullian, and Athanasius) of using supercharged rhetoric not only to advance but also *construct* orthodoxy and (by implication) heresy.[8] On Irenaeus' appeal to fellow church leaders to warn people of the dangers of irregular sects – "to avoid such an abyss (*profundus*, cf. Tehom) of madness"[9] – Keller asserts: "Tehomophobic ridicule seems to have become a standard weapon of

---

[6] Erasmus, *The Collected Works of Erasmus*, 12:295.
[7] *Haer.* i.preface.2.
[8] *Face of the Deep: A Theology of Becoming* (London: Routledge, 2003). Using Genesis 1.2 as a point of departure, Keller's book offers an invitation to "rethink the darkness of beginnings," wherein a conception of *creatio ex profundis* unseats the familiar Christian doctrine of *creatio ex nihilo* (xvi).
[9] *Haer.* i.preface.2. Irenaeus' statement is a word-play on *profundus* which also refers to the first principle or deity in Valentinian cosmology, Bythus ("deep" / "abyss").

heresiology."[10] According to Keller, it is Irenaeus' "polemic" and unwarranted "rhetorical extrusion" from Scripture, not a "latent biblical logic," that is constitutive of his particular interpretation of the Genesis creation accounts.[11] In like manner, it is not just that Irenaeus distorts the alleged "heretical" positions of his opponents. Rather, it is Irenaeus' rhetoric and polemic that is actually responsible for constructing heresy. "Arguably, Irenaeus is one of the inventors of heresy, building on Justin's scheme by gathering all 'other' doctrines under one label of 'heresy' he *produces* the hybrid monster."[12] Keller states, "We will find *richly ambiguous motives* amidst the 'sensitive initial conditions' of the fathers' Christianity. What, for instance, is going on when *they construct* a heretical, hysterical Sophia-goddess at the very site of the chaotic matter of Genesis?"[13] While making use of the research of historian Gerhard May, Keller nonetheless laments that May "unquestioningly reinforces [Irenaeus'] ahistorical homogenization of scripture."[14] "Irenaeus' turbulently reactive coherence," she says, "comes to frame and be framed as the truth of church history...."[15] Thus from Irenaeus' polemically-inspired hermeneutical construction (and concurrent "invention" of the Bible[16]), his "heresiology becomes historiography."[17]

According to this view, Irenaeus' sleight of hand, regrettably, has not been unmasked until now. Like the Ophite interpreters of Genesis which we shall

---

[10] Keller, *Face of the Deep*, 50.
[11] Ibid., 43-44. Keller's suspicion of Irenaeus' motives is, of course, not unique. When Elaine Pagels grapples with the question of why Irenaeus found the Valentinians' portrayal of God to be "so utterly reprehensible" to warrant their expulsion from the church, she offers an explanation. By their "modification of monotheism," the Valentinians not only offered a religious and / or philosophical alternative, more crucially, they offered a *political* alternative. They attacked the church's "system of governance" predicated on "One God" and "one bishop" (*The Gnostic Gospels* [New York: Random, 1979], 33-34). As a bishop himself, Irenaeus correctly recognized that Gnostic teachings were a grave threat to the political hegemony enjoyed by the church's clergy. Though Pagels is reluctant to unequivocally reduce "Irenaeus' religious convictions" to mere "political tenets in disguise" (46), Keller seems less so.
[12] So Virginia Burrus, in personal correspondence to Keller (cited in Keller, *Face of the Deep*, 253 n. 30); emphasis is original. The "hybrid monster" in Burrus' citation is most likely an allusion to Irenaeus' description of the "many-headed beast" that "has been generated from the school of Valentinus" as a "Lernaean hydra" (cf. *Haer.* i.30.15).
[13] Keller, *Face of the Deep*, 44; emphasis is added.
[14] Ibid., 50.
[15] Ibid., 50. In view of Irenaeus' extensive reference to God's oikonomia, Marion Grau is suspicious: "Irenaeus's rhetorical economy attempts to control definitions of truth and power in a controlled patrilineal succession of hand-me-down texts and dogmas" (*Of Divine Economy* [London: T&T Clark, 2004], 59).
[16] Ibid., 50. This claim, which Keller endorses, is from Virginia Burrus' personal correspondence to the author.
[17] Ibid., 50.

assess later in this chapter, such readers deem that which the author is presumed to conceal through the text as being more significant than that which the author purports to reveal. However, scholarship operating under the assumption that Irenaeus' polemic intent inevitably results in defective or deceptive accounts tends to run roughshod over the text in a rush to judge (and frequently, to shelve) it. Ironically, Keller models the very same kind of rhetorical, broad-brushed dismissal of Irenaeus that she accuses him of doing to his opponents. Of course, if, as a radical hermeneut might suggest, there is scant possibility of objectivity (or even object) in texts, the only remaining hermeneutical task is to scrutinize the *rhetoric* so as to uncover the intentions that propel the writer's exertion of power. According to such a reading, it is difficult to see how Irenaeus could possibly be serving his own self-interest by providing reliable and fair descriptions of his opponents' positions. In his *Gnostic Return in Modernity*, Cyril O'Regan highlights the re-emergent influence of Valentinian Gnosticism on modern philosophy, theology, and aesthetics, particularly in the last two-hundred years. Without having Keller's critique of Irenaeus in mind, his words offer an appropriate counterargument nonetheless: "... [A] Foucaultian genealogy rules out attempts to adjudicate truth-claims, because this would perpetuate the illusion that knowledge is anywhere divorced from power." "But," continues O'Regan, "one can sustain the point that the battle of truth is always at the same time a battle of or for power *without reducing truth to power*."[18] It is only reasonable, of course, to suppose that observations about the writer, whether derived from authorial-disclosure or from hypotheses based on "higher critical data," should inform a reader's critical assessment of writer and text. Yet it is regrettable when such evidence is marshaled principally to discredit the writer and thus enforce a silencing of the text as a whole. Instead, it would be more constructive if the explanatory potential of such observations were focused on the intra-textual interpretative level. We might ask: How can an awareness of Irenaeus' intent empower a greater sensitivity to particular qualitative features internal to the text of *Adversus Haereses*? How might it illumine an understanding of the text in its own right? Such are the kinds of questions that may be recommended to skeptics like Keller (presuming they agree on the value in close readings of the text as it stands). As we shall see, it is by no means assured that Irenaeus would have deemed his polemical intent to be served by deliberately misrepresenting his competitor's teachings.

---

[18] O'Regan, *Gnostic Return in Modernity*, 16; emphasis is added.

Competition: Gnostic Interpretations of Genesis 47

Objection Two: Irenaeus was *Unable* to Provide a Fair Accounting of His Opponents

Some who refuse to dismiss Irenaeus' Gnostic accounts as rhetorical fabrications may still view these narratives with suspicion. Perhaps Irenaeus was willing to provide an accurate depiction, but was ultimately *unable* to do so. It is true that Irenaeus' skills as a writer have been reappraised by many who are dissatisfied with the view that Irenaeus was "orthodox but rather stupid."[19] Yet despite recent defenses of, for example, the formal unity of *Adversus Haereses* book four,[20] lingering doubts persist over Irenaeus' competence as a researcher of Gnostic systems.[21] Popular refrains and prejudices denoting Irenaeus' sloppy scholarship and overreach are still too often repeated rather than challenged. Hans von Campenhausen's dated, though still influential work is representative. Irenaeus is praised for his writings on the "positive exposition of the Church's faith." Yet, as for his accounts of Gnostic teachings, von Campenhausen concludes that Irenaeus "lacked the clarity, *unprejudiced objectivity* and organizing expository power which were needed for the task."[22] "Lacking intellectual superiority," Irenaeus could only muster an "unorganized and tiresome attack on heretics."[23] It is true that Irenaeus' mistranslations of Hebrew reveal gaps in his knowledge of early Judaism.[24] Naturally, his perspective was limited as were his sources of information. Yet despite the fact that Irenaeus was neither a disinterested observer, nor a thoroughly equipped researcher, we find reason to suppose that he saw his objectives best advanced by writing as *accurately* as possible about his opponents' doctrines. To support this claim, we turn to the text itself.

In the prefaces to *Adversus Haereses* books one and two, Irenaeus states his two-fold strategy: to "disclose" (*manifestare*) his opponents' teachings so as to "overthrow" (*evertere*) them. Whereas books two through five offer specific refutations of his opponents' positions based on philosophical and (primarily) scriptural grounds, in book one Irenaeus undertakes the self-appointed charge of

---

[19] Cf. Robert M. Grant, "Irenaeus and Hellenistic Culture," *HTR* 42 (1949): 51. Thomas C. K. Ferguson, who recalls this citation, credits Robert Grant for helping to turn the tide toward a more sympathetic view of Irenaeus' abilities ("The Rule of Truth and Irenaean Rhetoric in Book 1 of *Against Heresies*," *VC* 55 (2001): 357.
[20] Cf. the aforementioned study by Philippe Bacq.
[21] A survey of recent scholarship suggests that Ferguson's claim that "the general consensus" now finds Irenaeus to be "fairly reliable" in relating Gnostic beliefs (ibid., 358) is exaggerated.
[22] Hans von Campenhausen, *The Fathers of the Greek Church* (trans. Stanley Godman, revised by L. A. Garrard; London: A&C Black, 1963), 20; emphasis is added.
[23] Ibid.
[24] Cf. Robert M. Grant, *Irenaeus of Lyons* (London: Routledge, 1997), 29-31.

bringing those "heretical" positions (and their variants) to the light of public exposure. Irenaeus considers this duty, exposing what these rival sects actually teach, to be a crucial service, claiming that "error is not shown forth such as it is, for fear that when stripped it may be recognized, but is fraudulently adorned with persuasive attire and appears more true than the truth itself...."[25] To those "sheep" who had been "cunningly allured" by "wolves," the extent to which Gnostic doctrine departed from that which was widely held by the church would probably not be initially apparent.[26] In Ptolemy's *Letter to Flora* we see modeled the process of gradual instruction that was likely characteristic of Valentinian initiation.[27] Outsiders to these groups, however, could be expected to have little or no clear knowledge of their systems of beliefs. But Irenaeus envisions himself not only as a shepherd, but as a medical doctor for whom accurate information is crucial for diagnosis and treatment: "The person who would undertake [the "heretics"] conversion must possess an accurate knowledge of their systems or schemes of doctrine. For it is impossible for anyone to heal the sick, without knowledge of the disease of the patients."[28] Insofar as he saw the intended recipients of *Adversus Haereses* also as would-be doctors, Irenaeus was motivated to provide them with the most reliable information possible about this "disease."

In the material extending through the first seven chapters of book one, Irenaeus describes the system of Ptolemy's disciples – the beliefs of a group he describes as a "bud" from the school of Valentinus.[29] This system attracts his greatest scrutiny and fullest description, given its influence upon the beliefs and practices of the Marcosians,[30] and Irenaeus' judgment of its archetypal status within a diverse, yet discernibly common Gnostic lineage. Given his impassioned pronouncement that the danger of Valentinian teaching could scarcely be overestimated, what is remarkable is the degree of *restraint* and patience Irenaeus shows in this section. In the entire account spanning seven chapters, Irenaeus' writing style is meticulously descriptive and nearly free of invective or even evaluation. Only in three places does Irenaeus interrupt his "reporter" mode: critical comments in i.3.6, a sarcastic outburst in i.4.3-4, and a heated response to what he perceives to be a Valentinian slander of the church (i.6.3-4). In contrast to Irenaeus' generally non-polemic exposition, Tertullian's

---

[25] *Haer.* i.preface.2. English translation by Grant, *Irenaeus*, 57.
[26] Cf. *Haer.* i.preface.1.
[27] Writing later, Tertullian asserted that the Valentinians "require a long initiation before they enroll (their members), even instruction during five years for their perfect disciples..." (*Val.* 1.1; cf. *ANF* 3:503; *SC* 280 [78.8-10]).
[28] *Haer.* iv.preface.2.
[29] *Haer.* i.preface.2.
[30] The followers of Marcus seem to be Irenaeus' immediate concern (cf. i.13-21), particularly in light of his personal experiences.

later work on the same subject does not conscientiously separate description from critique. His discussion is a running commentary, laced with pejorative remarks and even "ridicule." Tertullian reasons, "Even the truth may indulge in ridicule, because it is jubilant; it may play with its enemies, because it is fearless."[31] Irenaeus' greater sense of reserve suggests his attempt to redress the lack of clear information which had apparently hampered open debate between Gnostic and non-Gnostic groups within the church. In Irenaeus' estimation, exposure is the critical first step in confronting the Gnostic challenge. Rather than rushing in to capture the wild "beast" in the dense woods where it hides, the church would do better to flush it out into the open field where it can be slain without extraordinary skill.[32] Irenaeus' methodology supports this strategy: the expansive scope and copious detail found in his portrayal of the "opinions" of the adherents of at least twenty sects suggests his esteem for systematic investigation. Even a cursory reading shows that this text is not merely haphazard, frenzied polemic. Embarking on a research program, Irenaeus had somehow managed to acquire certain Valentinian commentaries, as well as to interview sect members personally for insider accounts.[33] Perhaps his awareness of the multifaceted nature of Gnostic systems, along with a recognition that Valentinian teachers indeed aspired to provide serious, credible interpretations of Jewish / Christian texts as Scripture spurred him to adopt a more rigorously empirical, rather than superficial methodology. Irenaeus recognized that he was tracking a moving target. In the second-century Roman world, religious groups of all sorts were emerging, mutating, coalescing and dividing at a frenetic rate.[34] Thus his widely-conceived objective in writing required some sort of methodical and analytical investigation into the common roots of the varied groups, as well as offers to "reply to them all according to their special characters."[35]

Given Irenaeus' concern to provide an informed exposition of Gnostic systems, it is not surprising that his rhetoric and arguments clearly rely on the force of *reason* to establish their credibility. In book two, for example, Irenaeus' theological case is dependent primarily not on biblical exegesis or confessional

---

[31] Tertullian, *Val.* 6.3 (*ANF* 3:506; *SC* 280 [90.20-21]). Such a comparison between Tertullian and Irenaeus on this point somewhat relativizes the complaint, raised by Ismo Dunderberg (among others), that Irenaeus' account in *Haer.* i.1-7 "is no objective description; it is often seasoned with irony and sarcastic remarks" ("The School of Valentinus" in *A Companion to Second-Century Christian "Heretics"* [ed. Antti Marjanen and Petri Luomanen; Leiden: Brill, 2005], 65).
[32] Cf. *Haer.* i.31.4.
[33] Cf. *Haer.* i.preface.2; i.13.3.
[34] This ongoing process of metamorphosis is, according Irenaeus, an inherent feature of groups of this doctrinal orientation because "no one is deemed 'perfect' who does not develop among them some mighty fictions" (*Haer.* i.18.1; cf. i.28.1).
[35] *Haer.* i.22.2.

appeal, but on philosophical reasoning.[36] Although his employment of systematic investigation and appeal to reason do not ensure accuracy (to modern standards, at least), such textual observations as these are relevant. They reveal Irenaeus' full confidence that methods of reasoned explanation and illumination, rather than belligerent rhetoric or deliberate obfuscation, would ultimately be more effective in dissuading the uninformed, vulnerable "sheep" from following these new teachers.[37] Therefore it would be unwarranted to characterize and discredit Irenaeus' account either as blindly belligerent or utterly naïve. Close readings of *Adversus Haereses*, along with external evidences (on balance, more corroborative than contradictory of Irenaeus' descriptions of Gnostic sects[38]) render dubious the charge that Irenaeus actually "constructed" a "heretical, hysterical Sophia-goddess."[39] It is much more plausible to conclude that, consistent with his own scholarly and polemical interest, Irenaeus' depictions described an objective phenomenon (i.e. external to himself and to his own rhetoric) to a reasonable (albeit not unflawed) degree of accuracy. At any rate, it is in pursuit of our primarily theological and hermeneutical interests, rather than historical, that our enquiry takes shape. Given Irenaeus' competition with other would-be Christian hermeneuts, how do his readings of Genesis 1-2 imply a conviction that these texts were somehow unique and indispensable? How does Irenaeus relate these readings to his larger project of presenting himself as a better reader of Scripture, *in toto*, than his opponents?

---

[36] E.g., *Haer.* ii.1.2, et al. Irenaeus speaks approvingly of "right reason" (*Haer.* ii.25.1) and "common sense" (*Haer.* ii.26.3). However, by placing these philosophical arguments first, rather than in a later climactic position, Irenaeus appears to concede that they will not be decisive in comparison with his theological / scriptural arguments (Gérard Vallée, *A Study in Anti-Gnostic Polemics* [Waterloo, Canada: Corporation Canadienne des Sciences Religieuses, 1981], 16). On Irenaeus' familiarity with Hellenistic rhetorical methods of "refutation" and "confirmation," see Pheme Perkins, "Ireneus and the Gnostics: Rhetoric and Composition in *Adversus Haereses* book one," *VC* 30 (1976): 193-200.

[37] Cf. *Haer.* i.preface.2.

[38] Iconography, as well as textual sources (both primary and secondary), contributes potentially relevant evidence. Birger Pearson, for example, describes an Egyptian Gnostic amulet, the "Jasper Pendant," whose image of Ialdabaoth and seven names correspond identically to the Ophite Gnostic system that Irenaeus describes in *Haer.* i.30 (*Gnosticism and Christianity in Roman and Coptic Egypt* [London: T&T Clark, 2004], 258-59).

[39] Keller, *Face of the Deep*, 44.

Why include the Ophite interpretation of Genesis 1-3?

At the onset, Irenaeus identifies the doctrines of the disciples of Ptolemy, who stand in the tradition of Valentinus, as his primary target.[40] Valentinian doctrine in general, asserts Irenaeus, represents a "recapitulation of all the heretics."[41] Accordingly, a close look at Valentinian readings of Genesis 1-3, (from Irenaeus' perspective, of course) is essential for our purposes. Yet it is profitable and, we will argue, justifiable also to include the interpretation of the Ophites (as provided in *Haer.* i.30) within the scope of our examination.

Among all the Gnostic systems described by Irenaeus in book one, the Ophite account stands out. It showcases some of the richest uses – and subversions – of Genesis 1-3 to expound an articulate, multifaceted system of theology, anthropology, and soteriology. Methodologically, its readings of Old Testament texts reveal key underlying hermeneutical assumptions in a way not explicitly found in the other Gnostic accounts described by Irenaeus. For example, the Ophite narrative alleges a close association between the traditionally-recognized author of the Pentateuch (Moses) and the Demiurge figure (Ialdabaoth). When the Ophites "distribute" the Hebrew prophets to various deities, Moses is designated as belonging to Ialdabaoth (i.30.11). Therefore, for the Ophites, errors or omissions in the "Mosaic" Genesis narrative simply reflected Ialdabaoth's deceitfulness or ignorance, as channeled through his inspired mouthpiece. Yet at the same time, since Sophia also is said to impart revelations through the text, some portions of the Old Testament are recognized as witnessing to a higher "spiritual" reality (cf. i.30.11). Noticing certain points of resemblance (as well as of contrast) between the Valentinians and the Ophites, we may naturally seek to know more about the Ophite narrative and how it might be related to those of the Valentinians.

After the first twenty-eight chapters on the Valentinians and their alleged extended family (so to speak), there is a discernible shift in Irenaeus' attention at the beginning of chapter 29: *Super hos autem ex his, qui praedicti sunt Simoniani, <u>multitudo Gnosticorum</u> Barbelo exsurrexit....*[42] The Ophites are one of the sects that Irenaeus subsequently addresses. While a literary division

---

[40] See especially *Haer.* i.preface.2; i.31.3; iv.33.3. Taken together, the entire section of *Haer.* i.1-28 shows Irenaeus' concern to address the Valentinians and the long, dubious "Simonian" heritage that, he claims, preceding them. Contemporary scholars, however, are generally unwilling to identify the "historical" Simon of Samaria (cf. Acts 8.9-24) as the chief progenitor of Gnosticism.

[41] *Haer.* iv.preface.2.

[42] "However, in addition to those out of these who were spoken of as Simonians, a multitude of Barbelo-Gnostics has risen up..." (*Haer.* i.29.1; SC 264 [358.1-2]; emphasis is added). *Super* may be taken to be an accusative of measure meaning "in addition to."

between the units i.23-28 and i.29-30 is commonly acknowledged,[43] the meaning of the phrase *multitudo Gnosticorum* is quite contested. Some scholars argue that Irenaeus tends to use the term "Gnostic" only in a generic, non-technical (or even confused) sense. Others believe that in some uses he has clear historical referents in mind: groups whose teachings are sufficiently distinctive so as to be distinguished from the Valentinians. Contemporary scholars, having the benefit of an extant Gnostic corpus augmented by the Nag Hammadi texts, likewise often discern both "Sethian" and "Valentinian" strands in second-century Gnostic tradition.[44] Harold Attridge, for example, recognizes one significant point of differentiation. Whereas Sethian writings manifest "apocalyptic literary conventions," Valentinian writings "eschew" such conventions in favor of a more "eschatological" view of history – perhaps one deemed more "philosophically respectable."[45] In light of such external evidence from Nag Hammadi, we might suspect that Irenaeus' statement in i.29.1 exhibits his awareness of these two strands (broadly speaking) within Gnostic tradition. The Barbelo-Gnostics, Ophites, and Cainites of *Haer.* i.29-31 share identifiable characteristics common to other Sethian writings such as *Apocryphon of John*.[46]

Yet in developing this new subdivision of i.29-31, Irenaeus asserts not only that the systems of the *multitudo Gnosticorum* are distinguishable from the Valentinians' "Simonian" heritage, but that these other Gnostic sects *preceded* and served as resources for the Valentinians. Only limited evidence is available

---

[43] Cf. Alastair H. B. Logan, *Gnostic Truth and Christian Heresy*: A Study in the History of Gnosticism (Edinburgh: T&T Clark, 1996), 1.

[44] Hans-Martin Schenke's prominent research has attempted to categorise Nag Hammadi texts based on these lines of traditions. Cf. Schenke, "Das sethianische System nach Nag-Hammadi-Handschriften," in *Studia Coptica* 45 (ed. Peter Nagel; Berlin: Akademie, 1974), 165-73.

[45] Harold W. Attridge, "Valentinian and Sethian Apocalyptic Traditions," *JECS* 8 (2000): 178-79. Attridge's claim builds upon observations made David Frankfurter and Brian Daley.

[46] Cf. Attridge, "Valentinian and Sethian Apocalyptic Traditions," 190. John Turner attempts to reconstruct the early historical progression of a Sethian tradition. He sees stage one (pre-100 C.E.) as represented by the portion of a hymn found in *Apocryphon of John* pertaining to ascent and baptism; stage two (100-125 C.E.) is found in the Barbeloite cosmogony in the short revision of *Apocryphon of John* and in *Haer.* i.29 ("Sethian Gnosticism: A Literary History," in *Nag Hammadi, Gnosticism, and Early Christianity* [ed. Charles W. Hedrick and Robert Hodgson, Jr.; Peabody, Mass.: Hendrickson, 1986], 55-66). Turner furthermore suggests that *Haer.* i.30 may represent an earlier stratum of tradition than that in *Haer.* i.29 (cf. John Turner, "Typologies of the Sethian Gnostic Treatises from Nag Hammadi," in *Textes de Nag Hammadi et le problème de leur classification: Actes du colloque tenu à Quèbec du 15 an 19 septembre 1993* [ed. Louis Painchaud and Anne Pasquier; Quèbec: Presses de l'Universitè Laval, 1995], 169-217).

in the search to identify the groups who produced Sethian texts and to posit their relationships to other religious groups (whether predecessor, successor, or contemporaneous). Moreover, the mere presence of Sethian literary features in a given text does not provide a sufficient basis for making definite conclusions. However, in light of what may be gleaned from extant texts of the period, Hans-Martin Schenke offers a reasonable observation. We should, he recommends, proceed under the assumption that "the Sethian scriptures, though spiritual products of the Gnostic group of Sethians, did not remain only in the hands of the Sethians, but circulated and were used also in other Gnostic circles and even in non-Gnostic communities."[47] Accordingly, "Sethian mythic concepts and ideas could easily spread beyond the limits of the group and thus, for example, gain entry into writings of quite a different origin, into the scriptures of other Gnostic communities as well as into writings which came into being only as isolated literary works of single individuals."[48] A literary relationship between the Ophite narrative (i.30) and the Valentinian (Ptolemaean) narrative (i.1-8) is not implausible.[49] There are two texts in this section where Irenaeus speaks of this relationship. In the first, Irenaeus concludes his presentation of the Ophite system by declaring, "Such are the opinions which prevail among these persons, *from which* (*a quibus*), like the Lernaean hydra, was generated the many-headed beast of the school of Valentinus (*de Valentini schola generata est*)."[50] A bit

---

[47] Hans-Martin Schenke, "The Phenomenon and Significance of Gnostic Sethianism" in *The Rediscovery of Gnosticism: Proceedings of the International Conference on Gnosticism at Yale* (ed. and trans. Bentley Layton; 2 vols.; Leiden: Brill, 1981), 2:595.
[48] Ibid.
[49] On the Gnostic accounts in *Adversus Haereses* book one, Pheme Perkins contests the influential suggestion made by F. Wisse that Irenaeus composed only the discussion of the Ptolemaic system (*Haer.* i.1-8) and a few other pieces, but that he borrowed the accounts in *Haer.* i.29-30 (as well as i.11-12 and i.22-28) from an earlier heresiologist ("Irenaeus and the Gnostics," 194). Instead, Perkins claims that i.29-30 attest a different rhetorical style and method than the materials Wisse wants to attribute to this earlier external source, and better match Irenaeus' own reporting of the Ptolemaic system in i.1-8. Since it is widely known that Gnostics "preserved and used many diverse materials," Perkins finds a better explanation by supposing that i.29-30 represent Gnostic sources that were "current among the Valentinians" (199). Might they have been among the Valentinian commentaries with which Irenaeus claimed to have familiarized himself (cf. *Haer.* i.preface.2)? Perkins suggests that Irenaeus could have found these "sources" of Valentinian systems: "He is a good enough student of Gnosticism to realize that they are not strictly speaking Valentinian. They also serve his purposes admirably, since they allow him to provide ancestors for the Valentinians. Having no name for these people, Irenaeus simply refers to them as 'Gnostics' (*Haer.* i.11.1; i.29.1)" ("Ireneus and the Gnostics," 200).
[50] The complete sentence reads: *Tales quidem secundum eos sententiae sunt: a quibus, uelut Lernaea hydra, multiplex capitibus fera de Valentini schola generata est* (*Haer.*

later, since Valentinian doctrine remains his central concern in writing, Irenaeus feels it necessary to explain his inclusion of the doctrines of these non-Valentinian *multitudo Gnosticorum* in i.29-31: "It was necessary clearly to prove, that, as their very opinions and regulations exhibit them, those who are of the school of Valentinus *derive their origin* from such mothers, fathers, and ancestors...."[51] Tertullian's comments seem to lend support to Irenaeus' claim that the Valentinian system was indebted to those of predecessor Gnostic groups (perhaps including the Ophites). In *Adversus Valentinianos*, Tertullian implies that Valentinus himself did not contrive the system attributed to him, but rather borrowed and possibly modified it: "...[F]inding the clue of a certain old opinion, he marked out a path for himself with the subtlety of a serpent."[52] In light of this statement, Werner Foerster suggests that Valentinus' system "could have been that of the 'Ophites,' which Valentinianism changed."[53]

If Irenaeus' assertion about the direction of influence between these two Gnostic traditions can be trusted, then clearly there is value in a closer study of the predecessor Ophite interpretations of Genesis 1-3. Simone Pétrement, however, has challenged Irenaeus' credibility on this point. She claims that the relationship ran the opposite direction: the sects in i.29-31 were actually indebted to the Valentinians.[54] According to Pétrement, the sentences from i.30.15 and i.31.3 (cited above) are "unclear."[55] Regarding the former, she does not believe that the syntax necessarily supports an identification of the "wild beast" with the school of Valentinus, nor are the referents of the Valentinians' "mothers, fathers, and ancestors" in the latter statement sufficiently evident. Furthermore, says Pétrement, the fact that heresiologists who follow Irenaeus fail to identify this particular linkage warrants her skepticism.[56]

In response, Alastair Logan affirms the credibility of the plain sense of Irenaeus' statements based on other evidence from *Adversus Haereses*. Much of

---

i.30.15; *SC* 264 [384.277-79]; emphasis is added). Cf. below for discussion on the syntactical function of *de*.

[51] *A talibus matribus et patribus et proauis eos qui a Valentino sint...* (*Haer.* i.31.3; *SC* 264 [386.24-25]; emphasis is added).

[52] Tertullian, *Val.*, 4.2 (*ANF* 3:505; *SC* 280 [86.9-11]). Werner Foerster translates this as: "He found the seed of an older doctrine." (*Gnosis: A Selection of Gnostic Texts* [ed. and trans. R. McL. Wilson; 2 vols.; Oxford: Oxford University Press, 1972], 1:122).

[53] Foerster, *Gnosis*, 1:122. To Foerster, the fact the Ophite account traces cosmic origin not to the "fall of a heavenly figure (cf. the Valentinian account in *Haer.* i.2), but to the fact that she simply cannot contain and hold the abundance of 'light' set in her" (cf. Ophite account in *Haer.* i.30) implies that the Ophite account is likely an earlier "stage of a speculation" than the Valentinian one (Foerster, *Gnosis*, 1:84).

[54] Cf. Simone Pétrement, *A Separate God: The Christian Origins of Gnosticism* (trans. C. Harrison; London: Darton, Longman & Todd, 1991), 40.

[55] Ibid., 362.

[56] Ibid., 363-64.

the ambiguity which Pétrement finds in i.30.15 can be resolved by supposing that the Latin *de* is meant to translate a genitive construction from the (non-extant) original Greek.[57] Logan then points to other occurrences of such grammatical constructions in the Latin text of *Adversus Haereses*.[58] Additionally, he claims that Pétrement has overlooked evidence earlier in *Adversus Haereses* book one that corroborates the plain sense of i.30.15 and i.31.3. Irenaeus observes that insofar as Valentinus posits both a Demiurge and a "left-hand power" he "agrees with those falsely called Gnostics, of whom to we have yet to speak" (i.11.1). This Valentinian "left-hand ruler," claims Logan, "seems close enough" to the Ophite "serpentine son of Ialdabaoth" later discussed in i.30 so as to "establish the connection and relationship of dependence."[59] Logan also cites evidence from *Adversus Haereses* to support the assertion, contra Pétrement, that Irenaeus indeed used the label "Gnostics" not only in a general sense but also as a technical term to identify the very specific sects described in i.29-31.[60] He argues that it was in their innovation of the concept of "emission of mental states or attributes of the Father like intelligence (*nous*) and reason (*logos*) as hypostases" that these earlier "Gnostics" (of i.29-31) were to be recognized as ancestors to the Valentinians: "The reference in 1.11.3 and 5 and elsewhere to Valentinian claims to be 'more gnostic than the Gnostics' must be seen in this context of primal emanations...."[61] The fact that heresiologists either before or after Irenaeus tended not to identify these progenitor "Gnostics" as distinct sects can perhaps be attributed to the dispositions of these Gnostics as "literary creatures, exegetes of texts, whose myths feed on existing ones."[62] Because they "do not seem to see the need for fixed interpretations and set groupings" it is difficult, then, to identify and differentiate these groups from others.[63] Logan's hypothesis is that the system in *Haer*. i.29 "represents an excerpt from the classic Christian Gnostic myth as far as the cosmogony and blasphemy of the Demiurge" which Irenaeus then "complements" with a "full account of the related myth in 1.30, more relevant to his purpose of demonstrating the spiritual ancestors of the Valentinians...."[64] If the Valentinian system, (as described by Irenaeus) is presumed to represent a later stage in the evolutionary development of this

---

[57] Cf. the Latin from *Haer*. i.30.15 in our footnote 50 above.
[58] Logan, *Gnostic Truth and Christian Heresy*, 7. As an example, he notes the use of *de mediis* in *Haer*. i.8.3.
[59] Ibid., 8.
[60] Ibid. Specifically, Logan points to Irenaeus' use of the label "Gnostics" in *Haer*. ii.13.8 and ii.13.10.
[61] Ibid., 9.
[62] Ibid., 12.
[63] Ibid.
[64] Ibid., 17.

myth, we may anticipate finding traces of adaptation and modification to the received Gnostic tradition.

Michael Allen Williams opposes any depiction of doctrinal development within sects like the Sethians or Valentinians as a matter of simple, straight-line progression.[65] Yet if Valentinian interpretation of Scripture (specifically Genesis 1-3) shows a critical awareness of and engagement with previous Ophite hermeneutical strategies, then exploring Ophite readings exposes some of the exegetical roots of the Valentinian tradition. Hopefully, such exposure will provoke a greater sensitivity to the modifications that Valentinians made in order to read Genesis 1-3 as Christian Scripture, and will, accordingly, sharpen the relief of Irenaeus' proffered counter-position. In the remainder of this chapter, we will examine Irenaeus' accounts of the Ophite and Valentinian readings of Genesis 1-3, in turn. Since we are primarily concerned with evaluating Irenaeus' critique of Gnosticism (as he saw it), other texts such as *Apocryphon of John* and *Gospel of Truth* will be accorded only peripheral attention insofar as they may assist our understanding of Irenaeus' *Adversus Haereses*.

Valentinians and Ophites as Readers of Genesis

We have previously noted that Genesis is the third-most frequently cited biblical text in *Adversus Haereses* (following Isaiah and Psalms). Now, as we introduce Gnostic interpretations of the biblical creation accounts, we return to the question of "protological orientation." Pheme Perkins points out that "[w]hile there is some evidence for gnostic use of other Old Testament texts… Genesis (with Jewish apocryphal traditions developed around its opening chapters) is the only Old Testament book which is widely used and foundational to understanding key features in gnostic and Valentinian speculation about the origins of the world."[66] Notably, Gnostic readers did not follow in the footsteps of the earliest Christian interpreters by interacting on a large scale with the Old Testament prophets. In fact, observes Perkins,

> The only text which is consistently "rewritten" is Gen 1-11. This focus suggests that gnostic exegetes were only interested in elaborating their mythic and theological speculations concerning the origins of the universe, not in appropriating a received canonical tradition… Within the larger culture, any myth or text that enjoyed public

---

[65] Cf. Michael Allen Williams, *Rethinking Gnosticism*, 224.
[66] "Gnosticism and the Christian Bible," in *The Canon Debate* (ed. L. M. McDonald and J. A. Sanders; Peabody, Mass.: Hendrickson, 2002), 370.

acceptance was expected to convey deeper philosophical and religious truth. *Hermeneutics*, not canon formation, is the central point at issue between Irenaeus and his Valentinian opponents.[67]

Perkins' deduction that Gnostic exegetes were "only interested" in using the Genesis texts for advancing their speculative myths is an ungenerous and unnecessary leap. However, on the larger question, she is right to critique the opinion of Gerard Luttikhuizen who asserts that Gnostic use of Genesis material is "secondary to what was an essentially pagan myth." Luttikhuizen, claims Perkins, "fails to account for the attention to *details* in the Genesis material that are crucial to the shape of the gnostic and Valentinian myth."[68] Furthermore, her conclusion identifying hermeneutics as the "central point at issue" is sound. Our task, then, is to put Perkins' claim to the test by in fact looking at these details in Ophite and Valentinian readings of Genesis.

Gnostic hermeneutics in practice: Ophite readings of Genesis 1-3

As noted above in section 2.1.2, we presume that the myths underlying *Haer.* i.29 and 30 represent associated strands of Gnostic tradition. Based on his statement in i.29.1[69] and their placement in textual apposition, we may infer that Irenaeus also recognized a kinship of some sort between these two myths: Barbelo-Gnostic and Ophite. The account in i.29 speaks of divine emanations and primordial events without making explicit recourse to Genesis 1-3. Yet the subsequent myth in i.30 communicates a Gnostic narrative by means of a conscious reinterpretation of biblical materials, attending to the creation, Adam and Eve, Noah, the Hebrew prophets, and the Christian gospels. Few of the details in the narratives of i.29 and i.30 are the same. Although both posit an originating tripartite deity, the hierarchy is differently structured: Father, Mother, and Son in i.29, but First Man, Second Man, and First Woman (or Holy Spirit) in i.30. In addition to theogony, cosmogony is also described differently. Yet Irenaeus highlights one conspicuous point of overlap. At the end of the Barbelo-Gnostic account (i.29.4) and in the Ophite myth which follows, the narrator places these words from Isaiah 45.5-6 in the mouth of the inferior Demiurge: "I am a jealous God [or "father and God"], and besides me there is

---

[67] Ibid., 370-71; emphasis is added.
[68] Ibid., 370; emphasis is added. Perkins cites Gerard Luttikhuizen, "The Thought Patterns of Gnostic Mythologizers and Their Use of Biblical Traditions," in *The Nag Hammadi Library After Fifty Years* (ed. John D. Turner and Anne McGuire; Leiden: Brill, 1997), 89-101.
[69] "However, in addition to those... a multitude of Barbelo-Gnostics has risen up...."

no one." Since, in the Gnostic narrative, this boast is recounted in order to expose the Demiurge's ignorance – and insolence – Irenaeus cites it twice perhaps to alert his readers to a key presupposition in an Ophite hermeneutic of Scripture (cf. i.30): insofar as Moses is the prophet of an uninformed and lesser god, the "Mosaic" texts, as written, cannot be trusted to accurately reflect the true nature of affairs.

The grand Ophite narrative tells the story of how a bit of divine power (*virtus*[70]) was lost to its legitimate owners in the Aeons above, and subsequently how the intermediary figure Sophia endeavors to work through humanity to reclaim and restore this power from her son Ialdabaoth, the Demiurge. Only after articulating a particular theogony and cosmogony does the story explicitly connect with words from Genesis. Ialdabaoth cries out, "Come, let us make man after our image."[71] Yet if Genesis 1-3 is presumed to represent the limited perspective and parochial interests of Ialdabaoth, then it is only to be expected that this text's writer is not privy to events that supersede Ialdabaoth in rank and precede him in terms of sequence. Genesis 1.1 may truly speak of the Demiurge's action of creating heaven and earth, but this is not, in fact, the very beginning. Vestiges in the text of Genesis suggest that Moses' story is merely a partial and superficial appropriation of a deeper, more complex story. The Ophites claimed that Genesis 1-3 ought to be read in a broader, even unexpected context wherein some event-sequences are rearranged, certain referents of textual elements reassigned, and Mosaic interpretations corrected. Yet, despite their somewhat radical re-contextualization of these texts, the Genesis material was, for the Ophites, exceptionally crucial for explaining reality. It informed a proper understanding of deity, the cosmos, humanity, Christ, and salvation (among other things). As such, the Genesis story was never far removed from the wider sweeping Ophite story.

SCENE ONE: BEGINNINGS BEFORE "THE BEGINNING" – WHAT MOSES DID NOT DISCLOSE

And when it [Sophia] had received power from that besprinkling of light... it sprang back again, and was borne aloft; and being on high, it extended itself... and formed this visible heaven out of its body...
(i.30.3).

The Ophite theogony begins by describing a supreme divine trinity, of sorts. Bythus (First Man) generates a son (Second Man), and both of them have intercourse with Holy Spirit (First Woman) who is third in the hierarchy (i.30.1). Under the Holy Spirit are the "separated elements" over which she is borne

---

[70] Cf. *virtus* in *Haer.* i.30.3; i.30.14.
[71] Cf. Genesis 1.26; *Haer.* i.30.6.

(*super quae ferri*): aqua, tenebrae, abyss, and chaos. After having relations with First Man and Second Man, the Holy Spirit cannot contain within herself the "greatness of the lights" and so produces two Aeons: Christ, who is caught up with his Mother to form an Aeon in the Pleroma above, and Sophia[72] who falls downward. While falling, Sophia determines to hold on to the portion of light[73] that she possesses. She descends into the waters "while they were yet in a state of immobility," and "imparts motion to them also, wantonly acting (*petulanter agentem*) upon them all the way to the depths" (i.30.3). From the waters, Sophia assumes a sluggish body constituted by *materia* that has been attracted to the divine light and has imprisoned (*circumtenēre*) it. Eventually, the divine light inside Sophia empowers her to spring upwards and to be "borne aloft" above the waters where she then forms the "visible heaven" out of her body. Although this particular narrative does not provide the details, it affirms that Sophia subsequently bears a son, Ialdabaoth, without the approval of her superiors.

While Ialdabaoth is a carrier of the divine *virtus* that his mother transmitted to him, he is defective because he was begotten from a female alone. Furthermore, his rebellious disposition brands him a threat to the divine order – the order wherein it is incumbent upon each member to be content with its placement in the hierarchy. Ialdabaoth grows powerful and, in that he "holds his mother in contempt," chooses to generate six sons without authorization (i.30.5). These seven archons, the father and his sons, comprise the "holy Hebdomad." They are identified as the seven "heavens" (cf. i.30.5; i.30.12), and the seven "angels" (or powers).[74] As such, they are further associated with the "seven stars" called "planets" (i.30.9) and the seven days of the week (i.30.10). Each member would later be assigned its own "herald" or prophet to engender human worship for itself. Together, the Hebdomad is said to "rule over things celestial and terrestrial" (i.30.5). But when his sons apparently challenge his authority, Ialdabaoth turns to the "subjacent dregs of matter" and begets a son, Nous (i.30.5). Ialdabaoth then "twist[s] him into the form of a serpent," perhaps to reinforce Nous' inferiority to his father. In his agitation, Ialdabaoth became "uplifted in spirit" and "boasted himself over all those things that were below him," exclaiming, "I am father, and God, and above me there is no one."[75] Sophia, having finally been enabled to relinquish her body and return to the lofty

---

[72] also called Sinistra and Prunicus

[73] Elsewhere this is termed also *virtus* (power), but in its basic sense it simply refers to *divina substantia* (cf. i.30.8).

[74] Cf. *Haer*. i.30.5. These are the seven heavens or divine potentates through which Christ is later said to descend by stealth in order to reach this world (i.30.12).

[75] *Haer*. i.30.5. Here, the general allusion is to Isaiah 45.5, thus Ialdabaoth is confirmed as the Hebrew God, Yahweh. These words from Isaiah are attributed to Demiurge also in the Valentinian account (*Haer*. i.5.4) and the "Barbelo-Gnostic" account (*Haer*. i.29.4).

company of the Aeons, is sharply disturbed at her son's audacious claim. From this point forward, the Ophite narrative reads like an epic war between mother and son. She strives to recover and restore the divine *virtus* ("sprinkling of light") to its rightful place above. He vies to maintain possession, serve his own interests, and thus thwart the efforts of his mother. Humanity is as a mere chess piece in this great duel between inferior deity figures.[76]

As the Ophites begin to tell the story of beginnings in view of Genesis, the fact that they locate a Trinitarian arrangement at the pinnacle of deity may suggest a familiarity with nascent Christianity, and thus with Christian readings of Genesis 1-3. Accordingly, they quite easily interpret the πνεῦμα Θεοῦ in Genesis 1.2 as referring to an entity that is both related to the highest Father God, yet somehow distinct. This "Holy Spirit" or First Woman is the lowest member of the trinity, and thus is able to directly interact with the "separated elements" just below her. Certainly Genesis 1.2 (LXX) provided the context from which the Ophites drew at this point:

ἡ δὲ γῆ ἦν ἀόρατος καὶ ἀκατασκεύαστος καὶ σκότος
ἐπάνω τῆς ἀβύσσου καὶ πνεῦμα Θεοῦ ἐπεφέρετο
ἐπάνω τοῦ ὕδατος.

Not only do the Ophites identify the "separated elements" as aqua, tenebrae, abyss, and chaos,[77] they speak of the "Holy Spirit" as being borne (*ferrī*; cf. ἐπεφέρετο[78]) upon them.[79] Yet, strictly speaking, the Ophites do not identify

---

[76] Hans Blumenberg comments on the "exceptional disposition toward myth that is built into Gnostic dualism." In such narratives, "two primeval powers, two metaphysical camps, oppose one another with every kind of stratagem and trick, and the history of man is only a sort of indicator of the changes in the distribution of power..." (*Work on Myth* [trans. Robert M. Wallace; Cambridge, Mass.: MIT Press, 1985], 179).

[77] The term Χάος may denote a formless mass or void.

[78] *Ferrī* is the passive infinitive of *ferre*; ἐπεφέρετο is the imperfect, passive / middle of ἐπιφέρω (see Genesis 1.2).

[79] In the process of telling and legitimizing its own story of cosmic origins, *Apocryphon of John* makes a similar use of Genesis 1.2. However, *Apocryphon of John* more overtly denies the trustworthiness of Moses. "Christ" himself is said to provide a hermeneutical warrant to depart from a straightforward, traditional reading. According to the narrator (Christ), the reader should interpret this event (darkness upon the face of the deep, and spirit / wind hovering over the waters) as Sophia beginning "to move to and fro..." and becoming "dark because her consort had not agreed with her [re: her generation of a son]." In an aside, Christ plainly gives interpretative guidance: "*Do not think it is, as Moses said*, 'above the waters.' No, but when she had seen the wickedness which had happened, and the theft which her son had committed, she repented... and the moving is 'to go to and fro' (*Ap. John* 13.18-26; emphasis is added). Thus *Apocryphon of John* seems concerned to emphasize that the Sophia / Spirit figure to which Genesis 1.2 is said to refer is an *inferior* deity rather than a participant in the Pleroma above. (All citations of

the First Woman as the "Holy Spirit" or "Spirit of God" in the Christian and Jewish writings. The First Woman presides in the purely spiritual realm that does not directly interact with this earthly world. Sophia, as the daughter of the First Woman acts as her counterpart in the lower realm, and as such emulates her mother.[80] Indeed, Sophia's ultimate goal is to return to her mother, from whom she fell. Ophite soteriology (sharing a common Gnostic theme) is the economy of re-collecting all of the traces of *virtus* present in "holy souls" (cf. i.30.14). They are to be absorbed into Christ, enabling Christ and Sophia to be fully united again and restored to their original place in Pleroma. Thus Ophite pneumatology is the story of Sophia's (not the First Woman's) work to effect this end. Sophia, then, is the one who speaks through the Old Testament prophets, facilitates the advent of Christ through Mary, and co-habits with Christ in Jesus during Jesus' earthly ministry (cf. i.30.11-13). Therefore, the highest members of deity identified by early Christian interpreters are reasserted by the Ophites to actually be counterparts on a lower tier of deity. The "God" of Hebrew Scripture (Ialdabaoth) is not Bythus, the "Father of All" but a creator deity two full levels below. The Christian "Christ" corresponds to a grandson of God; he is not the Second Man but the Second Man's son, Third Man. Accordingly, the "Spirit of God" is not the First Woman present with the "Father of All," but is her daughter Sophia (sister to Christ) (cf. i.30.1, 12). This reveals an Ophite theology that, despite contradicting the traditional Christian ascription of Christ and "Spirit" (Sophia) to the highest level, nonetheless views these two figures as superior in comparison to the creator God of the Hebrew Scripture.

Ophite hermeneutics of Genesis are built upon the presupposition that Moses was working with an incomplete or fraudulent knowledge base. As far as the Spirit's work in creation is concerned (Genesis 1.2), he only had access to knowledge of Sophia, not of the First Woman.[81] As Ialdabaoth's prophet (cf. i.30.11), his portrayals of cosmic beginnings are skewed so as to depict the creator God in the most favorable light. Thus some of the event-sequencing in Genesis 1-3 is viewed suspiciously. Moses incorrectly places Genesis 1.1 in the first position to portray Ialdabaoth's creation of the "heavens and earth" as ultimate starting point,[82] and Ialdabaoth as the highest god. Actually the account

---

Apocryphon of John are from *NHC* II in Michael Waldstein and Frederik Wisse, eds., *The Apocryphon of John* [*NHS* 33; Leiden: Brill, 1995]. See also *NHL* 98-116.)

[80] For example, after descending into the primeval ocean, Sophia "springs" up and is "borne aloft" over these waters (i.30.3). This experience, as does the statement about her mother's position, interprets Genesis 1.2.

[81] Furthermore, as we shall see, insofar as Moses speaks primarily as Ialdabaoth's prophet, he is not disposed to portray Sophia's work in favorable terms.

[82] For readers, such as the Gnostics, who turned to Genesis for explanations of ultimate beginnings (e.g., the origins of deity, humanity, the cosmos, good and evil), Genesis 1.1

of the Spirit's interaction with the primeval waters in Genesis 1.2 should have preceded 1.1. Ophite hermeneutics, then, do not recognize the "Mosaic" textual sequence to be normative. Moses also is reluctant (for reasons we shall see in the next section) to reveal the true referents of Genesis 1.1. The "heavens" which Ialdabaoth created (or generated) were his sons, the other archons (i.30.4-5). Although only inference is possible, it is reasonable to suspect that the Ophites believed that since each member of the holy Hebdomad is linked to one of the days in the week (cf. i.30.10), each member correspondingly oversaw one of the days in the week of creation as described in Genesis 1.1-2.4. Indeed in i.30.5, these archons are described as "creators." Furthermore, this teaching would be consistent with related Middle-Platonist and Sethian-Gnostic traditions, as represented in *Timaeus* and *Apocryphon of John* respectively.[83] Yet Moses appears either unable or unwilling to place the "true" events of which he speaks into their "true" contexts. For the Ophites, their initial suspicions were massively confirmed by what they read next in the Genesis narrative.

---

would likely have been seen as a rather abrupt and unsatisfying way to begin a narrative. Does this seemingly awkward, terse start to what should be a grand narrative suggest that Moses was not being entirely forthright? What might he have been withholding, and why?

[83] Plato's *Timaeus* speaks of delegation among deity with respect to creation. The "begetter of this universe" (*Demiourgos*) speaks to the lesser gods after they have been begotten:

> O gods, works divine whose maker and father I am, whatever has come to be by my hands cannot be undone but by my consent... There remain still three kinds of mortal beings that have not yet been begotten... I shall begin by sowing that [immortal] seed, and then hand it over to you. The rest of the task is yours. Weave what is mortal to what is immortal, fashion and beget living things (41a-d [trans. Donald J. Zeyl;. Indianapolis: Hackett, 2000]).

Apocryphon of John, after an opening section on theogony and the origin of Sophia's unapproved son Yaltabaoth, picks up the "light" motif of Genesis 1.3-5 (first day of creation). Yaltabaoth

> ... shared his fire with [his Aeon offspring], but he did not send forth (any) of the power of the light which he had taken from his Mother, for he is ignorant darkness. And when the light had mixed with the darkness, it caused the darkness to shine... (*Ap. John* 11.7-12).

Furthermore, in step with the biblical narrative, *Apocryphon of John* observes that "when [Yaltabaoth] spoke, it happened" (*Ap. John* 12.13; cf. Genesis 1.3, 6, 9, et al.). *Apocryphon of John*, like the Ophite myth, links deity, ontology, and time. The seven days of the week and 365 days of the year are said to correspond to the archonic and angelic powers that comprise the foundation of the world (*Ap. John* 11.25).

Scene Two: Sophia's Opening Salvo – The Creation of Man

> ...[I]n order to lead [the other archons] away and attract them to himself... Ialdabaoth exclaimed, "Come, let us make man after our image (i.30.6).

In response to Ialdabaoth's boasting of being the highest God, Sophia cries out: "Do not lie, Ialdabaoth, for the father of all, the first Anthropos is above thee; and so is Anthropos the son of Anthropos" (i.30.6). Possibly Ialdabaoth's words remind Sophia of her responsibility for this deteriorating situation. It was she who had seized the divine *virtus* during her descent to the lower realm of *materia* and had subsequently (by procreating) fostered its dissemination outside of the divine hierarchy. Thus Sophia now takes up the task of rectification: restoring the state of harmony and unity wherein all entities recognize the true and superior hierarchy in the Pleroma above. Her scheme is to empty (*evacuare*) Ialdabaoth and his offspring of their *principalis virtus* by means of a created human being. In such a way, Ialdabaoth would be prevented from "lift[ing] up himself against the powers above" (i.30.6). Sophia's plan begins to be realized when Ialdabaoth, seeking to distract attention away from the thundering voice of his mother, calls to his six-archon progeny: "Come, let *us* make man after our image."[84] Following the particular "idea of a man" as secretly furnished by Sophia, the archons "formed a man of immense size, both in regard to breadth and length" (i.30.6). But in this condition, man could only "wriggle" on the ground. Formless substance thus receives its form. Sophia's plot progresses as planned when the archons present the proto-man to Ialdabaoth, who then "breathed into man the spirit of life" (i.30.6).[85] The πνοὴν ζωῆς of Genesis 2.7 thus refers to the heavenly "sprinkling of light" or divine *virtus*. By breathing this substance into man, Ialdabaoth is "secretly emptied of his power" while man is filled with "nous" and "enthymesis" (i.30.6).[86] Immediately, the human man gives thanks to the First Man, in effect snubbing Ialdabaoth and the other archons.[87]

This section of the Ophite account shows a clear engagement with Genesis 1-2, exemplifying the interpretation and use of Scripture by the Sethian-Gnostic tradition.[88] It also reflects a keen sensitivity to points of exegetical tension that

---

[84] *Haer.* i.30.6; emphasis is added. Cf. Genesis 1.26; cp. *Ap. John* 15.11-13.
[85] *Illo autem insufflante in hominem spiritum vitae.* Cf. Genesis 2.7; *Ap. John* 19.15-33.
[86] ἐνθύμησις involves the notion of "thought, reflection, or idea" (cf. *BDAG*).
[87] Cp. *Ap. John* 20.32-21.13.
[88] Another example of a Sethian-Gnostic reading of Genesis 2.7 is found in the later (probably early third century) text, *The Hypostasis of the Archons*, which would appear to share certain narrative elements with "Sethian Ophites" (Bentley Layton, "Hypostasis of

were almost certainly recognized by Jewish and Christian readers of Genesis at that time. By supplying explanations and corrections in order to resolve these tensions, the Ophite interpretation effectively issues an indictment on the Mosaic text as it stands. According to them, the text shows signs not merely of simple omissions, but of deliberate concealment so as to introduce deception. First, although Moses was right to describe the creation of man and woman as occurring in *paradisus* (i.30.9; cf. παράδεισος in Genesis 2.8), in fact it was a celestial paradise wherein the creator god(s) formed Adam and Eve's *spiritual* – not physical – bodies (cf. i.30.9).[89] The entire scene, including humanity's transgression of Ialdabaoth's command not to eat of the forbidden fruit, is set in a heavenly realm that is lower than the Aeons above but higher than the material world. Only after Ialdabaoth passes judgment upon them are they cast down to the lower world and assume material bodies. The Ophite interpretations with respect to the second and third points of tension are more radical in their accusations. Why is the first common plural ending of ποιήσωμεν (Hebrew: *na'ăśeh*) used in Genesis 1.26? Genesis 1.1-25 scarcely gives the impression that other personalities are present alongside the creator God. Is this not proof that Moses, as Ialdabaoth's servant, has tidied up the story of creation so as to portray Ialdabaoth to humanity as the one and only "father of all" – a recognition he desperately craved? Is the plural verb in Genesis 1.26 a vestige of the true story that Moses forgot to change? The truth, says the Ophite account, is that Genesis 1-2 contains only fragments of the grand narrative – fragments that have been deceptively altered and paraded as the whole story. The creation of man was actually a collaborative work of the Demiurge and his archonic sons (hence the plural form of the verb). Finally, why does Genesis provide two separate accounts of the creation of man (Genesis 1.26-27 and 2.7)? Is this not

---

the Archons," *HTR* 67 [1974]: 367). Based on its opening reference to Paul and extensive recourse to Pauline and Genesis texts, Elaine Pagels remarks that this text demonstrates an "intention to read Genesis through Paul's eyes" ("Exegesis and Exposition of the Genesis Creation Accounts in Selected Texts from Nag Hammadi," in *Nag Hammadi, Gnosticism & Early Christianity* [ed. Charles W. Hedrick and Robert Hodgson, Jr.; Peabody, Mass.: Hendrickson, 1986], 266). Birger Pearson, in fact, more specifically labels this myth "an epexegetical comment on Genesis 2.7, i.e. on how man has derived his spiritual nature" (*The Pneumatikos-Psychikos Terminology in 1 Corinthians: A Study in the Theology of the Corinthian Opponents of Paul and its Relation to Gnosticism* [Missoula, Mont.: Society of Biblical Literature, 1973], 73).

[89] It is possible that the Ophites, like Philo, presumed the Genesis account to invite an allegorical interpretation on this point. Philo comments, "These themes, it seems to me, are philosophized symbolically rather than in the proper sense of the words (κυρίως)... it would seem that with the garden of delights [Moses] hints at the ruling part of the soul, which is filled with countless opinions just like plants" (Philo, *Opif.* 154; cited in *Philo of Alexandria: On the Creation of the Cosmos According to Moses*, [ed. and trans. David T. Runia; Leiden: Brill, 2001], 88. Cf. LCL 226: 122-23).

the clumsy work of an editor working for Ialdabaoth, that is, another Mosaic obfuscation? Undoubtedly Ialdabaoth must have been humiliated and embarrassed for falling for Sophia's trickery. He had unwittingly handed down his greatest treasure, divine *virtus*, to feeble man – the very creature he had made to provide himself with worship and honor (cf. i.30.10)! Maybe his own sons (the other archons) laughed at his disgrace, thus recalling the memory of the previous time when they had challenged his authority and refused to pay him due respect (cf. i.30.5). Indeed, Ialdabaoth would want to conceal the truth. Moses would need to portray him simply as the all-powerful Father of all and the sovereign creator of humanity. Genesis 2.7 is crafted so that the two events (formation from dust and the inbreathing of the breath of life) would appear to be a part of one continuous act of creation. Rather then omitting the event of the inbreathing, then, he could actually spin it to his own advantage: The benevolent creator had indeed *intended* his human creatures to have his πνοὴν ζωῆς. It was an essential component of their humanness and they owed it entirely to him. Of course, the Mosaic account must make no mention of what this "breath" actually is, nor reveal the tremendous implications of humanity's possession of it. Being convinced that Moses' falsehoods must be uncovered, the Ophites told the more complete story behind the creation of man, explicating what happened before, between, and after the events of Genesis 1.26 and Genesis 2.7b. By casting Genesis' account of the creation of man in a more expansive narrative, the Ophites fielded a stirringly competitive exegetical option for earnest readers of Genesis.[90]

SCENE THREE: IALDABAOTH'S COUNTERATTACK – THE CREATION OF WOMAN

But Ialdabaoth, feeling envious at this, was pleased to form the design of again emptying man by means of woman... (i.30.7).

---

[90] While denying that Gnostics "mercilessly plundered" Genesis material when constructing anthropogonic narratives (88), Giovanni Filoramo offers reasons for its attractiveness. Biblical accounts of human origins held a "richness of detail" that classical mythology lacked. Furthermore, biblical figures were widely known, as attested by the apocryphal traditions of Adam. Yet Filoramo insists that such Sethian (cf. Ophite) accounts were not propounded to be "exegeses (however much they claim to be) of the Biblical text." They were "put forward as the true Bible" (*A History of Gnosticism* [Oxford: Blackwell, 1990], 88). However, given how little is known about the Ophite communities and their ties to Jewish or Christian groups (or lack thereof), Filoramo's conclusion would seem to be conjecture. It is equally plausible to suppose that Genesis may have enjoyed such status that Ophite interpretation would have been couched as "exegesis" to initiates, albeit of a subversive type.

Although Sophia had won the first battle, "envy" spurs Ialdabaoth to strike back. Since man now has possession of *virtus*, and this new-found *nous* affords him the capability to know things beyond the circumscribed limits of Ialdabaoth's world, man refuses to acknowledge Ialdabaoth as the "highest." Ialdabaoth's strategy is to draw out (*educere*) from his own enthymesis (i.e., thought) a woman.[91] This woman will then be the means by which he can empty man of the divine light.[92] Unfortunately for Ialdabaoth, his plan will be thwarted when Sophia lays hold (*suscipere*) of the woman and secretly empties her of power. This appears to be an anticipatory summary statement. When the woman later eats of the tree that Ialdabaoth had designated as forbidden, this action enabled Sophia to "empty" the woman of her power, thus rendering her unable to empty the man. Yet before this happens, while the woman still has this power, the "others" (Ialdabaoth's original six progeny) are said to have come and "admired" her beauty. They then "named her Eve, and falling in love with her, begat sons by her, whom they declare to be the angels" (i.30.7). Apparently she is swayed by their flattery, accepting their name for her, "Eve" ("mother of the living"), and acts accordingly. Yet her reception of this title is illegitimate since there is only one true "mother of the living": the First Woman above. While at this point the narrative does not reproach the human woman for having procreated out of naïve pride, it apparently implicates her later based on a statement that draws a parallel between the attitudes and actions of Ialdabaoth and Eve. In Sophia's estimation, "…since there was already an incorruptible Father, he [Ialdabaoth] who called himself the Father was a liar; and since there was already a Man and a First Woman, she [Eve] sinned [by] committing adultery" (i.30.7).[93] Possibly, this portion of the Ophite narrative draws from Genesis 6.1-4:

---

[91] This follows the familiar pattern in Gnostic theogonies of generation through reflection (cf. *Haer.* i.29.1).

[92] The motif of a woman being employed to put man at a disadvantage echoes Genesis 3. However, in the Ophite story, the instigator of this exploitation is the creator himself rather than the serpent working against the creator.

[93] *…quoniam, cum esset Pater incorruptibilis olim, hic semetipsum uocans Patrem, mentitus est, et cum Homo olim esset et Prima Femina, et haec adulterans peccauit* (SC 264 [372.127-374.129]; emphasis is added). Robert Grant's translation differs entirely. Ialdabaoth is the one who commits the adultery, as well being the liar: "…since the imperishable Father already existed, Ialdabaoth lied when he called himself Father, and since Man and First Woman already existed, he sinned when a [sic] made an imperfect copy" (Grant, Irenaeus, 101). However, it is difficult to see how the text supports Grant's translation, given the parallelism, yet gender distinction of *hic* (nominative masculine) and *haec* (nominative feminine). If Genesis 6.1-4 were assumed to operate in the background, our interpretation would at least seem to be a possible reading.

> It came about when men began to be numerous upon the earth and daughters were born to them, that the sons of God (οἱ υἱοὶ τοῦ Θεοῦ) – having seen that the daughters of men were beautiful – took to themselves wives of all whom they chose (ἐξελέξαντο). And the Lord God said, "My spirit shall certainly not remain among these men forever, because they are flesh, but their days shall be one hundred and twenty years." Now the giants were upon the earth in those days, and afterward, when the sons of God went into (εἰσεπορεύοντο) the daughters of men, they caused them to bear children. Those were the giants of old (οἱ γίγαντες οἱ ἀπ' αἰῶνος), the men of renown.

The "sons of God" (in Genesis 6.1-4) could be naturally interpreted as referring to Ialdabaoth's six-archon progeny, and their hybrid divine-human offspring could be the "angels" to which the Ophites refer (cf. i.30.7). It appears that Ialdabaoth's plan is entirely frustrated by this turn of events. He had produced a woman from himself and had endowed her with his own divine substance so that she could empty the man and also bear Ialdabaoth's sons. These new sons would have enhanced his prestige and extended his rule because they would presumably recognize *him* as highest god (cf. i.30.8).[94] But Ialdabaoth's first offspring, the archons, had seduced the woman before he could seize the opportunity for himself. Furthermore, Ialdabaoth's "wish" (from *adipīscare*, cf. i.30.8) would never be fulfilled because of Sophia's new scheme. Sophia had been adapting her strategy in light of the woman's arrival. This "Eve" must not be permitted to continue to bear angelic offspring who would look to her, rather than to the true First Woman above, as the "mother of the living." In the garden, Sophia would implement the plan she had devised to empty the woman of her divine power.

In like manner to their correction of the "Mosaic" account of man's creation, the Ophites also seek to straighten out Moses' story of the creation of woman. Genesis 2.21, they imply, may have correctly stated that woman was drawn out from another living being rather than being formed from the dust as was man. But she was not molded from Adam's rib, but was actually drawn from Ialdabaoth's own "thought." Perhaps the Ophite "hermeneutic of suspicion" detects another Mosaic revision meant to conceal yet another humiliation endured by the creator God. After all, it was the woman whom Ialdabaoth had formed from his own substance who later instigates the human rebellion against him by disobeying his commandment not to eat of the forbidden tree. For Ialdabaoth, the truth is quite embarrassing: He cannot control

---

[94] This motivation to beget inferior beings over which to exult may be seen in Ialdabaoth's earlier formation and disfigurement of Nous (*Haer.* i.30.5-6).

a lesser being even when it is derived directly from himself! Despite his grandiose claims and attempts to cast himself as the highest Father, the circumstances keep proving him wrong. (Of course, thanks to Sophia, his futility is virtually guaranteed.) The First Man had sent forth his Ennoea to produce a son, Second Man. He also had "delighted" over the beauty of the First Woman, and had begotten Christ and Sophia by her. Both Second Man and First Woman were faithful to him, recognizing him as Father of All. But alas poor Ialdabaoth – his attempts to imitate the First Man never bring the same kind of results. His first brood of sons "deeply grieve" him when they "quarrel with him about the supreme power" (i.30.5). Next, upon creating man he is tricked into giving him *virtus* so that this human son worships the highest Father instead of him. Then, possibly learning from his mistakes, he creates a woman from his own *enthymesis* so that she might serve his interests. First, she is to empty man of *virtus*, and secondly, bear offspring by him (cf. i.30.8), perhaps to replace his first set of ungrateful sons. But as to his plans for woman, he is thwarted in both respects. Regarding the first, Sophia will spoil his scheme by enticing the woman (and man) to rebel against him in *paradisus*. Regarding his second intent (generate new offspring), his existing sons add insult to injury. They are the ones who seduce the woman, and *they* – not he – have offspring by her! But (if we are right that the Ophites have Genesis 6.1-4 in mind) Moses orchestrates a blatant cover-up of this matter. This event is taken out of its proper sequence (between the creation of Eve and the transgression in the garden) and relocated to the beginning of Genesis chapter 6. This extant fragment does speak truthfully of the archons having relations with humanity, and of their father's anger and subsequent punishment.[95] But insofar as Moses de-contextualizes the pericope from its original place and re-words it to be quite generic (it no longer names Eve as the one who is seduced but only vaguely speaks of γυναῖκας), the true story is somewhat buried and Ialdabaoth's name is not besmirched. In all likelihood, the Ophites could have defended this analysis based on the fact that in its current location, the pericope of Genesis 6.1-4 appears out of place and devoid of context. It is located immediately after the genealogy in chapter 5 ending with Noah, and before the story of Noah and the flood (6.5). The narrative would seem to flow uninterrupted if 6.1-4 were omitted. From Ialdabaoth's perspective, there is one more cruel irony. Even though Adam and Eve were *his* creations and were made to serve him so that he could bear the likeness of the First Man, these recalcitrant human subjects were the ones who increasingly resembled the First Man and First Woman above. As earthly prototypes of this heavenly couple, Adam and Eve were a bitter reminder of his own inferiority.

---

[95] Cf. Genesis 6.3.

SCENE FOUR: SOPHIA'S SCHEME UNFOLDS – REBELLION IN THE GARDEN

> ... But their mother (Sophia) cunningly devised a scheme to seduce Eve and Adam, by means of the serpent, to transgress the command of Ialdabaoth (i.30.7).

According to the Ophite narrative, Genesis 3 tells of the next phase in Sophia's epic struggle against Ialdabaoth. This time, she will gain a significant strategic victory. Previously (according to Genesis), Ialdabaoth had commanded the man, "You may freely eat of every tree of the garden; but of the tree of the knowledge of good and evil you shall not eat, for in the day that you eat of it you shall die."[96] Now, through the serpent, Sophia seeks to "seduce" Eve and Adam to transgress (*supergredere*) Ialdabaoth's injunction (*praeceptum*). Sophia's plan would accomplish two purposes. Upon eating the forbidden fruit, Adam and Eve would "attain knowledge of that power which is above all" and would subsequently "depart from those who had created them" (as Adam had done previously) (i.30.7).[97] The current wedge of enmity between Ialdabaoth and the human beings would be exploited and further widened. Secondly, their eating the fruit would enable Sophia secretly to empty Adam and Eve of the divine sprinkling of light. This is necessary "in order that that spirit which proceeded from the supreme power might participate neither in the curse nor opprobrium" (i.30.8). As suggested above, perhaps Sophia thought it necessary to empty Eve in order to prevent the further dissemination of *virtus* that would result from her propagation through the archons. The Ophite account of Adam and Eve's transgression nearly follows the Genesis 3 narrative.[98] The serpent, apparently Nous whom Sophia had incited to act against Ialdabaoth, spoke to Eve.[99] Eve "listened to this as if it had proceeded from a son of God" and readily

---

[96] Genesis 2.16-17.
[97] *Manducantes autem eos cognouisse eam quae est super omnia Virtutem dicunt, et abscessisse ab his qui fecerunt eos* (SC 264 [372.122-124]). Thus, presumably, Eve would have been made aware of the error of her presumption. It is not clear whether Adam, after "giving thanks" to the First Man after receiving the "spirit of life" (30.6) had subsequently become corrupted, perhaps as Eve had become, thus making necessary Sophia's plan to renew their knowledge by means of the fruit of the tree.
[98] In *Apocryphon of John*, however, Genesis 3 is appropriated in greater detail and to a greater degree of subversion. The archons are portrayed as unswervingly malevolent and deceptive toward man and woman, and the effect is to demonstrate that reality is precisely opposite to the Mosaic interpretation given in Genesis 3, with its accompanying depiction of the creator God. The details of Genesis 3 (e.g., the tree, the actions of the characters) point to a real event, but the Mosaic interpretation is purely deceptive (cf. *Ap. John* 21.17-22.9).
[99] According to 30.5, Nous is Ialdabaoth's son who was "twisted into the form of a serpent."

believed (*facile credidit*) (i.30.7). Next, Eve persuaded (*suadēre*) Adam to eat of the forbidden tree. Sophia then greatly rejoices, since she sees that the archons have been overcome (*victi sunt*) by their own creature. She exclaims that this vindicates the position of the incorruptible Father and proves Ialdabaoth to be a "liar."[100] Emptying the *virtus* from Adam and Eve is an act of separation that furthermore precludes the possibility that this divine substance would be tainted by being co-mingled with soulish and material elements. Ignorant of his mother's involvement in this situation, Ialdabaoth directs his vengeance against Adam and Eve, casting them out of the heavenly Paradise down to "this world" (*hunc mundum*), and cursing them. The serpent, Nous, is likewise cast down into this lower world (cf. Genesis 3.14) and forms an inferior copy of his father's Hebdomad through which he is said to rule. The lower Hebdomad, according to the Ophites, consists of the "seven mundane demons, who always oppose and resist the human race, because it was on their account that their father was cast down to this lower world" (i.30.8).

Upon entering this lower world, the "light and clear" spiritual bodies of Adam and Eve became bodies that were "opaque, and gross, and sluggish" (i.30.9).[101] Additionally, "their soul also was feeble and languid, inasmuch as they had received from their creator merely a mundane breath" (i.30.9). Even though it would seem that Sophia has already achieved her mission, she does not forget the human beings who have, in fact, incurred the cost. Being moved with compassion (*misererī*), she restores (*reddere*) the "sprinkling of light" to Adam and Eve and in so doing enables them to "come to a remembrance of themselves" (i.30.9).[102] They "knew that they were naked, as well as that the body was a material substance, and thus recognized that they bore death about with them" (i.30.9). But this new awareness of their nakedness and mortality is not a negative development (as the Genesis narrative implies), but a positive one. Their imprisonment in sluggish corporeality is thankfully only a temporary

---

[100] The Gnostics' interest (embodied here by the iconic figure, Sophia) in vindicating the highest Father, that is, upholding his supremacy, purity, and goodness in contrast to the claims and efforts of the creator, is also discernible in the Valentinian *Gospel of Truth*. As we shall note later, the narrator of *Gospel of Truth* goes to great lengths to assert that, contrary to what might be assumed, the highest Father is not to be blamed.

[101] *demutasse in obscurius, et pinguius, et pigrius* (30.9). In a Middle-Platonist framework, perhaps this alludes to the inability of these bodies to generate proper internal motion. See also *Ap. John* 19.25-21.13.

[102] Perhaps Sophia empathizes with the humans because she had experienced a similar fall from a higher realm (cf. the bond between the Gnostic "spiritual seed" and the Sophia figure in *Haer.* i.7.1 et al.). Yet she also may be willing to entrust the *virtus* to the humans again because now that they have been cast down from the heavens (the realm of the "holy hebdomad"), the threat that Ialdabaoth and / or the other six archons will attempt to propagate through Eve has been eliminated.

state. Death would provide the means of liberation. Thus Sophia reveals that even Ialdabaoth's punishment contains the seeds of hope. Sophia's complete victory over her son is assured, and Adam and Eve had grounds for being patient in the meantime. After Sophia had guided them to food, they came together and begat Cain[103] (who was later "destroyed" by the serpent who planted in him the urge to kill his brother Abel), and then Seth and Norea. All of humanity, say the Ophites, has descended from these latter two. This claim is based on the genealogy of Genesis 5 that bridges the gap between the narratives of the first human family and the story of Noah and the flood.

In assessing the Ophite reading of the Genesis 3 "temptation" narrative, it is clear that the Ophites sought to address relevant theological questions that, apparently, Moses could not or would not answer regarding both the transgression itself and its consequences: Who, exactly, is the "serpent?" Who stands behind him? What are his motivations for inciting the human rebellion against their creator? How, specifically, did the transgression result in a changed relationship between creator and humanity? How does this incident explain certain features of current human experience? In Genesis, Moses points to the gravity of this particular event in paradise, yet his sketchy account seems not to explain its full implications for the "bigger picture," that is, a vision of God, humanity, and God's economic activity in light of the revelation of Christ.

Concerning the first, the Ophites reveal that Sophia stood behind the serpent, Nous, though he may have been unaware of this. Since Nous already disdained his father (Ialdabaoth, who had "contorted" him), he was the ideal instrument for Sophia's scheme against her son. Eve so willingly heeded the words of the serpent perhaps because she was familiar with Nous.[104] Adam and Eve's transgression was not sin in an absolute sense, but rather sin from the perspective of Ialdabaoth whom they had disregarded. Concerning the second set of questions, the Ophites assert that this first human sin explains the antagonistic relationship not only between the creator and humanity, but also between the demons (Nous' progeny) and humanity. After all, it was on account of Adam and Eve that Nous was also cast down from Paradise. Subsequently, Nous would work against humanity. Yet the serious ramifications of humanity's fall cannot be adequately accounted in terms of a supposed loss of "imputed" relationship. There was more significantly also a loss of "imparted" substance: Until its restoration by Sophia, Adam and Eve's composition no longer included the divine light.

In that Genesis seemed less than willing to provide a more comprehensive explanation of the human transgression and its consequences, perhaps the text

---

[103] Cf. *Ap. John* 24.15-25.
[104] Another plausible scenario, given the text, is that Sophia disguised herself as Nous, the serpent. Thus Ialdabaoth's later judgment of Nous is cruelly misplaced.

was reckoned to invite such speculation. Yet, from the Ophite perspective, Moses' silence was expected given that the truth would be embarrassing for Ialdabaoth to acknowledge. Not only have his human creatures rebelled against him (which he does admit in the text), but also Sophia, by means of his wretched son Nous, has bested him again. Ialdabaoth's hopes for bearing a new set of offspring through Eve are dashed now that she no longer possesses the divine light. The segment in which Adam and Eve discover their nakedness has been re-contextualized. Rather than this awareness being the negative consequence of their eating the forbidden fruit, it is a sign of hopefulness recognized after Sophia has restored *virtus* to them. For the Ophites, the fall represents Sophia's – and also humanity's – victory over the malevolent god who made them. Thus nakedness and the bearing of death are not signs of human subjugation beneath Ialdabaoth's judgment, but rather are human blessings working toward an ultimate soteriological benefit. In its struggle against a vengeful creator god, humanity has a more powerful, higher ranking ally, Sophia.

SCENE FIVE: OLD TESTAMENT HISTORY AND PROPHECY AS THE STORY OF THE ONGOING STRUGGLE

Ialdabaoth himself chose a certain man named Abraham from among these, and made a covenant with him, to the effect that, if his seed continued to serve him, he would give to them the earth for an inheritance (i.30.10).

For the Ophites, the utility of the biblical narrative was not limited to informing the story of origins. It also provided help for interpreting the Christian gospel texts. This conviction that a crucial linkage exists between the two is evidenced by their provision of a modified reading of the Old Testament historical and prophetic writings that connect Genesis with Jesus.

In the time subsequent to the dramatic events of Genesis 1-3, humanity (so they say) is engaged by powers from three realms: the physical, the psychic, and the spiritual.[105] Nous' lower Hebdomad is said to encourage humanity into "all kinds of wickedness... and to apostasy, idolatry, and a general contempt for everything by [Ialdabaoth's] superior holy Hebdomad" (i.30.9). Ialdabaoth is the one who sent a flood to destroy humanity "because they did not worship or honor him as father and God" (i.30.10). At the same time, Sophia worked invisibly, as in her assistance to Noah, to oppose the archonic powers and to

---

[105] Although the Ophite narrative does not use precisely these three terms, the tri-partite arrangement is clear. By comparison, the Valentinians are more explicit in translating their tri-partite ontology, theology, and cosmology into a tri-partite anthropology and soteriology (cf. *Haer.* i.6.1-2; i.7.1-5).

preserve what was "peculiarly her own," namely, the "besprinkling of light" (i.30.10).

In an attempt to secure the highest allegiance of at least some portion of humanity, Ialdabaoth chooses one man from among them, Abraham. He made a covenant (*testamentum*) with him that "if his seed continued to serve him, he would give to them the earth for an inheritance" (i.30.10).[106] Afterwards, through Moses, Ialdabaoth brought Abraham's descendants out from Egypt, gave them the law, and made them the Jews.[107] Each of the seven members of the "holy Hebdomad" above (who correspond to each of the seven days) chooses a "herald" (*praeconium*) from the Jews. Each herald is an Old Testament prophet who glorifies and proclaims his corresponding god (archon).[108] Thus the Ophites distribute the prophets as follows:[109]

Deity	Prophets
Ialdabaoth	Moses, Joshua, Amos, and Habakkuk
Iao	Samuel, Nathan, Jonah, and Micah
Sabaoth	Elijah, Joel, and Zechariah
Adonai	Isaiah, Ezekiel, Jeremiah, and Daniel
Eloi	Tobias and Haggai
Oreus	Michaiah and Nahum
Astanphaeus	Esdras and Zephaniah

---

[106] Cf. Genesis 12; 15.

[107] *Post per Moysen eduxisse ex Aegypto eos qui ab Abraham essent, et dedisse eis Legem, et fecisse eos Judaeos* (i.30.10; SC 264 [378.186-188]).

[108] The translations of Robert Grant (*Irenaeus of Lyon*, 102) and Dominic Unger (*St. Irenaeus of Lyons: Against the Heresies*, vol. 1 [New York: Paulist Press, 1992], 100) are preferable to that of the *ANF* edition on this point. Perhaps we find here an Ophite echoing of Psalm 19 ("The heavens are telling the glory of God..."). Not only are the motifs of day, night, time, and glorification shared, there is a similar connection between them. Each day is a herald proclaiming the glory of a certain deity, thus the structure of time itself reminds people to worship the gods.

[109] According to F. T. Fallon, given the number and names of the prophets, it is reasonable to suspect that the Gnostic author is deliberately alluding to "the canonical scriptures and to the accepted number of books in the canonical scriptures [i.e. twenty-two]" ("The Prophets of the OT and the Gnostics: A Note on Irenaeus, Adversus Haereses, 1.30.10-11," *VC* 32 [1978]: 194). Flaws in transmission could account for the omission of Hosea, and the misrepresentations of Malachi as Michaiah and Tobias (*Tobia / Abdia*) as Obadiah. Although it is true that Nathan does not have a text associated with him, his status in Jewish tradition is reflected by his inclusion in the (presumably) first century, C.E. Palestinian text, *The Lives of the Prophets*.

Yet even Sophia herself is said to have spoken many things through (*per*) the prophets.[110] These "things" concern the First Man, and "that Christ who is above" (i.30.11). In so doing, she is said to be "admonishing and reminding men of the incorruptible light, the First Man, and of the descent of Christ" (i.30.11). Such things "terrify" the archons, who are reported to "marvel" at the "novelty" of their announcement by the prophets (i.30.11).

SCENE SIX: CHRIST AND THE ESCHATON

Upon this, her [Sophia's] mother, the First Woman, was moved with compassion towards her daughter on her repentance, and begged from the First Man that Christ should be sent to her assistance... (i.30.12).

Even though humanity possessed the divine light inside, evidently it was not fully effectual in overcoming the workings of the powers in the higher and lower Hebdomads, for Sophia is said to have had no rest. In her distress, she then turned to her mother, the First Woman, and repented. The First Woman successfully lobbied the First Man to send Christ to the world below in order to help his sister, Sophia, and the "besprinkling of light." Sophia made Christ's way ready by announcing his coming through John, preparing a baptism of repentance, and adopting the human Jesus to be the pure vessel of Christ.[111] (Previously, in accordance with the revelation that she had supplied to prophets, Sophia had brought about emissions from barren Elizabeth and the Virgin Mary through an unaware Ialdabaoth.[112]) After Christ descended through the realm of the higher Hebdomad and emptied those archons of their power,[113] he was united with his sister. The Ophites called this pair "bridegroom and bride."[114] The united efforts of Christ and Sophia produced Jesus: Christ entered Jesus, whose body had been fashioned by Sophia (through Ialdabaoth) to be "wiser, purer, and more righteous than all other men" (i.30.12). Christ then worked miracles, "announced the unknown Father," and disclosed himself to be the son of the First Man" (i.30.13). The archons, including the "father of Jesus"

---

[110] Robert Grant observes that "the Gnostic theory of the inspiration of scripture by various angels is anticipated in the book of Jubilees. When Moses wrote the story of creation, he did so under the inspiration of an angel of the Lord (2.1)" (*Gnosticism and Early Christianity* [New York: Columbia University Press, 1959], 59; cf. Jubilees 17.16 versus Genesis 22.1; et al.).

[111] This reading follows Grant's translation which more naturally fits the syntax and context (Grant, *Irenaeus*, 103). By contrast, the *ANF* translation attributes these preparatory works to the descending Christ.

[112] Cf. Luke 1.

[113] In similarity with Sophia's primordial descent, the sprinkling of light rushed to Christ.

[114] Cf. John 3.29.

Competition: Gnostic Interpretations of Genesis 75

(Ialdabaoth) worked to destroy Jesus Christ, but Christ departed from Jesus,[115] as did Sophia. Jesus alone was crucified. Yet Christ subsequently sent power to Jesus to raise his body, termed *corpus animale et spirituale* (i.30.13). According to the Ophites, Jesus' disciples mistakenly thought that Jesus had risen in an *earthly* body, being unaware of this impossibility.[116] Before being taken up into heaven, "knowledge descended into him" and then he taught these mysteries to some of his disciples who were capable of grasping (*capessere*) them. Jesus[117] sits at the right hand of Ialdabaoth to receive the souls of persons who know him.[118] In the process, Jesus is enriched, while Ialdabaoth is emptied of power (i.30.14). "For he will not possess the holy souls so as to send them back into the world, but only those which are from his substance, that is, from the 'breathing'" (i.30.14).[119] In the consummation of all things, the entire sprinkling of light will be gathered (*conligere*) and snatched away (*abrapere*) into an incorruptible Aeon.

Such is the highly dramatized and idiosyncratic account which Irenaeus ascribes to Ophite interpreters of Scripture. Although it must have been found plausible and even serviceable by some, the Valentinian communities would have reasons for borrowing from it while also making certain strategic alterations.

Gnostic hermeneutics in practice: Valentinian readings of Genesis 1-3

VALENTINIAN ADAPTATION OF OPHITE NARRATIVE?

For Valentinians engaged in an ongoing effort to expound a distinctly satisfying and comprehensive Christian system, the (arguably) older Ophite tradition would likely have been seen as a valuable resource. In fact, as we proceed to examine Ptolemy's Valentinian account of origins, we arrive at the

---

[115] See the use of this text in the Valentinian *Gospel of Philip* wherein Jesus' words from Mark 15.34 (Matthew 27.46), "My God, my God, why have you forsaken me?" indicate a similar separation of the spirit of Christ from the body of Jesus (*Gos. Phil.* 68.26-28).
[116] Cf. 1 Corinthians 15.50.
[117] The Latin text reads "Christ," but presumably since Christ has been assumed into the Pleroma above, and thus only Jesus could be said to be in the middle realm with Ialdabaoth, Unger and Grant, following the *SC* recommendation, emend it to read "Jesus" which makes better sense.
[118] The Latin text (which Unger follows) reads "them," perhaps referring to Jesus and Christ, rather than Jesus / Christ and Ialdabaoth. However, for the reasons in the previous footnote, we tentatively go with Grant's emendation.
[119] Here we quote Grant's translation (104), which renders *sed tantum eas quae sunt ex substantia eius, hoc est quae sunt ex insufflatione* (*SC* 264 [384.272-273]).

plausible conclusion that the Valentinians may have treated Ophite readings of Genesis as a basis upon which to make further modifications, developments, and corrections. To the Ophites, Genesis 1-3 was both revelatory and indispensable. It was revelatory because it was a communications conduit: Sophia, representing the spiritual realm above spoke to humanity below through the Old Testament prophets – even through Moses, the Demiurge's servant (cf. i.30.11). Therefore, Genesis shows authentic traces of the true story of beginnings, though Moses has somewhat obscured the central concern, namely, the power struggle between Sophia and her son the Demiurge creator. Valid interpretation would assuredly require changes to the Mosaic presentation, but Genesis 1-3 remained nonetheless indispensable, for it revealed the anthropological and soteriological parameters within which the significance of Christ's person and work could be rightly situated. But although the Valentinians consented to some of the Ophite modifications of the Mosaic narrative, certain further revisions were made to ensure a harmonious relationship between the group's interpretations of sacred texts, and their distinctive doctrine and ethos. For instance, since they sought to be identified with (or as) the true Christian church and thus more explicitly draw from recognized Christian texts, the Ophites' portrayal of a spiteful Demiurge (i.e., Old Testament creator God) would need to be softened.[120] In fact, this is what is evident in both the Valentinian Ptolemaic system of *Haer.* i.1-7 and the derivative Marcosian system of i.17-18. The creator in Genesis was not vicious, then, only hemmed in by limitations and ignorance.[121] Also, the privileging of

---

[120] It is possible that the Sethian-Ophite depiction of the world's ruling spirits as hostile to humanity originated not in orthodox Platonism or Judaism, but in Iranian Zoroastrianism (cf. Grant, *Gnosticism and Early Christianity*, 56). Origen, for his part, would later vehemently deny any affinity between the beliefs of "sects called Ophites and Cainites" and the "teachings of Jesus" (*Cels.* 3.13; cf. 6.24; 6.28; 6.30; 7.40).

[121] Cf. the consideration of the Pentateuch of Moses in Ptolemy's *Letter to Flora*. Ptolemy denies the view that "this law has been ordained by God the father." Yet he also counts as error the view that "the law has been established by the adversary, the pernicious devil" to whom some falsely "attribute the craftsmanship of the world" (Epiphanius, *Pan.* 33.3.2, 6; trans. Bentley Layton, *The Gnostic Scriptures*, [Garden City, NY: Doubleday, 1987], 308). Ptolemy's three divisions of the law, those ordained by the Demiurge (who is neither good nor evil), Moses, and the "elders," do not exactly correspond to the three divisions of prophecies in the Ptolemaean narrative cited by Irenaeus (i.e., prophecies uttered by Achamoth, Achamoth's "seed," and the Demiurge [*Haer.* i.7.3]). However, Ptolemy's divisions nonetheless express a less antagonistic appraisal of Hebrew Scripture than had the Ophites. Campenhausen speculates that Ptolemy may be distancing himself from Marcion's teaching on this point (*The Formation of the Christian Bible*, 165). But if we suppose that Valentinian doctrine (including Ptolemy's) represents a modified version of received "classical" Gnostic myth, it is no less plausible to think that the teachings of a predecessor sect like the Ophites were in view. The difference, as seen in *Letter to Flora*, can be attributed to Ptolemy's

Competition: Gnostic Interpretations of Genesis

Christology ensured that greater attention would be paid to associating Genesis with the gospel and Pauline materials in some manner. Although the Valentinian narratives in *Adversus Haereses* manifest comparatively less direct appeal to the text of Genesis 1-3 than do those of the Ophites, it will become evident that their readings of the gospels presuppose a Genesis background. The Valentinian enlistment, for example, of the Johannine prologue and the Pauline Corinthian letters to enlighten gospel readings depended upon their abilities to relate these texts first to the framework of Genesis 1-3.

In our study of Valentinian readings of Genesis, we shall draw from *Haer.* i.1-8 rather than *Haer.* i.11. Although the latter account is claimed by Irenaeus to represent the opinions of Valentinus himself, it is clearly abbreviated and does not show the interaction with Genesis that is featured in the teachings of his star disciple, Ptolemy.[122] In light of Valentinus' extensive biblical appropriation in *Gospel of Truth*, as well as the popular interests of his day, it is difficult to conceive of him not interacting with the Genesis creation accounts. For our purposes, though, the question of Ptolemy's conformity or lack thereof to Valentinus is of little consequence.[123] In Irenaeus' eyes, the Ptolemaean system, which he describes in great detail, was representative of the Valentinian school that he was encountering in the western regions of the empire. Furthermore, it was apparently the basis for the teachings of Marcus, Irenaeus' immediate target. In Irenaeus' presentation of Ptolemy's Valentinian system which comprises *Haer.* i.1-8, two sections may be distinguished: doctrines concerning the intra-Pleroma realm (chapters 1-2), and doctrines concerning the extra-Pleroma realm (chapters 4-7).[124] Each subdivision is followed by a section

---

recourse to Christian writings – especially the Matthean sayings of Jesus – to suggest a more sophisticated stance toward Moses, which is simply in keeping with the apostolic tradition initiated by Paul.

[122] Grant notes the influential suggestion of Francois Sagnard (*La Gnose Valentinienne et le tèmoignage de Saint Ireneè* [Paris: J. Vrin, 1947]) that Ptolemy was a systematizer of Valentinus' thought and that much of *Adversus Haereses* book one is an exposition of Ptolemy's system. Certainly Ptolemy's *Letter to Flora* indicates his interest in biblical exegesis (cf. Grant, *Gnosticism and Early Christianity*, 139).

[123] *Pace* the concerns of Kendrick Grobel who doubts the reliability of the Ptolemaean system of *Haer.* i.1-8 on the grounds that it is "three times removed from Valentinus himself" (*The Gospel of Truth: A Valentinian Meditation on the Gospel*. [New York: Abingdon, 1960], 14). Grobel claims that the abbreviated account Irenaeus gives of Valentinus' own teaching in *Haer.* i.11 is also dubious because it would have been expected to be closer to orthodoxy than the later Ptolemaean system, but does not appear to be (15). Yet it is difficult to argue from silence. Irenaeus could have known that Valentinus' own teachings were closer to the mainstream than Ptolemy's but either chose not to highlight this feature, or found it unnecessary to rehearse these in detail since his battle was not with Valentinus himself, but with Valentinus' disciples and their teachings.

[124] Cf. descriptions at the beginnings of *Haer.* i.3.1; i.4.1; i.8.2.

which outlines how the Valentinians interpret Scripture to substantiate those doctrines proffered (chapters 3 and 8 respectively).

BACKGROUND TO GENESIS MATERIAL: INTRA-PLEROMA

> ... [I]n the invisible and ineffable heights above there exists a certain perfect, pre-existent Aeon... (i.1.1).

According to Irenaeus' account, Ptolemy's Valentinian theogony begins with an incomprehensible, "perfect, pre-existent Aeon, whom they call Proarche, Propator, and Bythus..." (i.1.1). Alongside Bythus existed another Aeon, Sige. Upon being impregnated by Bythus, Sige begat Nous (also called Monogenes, who has a privileged knowledge of Bythus) and emits Alēthia. From this first tetrad are derived the remaining members of the Pleroma. Nous emits Logos and Life, who in turn produce Anthropos and Ecclesia. In total, thirty Aeons within a hierarchical ranking comprise the Pleroma. In recognition, perhaps, of earlier Gnostic teaching,[125] the Valentinians also propose a tri-partite division of divinity. Pleroma is comprised of three sets of Aeons: "an Ogdoad, a Decad, and a Duodecad" (i.1.3). In a fit of passion, Sophia, the youngest and lowest ranking Aeon, oversteps her position when attempting to enquire into the nature of Bythus. Her futile efforts would have destroyed her, if not for the intervention of Horos (Limit). One consequence of Sophia's "impossible attempt" is that she generated from herself a formless substance which embodies her own desire, ignorance, and grief. Fortunately, Horos was able to separate Sophia's "desire" (termed Achamoth) from Sophia herself. Sophia is thus able to remain in the Pleroma above, while Achamoth is "crucified"[126] and expelled to the world below. In order to prevent other Aeons from repeating Sophia's mistake, Nous then generated Christ and the Holy Spirit "for the purpose of fortifying and strengthening the Pleroma" (i.2.5). Intra-Pleroma peace was effected as Christ ameliorated the Aeons' restlessness, while the Holy Spirit "taught them to give thanks." The resulting harmony and bliss evoked a grateful response. All the Aeons made their best contributions to form Jesus,[127] the "very star" and "perfect fruit" of the Pleroma (i.2.6). As suggested in our first chapter, the Ptolemaean account of Jesus' formation, then, is strictly a matter of scriptural interpretation. As Colossians describes it, he is the "image of the invisible God" and the "firstborn of all creation" (Colossians 1.15). The Father's "pleasure" is that all the "Pleroma" (πλήρωμα) would dwell in him (Colossians

---

[125] I.e., Ophite and Barbelo-Gnostic traditions?
[126] A proposed emendation reads ἀποσταυρωθῆναι ("fenced off") rather than ἀποστερηθῆναι.
[127] Also called "the second Christ" and *Sōtēr* (*Haer.* i.3.1, 4).

1.19). The text shortly reiterates that "in him the whole Pleroma of deity (τὸ πλήρωμα τῆς Θεότητος) dwells bodily" (Colossians 2.9; cf. *Haer.* i.3.4).

For the Ptolemaeans, the Genesis account gave insight into cosmic and anthropological origins, but what about divinity?[128] If the Christian tradition shed greater light on the identity and characteristics of God, should not then the Christian sacred texts be brought to bear upon Jewish texts? In fact, if both Old and New Testament materials were authoritative in some manner, was it not *obligatory* for any Christian interpreter to explain how they are interrelated? Taking their cue from the pre-cosmic theme in the prologue to John's gospel from whence they obtained the names of certain Aeon personalities (e.g., Logos, Alēthia, Zoe[129]), the Valentinians proposed to supply a narrative even more fundamental than the basic sketch given in Genesis. This interest is reflected in the (apparent) citation given by Irenaeus from Ptolemy's commentary on the gospel of John:

> John, the disciple of the Lord, wishing to set forth the origin of all things, so as to explain how the Father produced the whole, lays down a certain principle, – that, namely, which was first-begotten by God, which Being he has termed both the only-begotten Son and God, in whom the Father, after a seminal manner, brought forth all things. By him the Word was produced, and in him, the whole substance of the Aeons, to which the Word himself afterwards imparted form. Since, therefore, he treats of the first origin of things, he rightly proceeds in his teaching from the beginning, that is, from God and the Word. And he expresses himself thus: "In the beginning was the Word..." (i.8.5).

GENERAL FEATURES OF VALENTINIAN COSMOLOGY: EXTRA-PLEROMA

...and on this account they allege that the Savior created the world by his power (i.4.5).

---

[128] According to *Haer.* i.17-18, the Marcosians, whom Grant labels "magic-minded Valentinians," did, in fact, employ a numerological reading of the Genesis creation account to discern thirty heavenly Aeons (cf. Grant, *Gnosticism and Early Christianity*, 64).

[129] These Aeon entities are distinct from the "Jesus" whose earthly ministry is attested in the gospels.

Having been separated from Sophia in the Pleroma above, Achamoth (having neither form nor figure[130]) is said to have been "boiling over" in places of darkness and vacuity" (i.4.1). This recalls, and perhaps revises the Ophite motif in which Sophia "imparts motion" by acting upon the primordial waters (cf. i.30.3). Although at this point in the story, the Valentinian account in *Adversus Haereses* does not use exactly the same Greek terms as in Genesis 1.2 (LXX), it is likely that this Genesis text (along with Platonist sources) at least informed Gnostic accounts thematically.[131] Darkness, void, and shapelessness characterize conditions before the creation of the cosmos. Christ then shows compassion to Achamoth by imparting to her μόρφωσις and an "odor of immortality," though she must remain beneath the Pleroma in order that she may learn to desire "better things" (i.4.1).[132] Achamoth's very desire to return to Sophia constitutes the collection and substance from which the cosmos (including the Demiurge, and souls of this world) was made.[133] Where the

---

[130] *informis* (ἄμορφος) *et sine specie* (ἀνείδεος) While the concepts are similar, these terms differ from those in Genesis 1.2 regarding the earth being ἀόρατος (invisible) and ἀκατασκεύαστος (unformed).

[131] Gnostic interest in the allegorical interpretation of Genesis 1.2 is evidenced by Calcidius' commentary on Plato's *Timaeus* (4th – 5th c. C.E.). Calcidius comments that Origen claimed to be persuaded by certain Jews that, according to the original Hebrew, the text ἡ δὲ γῆ ἦν ἀόρατος καὶ ἀκατασκεύαστος meant *terra autem stupida quadem erat admiratione* ("the earth was lying speechless in a kind of admiration"). J. C. M. van Winden has discovered a link between this exegesis and the terms used in *Haer.* i.1-5 (and Tertullian's *Val.* 10.2-3) which recounts the Valentinian story of Sophia's fall from Pleroma ("Terra Autem Stupida Quadam Erat Admiratione: Reflexions on a remarkable translation of Genesis 1:2a" in *Studies in Gnosticism and Hellenistic Religions* [ed. R. van den Broek and M. J. Vermaseren; Leiden: Brill, 1981], 458-66). After Sophia's "plan" to know the highest Father is thwarted, her "speechless amazement" is the very origin of her pathos. In turn, this pathos comes to be identified with physical matter or earth itself. Van Winden's study thus points to the extent to which Gnostics – including the Valentinians – engaged with the creation texts of Genesis, as well as the attractiveness of their exegesis within Jewish and Christian communities of the day.

[132] In that Achamoth and her "spiritual seed" are kin, they have parallel paths of development and destiny. This Valentinian assertion about the necessity of dwelling in lower realms in order to give opportunity for moral development bears resemblance to the related section from *Timaeus* 90a-d.

[133] To P. Fredriksen, the linguistic associations among the terms "defect," "hyster," and "Sophia," as attested in Greek literature and medical writings, suggest a possible connection between Gnostic creation myths and popularised Greek views on gynaecology. In Irenaeus' account of the teachings of the Cainites, the Sophia figure is named *Hystera* (ὑστέρα, womb; cf. *Haer.* i.31.2). Ὑστέρα is "defective" (ὑστέρημα) because, by refusing a male consort, she lacks moisture / sperm. Sophia's ascent to Bythus, then, can be seen to parallel the supposition in Greek medicine that a womb which dries out due to lack of seed tends to rise in the body. In the case of Gnostic narrative, the defective part (cf. Achamoth) associated with female and matter is the

Valentinians actually identify the locus of that creation, however, is a bit ambiguous – at least according to Irenaeus.[134] *Sōtēr*[135] is the one who later descends and separates Achamoth's passions from her, though not entirely. The "incorporeal passion" is transmuted into "unorganized matter" (i.4.5). Thus *Sōtēr* was said to have created the world by his "power" (*virtute*) even before the Demiurge created it psychically and materially.[136] Given the fact that, according to Valentinian commentary on John's gospel, John desired to "set forth the origin of all things, so as to explain how the Father produced the whole," the claim in Genesis 1.1 would have to be reconciled with the apparent counter-claim in John 1.3. Although "In the beginning God created the heavens and the earth," yet "all things came into being through [the Word], and without him not one thing came into being...."[137] The Valentinian narrative positing two creations and two creators, therefore, adapts to accommodate this textual predicament. Regarding the origins of cosmic substances, the Valentinians supply reconciling details where the Genesis account stands silent.[138] Achamoth's tears constitute liquids; and her "grief and perplexity" is the basis for the formation of all corporeal elements. In a qualitative sense, two different kinds of concretions are brought forth from her desire. One type is irredeemably evil. The other, ψυχικός, is able to be converted, and is the substance from which she formed the Demiurge. In her joy of being released from her passion, Achamoth herself formed a third type of substance, πνευματικός, which is the spiritual "seed" that she sows into the world through an ignorant Demiurge. Like the Ophite Demiurge, the Valentinian Demiurge creates the powers of the seven

---

portion that falls downwards and is the basis for the consequently defective material world ("Hysteria and the Gnostic Myth of Creation," *VC* 33 [1979]: 287-90; cf. *Haer.* i.2.3-5). If Fredriksen is right, her analysis enhances an understanding of how Platonic tendencies to disparage physical material as "female," and thus defective, were expressed in religious (i.e., Gnostic) narrative.

[134] In a later section, Irenaeus asks whether the Valentinians locate creation "in the bosom of the Father" or in a "vacuity" outside and distinct from the Pleroma (ii.4.1-3). According to his accusation, if the former is true, then creation constitutes a stain on the "perfect" Father. If the latter is true, then such a void (assuming that the Father is not responsible for creating it) is at least on par with, if not more ultimate than is the Father. In this same section, Irenaeus asserts that the Valentinians hold the opinion that "the creator formed the world out of previously existing matter" and that the "world was formed by angels." These claims, however, are not a feature of the basic Ptolemaean narrative in *Haer.* i.1-7.

[135] *Sōtēr* is the aforementioned "second Christ" who was the pre-cosmic product of the contributions of all the Aeons in Pleroma.

[136] διὰ τοῦτο δυνάμει τὸν Σωτῆρα δεδημιουργηκέναι (*SC* 264 [74.460-61]).

[137] Genesis 1.1; John 1.3.

[138] According to Irenaeus' interpretation, Genesis portrays God as creating the cosmos *ex nihilo* (cf. *Haer.* ii.10.3-4).

heavens (i.5.2). However he is not part of this "holy Hebdomad" but exists above them as "Hebdomas." Whereas the Ophites posited a scheme in which members of the "lower" Hebdomad mimicked and rivaled those in the "higher" Hebdomad, in the Valentinian system, Achamoth somewhat models the role of Propator (Bythus), the Demiurge, that of Nous, and the "mundane" angels (formed by the Demiurge), that of the other Aeons in the Pleroma.

Upon forming the Demiurge, however, Achamoth conceals herself from him. By her power, she then impels him to create "everything outside of the Pleroma," both things ψυχικός and ὑλικός (i.5.2). There is a clear correspondence between the Valentinian figure of Achamoth and the Ophite Sophia, yet alterations are also evident. Unlike the Ophite Sophia, the Valentinian Achamoth (and the aforementioned heavenly *Sōtēr*) has an active, albeit hidden, role in the creation. Perhaps to demonstrate a closer alignment with emergent Christian teaching and tradition, the Valentinians sought to temper the radical anti-cosmic tendencies of earlier Gnostics like the Ophites. If the Demiurge were not solely responsible for the created order, and were not expressly a self-serving, deceitful, fiend to humanity, then genuine traces of heavenly truth could be found veiled in earthly realities. The Valentinian Demiurge is genuinely unaware that he is but the instrument, not the source, of creation. In summing up the Valentinian depiction of the Demiurge creator, Irenaeus, perhaps, parrots some of the group's own lyrics:

> He formed the heavens, yet was ignorant of the heavens. He fashioned man, yet knew not the Man [above]. He brought the earth to light,[139] yet had no acquaintance with the earth... (i.5.3).

This saying exemplifies not only a conscientious grappling with the Genesis 1-2 portrayal of God as "forming the heavens," and "fashioning man," but also the playful transposition of the theme of John 1.1-11: Through the Word, all things come into being, but the world "did not know him."[140]

Being merely ψυχικός and thus "incapable" of having knowledge of the πνευματικός (whether of Pleroma, his mother, or the spiritual seed), the Demiurge "imagined himself to be God alone" (i.5.4). Accordingly, say the Valentinians, the Demiurge "declared through the prophets, "I am God, and besides me there is none else" (i.5.4; cf. Isaiah 45.5-6; 46.9). Although their attribution of this Isaian saying to the Demiurge simply shows the Valentinians following a long-held Gnostic tradition, the significant question is: What do the Valentinians do with this motif? As in the Ophite story, the Demiurge's bold declaration is located in primordial time before the creation of humanity. But

---

[139] δείκνυμι/ *ostendere*
[140] John 1.10.

whereas for the Ophites, this saying establishes the group's contention that Demiurge creator was a willful liar (after all, he *did* know his mother, holding her in "contempt" [i.30.5]), in the Valentinian revision this saying manifests the Demiurge's veritable ignorance. "He was ignorant of the forms of all that he made, and knew not even of the existence of his own mother, but imagined that he himself was all things" (i.5.3). The Valentinians exploit the citations from Isaiah 45 and 46, then, to *recast* the Demiurge as a more credible figure. Yet though he may be relatively benign, his ignorance nonetheless renders him "defective."[141] Even the devil ("Cosmocrator") whom the Demiurge created is superior to him insofar as the devil, being a spirit, knows spiritual things.

THE DEMIURGE AND THE CREATION OF THE WORLD

> ...*the Demiurge imagined that he created all these things of himself, while he in reality made them in conjunction with the productive power of Achamoth* (i.5.3).

Whereas the Ophite account generally follows Genesis 1-2 by assuming that the being who "intends" creation (i.e., who supplies the "images") and the one who actually creates is one and the same, the Valentinians attribute these two functions to different protagonists.[142] In an ultimate sense, *Sōtēr* (Jesus) "conferred honor upon the Pleroma by the creation [which he summoned into existence] through means of the [Demiurge's] Mother, inasmuch as he produced similitudes and images of those things which are above" (ii.7.1).[143] In turn, Achamoth's intention for creating the physical world through the Demiurge was to provide the ψυχικοί the opportunity to be trained (παιδεύειν) through sensory experience (cf. i.6.1).[144] Likewise, her purpose for depositing this spiritual seed into the world was that, while being "carried as in a womb in this material body, it might gradually increase in strength and in the course of time become fit for the reception of perfect rationality" (i.5.6).[145]

---

[141] Cf. Irenaeus' analysis in *Haer.* ii.3.2; iv.33.3; passim.

[142] Cf. *Haer.* ii.16. This divergence is true of the Ophite Demiurge insofar as the creation of heavens and earth is concerned, but does not apply to their story of the creation of man. Sophia is said to supply the "idea" of a man to the archons who form him (i.30.6).

[143] *Haer.* ii.7.1.

[144] This echoes a standard Platonic theme. Cf. Plato, *Timaeus* 47b-c (Zeyl, 35-36): "... the god invented sight and gave it to us so that we might observe the orbits of intelligence in the heavens and apply them to the revolutions of our own understanding... So once we have come to know [the heavenly revolutions]... we should stabilize the straying revolutions within ourselves by imitating the completely unstraying revolutions of the god" (cf. 69c; 44d-45b).

[145] This motif coincides closely to that found in Plato's *Timaeus*, sections 69c-72d; 36a-b; 43a-44c and 90c-d.

84 Irenaeus and Genesis

Though the Savior and Achamoth may "intend," the Demiurge "creates" insofar as he forms (δημιουργειν / *fabricāre*) the world. As in the Ophite narrative, the Demiurge is said to have created the seven heavens which are termed "intelligent" angelic powers (i.5.2). It appears that the Valentinians (as their predecessors) derived this belief from Genesis 1-2. That these heavens were angelic beings whom the Demiurge had begotten would seem to be reasonable, if γενέσεως in Genesis 2.4 were interpreted in a more literal than figurative sense:

αὕτη ἡ βίβλος γενέσεως οὐρανοῦ καὶ γῆς ὅτε
ἐγένετο ᾗ ἡμέρᾳ ἐποίησεν ὁ θεὸς τὸν οὐρανὸν καὶ
τὴν γῆν.[146]

If the "generation" of the heavens in Genesis 2.4 is viewed in tandem with the superscription in Genesis 1.1, then the seven days of creation that follow in Genesis 1.3-2.3 could naturally be viewed as speaking not just of the seven subdivisions of the cosmos, but of the seven correspondent angels.[147] In cosmogony, as in other concerns, the Valentinian narrative shows an attempt to credibly engage not only Genesis 1-2 and Ophite (and other Gnostic) interpretations, but also Plato.[148]

In the Valentinian hierarchy, the Demiurge occupies the middle "heavenly" realm – above the "worldly" realm of the Cosmocrator, but below the sub-Pleroma "intermediate habitation" of Achamoth. Though Achamoth had designated her son to be the fashioner of the world, her own passions (as mentioned above) constitute the cosmic building-blocks. Her "state of stupor" gives rise to earth; her fearful "agitation" elicits water; the "consolidation of her

---

[146] "This is the record of the generation of heaven and earth when they were made, in the day in which the Lord God made the heaven and the earth."

[147] As noted above, the Ophite narrative identified the seven archons whom the Demiurge created with the seven days of the week. Whereas the Valentinian account in *Haer.* i.1-7 does not employ a hermeneutic of gematria when reading Genesis 1, the Marcosians did. According to Irenaeus, they believed that the Demiurge's very creation of time and seasons manifested inherent defect and the creator's weakness (cf. *Haer.* i.17.2). Though Irenaeus does not suggest that the followers of Marcus had Genesis 1.3-5 and 1.14-17 in mind, such an association is plausible.

[148] *Timaeus* 38c-40d describes the "father who had begotten the universe" (37d) creating the lesser deities of the heavenly bodies (πλανήτης, cf. 38c), and the stars (deities made from fire, cf. 40a). John Dillon labels the Valentinian depiction of the Demiurge as "an explicit parody of the *Timaeus*, and through it of Platonic metaphysics in general, as well as an attack on Jehovah as portrayed in the Old Testament" (*The Middle Platonists: A Study of Platonism, 80 B.C. to A.D. 200* [London: Duckworth, 1977], 387). However, even on the basis of Irenaeus' admittedly non-neutral presentation, Valentinian teachings show no trace of satire but rather reflect a serious reading and adaptation of multiple authoritative sources in light of Christian beliefs.

grief" constitutes air; and all of these passions are associated with the emergence of fire (i.5.4). "Ignorance" is said to "lie concealed" within all of these passions (i.5.4).

Two notable characteristics may be observed in this section of the Valentinian account dealing with the Demiurge and the creation of the world. First, the Valentinians seem relatively uninterested in highlighting the pluriformity of natural creation as it is differentiated in the works of each of the "days" of creation in Genesis 1. This silence is not unexpected given the Valentinians' primarily soteriological focus. The subsequent biblical account of the creation of *humanity* was the section most helpful for explaining and defending one of their cornerstone doctrines, namely a tri-partite anthropology. Secondly, in contrast to the Ophites, the Valentinians are quite eager to speak of creation in terms of composition, a differentiation of primordial elements and substances. To do so, they drew from *Timaeus*, which in the second century C.E. enjoyed widespread cultural dissemination not only among Middle-Platonist philosophers but among virtually all educated persons. "Indeed," argues David Runia, "the *Timaeus* was the only Greek prose work that up to the third century A.D. every educated man could be assumed to have read."[149] Where *Timaeus* denotes the basic constituents of air, water, fire, earth simply as "lumber for carpenters"[150] (the "carpenters" being the Demiurge and lesser gods), the Valentinians connect these same cosmological elements to the more fundamental context of theology. They are Mother Achamoth's own passions. In so doing, the Valentinians address what they see as *Timaeus'* incomplete and confused understanding of primeval matter. First, *Timaeus* does not explain where such matter originates. Second, though it perceptively presents matter in somewhat feminine terms (matter is associated with the rather obscure concept of "receptacle," the "wetnurse of becoming"[151]) *Timaeus* does not adequately clarify the relationship between "ideas," creator, and "becoming."[152] The Valentinian account proposes to correct and inform *Timaeus* on these two points.

---

[149] *Philo of Alexandria and the* Timaeus *of Plato* (Leiden: Brill, 1986), 57. The extensive citations and allusions from *Timaeus* found in early Christian patristic writings also confirm this point. Bentley Layton supposes that Philo's efforts to show the compatibility of the Genesis creation narratives with *Timaeus* prepared the way for such later Gnostic-Christian adaptations from these texts (*The Gnostic Scriptures*, 16).
[150] Plato, *Timaeus* 69a-b.
[151] Ibid., 49a.
[152] *Timaeus* more precisely attempts to address the (related) relationship between "Necessity," "Intellect," and "becoming." Yet it admits that to "illuminate in words" the concept of the "receptacle of all becoming – its wetnurse, as it were" is "difficult and vague" (*Timaeus* 49a [Zeyl, 38]; cf. 49a).

As Middle-Platonism became increasingly characterized by dogmatism, one of the "most striking features" was that many readers of *Timaeus* were espousing an "uncritical acceptance of a literal cosmogony."[153] From the *Didaskalikos* of Albinus, David Runia points out representative philosophical features that emerge, in large part, on the basis of hermeneutical approaches to *Timaeus*. For example, ideas have a function that is "more 'physical' than epistemological, i.e. to serve as paradigm for the cosmos and all its natural parts...."[154] Insofar as ideas are "God's thoughts," they are "located in God's νοῦς as the object of his thought. Creation takes place when God looks to his thoughts as cosmic paradigm."[155] On the subject of creation, the influence of *Timaeus* led many to explain "the structure of reality... in a creationistic way, even if a literal creation is denied."[156] Furthermore, "[t]he question of whether the γένεσις did or did not take place in time (i.e. whether the *Timaeus* should be read literally or not) was endlessly discussed."[157] Valentinian teachings on composition, whether describing the basic elements of Achamoth's passions or the three "substances" that constitute the qualitative distinctions within the cosmos and humanity, enabled them to propose a more comprehensive and nuanced understanding of reality. The Genesis account, valuable though it was, did not satisfactorily explain how the cosmological and the theological are related, and thus was a partial account requiring supplementation. If Christianity truly sought to provide an all-encompassing view of reality, then the *Timaeus* could assist. By the same token, *Timaeus* on its own was also an incomplete account, and thus needed to be read together with Genesis.[158]

A secondary benefit of the use of *Timaeus* is that it gave the Valentinians authoritative resources by which to rehabilitate the Demiurge's image. The very fact that the Valentinians recovered the Platonic label Δημιουργός to describe the Old Testament creator God may suggest their desire to distance themselves from such Gnostic predecessors as the Ophites. Although "Ialdabaoth" was of Hebraic derivation, to persons steeped in Christian tradition this rather foreign-sounding name could have been off-putting. The Ophite creator, inasmuch as his depiction relied on a "hermeneutic of suspicion," was plainly not consonant with

---

[153] Runia, *Philo of Alexandria and the* Timaeus *of Plato*, 49.
[154] Ibid., 53.
[155] Ibid.
[156] Ibid., 54.
[157] Ibid.
[158] Runia argues that from the beginning of the reception of Plato's *Timaeus*, its argument was acknowledged in some respects to be less than fully satisfying. He finds an example where the text itself expresses a "measure of discomfort" in *Timaeus* 52c4: "...it stands to reason that the image should therefore come to be in something else, *somehow* clinging to being [οὐσίας ἀμωσγέπως ἀντεχομένην], or else be nothing at all" (Runia, *Philo of Alexandria and the* Timaeus *of Plato*, 41 n. 18; Zeyl, 42; emphasis is added).

mainstream Christian teaching. Thus in a revolutionary manner, the Valentinians turned to *Timaeus*. Though he is certainly limited – in *Timaeus*, Δημιουργός must work within the confines of Necessity[159] – the Demiurge is not a surly character, nor is he the cause of evil. Indeed Δημιουργός is ascribed respect: "He [the framer of the universe] was good, and one who is good can never become jealous of anything. And so, being free of jealousy, he wanted everything to become as much like himself as possible... The god wanted everything to be good and nothing to be bad so far as that was possible...."[160] The Demiurge, therefore, is simply working within the limitations imposed upon him (unawares) by the higher deities. He arranges the universe in an ordered manner, and sows human souls into the world.[161] Yet *Timaeus* is not accepted uncritically. The abstraction of a higher constraining force, "Necessity," could at times be personalized and more intricately described in terms of higher deity. Quite easily, *Timaeus'* conception of Δημιουργός is emended so as to emphasize his instrumental function. Given his notoriety, it would be unsurprising that some uninformed persons (e.g., those in the "mainstream" Christian tradition) would suppose him to be the source of goodness, though he is but a conduit through which higher deity works.

THE DEMIURGE AND THE CREATION OF HUMANITY

...[The Demiurge] fashioned man, yet knew not the Man... (i.5.3).

Just as there are three types of material which Achamoth brought into existence (πνευματικός, ψυχικός, and χοϊκός), so also are there three (mutually exclusive) corresponding human γενεαί. Adam, apparently, was an exception in that all three natures were present in him.[162] Mindful of Genesis 2.7 (and the sequence of creation in Genesis 1), the Valentinian account depicts the Demiurge as making (ποιεῖν / *fabricare*) man after having fashioned the world.[163] Yet the narrative suggests a conscious reinterpretation of Genesis 2.7:

---

[159] As implied in *Timaeus* 47e-68d.
[160] Plato, *Timaeus* 29e-30a (Zeyl, 15).
[161] Cf. Plato, *Timaeus* 30a; 53b-c; 42d-e; cf. *Haer.* i.5.6.
[162] Cf. *Haer.* i.7.5: "They conceive, then, of three kinds of men, spiritual, material, and soulish, represented by Cain, Abel, and Seth. These three natures are no longer (οὐκέτι) found in one person, but constitute various kinds [of men]." Earlier (*Haer.* i.5.6), Adam was said to have received a spiritual nature from Achamoth in addition to having a soul and body.
[163] It is interesting that in the Valentinian narrative described in *Adversus Haereses* (in contrast to that of the Ophites) there is no mention of the creation or role of woman as described in Genesis 2.20-3.21. Perhaps on this point the Valentinians are influenced by *Timaeus* (among other factors), in which the origin of women is discussed only as an afterthought. Female humans, according to Plato's text, are merely "reborn" males who

The Demiurge "created the earthy man (τὸν ἄνθρωπον τὸν χοϊκόν)[164] *not taking him from this dry earth, but from an invisible substance consisting of fusible and fluid matter* (οὐσία / *substantia*)."[165] As in their narration of the creation of the cosmos, the Valentinian account is again concerned to speak of composition, and Moses' report is found to be incomplete and inaccurate. Furthermore, this "earthy man" is not to be understood as referring to physical flesh. Rather the "covering of skin" is associated with a later event in the Genesis narrative (cf. Genesis 3.21).

Next, the Demiurge is said to have "breathed" (ἐμφυσειν / *insufflare*)[166] into this man the soul (i.5.5). Since the Valentinian creator was ψυχικός in nature, it is logical that the Valentinians then assert that this inbreathed ψυχικόν is what was created after "God's" image (εἰκών) and likeness (ὁμοῖος). According to them, Genesis 2.7 ought to be read in concert with Genesis 1.26 in order to understand human composition. These texts implied a distinction between a "material" element that is after God's image while not coincident with God's substance, and a "soulish" element that is after God's likeness. However, the Demiurge's "breath of life" apparently communicated to humanity not only his ψυχικός nature, it also served as the moment of opportunity for Achamoth secretly to introduce her πνευματικός seed into the human race (cf. i.5.6). Thus Genesis 2.7 calls the man a "living spirit" (πνεῦμα ζωῆς) because his substance came from an indirect "spiritual emission" (i.5.5). Only after (ὕστερος / *post deinde*) this double-inbreathing is the human being "enveloped all round with a covering of skin (δερμάτινος / *dermatinam*), and by this they mean the outward sensitive flesh (αἰσθητὸν σαρκίον / *sensibilem carnem*)" (i.5.5).[167] Most likely, Irenaeus understood the Valentinians to base this doctrine

---

had previously "lived lives of cowardice or injustice" (91a [Zeyl, 87]). As such, women were deemed essentially and morally inferior to men.

[164] Cf. 1 Corinthians 15.47.

[165] *Haer*.i.5.5; emphasis is added. The Greek reads:
οὐκ ἀπὸ ταύτης δὲ τῆς ξηρᾶς γῆς, ἀλλ' ἀπὸ τῆς ἀοράτου οὐσίας, ἀπὸ τοῦ κεχυμένου καὶ ῥευστοῦ τῆς ὕλης λαβόντα... (*SC* 264 [86.558-60]; cf. *Haer*. v.15.4).
This contrasts with Genesis 2:7 (LXX):
καὶ ἔπλασεν ὁ θεὸς τὸν ἄνθρωπον χοῦν ἀπὸ τῆς γῆς καιἐνεφύσησεν εἰς τὸ πρόσωπον αὐτοῦ πνοὴν ζωῆς καὶ ἐγένετο ὁ ἄνθρωπος εἰς ψυχὴν ζῶσαν. The fact that in the Valentinian account, man is formed from "invisible substance" consisting of "fluid matter" rather than from the physical dry dust of the earth is a significant difference for Irenaeus, as we shall see in our fourth chapter on his anthropology.

[166] This Greek verb, the same as in Genesis 2.7, occurs nine times in the Septuagint and Apocrypha, though only once in the New Testament (John 20.22).

[167] Cf. Genesis 3.21 (LXX):
καὶ ἐποίησεν κύριος ὁ θεὸς τῷ Αδαμ καὶ τῇ γυναικὶ αὐτοῦ χιτῶνα δερματίνους καὶ ἐνέδυσεν αὐτούς.

on an allegorical reading of Genesis 3.21 as Philo had done earlier.[168] Both texts use the same Greek words for "covering of skin" (*Adversus Haereses*: δερμάτιον χιτῶνα; LXX: χιτῶνας δερματίνους). By highlighting the Valentinian distinction between "earthly" man (cf. Genesis 2.7) and human flesh (cf. Genesis 3.21), Irenaeus may be pointing to an incongruity between the Valentinian position and the plain sense of the Genesis text – a matter which might not have been clear to persons outside the Valentinian community.[169] (The anthropological sketch that Irenaeus will offer in response [cf. our chapter four] is decidedly non-Platonic insofar as flesh is proclaimed to be constitutive of the human creation.) In the next subsection, Irenaeus elaborates on the πνευματικός which Achamoth has surreptitiously sown into humanity. The spiritual seed was the fruit of her contemplation of *Sōtēr's* angels, and as such they will serve as their brides in the eschaton. In the present time, they are the *Ecclesia*, the antitype (ἀντίτυπος) of the true *Ecclesia* above.

Nothing in Genesis 1-3 would seem to provide source material for the Valentinians' teaching about the origin of this third human nature, the "spiritual seed" (cf. i.6.4; i.7.1).[170] Yet this omission is not unexpected, for the Valentinian Demiurge (Yahweh / Elohim in the Genesis story) is reckoned to be ignorant of the existence of the πνευματικοί. Moses, being Yahweh's prophet, must also have been unaware. However, the apostle Paul, unfettered by such ignorance, was found to offer penetrating insight into the event of humanity's creation. In 1 Corinthians 15, Paul twice refers to Adam by name,[171] and also retrieves from Genesis 2.7:

---

[168] Cf. Philo, *QG* 1.53.
[169] The abrupt movement in Irenaeus' Valentinian account from Genesis 2.7 (breath of life) to Genesis 3.21 (covering of skin) without a discussion of intervening Genesis events might upon first glance be surprising. However, this may reflect Irenaeus' use of a systematic and topical approach to explaining the Valentinian system. In first exploring anthropological origin (*Haer.* i.5.5), Irenaeus sets up the subsequent discussion (*Haer.* i.6 to i.7) in which a tri-partite anthropology (actually quadra-partite on the individual level, in that "earthy" is distinguished from "fleshly" [cf. i.5.6]) is related to Christology, soteriology, and eschatology. Thus the section on human origination covers, in sequence, the human components: earthy man, psychic man, fleshly man, and spiritual man.
[170] The Gnostic view that Seth was the archetype of the πνευματικοί would likely have been informed by strands of Jewish wisdom tradition and speculative readings of the Genesis 5 genealogy alongside Genesis 1-2. Genesis 5.1 reiterates that Adam was made "according to the image of God" (ἧ ἡμέρα ἐποίησεν ὁ θεὸς τὸν Αδαμ κατ εικόνα θεοῦ ἐποίησεν αὐτόν). As mentioned earlier, Adam was deemed to have received the spiritual deposit of Achamoth. Seth, the only son of Adam and Eve mentioned in the genealogy, is said to have been begotten according to the likeness and the image of Adam (ἐγέννησεν κατὰ τὴν ἰδέαν αὐτοῦ καὶ κατὰ τὴν εἰκόνα αὐτοῦ) (5.3).
[171] 1 Corinthians 15.22, 45.

οὕτως καὶ γέγραπται ἐγένετο ὁ πρῶτος ἄνθρωπος
Ἀδὰμ εἰς ψυχὴν ζῶσαν.[172]

Noting the expressly Christian anthropological statements in Paul's New Testament text, Valentinian interpreters quite naturally juxtaposed these alongside Genesis 2. Different types of ἄνθρωπος may be discerned: ψυχικὸς ἄνθρωπος, for example, cannot receive τὰ τοῦ πνεύματος.[173] "Not all flesh is alike" (Οὐ πᾶσα σὰρξ ἡ αὐτὴ σάρξ..." [verse 39]). A distinction is made between σῶμα ψυχικόν and σῶμα πνευματικόν (verse 44). Furthermore, "the first man was from the earth, a man of dust (ἄνθρωπος ἐκ γῆς χοϊκός); the second man is from heaven (ἐξ οὐρανοῦ) (verse 47). The Valentinian description of the Demiurge's human creation as an ἄνθρωπον τὸν χοϊκόν (*Haer.* i.5.5) appears to draw from verse 48. Here Paul similarly uses χοϊκόν as a collective noun preceded by the definite article:

οἷος ὁ χοϊκός, τοιοῦτοι καὶ οἱ χοϊκοί, καὶ οἷος ὁ
ἐπουράνιος, τοιοῦτοι καὶ οἱ ἐπουράνιοι[174]

Thus when the Valentinians speak of three human *geneai*, πνευματικός, ψυχικός, and ὑλικός, 1 Corinthians 15 is their authoritative source text. We shall discuss this matter in greater detail in our fourth chapter when we assess Irenaeus' response to this Valentinian hermeneutic.

Major differences exist between the Valentinian account of the creation of man and that proffered in *Timaeus*. Unlike *Timaeus*, the Valentinians distinguished between "spiritual" and "psychic" materials, each originating from deities of different levels. Yet echoes of *Timaeus* may be clearly heard. The supposition that the spiritual man is "deposited" into the world by Achamoth, the spiritual mother above, recollects Plato's description of deity "sowing" souls into the world which are, subsequently, "*of necessity* implanted in bodies."[175] The "psychic" material which the Demiurge "breathed" into Adam could be seen to correspond to "the most sovereign part of our soul... God's gift to us, given to be our guiding spirit."[176] "It raises us up away from the earth and toward what is akin to us in heaven" (cf. the Demiurge's psychic realm).[177]

---

[172] 1 Corinthians 15.45: "Thus it is written, 'The first man, Adam, became a living soul'...."

[173] according to the earlier statement in 1 Corinthians 2.14

[174] "As is the earthy, so also are those who are earthy; and as is the heavenly, so also are those who are heavenly."

[175] Cf. Plato, *Timaeus* 73c; 42a. The "starting point" of man's creation is said to be "the formation of marrow [the brain and peripheral extensions]... a 'universal seed' contrived for every mortal kind" into which souls are "implanted" (73b; Zeyl, 67).

[176] Ibid., 90a (Zeyl, 85).

[177] Ibid. (Zeyl, 86).

The Valentinian narrative (loosely) follows Genesis rather than *Timaeus* by asserting that the formation of the bodily "container" precedes the impartation of the spiritual or psychic material. Yet its description of the necessary function and purpose of the physical body points directly to a dependence on Plato. In *Timaeus*, the reason that souls were "*of necessity* (ἐξ ἀνάγκης) implanted in bodies" was that their growth and destinies (i.e., "acquir[ing] the nature of being the most god-fearing of living things") required a sensate external environment.[178] In accord with this, the souls needed a "carriage" in the form of a physical body with limbs to facilitate navigation in this world.[179] Sense perception was critical for the proper training and disciplining of the soul before it could return to its heavenly origin.[180] The marrow containing the soul required a protective "wrapping" of flesh, which should not be "dull and insensitive (ἀναισθησία)"[181] Rather, the physical body would be constructed "to make sure that the stimulations received by the senses... might register clearly upon the body as a whole."[182] In the Valentinian narrative, the man was "enveloped all round with a covering of skin... the outward *sensitive* (αἰσθητός) flesh" (i.5.5). The confinement of spiritual and psychic human life within a body of sensitive flesh in a physical, sensate world was a matter of necessity, for it enabled the requisite "training by means of the outward senses." Indeed, it is "on this account... [that] the world was created..." (i.6.1).

Yet the motif of *necessity* in a broader sense also firmly links the Valentinian account to that of the *Timaeus*. For the Valentinians, necessity circumscribes the potentialities and destinies of the three types of substance, and thus of humanity: "All that is material... must *of necessity* (κατ' ἀνάγκην) perish, inasmuch as it is incapable of receiving any *afflatus* of incorruption" (i.6.1). "It is impossible that material substance should partake of salvation... so again it is impossible that spiritual substance should ever come under the power of corruption."[183] "Spiritual substance has been sent forth for this end, that, being here united with that which is soulish, it might assume shape, the two

---

[178] Ibid., 42a (Zeyl, 29); emphasis is added. Cf.: "Of necessity... it came about that [man] lived his life surrounded by fire and air..." (*Timaeus*, 77a [Zeyl, 71]).

[179] Cf. Plato, *Timaeus* 69c-72d; and Zeyl, lxxix.

[180] "So, once the souls were of necessity implanted in bodies... the first innate capacity they would, of necessity, come to have would be sense perception..." (Plato, *Timaeus*, 42a [Zeyl, 29]).

[181] Ibid., 75e (Zeyl, 70).

[182] Ibid., 77e (Zeyl, 72). Cf. 74e (ἀναισθησίαν); 75b (αἴσθησιν); 75c (εὐαισθητότερα); 76d (εὐαισθησίας).

[183] *Haer.* i.6.2. Although Valentinian anthropology connotes a fairly strong element of determinism, the theme of divine grace is by no means absent. The Pauline texts which the Valentinians expounded frequently celebrate God's gracious activity toward his spiritual children (i.e., seed).

elements being simultaneously subjected to the same discipline" (i.6.1). "[A]nimal souls of necessity (κατ' ἀνάγκην) rest for ever with the Demiurge in the intermediate place" (i.7.5). The Valentinian perspective on a cosmic order crafted by both the Demiurge and Achamoth, thus reflect *Timaeus'* summation: "[T]his ordered world is of mixed birth: it is the offspring of a union of Necessity and Intellect."[184]

THE DEMIURGE AND THE OLD TESTAMENT PROPHETS

> ...[M]any things were spoken by this seed [of Achamoth] through the prophets, as it was endowed with a transcendently lofty nature (i.7.3).

Following the discussion that contrasts the natures and correspondent destinies of the three classes of human beings, *Haer.* i.7 briefly presents an overview of the time period between creation and the advent of Christ, from a Valentinian perspective. Perhaps the most notable feature is that the Demiurge is portrayed much differently than the Ophites' megalomaniac Ialdabaoth who constantly seeks to avenge humanity's rebuff. By contrast, the Valentinian Demiurge is almost congenial. He even has a special affection (ἀγαπειν / *diligere*) for the "superior" persons who "possess the seed of Achamoth" (i.7.3). Oblivious to the true cause of these feelings, the Demiurge thinks they are the way they are because of him. Thus he distributes (or classifies) them as prophets, priests and kings.[185] On the basis of this seed's transcendent nature, they are said to have spoken "many things" through the prophets (i.7.3). In a broader sense, there are three sources of prophetic revelation: Achamoth, the πνευματικοί, and the Demiurge. Though the Demiurge is at times a source of prophecy, on other occasions he is merely an unwitting channel for prophecies from Achamoth. Since he cannot know of spiritual things higher than himself, the Demiurge remained ignorant of Christ's future advent despite the prophecies. These he attributed to various causes: a "prophetic spirit," a mere uninspired man, or even to forces below himself. Not until Christ actually appeared did the Demiurge finally discern his coming. Subsequently, he is said to have "learned all things from [Christ], and gladly with all his power (δύναμεως / *virtus*) joined himself to him" (i.7.4). In fact, the gospel account of the centurion's encounter with Jesus is to be interpreted as depicting the Demiurge's recognition of Christ's authority.[186]

---

[184] Ibid., 48a (Zeyl, 36).
[185] Cf. Unger, *St. Irenaeus*, 39.
[186] Cf. Matthew 8.9 and Luke 7.8.

CHRIST IN VALENTINIAN READINGS OF THE GOSPELS

> ...[T]he Savior came to the soulish substance (which was possessed of free-will), that he might secure for it salvation (i.6.1).

The Valentinians, like the Ophites, assume that the Christian gospels attest the pre-existence of Jesus. However, the Valentinian narrative differs (perhaps representing an adaptation) in that Jesus (*Sōtēr*) is more involved in the pre-cosmic drama starring Sophia / Achamoth. As noted above, Christ sends Jesus to answer Achamoth's second cry for help. Upon seeing Jesus, Achamoth "ran forward to meet him" and insofar as he separated her passions from her, Jesus is credited with "virtually" (by power) creating the world (i.4.5). After Achamoth's offspring, the Demiurge, introduces the three types of substances into the world he creates, the strategy is set. The ψυχικοί are now to be "trained" through the senses. "That is why, they say, the world was made and why the Savior came to save this psychic element, since it possessed free will."[187] This Jesus, so the Valentinians claim, was equipped for his mission by "assum[ing] the first fruits of what he was going to save: from Achamoth, the spiritual; from the Demiurge he was clothed with the psychic Christ." Finally, "he was surrounded by a body[188]... prepared with ineffable skill. He received nothing material, for the material is not capable of being saved."[189] Jesus' ministry is then oriented toward revealing the "perfect knowledge of God" (cf. i.6.2). His teachings through parables, as recorded in the gospels, speak of divine realities – truths heretofore hidden from humanity. For example, the story of the prodigal (Luke 15) is the account of Sophia's fall and restoration to Pleroma. Because he is the embodiment of *Sōtēr* who constitutes the fullness of Pleroma,[190] Jesus is uniquely able to reveal and impart such divine fullness.[191] In the eschaton, "when all the seed shall have come to perfection," Achamoth is received into Pleroma and takes *Sōtēr* as her spouse (i.7.1). The component materials in humanity are separated and enter their destined abodes. The πνευματικοί rise to Pleroma, leaving their psychic material in the intermediate abode where the Demiurge and the "souls of the righteous" will abide. However, all substance of the material kind will be utterly destroyed by fire (i.7.1).

---

[187] *Haer.* i.6.1; trans. by Grant, *Irenaeus*, 64.
[188] This body is presumably the earthly Jesus, which can be distinguished from the divine *Sōtēr* who fills him (cf. the last sentence of 7.3).
[189] *Haer.* i.6.1; trans. by Grant, *Irenaeus*, 64.
[190] Cf. the origin of Jesus / *Sōtēr* in Pleroma (2.6); as noted above; see also Colossians 2.9; et al.
[191] Just as there are said to be three sources of Old Testament prophecy: Achamoth, the πνευματικοί, and the Demiurge (cf. Ptolemy, *Letter to Flora*), so also are there three sources behind the sayings of the Jesus of the gospels: *Sōtēr*, Achamoth, and the Demiurge (*Haer.* i.7.3).

The Valentinian interpretation of the Christ in the gospels resembles that of the Ophites insofar as the major contours of the plot are concerned. Yet Valentinian readings of the gospels highlight meanings that posit a reality much deeper and broader in scope, encompassing things spiritual, psychic, and material. Jesus is not simply the union of two Aeons, that is "Christ" (third Man) and "Sophia," but rather is the embodiment of *Sōtēr*, fullness of *all* deity. His marital union will eventually be with Achamoth, Sophia's enthymesis, whereby Sophia and thus all of Pleroma is fully restored. Jesus is not a mere competitor to the Demiurge, slowly eroding his power. He is uniquely sovereign, and his salvific work may be seen to enact the convergence and triumph of both "necessity" and "intellect" whereby all things (including the Demiurge) reach their ultimate destinies. In this way, unity is more satisfactorily demonstrated: Christ is "all in all."[192] Valentinian innovation has honed the received Gnostic narratives to yield a sharper christological edge. Not only is this evident in their readings of the gospels, but also in their appropriations of Genesis 2-3 to which we now turn.

THE GENESIS GARDEN AND TEMPTATION NARRATIVES IN THE *GOSPEL OF TRUTH*

> ... *He was nailed to a tree; he became a fruit of the knowledge of the Father which did not, however, become destructive because it [was] eaten, but to those who ate it, it gave (cause) to become glad in the discovery* (Gos. Truth 18.24-29).

Though the Valentinian narratives in *Adversus Haereses* do not overtly employ allusions or themes from the Garden and Temptation narratives in Genesis 2-3, their appearance in *Gospel of Truth*[193] suggests that the Valentinian tradition (broadly conceived) did find this material relevant to the formulation of their doctrines.[194] The remarkable typological readings found in *Gospel of Truth* attest to two Valentinian convictions. First, the coherence of the gospel narratives was to be explained and defended as a matter of highest priority. Second, the texts of Genesis 2-3 were essential in order to accomplish this essentially hermeneutical task. Unlike the Ophite account in i.30 or the even

---

[192] Cf. Ephesians 1.23; 1 Corinthians 15.28.

[193] Despite the reservations of some scholars, most now seem to be comfortable with attributing *Gospel of Truth* to the Valentinian tradition, even if not Valentinus himself. For an introduction into the debate over higher critical data concerning this text, see for example Jacqueline A. Williams, *Biblical Interpretation in the Gnostic Gospel of Truth from Nag Hammadi* (Atlanta: Scholars Press, 1988), 1-13.

[194] Robert Grant argues that since *Gospel of Truth* contains echoes of "nearly all the New Testament writings, except the Pastoral Epistles," Valentinus was evidently "providing a reinterpretation of the Christian doctrine" (*Gnosticism and Early Christianity*, 129).

more subversive *Apocryphon of John*, *Gospel of Truth* does not appropriate Genesis 2-3 systematically, nor does it show the slightest concern to read and interpret Genesis in its own right, apart from other texts. For example, Genesis 2-3 is not mined as an etiological source of insights into the origins of the cosmos, humanity, sin, death, divine-human enmity, work, and sexuality (to name but a few). Whereas the Ophites and *Apocryphon of John* contested the authority and reliability of Genesis 2-3 itself and the events it purports to narrate, *Gospel of Truth* views Genesis 2-3 instrumentally. It is a vital hermeneutical tool that promises to shed light on gospel readings concerning Christ's role in the economy of human salvation. Genesis 2-3 provides language and an interpretative framework for speaking soteriologically. It is apparent, then, that Valentinian interpretation of the gospels as a coherent narrative presupposes the foundational Genesis texts.

Riemer Roukema succinctly captures the general theme of *Gospel of Truth*, denoting it "a meditative, mystical address about redemption from ignorance and about the riches of the knowledge of the truth."[195] Whereas the "incomprehensible Father" is said to be the source of the "All," "Error" (personified) is the one who created matter and humanity.[196] But while Error has been the source of ignorance and oblivion concerning the truth of the Father, Jesus has come to bring revelation – to show humanity the way to the Father.[197] Jesus is a teacher, as well as the instantiation of divine revelation itself. He was "published" as a "book" when he was nailed to a tree.[198] As a result of this revelation, ignorance vanishes, the "All" is brought into unity with the Father, and rest is restored.[199] Most biblical allusions made in *Gospel of Truth* are to New Testament texts and themes. Yet Jacqueline Williams has identified four occasions where *Gospel of Truth* may reveal interaction with texts from Genesis 2-3, specifically Genesis 2.7, 2.15, 2.17 and 3.7, and 3.5.

The aforementioned motif of a divine figure breathing into a human being (Genesis 2.7) has been recontextualized in *Gospel of Truth*. Here it is Jesus (rather than the Demiurge), and he brings knowledge of the "incomprehensible" Father to ignorant humanity: "...[W]hen he had breathed into them what is in the mind, doing his will, when many had received the light, they turned to

---

[195] R. Roukema, *Gnosis and Faith in Early Christianity* (London: SCM, 1999), 143.
[196] *Gos. Truth* (*NHC* I, 3) 17.5-9; 17.14-20. The most common view is that "Error" is loosely identified with the Valentinian Demiurge. "While there is no clear separation of the Father from the creator, Error is evidently a surrogate for the latter; it 'elaborated its own matter,' and it was only imitating Truth when it modeled a creature" (Grant, *Gnosticism and Early Christianity*, 131). (All citations from *Gospel of Truth* are from *The Nag Hammadi Library in English* [ed. J. M. Robinson; Leiden, 1977], 37-49).
[197] *Gos. Truth* 18.15-21.
[198] Ibid., 19.10-21.25.
[199] Ibid., 24.9-25.19.

him."[200] Thus, the "Father's thought" is "transmitted by the Son's breathing."[201] Despite the obvious discrepancies between *Gos. Truth* 30.34-35 and Genesis 2.7, four common elements are presented in the same sequence in each: (1) a divine figure (2) breathes (3) into a human figure (4) a given divine content.[202] The discrepancies, then, do not point away from an appeal to Genesis 2.7, but rather suggest a Valentinian re-appropriation of it. Christ's unique action may be understood in terms of its continuities and discontinuities with the prior action of the Demiurge. There is contrast insofar as Christ and Demiurge are qualitatively different in terms of rank and motivation. Yet comparison is implicit in that Gnostic systems tend to hold together the concepts of "thought" (i.e., mind or knowledge), "light" (cf. *Gospel of Truth*), and "life" (cf. Genesis 2.7) in close association. This allusion may be an instance of a typological use of Genesis, perhaps one that even hints at an Adam-Christ typology.[203] Just as "God has breathed [the breath of life] into the first human being... the beloved Son has breathed into those who have listened to him...."[204] This breath "bestows light" and "this light is conversion."[205]

Another of the redemptive effects of divine revelation is that the Son enables the Father's children to embark on a return journey back the Father. It is in this context that *Gospel of Truth* possibly appropriates Genesis 2.15[206] to offer assurance that the Father will show goodness to his children. "He is good. He knows his plantings because it is he who planted them in his paradise. Now his paradise is his place of rest."[207]

Going backward in the narrative sequence of *Gospel of Truth* but forward in the Genesis story, we turn to examine the most substantial and unambiguous appropriation of Genesis 2-3: the christological reinterpretation of the "tree of the knowledge of good and evil." Because Christ brings knowledge that threatens to reveal the "oblivion of error,"[208] Error stridently opposes him.

> ...[E]rror grew angry at him, persecuted him, was distressed at him, (and) was brought to naught. He was nailed to a tree; he became a fruit of the knowledge of the

---

[200] Ibid., 30.34-31.1.
[201] Williams, *Biblical Interpretation*, 110. Williams concedes that since *Gospel of Truth* frequently appeals to similar motifs found in the gospel of John, it is only "possible" rather than probable that Genesis 2.7 is *Gospel of Truth*'s primary source at this point (111).
[202] Ibid., 110.
[203] Ibid., 111.
[204] Ibid.
[205] Ibid.; cf. *Gos. Truth* 30.36-31.1.
[206] καὶ ἔθετο αὐτὸν ἐν τῷ παραδείσῳ
[207] *Gos. Truth* 36.35-38; cf. Williams, *Biblical Interpretation*, 153.
[208] *Gos. Truth* 17.36-37

> Father, which did not, however, become destructive because it [was] eaten, but to those who ate it, it gave (cause) to become glad in the discovery. For he discovered them in himself, and they discovered him in themselves, the incomprehensible, inconceivable one, the Father....[209]

Clearly Genesis 2.17[210] and 3.6-7 are in view here. Both *Gospel of Truth* and the Sethian *Apocryphon of John* assert that human beings accrue the benefit of knowledge of the Father by eating fruit from a tree. Both identify the same antagonist. Error is the malevolent archon who creates the world. But since *Apocryphon of John's* narrative is circumscribed within and aspires to inform the *Genesis* context, it radically subverts the traditional meaning of Genesis 2-3. Being inspired by the Demiurge, "Moses" deceptively represents the tree of the knowledge of good and evil as deleterious, while depicting the tree of life as salubrious. From the perspective of "Christ" (the narrator of *Apocryphon of John* who supersedes the lower order Demiurge), precisely the opposite is true.[211] By contrast, *Gospel of Truth's* narrative is set within and seeks to inform a *christological* context. Thus when it speaks of the results of eating from the tree as positive, it is not subverting Genesis, but rather points to Genesis' radical eschatological fulfillment in Christ. The Genesis imagery of Adam and Eve partaking from a tree resulting in death highlights the *contrasting result* of Christ's encounter with a tree. His death yields knowledge of the Father, bringing gladness. Thus *Gospel of Truth* presupposes and incorporates a christological hermeneutic when reading Genesis 2-3, such as is done by New Testament writers. The Valentinian reading depends on recognizing an analogous relationship between Adam and Christ (cf. Romans 5), and a conception of Christ (through his death and resurrection) as "first fruits" (1 Corinthians 15.20-23; cf. *Haer.* i.6.1). As such it is best characterized as a typological reading of Genesis 2.17 and 3.6-7.[212]

The fourth possible allusion to Genesis 1-3, as noted by Williams, is also set within the context of Christ's redemptive revelation of the Father rather than the context of anthropogony. Again *Gospel of Truth* appears to use Genesis 3.5 typologically in order to point to the dramatic reversal enacted in Christ's revelation, when compared with the tragic narrative event of Genesis 3.5-7. In the Genesis account, the serpent asserts: "for God knows that when you eat of it your eyes will be opened, and you will be like God, knowing good and evil." After the woman and man ate the fruit from the forbidden tree, "then the eyes of

---

[209] Ibid., 18.22-33.
[210] "But of the tree of the knowledge of good and evil you shall not eat, for in the day that you eat of it you shall die."
[211] Cf. *Ap. John* 21.16-22.9.
[212] Cf. Williams, *Biblical Interpretation*, 28.

both were opened, and they knew that they were naked...."[213] In *Gospel of Truth*, the human state of ignorance is described as dream-like. But when the dreamers receive revelation, they leave the "terrors" and "fictions" of the dream world behind, esteeming them never to have been "solid" in the first place.[214] "The knowledge of the Father they value as the dawn... Good for the man who will come to and awaken. *And blessed is he who has opened the eyes of the blind...* Having extended his hand to him who lay upon the ground, he set him up on his feet, for he had not yet risen."[215] Though the mere reference to the opening of blind eyes is not sufficient to demonstrate an allusion to Genesis 3.5, its context in *Gospel of Truth* suggests it. Christ's revelation opens human eyes so as to enable clear self-awareness. In Genesis 3, the eyes of man and woman were opened when they ate the fruit, just as the serpent had promised, but with harmful results. In this case, *Gospel of Truth* may have drawn not only from the Genesis account, but also from Sethian interpretations of Genesis. In Irenaeus' retelling of the Ophite narrative (and similarly in *Apocryphon of John*), newly-created man is in a prone state. He is able only to "wriggle" upon the ground until he receives the divine inbreathing of the Demiurge. In parallel fashion, Christ's breath of divine knowledge opens the eyes of the sleepers and empowers them to arise.

In sum, by their allusions to Genesis 2-3 in *Gospel of Truth*, the Valentinians bolster their proposed Christian vision of humanity and of humanity's way of salvation. It is this vision that Irenaeus will oppose on the basis of his own revisited readings of Genesis 1.26 and 2.7.

Assessing Gnostic Readings of Genesis

As our chapter has demonstrated, looking closer at Ophite and Valentinian readings of Genesis 1-3 brings to the foreground some strikingly unusual exegesis as well suggests basic hermeneutical assumptions. Our objective in this chapter has been two-fold. First, we wish to provide evidence with which to contest popular misconceptions about Gnostic readers of biblical texts. Our approach assumes that Irenaeus' vehement opposition to Gnostic teachings did not preclude but in fact promoted his interest in representing them as accurately as possible. Yet, just as we began by refusing to prejudge Irenaeus' efforts before looking at his texts, so also we have initially aimed to give his antagonists a sympathetic hearing. Thus although *Adversus Haereses* is our

---

[213] Genesis 3.5, 7.
[214] *Gos. Truth* 28.32-30.4.
[215] Ibid., 30.4-23. The italicized portion (30.14-16) is that which Williams proposes as a possible allusion to Genesis 3.5 (*Biblical Interpretation*, 104-106).

primary source of content, it has been necessary at times to adopt a bit of critical distance. This gives room to consider the possibility that certain groups adhering to a mixture of Gnostic-Christian teachings might indeed have read Genesis not to denigrate or distort these texts but with the serious intention of expounding a richer Christian interpretation. This task has led us to consider the cases of two intriguing Gnostic interpretations of Genesis, those of the Ophites and the Valentinians, with an eye to their possible relatedness. After reading these narratives carefully, we find reason to challenge sweeping generalizations about Gnostic interpreters of Genesis. For example, it is at best incomplete, and at worst misleading to pronounce that, "in contrast to the church, the Gnostics rejected (*ablehnen*) Genesis and therefore emphasized (*herausstellen*) its defectiveness."[216] Secondly, we have endeavored to maintain a strict focus on Gnostic readings of *texts* rather than on doctrines. This prepares the way for our subsequent investigation into the hermeneutical dimensions of Irenaeus' counterproposals. Accordingly, we are not concerned to evaluate the Ophite interpretation of Genesis in its own right, but only insofar as it informs our understanding of Valentinian readings of Genesis as Christian Scripture, for these are the readings that Irenaeus disputes.

Generalizing and refiguring

First, we turn to the problem of oversimplification. In his detailed study of Irenaeus' Adam / Christ typology, J. T. Nielsen offers a summary of what he terms "the way the Gnostics make use of Holy Scripture."[217] It is difficult to discern whether Nielsen is simply repeating Irenaeus' judgment or offering one of his own, though it is most likely that we see a confluence of the two. Nielsen relates that "the Gnostics" use names, terms and concepts from the Old Testament in presenting teaching that "sternly rejects the Creator God of the O.T. and that which he created, and... set[s] a low value on man."[218] In succession, he cites *Haer.* i.30.7 and i.5.3 to describe Gnostic views of the Demiurge, before making further mention of Marcion's negative view of the Jewish creator God based on *Haer.* i.27.3. On the basis of these readings, "the meaning of the O.T. becomes exactly the opposite of what was intended."[219] Compared to their approach to the New Testament, the Gnostics are said to "undervalue" the Old Testament. "In Gnosticism," states Nielsen, "the O.T. has a typological function: what actually matters takes place in the Pleroma. That is

---

[216] Armstrong, *Die Genesis in der Alten Kirche*, 143.
[217] *Adam and Christ in the Theology of Irenaeus of Lyons* (Assen, The Netherlands: Koninklijke Van Gorcum, 1968), 50.
[218] Ibid., 51.
[219] Ibid.

pointed to by everything described in the O.T. The norm is the Pleroma, the O.T. is *subject* to it."[220] Cyril O'Regan also estimates the scope of Valentinian "disfiguration-refiguration" of the Christian narrative as "total": "Not a single important feature of the [biblical] salvation-history narrative is left intact and is not reconfigured in such a way that its meaning is totally changed... The negative estimation of the creator, as detailed graphically in [the Ptolemaean system], has obvious negative consequences for an evaluation of the created order."[221] Upon first glance, Nielsen and O'Regan are absolutely right. Yet it would seem that our analysis of Ophite and Valentinian readings of Genesis creation texts as Scripture could moderate their conclusions.

The first concern, as evident in Nielsen's summary though not O'Regan's, is sweeping generalization. The Genesis readings of the Ophites and Valentinians (not to mention Marcion's) express theological interests and hermeneutical uses that may, at best, overlap only partially. While historical scholars of Gnosticism have long been calling for more acknowledgement of diversity between groups, this variegation is also readily apparent in a straightforward reading of Irenaeus' *Adversus Haereses*. By differentiating Ophite and Valentinian readings of Genesis, along with suggesting their relatedness, it becomes clear that imprecise judgments about "Gnostics" promote an incomplete vision. Valentinian uses of Genesis are dependent upon and yet notably different from Ophite uses, and Irenaeus' counter-interpretations can be better understood with this in mind. The second question raised concerns the extent to which the Valentinians have "disfigured" and "refigured" a Christian narrative. Here, on the basis of Valentinian interpretations of Genesis, at least, we may hesitate at endorsing O'Regan's rigid judgment. We shall find similarities amongst Irenaean and Valentinian hermeneutics of Genesis, along with the admittedly more substantive discontinuities. To be certain, though, O'Regan is right to focus attention not on differences between the doctrines or terminologies (cf. "recapitulation") of Irenaeus and the Valentinians, but on their divergent configurations of a biblical "salvation-history" narrative. In any such rendition, the opening chapters of Genesis, insofar as they introduce the story, are peerless. However, any attempt to adjudicate between Irenaeus' reading of Genesis and that offered by the Valentinians would seem to invite the question: Can we speak of one "Christian" narrative in Genesis 1-3? O'Regan accuses Valentinian Gnosticism of being a "tradition of texts without being a tradition of scripture in the strict sense" because "scriptural assignation depends not only on texts having authority and community use but also on a given number of texts

---

[220] Ibid., 52; emphasis is added.
[221] *Gnostic Return in Modernity*, 150; 151. In O'Regan's view, the "Christian mythos" in the hands of the Valentinians has been "so swerved that it indicates proximally a new narrative formation, and ultimately a new narrative grammar" (59).

being regarded as constitutive of the community tradition and incapable of being added to, displaced, or fundamentally emended."[222] The Valentinians, he says, show a tendency "to *expand* the narrative, to make claims to have an exhaustive knowledge of the deep things of God, the mysteries of creation and evil in particular, and to place a supreme value on knowing, specifically knowing the new metanarrative, which reconfigures and thereby reinterprets the biblical and canonic narrative."[223] However, with regard to Genesis 1-3, we might argue that in the second-century church, there was no single pre-formulated and unambiguously Christian narrative. As we shall see in chapter four, Irenaeus himself can be fairly accused of "expanding" the creation narrative when he constructs a christological reading of Genesis 2.7 on the basis of John 9.6.[224] The Valentinian extension of the Genesis narrative relied upon the gospel of John as well as (it would seem) Ophite and Middle-Platonist traditions. The crucial factor, then, is hermeneutical: How is the biblical framework to be widened and how is this wider reading theologically warranted? In this respect, Irenaeus' "rule of truth" equating Creator God and Father of Jesus Christ comes into service. In order to test O'Regan's robust claim of the Valentinians' "total" deformation of Christian narrative grammar, we turn to review a few characteristic features of its Genesis interpretations, in comparison with possible sources and competitors.

The Valentinians and Genesis

In contrast with the Ophites, the Valentinians used Genesis 1-3 to ascribe ultimate significance and pre-eminence to the person and work of Christ. This *Sōtēr* was the nexus linking creation and salvation, humanity and divinity. At the same time, though, the Valentinians attributed greater respectability to the Old Testament creator God.[225] He may still be limited and unaware, but he is not malicious, as was the Ophite Demiurge. He looks nothing like the monstrous figure who happily exploited human beings to advance a war against his mother. The rehabilitated Valentinian Demiurge has a tender side: As he "continue[s] administering the affairs of the world as long as that is fitting and needful," he "exercise[s] a care over the church" (i.7.4). The Valentinians' portrayal of a

---

[222] Ibid., 59.
[223] Ibid., 64; emphasis is added.
[224] Cf. our chapter four below.
[225] Cf. Michael Allen Williams: "If it is true that some Valentinian mythmakers drew inspiration from traditions like those in *Apocryphon of John*, then the demiurge in Valentinian myths has certainly not been further degraded from what was found in *Apocryphon of John*, but rather rehabilitated to a great extent" (*Rethinking Gnosticism*, 224).

gentler creator God reflects their "aim" of an "accommodation to mainstream Christianity."[226] In moving toward more a more explicitly Christian hermeneutic, Valentinian teaching showed a greater resolve to connect the Genesis paradise narratives to the Christian story than had earlier Gnostics. While still making some theological use of Genesis 1-3 texts in their own right, Valentinian speculation on cosmogony and theogony now became more intentionally framed within the context of christological readings of gospel and Pauline materials.[227] Their Christian tri-partite anthropology traced its roots to Paul, and in particular to Paul's reading of Genesis 2.7. The Johannine prologue appropriately addressed vital questions of origin in a way that affirmed a harmony between cosmology and Christology, and between the Genesis and gospel narratives. Christ himself is the hermeneutical key by which the full richness of the text of Genesis 2-3 is brought to bear on human – and more precisely, *Christian* – experience. Thus as readers of the Old Testament as Christian Scripture, the Valentinians reasonably defended their claim that they stood in continuity with other Christian interpreters in the apostolic tradition. Nevertheless, the Ophite narrative is a silent witness testifying the extent to which Valentinian interpretation remained unreformed. Just as Ialdabaoth's inferiority was reinforced in his desperate, though futile attempts to imitate the First Man, so also the Valentinian creator could never realize his aspirations. He would be forever subordinate to the top tier of divinity. Likewise, creation itself was fundamentally fragmented and alienated. "Jesus" may have created the world by his "power," but lesser beings were responsible for the formation of material existence. The divine economy was not designed to renew and transform that which was not divine. Instead, it re-established God's unity by quarantining and disposing of the unworthy creation that was the by-product of regrettable primordial passion. While catching glimpses of the basic natures of God and humanity in the texts of Genesis 1-3, *Timaeus* also proved helpful. Certainly, there are obvious distinctions between the Ptolemaean system and that of *Timaeus*. Yet when one operates under the hypothesis that the Valentinians tempered an earlier more radicalized Ophite reading of Genesis (cf. *Haer.* i.11.1), it is the similarities between the Valentinian and classic Platonic narratives that are most interesting.[228] Genesis 3.21, rather than 2.7 describes the

---

[226] Foerster, *Gnosis*, 1:127. In addition, perhaps the Valentinians were keen to present a "philosophically respectable view" insofar as history is concerned (Attridge, "Valentinian and Sethian Apocalyptic Traditions," 179).

[227] For some examples, cf. *Haer.* i.3.1-6; *Gos. Truth* 17.4-21.1.

[228] *Pace* Christoph Markschies, who insists that the Ptolemaean system reported by Irenaeus is "markedly removed not only from Valentinus himself but also from classical Platonism by virtue of its radically pessimistic view of the world and creation" (*Gnosis*, 94).

covering of flesh which envelops soul or spirit and functions just as the needful "soul-carriage" of Plato's text. By giving a window into human composition, the Genesis creation accounts, then, distinguish the destinies of types of human beings and point to the security of their fulfillment, as dictated by necessity. Christ's advent is the harbinger of a full revelation that awaits the eschaton when temporal reality shall at last be extinguished.

In conclusion, contrary to Nielsen's statement, what we see in Valentinian readings of Genesis is not an opposition between a "norm" (i.e., a Pleroma myth) and the Old Testament which is made "subject" to this norm. The Old Testament is not so much "undervalued" as distinctively interpreted and used. The Ophites, Valentinians, and Irenaeus all affirmed that the opening sections of Genesis were pivotal as theological sources. The crucial variable was the method of interpretation developed. Even for Irenaeus, the Old Testament (here, Genesis 1-3) was not so much a text that stood independently as Christian Scripture, whose content could be set against another "norm" – say, the apostolic tradition in place of the norm of Pleroma. The Genesis accounts had to be read christologically in order to function as Scripture. They were not defined over against a norm; they themselves had to be normed by a particular hermeneutic. The specific cases of Irenaeus' normed readings and uses of Genesis 1.26 and 2.7 are the focus of our next two chapters. In them, we encounter Irenaeus' endeavour to achieve a better correlation between Genesis and the gospels than the Valentinians and other competitors had managed.

3. GENESIS 1.26 AND THE DIVINE ECONOMY

Investigating Irenaeus: Choosing our Path

Although our foray into the foreign territory of Gnostic biblical interpretation might seem a diversion from our primary concern, Irenaeus' hermeneutical uses of Genesis 1.26 and 2.7, it has helped to pave the way for a more profitable journey ahead. In light of the scholarly approaches to Irenaeus surveyed in our first chapter, three methodological options are evident. First, one might enquire into Irenaeus' influential role in history. According to this school, to which Catherine Keller lends her voice, Irenaeus is a compelling figure primarily because he stands at the vanguard of (so-called) orthodoxy. It is he who establishes the precedent for future church leaders to authorize and deploy doctrine as a means of repressing natural ecclesial diversity. By such acts of exclusion, then, religious elites are empowered to defend their political hegemony. In a sense this school of thought focuses on Irenaeus' methodology, though it is a methodology reducible to politics and rhetoric. Theological claims are deconstructed and unmasked. The second option is to give primary attention to the content of Irenaeus' doctrinal contribution. This is preferable for those who, from Wingren to Boersma, stand outside the more strident modernist and postmodernist critiques of the past century and suspect that there is yet more of value to be recovered in Irenaeus' theological legacy. His doctrine of recapitulation, for example, is a precious treasure to be dusted off and put to work in a new theological context – one different than that of either Irenaeus himself or the reformers. However, as we have previously suggested, both options have drawbacks. It is just as unnecessary to focus on doctrine at the expense of methodology as it is to focus on methodology at the expense of doctrine. The third option, then, would be to enquire into Irenaeus' method, not so much with an eye toward history or politics (as with the first) but with an interest in explaining the distinctive features of Irenaeus' theological reasoning. For Eric Osborn, such a mission is couched in detective-like terms: "tracking down an elusive thinker."[1] The magnificent "originality"[2] of Irenaeus is, perhaps, best understood by positing the latent, unacknowledged sources that likely had informed his thought. Osborn suspects that a "form of horizontal Platonism" lurks in the background, though Irenaeus was "not conscious" of its influence upon him.[3] For example, "Irenaeus used a Platonic move to explain the relation of man to God."[4] In speaking of Irenaeus' diverse uses of the "image and likeness of God" motif, Denis Minns offers a faint echo. Irenaeus may have left us with no paper-trail, but "it would be idle to deny that Irenaeus does draw upon various, and, at times, mutually opposed traditions of interpretation of this text."[5]

In our view, research into the background of Irenaeus' work – the possible philosophical, theological, or cultural sources standing behind him – is entirely commendable. All types of relevant evidence should be unearthed and hypotheses put forward for testing. For example, part of the value in examining Irenaeus' Gnostic competition lies in the quiescent associations that are brought to light. We have suggested that both Irenaeus and the Valentinians express a protological orientation by their respective approaches to scriptural interpretation. Additionally, Harnack's suggestion that Irenaeus' depiction of salvation by mystical union with Christ[6] was influenced by Gnostic theology and Platonist thought is not implausible. However, it should be recognized that this line of methodological enquiry into possible background influences is not the only option, nor is it necessarily the most reliable and constructive one. Hidden sources may be sought and linkages proposed in an effort to reconstruct the contents of Irenaeus' head (as it were). Yet, on balance, there is greater value to be found in a close study of how Irenaeus used the sources that he *openly* acknowledges as foundational to his arguments, namely the traditioned texts of Scripture. What he did, of course, is more observable and significant than what he may have thought. We could ask, then, how does Irenaeus interpret scriptural texts and, by them, forge theological proposals?

---

[1] Osborn, *Irenaeus of Lyons*, 16.
[2] Ibid., 15-17.
[3] Ibid., 15-16.
[4] Ibid., 17. Irenaeus employs "the Platonic concept of participation" to "express man's real but incomplete participation in the life of God" (17).
[5] Minns, *Irenaeus*, 60. To Minns' credit, though, he goes on to focus on Irenaeus' text rather than speculate as to source materials.
[6] I.e., the so-called "physical" doctrine of atonement.

Irenaeus the exegete?

Such a question is likely to elicit a related objection. Is Irenaeus' methodology with regard to Scripture even relevant to contemporary readers? More specifically, should his work be considered biblical "exegesis"? Many modern scholars have reservations on this point. One recent voice aptly summarizes this view:

> Most ancient interpreters turned to Scripture with intentions which modern exegetes would consider inappropriate, for they did not study the text in its own right but for what it meant for their community of believers... In Irenaeus's work, *Against the Heresies*, we can scarcely speak about "exegesis" in the technical sense, though we find in it a vibrant defence of biblical truth....[7]

We may wonder, however, whether in a current age increasingly sensitized to the irreducibility of interpretation such a distinction between pristine, "technical" exegesis and other uses of Scripture is helpful. Insofar as Irenaeus predates the differentiation of exegesis and doctrine, all discussion of Scripture was simply speech about God. Admittedly, part of the dilemma is a matter of semantics. Yet, the claim that a theologian who studies the scriptural text with an aim to discern its meaning for a "community of believers" cannot be said to be doing exegesis would seem to imply an overly constrictive understanding of that notion. One need not fly to the other extreme and reduce the substance of a given message to social and political variables to recognize that these particulars are inextricably fused with content when doing exegesis or any other work meant for public transmission. In other words, it is fair to term Irenaeus an exegete of Scripture, and, accordingly, to maintain a certain degree of openness when attempting to follow the logic of his readings.

Unfortunately, as we asserted in our introductory chapter, even when Irenaeus' interpretation of Scripture does attract attention, his readings of Paul (and to a lesser extent, the gospels) garner the lion's share of scrutiny. Genesis remains underappreciated.[8] There may not be a single "key" to Irenaeus' theology and hermeneutical approach, but his exegesis and carefully tailored uses of the Genesis creation texts notably stand out amongst a crowd of

---

[7] Charles Kannengiesser, "The 'Speaking' God and Irenaeus's Interpretive Pattern: The Reception of Genesis," *Annali di storia dell' esegesi* 15 (1998): 337.

[8] On Irenaeus' use of New Testament texts, see, for example: D. Jeffrey Bingham (*Irenaeus' Use of Matthew's Gospel in Adversus Haereses* [Leuven: Peeters, 1997]), and Rolf Noormann (*Irenaus als Paulusinterpret* [Tübingen: Mohr, 1994]), David Balas, and Richard Norris on the Pauline corpus. Gregory Armstrong's brief study, *Die Genesis in der Alten Kirche*, is one of the few exceptions to this tendency.

candidates. Doing justice to the integrity of sacred text "in its own right" (to use Kannengiesser's words) and employing it for a diverse set of theological and ecclesial tasks were not, for Irenaeus, mutually exclusive goals. Indeed, he would have denied that this dichotomy were even possible.

Methodology and theology

On the basis of Irenaeus' presentations of Valentinian (and Ophite) systems, it is clear that these groups ascribed significant import to the texts of Genesis 1-3 as means by which to explain and commend their doctrines. As Christian interpreters, the Valentinians were concerned to account for Christ's function in the economy of salvation, and Genesis provided crucial narratives and motifs in order to express this. As we shall see, Irenaeus' own theological response demonstrates a basic agreement with his adversaries on this point. Because Scripture was read particularly from a protological orientation, the creation texts were irresistible and irreplaceable. Without them, Christ's soteriological work could not be connected with the larger narratives that related humanity to divinity and to the cosmos. Of course, Irenaeus did adopt a different tack, and the manner in which his christological depictions and uses of Genesis differed from those of the Gnostics provided not only a theological rebuttal but also hermeneutical guidance for leaders in the wider sphere of proto-orthodox Christianity. Thus Manlio Simonetti, for example, rightly underlines the "global importance" that Irenaeus ascribed to Christ's presence in Scripture: Christ is made the subject of Old Testament theophanies, not only the "object of the *logos* and prophetic types."[9] Yet we are keen to insist that Irenaeus' hermeneutic of Scripture has, itself, a very specific *textual* basis – one in which his christological readings of Genesis 1.26 and 2.7 are central.[10] These texts were unique. So richly fertile and exceedingly flexible, they could be marshaled at a moment's notice to enable Irenaeus to say almost anything necessary about Christian doctrine.[11] In this chapter and the next, we shall present examples of

---

[9] M. Simonetti, "Per typica ad vera," *VetChr* 18 (1981): 367.

[10] In *Haer.* books 3-5, Irenaeus intentionally makes use of a number of Genesis motifs including image and likeness of God, breath of life, the garden, virginity and fertility, the temptation, the tree(s), and the (so-called) protoevangelion. However, the first two motifs have starring roles, as evident by their capacity to carry greater theological loads in discourse about God and humanity. This will become clearer when we begin to look at specific passages from *Adversus Haereses*.

[11] Recognizing that the "use of the Old Testament and especially Genesis, was of greatest significance for the spread of Christianity" in its first two centuries, Gregory Armstrong distinguishes two relevant questions (*Die Genesis in der Alten Kirche*, 15). The first concerns the selection of the texts and the "forms of interpretation" to be used. The "all-important" second question, "Was hat diese Sachlage zu bedeuten?" assesses the "inner

Irenaeus' exegetical work and multifaceted uses of these texts. Although we argue that these Genesis texts hold a privileged status, our study is, in one sense, merely a case in point illustrating how Irenaeus read the Old Testament as Christian Scripture. Additional texts invite further research.

A perusal of *Adversus Haereses* suggests that although Genesis 1.26 and 2.7 are both used extensively for theological purposes, they are not used in the same ways. Isolated references to the image and likeness of God are scattered liberally throughout books three, four and five. This text evidently functioned like a hermeneutical tool, ready at hand wherever needed. Accordingly, we have brought forward three representative examples that summarize its wide-ranging utility. The image and likeness language of Genesis 1.26 supplies the paint, as it were, for picturing humanity and God at each crucial stage in the sweep of God's grand economy. If flexibility is the hallmark of Genesis 1.26, Genesis 2.7 is found well-suited for wide typological readings. This text, with its imagery of "formation from dust" and "breath of life," is a crucial pillar in Irenaeus' extended anthropological argument in book five concerning the right interpretation of 1 Corinthians 15.50.[12] Thus in our fourth chapter, we shall carefully trace the uses of this text only in the section *Haer.* v.1-16. Our current chapter, however, sets the stage for this latter task, both as regards Irenaeus' method and his theology. As to the former, it will be evident that Irenaeus interprets both Genesis 1.26 and 2.7 in a manner more flexibly than is typically granted. Irenaeus may have referents in mind for image of God and breath of life, but he frustrates attempts to identify their fixed meanings because his immediate concern is not to define them but to use them to point to other theological realities or states of being.[13] Our study of Genesis 1.26 sets the stage

---

connection" between Genesis interpretation and the theologies of Justin, Irenaeus and Tertullian (17). Furthermore, there are two basic standpoints in this relationship between theology and interpretation. "One provides the grounds for creative [*schöpferischer*] theological work." The other is more of a "receptacle for the interpreter's already characteristic general attitude [*Gesamthaltung*]" (David Lerch, *Isaaks Opferung christlich gedeutet* [Tübingen: Mohr, 1950], 2; cf. Armstrong, 17). Lurch qualifies this differentiation by acknowledging that in reality, both processes are effectively at work in the interpretation of any text. While not denying this, our study is especially concerned to highlight the first standpoint, Irenaeus' creative theological work with the texts of Genesis 1.26 and 2.7 that illumine the "inner connection" between his exegetical readings of Genesis and his theological system.

[12] I.e., the Pauline reference to the inability of "flesh and blood" to inherit the kingdom of God.

[13] There is truth in Richard Norris' general assessment of Irenaeus' "unusually influential theological synthesis." This, he says, enjoys the "double advantage of being relatively clear in its outlines and at the same time fuzzy in its details, so that those who followed him could manage at once to be persuaded of his essential rightness, and to sit loose to his particular notions on any given subject" ("The Transcendence and Freedom of God:

theologically for that of Genesis 2.7 insofar as both texts, given Irenaeus' christological reading, describe the divine economy. Genesis 1.26 plots the timeline while Genesis 2.7 fills in the details of the triune God's work to achieve his goal of fashioning the *homo vivens*. As we progress through these sections from *Adversus Haereses*, we aim to substantiate the primary assertions adopted thus far. Irenaeus' discourse essentially attests a hermeneutical battle with his Gnostic opponents – a crucial aspect of which concerns the way Genesis 1-2 is construed and deployed as Christian Scripture. Indeed, Irenaeus' doctrine of recapitulation is best described as a subset of his interpretative strategy regarding these Genesis creation texts.

Genesis 1.26: Humanity made according to God's image and likeness

Over forty years ago, Gustaf Wingren observed in a footnote that "Gen 1.26f. keeps recurring in Irenaeus in widely different contexts."[14] The impression given in recent works by Minns, Osborn, and MacKenzie is that such varied uses are best seen as invitations to solve a mystery – to discover the original coherent, consistent theological anthropology that Irenaeus must have had in mind. Various keys are put forward as candidates to unlock this stubborn strongbox. Some scholars eventually abandon this quest as futile, branding Irenaeus either as utterly confused or sloppy. But most approach Irenaeus' "image and likeness of God" as a concept whose meaning can be distilled through contextual reconstruction and synthesizing (or harmonizing) the scattered references in which it occurs. Denis Minns' remarks are representative:

> More recently, scholars have found [Irenaeus'] use of the text [Genesis 1.26] to be self-contradictory and to reflect his uncritical use of various, mutually incompatible sources. Others, again, have proposed elaborate defenses of his fundamental consistency...That [Irenaeus] drew upon various exegetical and theological traditions current within the Church of his time is neither surprising nor reprehensible, and should not at once rule out the possibility that his theology on this point was *coherent and consistent*.[15]

Irenaeus, the Greek Tradition, and Gnosticism" in *Early Christian Literature and the Classical Tradition, In Honorem Robert M. Grant* [ThH 53; ed. W. R. Schoedel and R. L. Wilkens; Paris: Beauchesne, 1979], 87).

[14] *Man and the Incarnation*, xiv.
[15] Minns, *Irenaeus*, 60; emphasis is added.

Iain MacKenzie apparently has a similar idea of the kind of goal worthy of pursuit: "Irenaeus is certainly flexible in his application of the phrase 'the image of God.' Yet... I think that a *synthesis* of his scattered and sometimes apparently contradictory statements can be achieved" after a "careful marshalling and comparison of the texts."[16] Eric Osborn's recent study addresses Genesis 1.26 in Irenaeus under the subheading "Image and Likeness: *The Puzzle*."[17] Subsequently, Osborn undertakes to resolve the commonly perceived dilemma that "[t]he great theme of man as the image of God seemed to *lack cohesion*."[18] These recent assessments roughly follow the judgments of previous scholars such as David Cairns. We must "admit," he says, that Irenaeus was "more directly interested" in themes such as the unity of history and recapitulation "than in making unmistakably clear his views on the image and the likeness."[19] Certainly much ink has been spilt over the related question of whether Irenaeus used image and likeness synonymously or not.[20]

The accumulating research of these and other scholars has undoubtedly shed much light on the Genesis 1.26 motif in *Adversus Haereses*, and there is no denying the attractiveness – and merit – of attempts to clarify and systematically understand the notions of image and likeness.[21] After all, Irenaeus can be

---

[16] Iain M. MacKenzie, *Irenaeus's Demonstration of the Apostolic Preaching: A theological commentary and translation* (Aldershot: Ashgate, 2002), 107-108.

[17] Osborn, *Irenaeus of Lyons*, 211.

[18] Ibid.; emphasis is added.

[19] *The Image of God in Man* (London: SCM, 1953), 74. Cairns agrees with Ernst Klebba (*Anthropologie des hl. Irenaeus eine dogmenhistorische Studie* [Münster i. W.: H. Schöningh, 1894], 22) that confusion results from Irenaeus' "careless use of terms" and the fact that Irenaeus' referents differ (74). He further notes Arnold Struker's concern that some uncertainty may be due to the Latin translation – a language which is "much poorer than the original Greek" (74; cf. Struker, *Gottebenbildlichkeit des Menschen, ein Beitrag zur Geschichte der Exegese von Gen., 1.26* [Münster i.W., 1913], 92). However, such laments are not particularly helpful, at least when compared with Lawson's simple observation that "The terms 'image' and 'likeness' are somewhat fluid. It has not always been remembered that Irenaeus can use them of Adam both before and after the Fall" (*Biblical Theology*, 200).

[20] See, for example, E. Brunner's synopsis of the history of interpretation on this point in *Man in Revolt: A Christian Anthropology* (trans. Olive Wyon; London: Lutterworth, 1939), 93. Frequently, passages such as *Haer.* iv.33.4 and v.16.2 are cited to distinguish an "inamissible" image of God tied to our created-ness and a "status" of God-likeness, which is based on the gift of "friendship and communion with God" (Bernard Sesboüé, *Tout récapituler dans le Christ* [Paris: Desclée, 2000], 149).

[21] In an article cognizant of post-war societal concerns, Zachary Xintaras gives a profitable overview of referents of image of God found in the Greek Orthodox tradition. Irenaeus is credited for associating the image of God with "man's rational and free being" as well as with "the capacity to know his Creator and enjoy communion with Him" ("Man - The Image of God According to the Greek Fathers," *GOTR* 1 [1954]: 51; 58).

frustratingly imprecise from an analytical standpoint (i.e., *what* exactly did Irenaeus think was the image and / or likeness of God given to humanity, and precisely *how* was it / will it be given?). Yet such endeavors to clarify the matter by viewing it as a riddle to be solved may actually leave a more significant question unanswered or, worse, unacknowledged: *Why* does Irenaeus continually return to Genesis 1.26 in the course of his treatise? From a different vantage point, then, Irenaeus' alleged inconsistencies may instead be treated as potential insights into the catholic-Christian[22] hermeneutic of Scripture he intentionally models. Apparently, Irenaeus believed that Genesis 1.26 can be used in a variety of theological contexts. It speaks of original human constitution, human fallenness and restoration, and human eschatological destiny. We choose to focus on these three (at the possible exclusion of others) because they encapsulate Irenaeus' primary theological interest of portraying God's activity toward humanity as coherent, purposeful, and unitary.[23] Irenaeus is not the first post-apostolic theologian to draw on Genesis 1.26,[24] yet his extensive reliance upon it marks him as a pioneer. Therefore, instead of attempting to "tidy up" the concept of divine image and likeness in *Adversus Haereses*, we now turn to examine the first of three "widely different contexts" (to use Wingren's words) in which Irenaeus puts it to work. When facing his enemy on a theological battleground, Genesis 1.26 proved essential for both defensive and offensive maneuvers.

Using Genesis 1.26: The original human constitution

In discussions about God and God's economy, Irenaeus' deep antipathy toward narratives that presumed to speak of events before creation is well-known.[25] As we saw in our sections on Gnostic interpretations of Genesis, even close adherence to the biblical text was not a sufficient criterion for distinguishing a catholic-Christian narrative from challengers. One's

---

However, it is difficult to accept Xintaras' claim that Irenaeus "tried to define [this expression] in a systematic way" (51).

[22] Labeling Irenaeus' distinctive approach as "catholic-Christian" (i.e., "mainstream") is, in a sense, anachronistic. However, our use of this descriptor for Irenaeus' alternative does have some textual basis in *Adversus Haereses*, albeit indirect (cf. *Haer.* i.10.1-3; iii.3.1; iii.4.3).

[23] Thus questions over such issues as the relation between Son and Spirit to "God," or the origin of evil are relevant primarily to Irenaeus within the context of the divine economy and not in isolation.

[24] On limited reference to Genesis 1.26-27 in early Christian literature, cf. *Barn.* 5, 6; *1 Clement* 33.4-5; Ign. *Magn.* 5; Ign. *Smyrn.* 9; Justin, *Dial.* 62; Athenagoras, *De resurrectione* 12; *Diogn.* 10.2.

[25] Cf. especially *Haer.* ii.7-11.

hermeneutic was the determining factor. By declaring God to be Creator (i.e., a *terminus a quo*), Irenaeus' rule of truth effectively stipulated that any accounting of God's activity – or Christ's – must begin with anthropogony rather than with theogony.[26]

CONTEXT OF *ADVERSUS HAERESES* IV.20: EPISTEMOLOGY

In the section leading to *Haer.* iv.20, Irenaeus' critique of his opponents focuses on their "imaginations" (*cogitationes*) concerning God. By refusing to identify the true, supreme God as Creator, so Irenaeus argues, their very thoughts are impious responses to God. Thoughts that aspire to "range beyond (*supra*) God" in fact constitute a "turning away from the true God,"[27] whose greatness is said to surpass all human comprehension (iv.19.2).[28] As the πνευματικοί, the Valentinians had declared their freedom to transverse the ontological and epistemological boundary separating Pleroma from created cosmos. If the realms of the two gods are presumed to be discrete (for Irenaeus,

---

[26] On this point, an interesting comparison may be made between Irenaeus and the exegetical guidance found in the fifth-century rabbinic text Genesis Rabba. According to Philip Alexander, the firm restrictions on rabbinical exposition of Genesis 1 dating back to the Tannaitic period were an acknowledgement of this text's "theological importance" ("Pre-Emptive Exegesis: Genesis Rabba's Reading of the Story of Creation," *JJS* 43 [1992]: 245). Genesis Rabba "suggests the idea that within the Account of Creation one can only engage in *derashah* [i.e., a type of enquiry] from the point in the narrative where man was created. The implication seems to be that what lies before that point belongs to the realm of the esoteric" (235; cf. *Gen. Rab.* 9.1; emphasis is original). Irenaeus avers, for example, "If... anyone asks, 'what was God doing before he made the world?' we reply that the answer to such a question lies with God himself" (*Haer.* ii.28.3). William Schoedel suggests that the "basic contrast" drawn by Irenaeus "is between the assertions of Scripture... and speculation about such assertions" ("Theological Method in Irenaeus," *JTS* 35 [1984]: 35). However, even if Irenaeus himself makes such a claim, we shall highlight evidence in his treatment of Genesis 1.26 and 2.7 that indicates that the determining factor is not the presence or absence of speculation, but the interpretative lens chosen. (In chapter four, we will consider, as an example, Irenaeus' reading of John 9.6.)

[27] *Haer.* iv.19.1. See also *Haer.* ii.28.1: "Having therefore the truth itself as our rule, and the testimony concerning God set clearly before us, we ought not, by running after numerous and diverse answers to questions, to cast away the firm and true knowledge of God." Norbert Brox suggests that Irenaeus consciously adapts the ancient tradition of "*Wissenskritik*" for use in biblical hermeneutics. In such discussions, human curiosity (περιεργία) was reckoned to lead to the "acute danger of self-overestimation," which was a fundamental moral lapse ("Die biblische Hermeneutik des Irenaeus," *ZAC* 2 [1998]: 34).

[28] Irenaeus can imagine no greater "conceit" than the exaltation of one's "own thought above the greatness of the Creator" who "made and fashioned him, and imparted to him the breath of life" (*Haer.* ii.26.3, 1).

Genesis 1.26 and the Divine Economy 113

this implies two contained and thus limited gods[29]), it follows that human knowledge of Bythus does not correlate with intimate knowledge of the Demiurge who actually formed human bodies and souls. Yet this was hardly problematic since knowledge of an inferior god was of limited value anyway. For Irenaeus, any assessment of human knowledge of the divine (i.e., the bounds and purposes of such knowledge[30]) must naturally account for original human constitution: the know-er. This, then, points to the pivotal concern, namely, the God responsible for making humanity (body and soul) and the distinguishing characteristics of his creating act.

Adapted for precisely this theological task (how to speak of the Creator God in relation to humanity), Genesis 1.26 is an indispensable hermeneutical tool in Irenaeus' hands. It enables the emphatic assertion that the divine creation of humanity was unmediated. The one, boundless, highest "Father of all things" (iv.20.1) was *directly involved* in making humankind.[31] Whatever else might be added when describing original human constitution, this claim of divine directness in creation must be seized upon as the point of departure. Indeed, this tenet is a gravitational center that renders orbital all other speech about human origination.

SELECTED TEXT AND COMMENTS ON *ADVERSUS HAERESES* IV.20.1

Irenaeus states:

> ...[I]t is he who by himself[32] has established, and selected, and adorned, and contains all things; and among the all things, both ourselves and this our world. We also then were made (*facti sumus*), along with those things which are contained by him. And this is he of whom the Scripture says, "And God formed man, taking clay (*limus*) of the earth, and breathed into his face the breath of life." It was not angels, therefore, who made us, nor who formed us, neither had angels power to make an *image of God*, nor any

---

[29] Cp. *Haer.* iv.19.3: "And that his greatness is not defective, but contains all things, and extends even to us, and is with us, everyone will confess who entertains worthy conceptions of God."

[30] Cf. *Haer.* ii.28.1-3; passim.

[31] Cf. *Epid.* 11. Irenaeus' contemporary, Theophilus of Antioch's comments: "When God said, 'Let us make man after our image and likeness'[Gen. 1:26], he first reveals the dignity of man. For after making everything else by a word, God considered all this as incidental; he regarded the making of man as the only work worthy of his own hands" (*Autol.* 2.18 [OECT, *Theophilus of Antioch*, 57]. Cf. Clement of Alexandria, *Paid.* 1.3).

[32] *et ipse est qui per semetipsum*

one else, except the true God,[33] nor any power remotely distant (*longe absistens*) from the Father of all things. For God did not stand in need of these [beings], in order to accomplish what he himself had predetermined with himself to do, as if he did not possess his own hands. For with him were always present (*adsum*) the Word and Wisdom, the Son and the Spirit, by whom and in whom, freely (*libere*) and spontaneously (*sponte*), he made all things, to whom also he speaks, saying, "*Let us make man after our image and likeness*"; he taking from himself the substance of the creatures [formed], and the pattern of things made, and the type of the adornments in the world ("*Faciamus hominem ad imaginem et similitudinem nostram,*" *ipse a semetipso substantiam creaturarum et exemplum factorum et figuram in mundo ornamentorum accipiens*) (iv.20.1).[34]

Irenaeus' point is to contrast Bythus with the highest God as portrayed in Genesis. Unlike Bythus, the true Father of all things is, categorically, not distantly withdrawn (*longe absistens*) from creation but is present insofar as his own two hands formed the man from clay. The twin modifiers *libere* and *sponte* highlight the unaided and unrestricted manner of God's "making." Genesis 1.26 is thus used to establish that God's creation of human beings was *direct*. Irenaeus employs it twice in this passage. The first is an allusion (no other power but the true God was able "to make an image of God"), and the second, a few lines down, is a fuller citation of the verse. It may be helpful to examine these references in reverse order. According to Irenaeus, God's created activity is unmediated. Explicating Genesis 1.26, which he has just quoted, Irenaeus states that God takes *ipse a semetipso substantiam creaturarum*. The plural *creaturarum* denotes creation in general, that is, the quality of created-ness.[35] On

---

[33] We follow the *SC* edition in preferring the Armenian variant *verum Deum* to the *Verbum Domini* of the Latin tradition (*SC* 100 [626.14]) although either option is conducive to our interpretation in this context.

[34] *SC* 100 (624.5-626.23).

[35] *SC* 100 (626.21). MacKenzie insists that this should be interpreted as "God taking among himself" because "[a]ny idea that Irenaeus is advocating a mythological synthesis between the substance of the dust of the earth and the substance of the Creator... would entirely contradict his insistence of man being in a community of union with God" (*Irenaeus's Demonstration*, 103-104). MacKenzie's point is understandable, though we may alternatively find Irenaeus' claim as intentionally contradicting Valentinian (and Middle-Platonic) speculation about possible primal substances underlying the human amalgamation (cf. our chapter two above). For God to create "from his very substance," rather than from external composite materials, better supports a viewpoint of *creatio ex nihilo*. According to Richard Norris, the doctrine of *creatio ex nihilo* attributed to

the one hand, Irenaeus is keen to locate humanity as a subset of a wider created order.[36] But Irenaeus' use of Genesis 1.26 several sentences before, set alongside Genesis 2.7, implies that the directness of God's creating applies supremely to his creation of the human creature. This loftiest of all creatures, whose constitution was pre-appointed (*praefinire*) to be made *ad imaginem et similitudinem Dei*, could be made by no being with lesser status or power than this one "true God" himself. Countering perceived Valentinian presumption, Irenaeus contends that by virtue of its original constitution, humanity is inescapably classified as created. Yet at the same time, to this particular creature, stamped with the image of the supreme God, has been ascribed immense worth and dignity by virtue of its being created by this God. If the Creator God of Genesis 1-2 is indeed the one supreme God rather than a lower bounded god, Valentinian disparagement of the mundane works of the Creator is unsustainable.

Despite his nod to humanity's lofty position, in this section Irenaeus uses Genesis 1.26 (in conjunction with Genesis 2.7) to say something more crucially about *God* than about humanity. His wording witnesses to a steadfast theocentric emphasis. *Et hic est de quo Scriptura ait:*[37] "And God formed man, taking clay of the earth, and breathed into his face the breath of life." It is *this* God's Word and Wisdom, that are the *per quos* and *in quibus* he made all things. He speaks to *these* two when he says (*ad quos et loquitur*), "Let us make man after our image and likeness." Thus the God who acts directly is more precisely God-as-triunity. The significance of Irenaeus' early Christian use of Genesis 1.26 to speak of divine triunity is apparent when compared to a rather binitarian view in the Epistle of Barnabas: "For the Scripture says concerning us, while he speaks to the Son, 'Let us make man after our image....'"[38] After the Lord commands the man to "increase" and "multiply," Barnabas adds "These things [were spoken] to the Son."[39] Justin also cites Genesis 1.26 only to argue that

---

Irenaeus is a necessary corollary to his doctrine of God, which emphasises God's absolute "inclusiveness" and power. "What there is, is there because God wills it, and for no other reason. Such a conception naturally excludes any notion of a preexistent or resistant matter which God forms, just as it excludes any notion that 'the way things are' can be accounted for by appealing to the operation of agents inferior to God" ("The Transcendence and Freedom of God," 97).

[36] Among the "all things" that God has "established," "selected," "adorned," and "contained" are "both ourselves and this our world." "We also then were made, along with those things which are contained by Him" (*Haer.* iv.20.1).

[37] *SC* 100 (624.9-10).

[38] *Barn.* 6 (*ANF* 1:140).

[39] Ibid. In the reference immediately before Genesis 1.26 is cited, Barnabas reads "He has made us after another pattern, that we should possess the soul of children, inasmuch as he

"Wisdom" was present with God from the beginning, not to intimate a divine triunity.[40] Irenaeus can exploit the plural inflection ("let us") without sacrificing directness because in his estimation, God's two hands are fully divine, not subordinates to whom the tasks are delegated (as in Platonist-influenced Ophite and Valentinian readings of Genesis 1). Where God's Word and Wisdom are working, this is to be recognized as God working – directly.[41]

If, as Irenaeus concludes from Genesis 1.26, God is directly and entirely responsible for the creation of humanity, the resulting knowledge of the Creator God's identity and the created human's nature is arrayed in contrast to the Valentinians' ambitious thoughts. The appropriate human response to its Creator is the proper governance of thoughts: to fix (*figere*) one's mind *in uno et vero Deo* (iv.19.1).[42] To conceive of God worthily (*digne*) means to eschew as futile any aspiration to know God in his inestimable greatness.[43] Instead the creature is to receive the knowledge of God enabled by his love, which ought to lead to a response of obedience.

CHALLENGING THE OPPOSITION: ORIGINAL HUMAN CONSTITUTION

Of course, the Ophites had found Genesis 1.26 to be essential for their narrative as well. But for readers who could see through Moses' textual ruse, Ialdabaoth's words "Come, let us make man after our image" had only reinforced the notion that the creator's work was actually indirect, uninformed, and involuntary. Sophia had supplied the "idea." He was the unsuspecting, blundering stooge whose initial best efforts produced a mere wriggling worm.[44] In the great human quest for self-understanding (and insight into the significance of Christ's life), knowledge of the creator was superfluous at best.

The Valentinians, like the Ophites and followers of Saturninus and Basilides,[45] also made explicit recourse to Genesis 1.26. However, a Valentinian adaptation of Ophite tradition fittingly melded with a more benign Platonic

---

has created us anew by his Spirit." Significantly, "his Spirit" is a later Latin addition, not present in the earlier Greek text.

[40] *Dial.* 62 (*ANF* 1:228).

[41] Cf. *Haer.* iv.20.3, 4. Although Irenaeus' descriptions of the divine economy might at times imply subordinationism, on balance he leans closer to modalism (cf. Minns, *Irenaeus*, 38). The Word and the Spirit are not different gods, but hands of the one God. Where the hands are present, the one highest God is present.

[42] *SC* 100 (616.16).

[43] Ironically, it seems that Irenaeus accuses the Valentinians of the same sin or defect as their mother, Achamoth / Sophia: an ill-advised initiative to grasp knowledge of the highest God.

[44] *Haer.* i.30.6.

[45] Cf. *Haer.* i.24.1.

metaphysic had different interests in the text. The Demiurge who made humanity was indeed an intermediate, constrained deity who thus had an instrumental rather than originating role in creation.[46] But the Valentinians were keen to explain the particulars of cosmos and humanity in terms of generalized underlying substances. Genesis 2.7 (God's breathing the breath of life into the man) helped them to sketch a broader narrative about the three types of humanity. Genesis 1.26 was marshaled to illumine Genesis 2.7. It was insofar as the Demiurge imparted his psychic nature through insufflation that the man was created "according to the image and likeness of God."[47]

According to Irenaeus, the Valentinian disciples of Marcus followed a more radical hermeneutical path when interpreting the two Genesis texts on original human constitution – texts which could be viewed not only as distinctive, but incongruent. From a Platonist standpoint, how can a man be both made "after the image and likeness of God" (Genesis 1.26) *and* formed out of mundane earth (Genesis 2.7)? The mainstream Valentinian position (at least as cited by Irenaeus) solves this problem by interpreting the earth-man of Genesis 2.7 as being formed of "fusible and fluid" substance (οὐσία).[48] The covering of flesh (σάρξ) comes only later in Genesis 3.21. But the Marcosians reckoned, as had the Ophites previously, that Genesis 1.26 and 2.7 refer to two separate events and two separate men.[49] One, the "spiritual man," was "formed after the image and likeness of God, masculo-feminine." The other man was "formed out of the earth."[50] As Plato's *Timaeus* had located the "most sovereign part of our soul... god's gift to us" in the human head,[51] these Marcosians asserted that "man... being formed after the image of the power above" had this "ability (δύναμις / *virtus*)... seated in the region of the brain."[52]

By directing attention to what the text unambiguously states about humanity's Maker, Irenaeus' narrowed, kerygmatic use of Genesis 1.26 vigorously aims to undermine Gnostic exploitation of this passage. The

---

[46] Irenaeus remarks that the Valentinians "go on to say that the Demiurge imagined that he created all these things of himself, while he in reality made them in conjunction with the productive power of Achamoth" (*Haer.* i.5.3).
[47] *Haer.* i.5.5.
[48] Ibid.
[49] This supposition originates even before Philo, who addresses the question: "Why did [God] place the molded man in Paradise, but not the man who was made in his own image?" (Philo, *QG* 1.8; cf. Michael Goulder, "Exegesis of Genesis 1-3 in the New Testament" *JJS* 43 [1992]: 228). Philo confirms a distinction between the man who is made according to the image of God (i.e., according to the "Logos" [cf. *QG* 2.62]) and "man as generated now," which "Moses" describes as being made from earth (*Opif.* 134).
[50] *Haer.* i.18.2.
[51] *Timaeus* 90a [Zeyl, 85-86].
[52] *Haer.* i.18.1.

Valentinians sought to expand and deepen the narrative context of Genesis 1.26 in order to explain Scripture's account of divine oikonomia in light of an even broader story. By contrast, Irenaeus deploys his hermeneutical tool, Genesis 1.26, with a tighter focus dictated by his theological parameters.[53] This passage chiefly *proclaims* the directness of God's creation of humanity rather than *explains* exactly what image of God is or how it is bestowed. In context, then, being "made after God's image and likeness" means being made by a God who, despite his peerless and supreme rank, was intimately present in our very creation and bodily formation.[54] Genesis 1-2 attests that no mediation was *possible* because God-as-Creator has no rivals or counterparts. No mediation was *required* because there is no distance or barrier to be overcome. In *Haer.* iv.20.1, Irenaeus is concerned to make a further point, however. By using Genesis 1.26 together with Genesis 2.7, he sees that the immediate and purposive qualities of God's creative activity characterize not just the human soul (the breath of life) but also the human body.[55] God's extravagantly direct and intimate participation in the creation of the human being is portrayed in fully concrete images: God's own hands mold the fleshly human frame from clay, and God's mouth breathes the soulish breath of life into his body. This claim that humanity's original constitution was comprehensively patterned after the image of God has great implications for Irenaeus' doctrine of recapitulation. Furthermore, Irenaeus connects his theological point from Genesis 1.26 to the original issue of human epistemology. Simply learning *"that* there is so great a God" who has created us directly with his own two hands is not only sufficient knowledge, but it is the knowledge of most profound consequence.[56]

---

[53] Please see the caveat offered in our introduction: To attend to the more utilitarian features of Irenaeus' hermeneutic need not cause one to doubt Irenaeus' intention to hear and explicate the theological truth claims made by the biblical text itself.

[54] Furthermore, by reading Genesis 2.7 together with 1.26 (*pace* Philo, et al.), Irenaeus asserts that "the 'modeling' (πλάσις) of man in Genesis 2.7 is not an inferior act to its 'fabrication' (ποίησις) in the image of God, since Adam is at the same time made and modeled by the 'Hands of God'..." (Ysabel de Andía, *Homo vivens: incorruptibilité et divinisation selon Irénée de Lyon* [Paris: Études Augustiniennes, 1986], 63). God's immediate, participatory, and purposive act in creating humanity, extends both to the human soul (the breath of life) and the human body of clay (cf. Irenaeus, *Epid.* 11).

[55] Cf. *Epid.* 11: "... for the formation he outlined his own form, that also what would be seen should be deiform" (trans., J. Smith, *Proof*, 148-49).

[56] *Haer.* iv.20.1; emphasis is added. With *Haer.* ii.25-28 in view, Schoedel reckons that Irenaeus shows an affinity with the empiricists' attitude in the empiricist / dogmatist debates of Greek philosophy. Instead of addressing "*how* each thing becomes systematic knowledge" (a divisive task), empiricists focus on the fact "*that* it becomes what we can clearly consider as agreed on" (Galen, *De sectis* 3 as cited, with emphasis, by Schoedel, "Theological Method," 32). Irenaeus' hypothetical alignment with the empiricists is

Using his tool, Genesis 1.26, to assert that humans are divine handiwork in the fullest sense insofar as God created them directly, Irenaeus not only challenges the Valentinian scheme of human creation as mediated, but also critiques predecessor cosmogonies and anthropologies to which this system is indebted. In effect, Irenaeus employs Genesis 1.26 to set forth a grand non-Platonic ontology. Irenaeus' claim that the Creator God was directly involved in human origination supplies a contrasting view not just of divine agency but also of metaphysical "distance." The Valentinians aimed to maximize the distance (which they alone could traverse) between Bythus and the ordinary mundane realm of bodily human existence. On the other hand, in boasting of detailed knowledge about divinity, the Valentinians could be reckoned to minimize the distance (or expanse) internal to the supreme God himself.[57] But Irenaeus claims the reverse to be true. Whereas it is impossible for the supreme God himself to be measured (iv.20.1), yet God's love and intimate relation to humanity (expressed in that his very hands molded us in his own image and likeness) testify to a comparatively minimal epistemological distance between the created human and the supreme God.[58] At the same time, Irenaeus does not minimize the *ontological* distance between Creator and creation. Ironically, his use of Genesis 1.26 results in an even stronger doctrine of divine transcendence than that of the Valentinians. Bythus must be safeguarded against contamination from the mundane creation existing on the other side of the boundary. For Irenaeus, God's transcendence is magnified insofar as this supreme, perfect God interacts directly with humanity as its Artisan, without compromising his own integrity. In other words, Irenaeus denies a Valentinian view that characterizes divine and human activity on earth (or heaven for that matter) as competitive.[59] In light of *Haer.* iv.20, Emil Brunner's summary is apt: "'Created in his image, in his likeness' is a parable, hence its meaning does not lie on the surface... it says that the nature of man – in his origin or in general – is nothing in itself... but that its ground of existence and of knowledge is in God."[60] The fact that Irenaeus gains such theological leverage from a succinct clause in Genesis 1.26 intimates his view that the "image and likeness" motif is not merely a store of

---

understandable, given his insistence that the one church proclaims a universally-recognized interpretation of the apostolic and Scriptural tradition.

[57] Cf. Irenaeus' critique in *Haer.* iv.19.2 which cites Isaiah 40.12. He concludes, "As regards his greatness, therefore, it is not possible to know God, for it is impossible that the Father can be measured; but as regards his love... we do always learn *that* there is so great a God..." (*Haer.* iv.20.1; emphasis is added).

[58] Cf. *Haer.* iv.19.3; 20.1.

[59] That is, Irenaeus insists that a divine being can genuinely act in the physical world of humanity without this action constituting competition with humanity, and without incurring self-contamination (many thanks to John Webster for this relevant observation).

[60] *Man in Revolt*, 96.

doctrinal content but a dynamic, effective tool for theological work. Further examination of Irenaeus' citation of this text lends support to this conclusion.

Using Genesis 1.26: Human fallenness and restoration

If the "image of God" language in Genesis 1.26 (in conjunction with Genesis 2.7) is taken to supply the starting premise for speaking of the original human constitution – we are made by God's direct action – a dilemma quickly emerges. Challenging Valentinian explanations of the relationship between extra-Pleroma and intra-Pleroma beings, Irenaeus had noted the logical expectation that "similitudes and images of [eternal] things which are above" ought "always to endure," just as the original does.[61] Yet human experience and Scripture itself witness to the body's mortality. Especially striking is the oft-repeated phrase in the genealogy of Genesis 5: "Thus all the days of [so and so] were [this many years] and he *died*." If, as Irenaeus interprets Genesis 2.7, the handcrafted body (along with the inbreathed soul) was made after the eternal God's image, how is this body's eventual disintegration to be understood? In order to explain the change in human condition between Genesis 1-2 and Genesis 4-5, Irenaeus finds it necessary to use Genesis 1.26 again, though in a different way and for a different theological task. Using this hermeneutical tool, Irenaeus makes this theological point: human refusal to offer God obedience and thanks manifests the operations of sin, death, and barrenness that are characteristic of human fallenness. Through Adam's disobedience, humanity has squandered and lost the "image and likeness of God" (i.e., that direct, intimate connection with its Creator). One particularly notable feature in *Adversus Haereses* is that Irenaeus appears rather uninterested in talking about human fallenness as a subject of its own.[62] He does invoke Genesis 1.26 to speak of humanity's loss, but he often finds irresistible the urge to subsume this topic into the larger context of human restoration. These two sides of soteriology, constituting that span of God's economy between human origin and eschaton, are typically mentioned in the same breath. Therefore, as we examine a representative passage (*Haer.* iii.18.1) we will follow Irenaeus' lead. Since Irenaeus' primary concern in this section is Christology, we shall first assess his use of Genesis 1.26 to speak of how humanity is restored through Christ's recapitulation. Then we will return to suggest how Genesis 1.26 serves as

---

[61] *Haer.* ii.7.1.

[62] O'Regan observes that "outside of what it excludes, Irenaeus's position on sin is relatively undeveloped." Irenaeus "does not attempt to correlate *disobedience* with all the biblical namings for sin" nor does he "probe in the way an Augustine does the motivational structure of sin, in which the categories of *self-love* and *pride* loom large..." (*Gnostic Return in Modernity*, 165; emphasis is original).

Irenaeus' tool for articulating humanity's fallenness, albeit an adjuvant role for this text. Before discussing these uses, though, we turn to consider the context of *Haer.* iii.18.

CONTEXT OF *ADVERSUS HAERESES* III.18: CHRISTOLOGY

Irenaeus' project in book three, to "adduce proofs from the Scriptures"[63] depends upon his assertion that Scripture – as defined and interpreted in the apostolic tradition[64] – is the normative source of truth. Irenaeus, like his opponents, appeals to Scripture in an effort to discern the logic in the church's powerfully compelling christological traditions. Many questions arise: Who was / is Christ? How is he related to humanity? How is he related to the supreme God? How does he illumine our knowledge of the highest God? How is he related to the Creator of the cosmos (if not the supreme God)? What did Christ "do" in his advent and why?[65] How is his work significant for present-day living? In this section as elsewhere, Irenaeus anchors his challenge of Gnostic christologies[66] to his two-part *regula veritatis*:

> *id est*...[1] *sit unus Deus omnipotens qui omnia condidit per Verbum suum...;* [2] *hic Pater Domini nostri Iesu Christi....*[67]

That Irenaeus considers God's identity as Creator to be decisive in any accounting of Christ's advent is clearly manifest. In the section of book iii leading up to chapter 18, there are at least *seventy-seven* occurrences of "Creator," "Maker," or creation-related terms.[68] Christ and the Scriptures speak with one voice, says Irenaeus, in proclaiming only one God as Creator and highest Father.[69] As for Christ himself, he is not an additional or intermediary god but is in fact the eternal Word, one of God's own hands through which creation came to be.[70] Thus, contrary to what some Gnostics may conclude, "this creation to which we belong" is *not* "shut off from communion with the things

---

[63] *Haer.* iii.preface
[64] Cf. *Haer.* iii.4.1; 5.1.
[65] Cf. *Haer.* iii.18.2. Irenaeus cites Paul in Romans 14.9 as revealing the "reason [*rationem*] why the Son of God did these things...."
[66] Cp., especially for our purposes, *Haer.* i.6.1; 7.2; i.30.11-13.
[67] "That is... there is one God almighty who made all things by his Word... this is the Father of our Lord Jesus Christ" (*Haer.* i.22.1; *SC* 264 [308.1-310.20]). Irenaeus' *regula veritatis* appears in various slightly different forms, but this citation is representative.
[68] These references from *Haer* iii.1-17 include derivatives of *facio, plasmatio, condo,* and *artifex* where used to speak of specifically of God as Creator or of God's created work.
[69] Cf. especially *Haer.* iii.5.
[70] Cf. *Haer.* iii.6.5; 8.2-3; *passim*.

invisible and ineffable."[71] According to Irenaeus, Christ's protological activities must be manifestly connected to (and be fulfilled in) his soteriological work. The christological doctrines which Irenaeus attacks in iii.18 are those that regard the Jesus Christ of the gospels as a divided being. Though Christ appeared to suffer, some argued that he was not truly a *passibilis homo*. The Ophites reckoned that "Christ" had descended and taken up residence in "Jesus" (the body prepared by Sophia), but had "flown away" before the bodily Jesus suffered.[72] According to Valentinian interpreters, *Sōtēr* descended from Pleroma and was "clothed with a psychic Christ" by the Demiurge, yet "received nothing material, for the material is not capable of being saved."[73] Irenaeus argues that by holding errant views of Christ, the Gnostics accordingly "set the Spirit aside altogether."[74] Furthermore, since Irenaeus discerns that the divine economy (as attested in law, prophets, gospels, and apostolic writings) speaks of soteriology as the co-working of Son and Spirit as God's two "hands," Gnostic doctrines of salvation are flawed because they are built on faulty understandings of Son and Spirit. The *imago Dei* motif from Genesis 1.26 again becomes a finely honed hermeneutical device, enabling Irenaeus to speak of human fallenness in a way that is in continuity with apostolic traditions of Christology and soteriology. By means of Genesis 1.26, Irenaeus explains the human situation addressed by Christ: the nature of human fallenness, its remedy, and its relation to the human *telos*. In short, the most apropos way to describe human fallenness is to say that in Adam, humanity lost its being "according to the image and likeness of God" (iii.18.1).

A few paragraphs before iii.18.1, Irenaeus had used the image motif while comparing humanity's state of fallenness to that of the wounded man in the gospel parable of the Good Samaritan (cf. Luke 10.29-37). When the Lord's own human creation (*suum hominem*) had "fallen among thieves," the Lord had compassion upon him and "bound up his wounds." Like the Samaritan who gave two denaria to the innkeeper to provide for the wounded man's recovery, the Lord "gives two royal denaria so that we, receiving (*accipere*) by the Spirit the image and superscription of the Father and the Son, might cause the denarium entrusted to us to be fruitful."[75] Irenaeus summons this effervescent confluence of motifs – the parable of the Samaritan, Jesus' reference to an imperial coin,[76] and the fruitfulness / vineyard language – to speak of the Son and Spirit's work in the ministry of Christ. That he intends these metaphors to illumine and

---

[71] *Haer*. iii.11.1.
[72] *Haer*. i.30.12-13.
[73] *Haer*. i.7.3.
[74] *Haer*. iii.17.4.
[75] *Haer*. iii.17.3.
[76] Cf. Luke 20.24; Mark 12.16; Matthew 22.20.

contextualize Genesis 1.26 in relation to the fall and restoration of humanity is evidenced by the subsequent reemergence and expanded use of the image of God motif in iii.18.1. Here Irenaeus explains the specific kind of remedy provided by Christ: *recapitulation*. In other words, the first use of image in iii.17.3 envisions the restoration of the divine image in humanity and thus anticipates the second use of image in iii.18.1 (and following). The peculiar condition of human fallenness required the pre-existent Christ to become "a man liable to suffering" so as to restore humanity to its intended state of bearing God's image and likeness.

SELECTED TEXT FROM *ADVERSUS HAERESES* III.18.1-2

Although Irenaeus speaks in many places about Christ's recapitulation of humanity and of the efficacy of God's salvation, it is in *Haer.* iii.18 that he most explicitly illuminates and particularizes the nature of human fallenness by contending that Genesis 1.26 – better than any other Scripture passage – tells what was lost, and what kind of Christ (and work) was needed in order to recover that which was lost.

> For I have shown that the Son of God did not then begin to exist, being with the Father from the beginning; but when he became incarnate and was made man, he *recapitulated* in himself the long line of human beings, and furnished us in a brief, comprehensive manner with salvation (*longam hominum expositionem in seipso recapitulauit, in compendio nobis salutem praestans*), so that *what we had lost in Adam – namely to be according to the image and likeness of God* – that we might recover in Christ Jesus (*ut quod perdideramus in Adam, id est secundum imaginem et similitudinem esse Dei, hoc in Christo Iesu reciperemus*). For as it was not possible that the man who had once for all been conquered and destroyed through disobedience (*qui semel uictus fuerat et elisus per inobaudientiam*), could reform (*replasmare*) himself, and obtain the prize of victory; and as it was also impossible that he could attain to salvation who had fallen under the power of sin, the Son effected both these things, being the Word of God, descending from the Father, becoming incarnate, stooping low, even to death, and consummating the economy (*dispensatio*) of our salvation....[77]

---

[77] *Haer.* iii.18.1-2; *SC* 211(342.7-344.21); emphasis is added.

It is intriguing that by asserting that human fallenness means a *loss*[78] of the image and likeness of God (in whatever respect and degree), Irenaeus quite unabashedly goes beyond the description of this drama given by the narrator of Genesis 3. For example, Karl Barth (perhaps the most widely cited scholar on the issue of *imago Dei* since 1945[79]) concludes that he can find no exegetical basis for the notion that humanity lost the image of God in the fall.[80] Irenaeus' interpretation certainly appears to be inventive, but is it reckless or unwarranted? It may be helpful to enquire as to why Irenaeus found Genesis 1.26 so valuable in thinking about the human condition. This text explains not just what is specific to the creation of human beings, but also why the fall in Genesis 3 was such a disaster for humanity and how it is counteracted. As we have seen, his usage of "image of God" in the preceding context (chapters 17-18) is extraordinarily rich – embedded, as it were, in the fertile theological soil of diverse scriptural narratives. In iii.18.1, the image of God motif anchors and orients Irenaeus' understanding of salvation. First, it reveals the "from what" and "to what" in a locative sense: humanity as having lost (pluperfect of *perdere*) its "being according to the image and likeness of God," and then as finally recovering it. Second, it identifies the "how" of salvation as Christ's recapitulation of humanity according to the divine image. Insofar as Irenaeus' primary concern here is to confront his opponents with an alternative view of Christ as informed by Genesis 1.26, we will look first at his characterization of this "how" of salvation, namely, Christ's recapitulation. Using Genesis 1.26 as a tool, Irenaeus suggests a more satisfying way to understand how Christ enables humanity to realize God's intention for it. After this, we will be better prepared to address the original issue we raised, namely, how Irenaeus uses Genesis 1.26 to speak of human fallenness (i.e., that particular condition that is remedied through Christ's restoration).

GENESIS 1.26 AND RECAPITULATION

The text under consideration (iii.18.1-2) begins by declaring that the Son of God, though always present with the Father, was made man (*homo factus*). As a human being, he recapitulated the long human narrative.[81] Christ, then, is both

---

[78] The semantic range of *perdere* may include not only the sense "to lose" but also "to marr" or "to destroy."

[79] Cf. Gunnlaugur Jonsson, *The Image of God: Genesis 1.26-28 in a Century of Old Testament Research* (Stockholm: Almqvist and Wiksell), 1988), 65. Jonsson summarizes the vigorous twentieth-century debate between Barth and Brunner on this point (65-76).

[80] The *imago Dei* "does not consist in anything that man is or does. It consists as man himself consists as the creature of God" (*Church Dogmatics* III/1 [ed. G. W. Bromiley and T. F. Torrance; Edinburgh: T&T Clark, 1958], 184).

[81] For *expositio*, the SC edition suggests the Greek retrojection ἱστορία.

compared with and contrasted to Adam; he repeats Adam and reverses Adam. As to the *comparison*, Irenaeus emphasizes three fundamental ways that Christ was genuinely human, each of which is crucial to the possibility of Christ's work of recapitulation.[82] First, like Adam, the incarnate Christ was made through God's direct initiative rather than through some sort of mediation. Not surprisingly, then, the doctrine of the virgin birth plays an essential role in his Christology. Secondly, Christ had a fleshly, human body as did Adam – a body fully capable of suffering.[83] But, as Irenaeus seems to conclude, to be made of human flesh is not a sufficient condition by which one can be rightly termed human. Finally, then, Christ's life must necessarily be a life of human temporal development:

> Wherefore also [Christ] passed through every stage of life, restoring to all communion with God. Those, therefore, who assert that he appeared putatively, and was neither born in the flesh nor truly made man, are as yet under the old condemnation... (iii.18.7).

In Irenaeus' estimation, if Christ were to sum up humanity in himself, he would need to experience and re-claim through his sanctifying obedience every temporal location in human development from infancy to old age.[84] In such a way, time is to be properly understood as an ontologically fundamental category for humanity. Such a claim would likely have been interpreted as a direct challenge to the Platonic-informed metaphysic popular in Gnostic circles.

Central to the *contrast* he sets up between Christ and Adam is Irenaeus' use of the term *recapitulare* (ἀνακεφαλαιώσασθαι) in iii.18.1 and iii.18.7. Originally a rhetorical term denoting the summary of a narrative,[85] Irenaeus extends its semantic range when he presses it into the service of theology. In the context of chapters 17-19, Irenaeus uses *recapitulare* to affirm that Christ effected unity through his in-gathering and summation of humanity.[86] He is human in the fullest possible sense. But *recapitulare* also involves a reversal – a

---

[82] Cf. *Haer.* iii.17.4 (*SC* 211 [338.6-7]):
"the Word of the Father, coming in the fullness of time, having become incarnate in man for the sake of man, and fulfilling all the conditions of human nature (καὶ πᾶσαν τὴν κατὰ ἄνθρωπον οἰκονομίαν ἐκπληρώσαντος)."

[83] Cf. *Haer.* iii.18.3.

[84] See, for example, *Haer.* ii.22.4. This may be contrasted with Athanasius' focus on the soteriological significance of Christ's birth and death to the relative exclusion of that of his earthly life (cf. *Inc.* 8-9).

[85] Grant, *Irenaeus of Lyons*, 50.

[86] "He caused man to cleave to and to become one with God... unless man had been joined to God, he could never have become a partaker of incorruptibility" (*Haer.* iii.18.7).

reversal that emphasizes Christ's discontinuity with Adam and his continuity with God as Adam's Creator.[87] Thus Christ is said to *reform* (*replasmare*) humanity, and this re-formation corresponds to God's original formation of Adam's physical body. As God's Son, Christ is obedient to God in every way that Adam was disobedient.[88] Whereas "by the disobedience of the one man... the many were made sinners, and forfeited life," Christ's obedience brings justification and salvation (iii.18.7).[89] Christ came to "kill sin, deprive death of its power, and vivify man" (iii.18.7). Christ's bodily resurrection is the "first fruits of the resurrection of man."[90] Human bodies, now reformed, can partake of eternal life as was originally intended by their Craftsman.

Yet there is a further, second step in God's salvation after Christ's recapitulation. The Son "commends" "his own man"[91] whom he has re-made to the Spirit, so that the Spirit can be received just as Adam had received the original insufflation of the breath of life (Genesis 2.7). No longer "dry earth" or a "dry tree," humanity is enabled to be "fruitful... to the Lord" (iii.17.3).[92] The extraordinary result of God's oikonomia, the outworking of his own two hands, is that humanity will recover (*recipere*) its being *secundum imaginem et similitudinem... Dei* (iii.18.1). In other words, Irenaeus' notion of recapitulation in this crucial section (chapters 17-19) begins and ends with the text of Genesis 1.26. Christ and Adam are alike in that they both originally bore the image of God. Yet the crucial point of contrast is that whereas Adam lost (or marred) his creaturely-existence after the image of God, Christ *retained* it and thus restores it to the human race.

---

[87] In Ephesians 1.10, the only New Testament reference where ἀνακεφαλαιώσασθαι occurs in a christological context (Romans 13.9 employs the traditional meaning), the word denotes an in-gathering or summation, but not necessarily a reversal as does Irenaeus': εἰς οἰκονομίαν τοῦ πληρώματος τῶν καιρῶν, ἀνακεφαλαιώσασθαι τὰ πάντα ἐν τῷ Χριστῷ, τὰ ἐπὶ τοῖς οὐρανοῖς καὶ τὰ ἐπὶ τῆς γῆς ἐν αὐτῷ ("as a plan for the fullness of time, to recapitulate all things in Christ, things in heaven and things on earth").

[88] Cf. *Haer.* iii.18.4, 7; cp. Adam in iii.18.2.

[89] Only a man could destroy sin and thus death (cf. Romans 5.14, 19).

[90] *Haer.* iii.19.3.

[91] *suum hominem* (Haer. iii.17.3).

[92] Thus the second step involves "access to the divine life which Christ affords to individual believers by being the mediator... [who] accommodates God to men and accustoms men to receiving God" (Norman Russell, *The Doctrine of Deification in the Greek Patristic Tradition* [Oxford: Oxford University Press, 2005], 108; cf. *Haer.* iii.18.7; iii.20.2; iv.28.2). Cf. the next section in this chapter.

GENESIS 1.26 AND HUMAN FALLENNESS

If Christ puts humanity right, what does this say about how humanity went wrong? In light of Irenaeus' theological construct of recapitulation, we now turn to his depiction of human fallenness. It is by applying Genesis 1.26, his ready hermeneutical tool, that Irenaeus assesses and interprets the protological narrative of Genesis 3 as it relates to Christ. In so doing, he aims to provide a reading of Genesis 1-3 that gives more insight into the human condition than does the Valentinian version.

For Irenaeus, human fallenness speaks of the loss (*perdere*) of the image and likeness of God, and this theme of "lostness" is one he returns to again and again throughout *Adversus Haereses* In some instances, "lost" is a predicate of humanity, describing a condition (i.e., human beings are "lost sheep" to whom Christ comes as Shepherd).[93] In other passages, "lost" is an object set in relation to humanity as the subject. For example, Irenaeus asserts that humanity lost the "sure Word of God... by means of a tree."[94] Whether "lost" refers to a condition or an object, however, this major theme is always either explicitly or implicitly grounded in the text of Genesis 1-3. When, in *Haer.* iii.18.1-2 and surrounding context Irenaeus uses the language of Genesis 1.26 to speak of the root of human fallenness, he focuses on two clusters of motifs (or categories) to explain and express this loss. Losing the image and likeness of God entails a loss of *life*[95] and a loss of *fruitfulness*.[96] Salvation is in essence the recapitulatory work of God's two hands, Son and Spirit, to restore each of these in turn, to humanity.

Human fallenness means that Adam lost life. Irenaeus summarizes Genesis 3 as follows: Through his disobedience, Adam had been "conquered" and "destroyed" (*uictus fuerat et elisus*), having "fallen under the power of sin" (*sub peccato ceciderat*).[97] As mentioned above, Irenaeus vividly portrays the human condition as one of woundedness. We are like the traveller who, having been beaten up by thieves, lies bleeding and abandoned in the wayside.[98] To be sure, Irenaeus does not present Adam purely as innocent victim, for he bears the guilt and suffers the consequences of his own disobedience. Yet humanity has also been cruelly buffeted and blinded by the serpent, the deceiver.[99] Having been, in the beginning, carefully crafted by God after his own image, humanity now finds itself in dire need of reformation (*replasmare*) but is powerless to bring it

---

[93] Cf. *Haer.* iii.23.1; v.12.3.
[94] *Haer.* v.17.4; cf. iii.23.5; iv.4.3; iv.39.2.
[95] Cf. *Haer.* iii.18.2-3, 7; iii.19.1.
[96] Cf. *Haer.* iii.17.2-3.
[97] *Haer.* iii.18.2; *SC* 211 (344.15-18).
[98] *Haer.* iii.17.3; Luke 10.35.
[99] *Epid.* 12; *Haer.* iii.20.1 ("blinded").

about.[100] Salvation and the "prize of victory" are completely out of reach. Humanity's wounds, the result of Adam's disobedience, are terminal. They will lead inexorably to the death of the body that was meant to bear the image and likeness of the immortal God. In addition to his referencing of Paul (especially Romans 5), Irenaeus hints at how he may understand death to be the unavoidable consequence of sin:

> [T]hose who assert that [Christ] was a mere man begotten by Joseph, remaining in the bondage of the old disobedience (*pristinae inobaudientia*), are in a state of death, insofar as they have not yet been *joined* (*commiscere*) *to the Word* of God the Father... (iii.19.1).[101]

Given Irenaeus' fondness for comparisons, it is not completely unfair to suggest a generalization from this particular statement. Disobedience somehow separates the human being (the *facti*) from the divine Word (its *Fabricator*), so destroying the conjunctive bond between them. To press the language a bit, one might say that humanity, originally "capitulated" by virtue of its relationship to its "head," has found itself "de-capitulated" (or decapitated). What is needed is a re-capitulation wherein the original connection between creation and Creator is restored, thus replacing death with life. In this respect, Christ, the compassionate Good Samaritan, binds the wounds of fallen humanity and enables the re-reception of God's image and likeness by the Spirit (iii.17.3). The Shepherd has restored his lost sheep to the "fold of life" (*in cohortem restituens vitae*).[102]

The Son's bodily recapitulation of humanity through his life, death, and resurrection restores the image of God insofar as the human body (so to speak) is healed of its injuries. Disobedience is reversed, and its destined end, death, is thwarted in a decisive (albeit proleptic) manner. Yet humanity's recovery of the image and likeness of God also requires the consequent work of God's other hand, the Spirit. The communication of the Spirit to humanity through the Word (cf. iii.17.4, passim) is essentially God's second and qualitatively superior

---

[100] Haer. iii.18.2; cf. Nielsen, *Adam and Christ in the Theology of Irenaeus*, 11.

[101] *SC* 211 (370.3-372.4). For the connection between disobedience and death, see especially *Haer*. v.23.1.

[102] *Haer*. v.15.2; cf. iii.19.1 ("antidote of life") and iv.36.7 (the knowledge of divine Son is immortality). F. Altermath attempts to reconcile the meaning of Adam's loss of the *imago Dei* in *Haer*. iii.18.1 with Irenaeus' assertion that Adam and Eve's original created state was immaturity (iv.38). Thus, claims Altermath, it was not immortality that Adam lost through disobedience but rather the "character of God's son" ("The Purpose of the Incarnation according to Irenaeus," *StPatr*. 13 [1975]: 67). Although Irenaeus repeatedly insists that the fall implies a loss of life of some sort (it is debatable whether this is life proper to the uncreated or the created), Altermath is right to see the primary focus on humanity's loss of communion with God. Indeed, the two losses cannot be separated (cf. *Haer*. v.23.2).

insufflation of the breath of life. The ministry of the Spirit reverses the utter barrenness in humanity that had accompanied the loss of the divine image and likeness. In discussing the human need for God's Spirit, Irenaeus returns to motifs from Genesis 1-3 to draw a comparison.

> And as *dry earth* (*arida terra*) does not bring forth unless it receives moisture (*humorem*), in like manner we also, being originally a *dry tree* (*lignum aridum existentes primum*), could never have brought forth fruit unto life without the voluntary rain from above. For *our bodies* have received unity among themselves by means of that laver which leads to incorruption, but *our souls*, by means of the Spirit. Wherefore both are necessary, since both contribute towards the life of God... (iii.17.2).[103]

Irenaeus makes the point that human fruitfulness requires both unity (effected by Christ's recapitulation) and the water of the Spirit (iii.17.2). Thus while humanity's fallenness is again affirmed to be, at its root, a state of disjunction with its head, the Logos Creator, a closely related characteristic is unfruitfulness. Since humanity had been made after the image and likeness of God in both its molded frame and inbreathed soul,[104] losing (or marring) the image of God involved not only disunion with God but the loss of the divine breath, that is, the moisture-infusion of the Spirit.[105] Barrenness and death resulted. The "image and superscription of the Father and the Son" once "entrusted" to humanity no longer "count[ed] out the increase to the Lord" (iii.17.3). Fruitfulness is thus associated with the human capacity to grow, progress, and develop. But for Irenaeus, this production stemming from the imprint of the divine image chiefly means an outward giving toward God, acknowledging and thanking one's own Creator. The most significant area of human growth is in the knowledge of God. Disrupted by the fall, such fruit-bearing toward the Creator should have been the most natural, fulfilling human expression and pursuit, given Genesis 1.26's proclamation that humanity is made through the Creator God's direct and willing action.

---

[103] *SC* 211 (332.35-42). In *Epid*. 99, Irenaeus reiterates that those who do not receive the "gifts of the Holy Spirit" and the "charism of prophecy," that is, the water "whereby man bears fruit of life to God," remain incapable of bearing fruit.

[104] Cf. Irenaeus, *Epid*. 11.

[105] Cp. Gnostic depictions of the heavenly "sprinkling" / divine *virtus*.

CHALLENGING THE OPPOSITION: HUMAN FALLENNESS AND RESTORATION

Irenaeus' hamartiology in *Haer.* iii.17-18 is stamped with a distinctive hermeneutical footprint. Given his christological reading of one eminent text, Genesis 1.26, Irenaeus interprets the human condition attested in Genesis 1-3 by means of this filter. While sharing the protological interest of his Gnostic opponents, Irenaeus hopes to undermine the credibility of their Genesis readings and ultimately their system as a whole. Whatever the image of God might be, if it is an essential feature of human original formation, it must play an important part in the divine-human interaction that is the economy of salvation. With the Ophites and Valentinians, Irenaeus recognizes that bodily death is a hindrance to the full human expression of the divine image (or *virtus*). However if, as Irenaeus affirms in contrast to his opponents, Genesis 1.26 indicates the supreme Creator God's direct connection with and free intentions toward his human creation (in both soul and body), then subsequent Ophite and Valentinian depictions of divine-human estrangement in Genesis 3 are patently misleading.

The Ophites had claimed that the man's reception of the inbreathed divine *nous* and *enthymesis* – unintended by the creator god – was the catalyst enabling him to grasp knowledge of the divine realm that transcended Ialdabaoth.[106] Newly enlightened, the man now justly refuses to offer thanks to his creator, but redirects it to First Man in Pleroma. For Irenaeus, any presumption to scorn one's Creator marks the obliteration of that divine image and results in human barrenness. In the Ophite interpretation of Adam and Eve's disobedience, a member of divinity (Sophia) seeks to *steal* the *virtus* (cf. image) from humanity so as to prevent it from becoming tainted in the lower world of creation. Adam's disobedience to his creator resulted in banishment to a bodily existence of corruption and death. Irenaeus, however, affirms the plain sense of the "Mosaic" account. Humanity is responsible for losing the divine image, thus cutting itself off from its life-giving, loving head. An Ophite Jesus, who was not truly human but rather a heavenly emissary bearing mystic knowledge, could not procure salvation if salvation were to be understood as the comprehensive realization of the divine image. Salvation required the re-capitulation of humanity into the divine so that body and soul could be enabled to bear the divine image of life and fruitfulness according to the original vision of Genesis 1.26.

As previously suggested, Irenaeus' contrast to the Valentinian depiction of human fallenness also depends upon his use of Genesis 1.26 as a precision tool. Unlike the Ophite interpretation, the somewhat benign Valentinian Demiurge had neither bestowed the divine image unintentionally, nor had he tried to steal it back from humanity. But Irenaeus recognized the cost of this Valentinian

---

[106] *Haer.* i.30.6.

rehabilitation act: the value of the divine image for human beings *as creatures* was significantly diminished. In that this image was only the psychic nature of the Demiurge, it offered no connection to the supreme God (this was the role of the "spiritual seed" sown by Achamoth). Nor did it enfold bodily created-ness into the scope of salvation. The loss of such an image would be no great tragedy, having bearing neither on bodily death nor spiritual eternal life.[107] At the core, the Valentinians – no less than the Ophites – were more monist than dualist in their view of reality. If the problem to be overcome was ontological plurality, then "the doctrine of evil and the notion of a fall [must be found] *within* the doctrine of creation – not, as does the book of Genesis, after and alongside it." [108] Valentinian soteriology, then, depicts Christ "breathing into them what is in the mind" (i.e., spiritual substance from Pleroma, rather than the creator's original, merely psychic breath).[109] Of the other substances in this plurality, the psychic nature might be salvaged, but the material nature would certainly be destroyed.

Irenaeus however, argues that Genesis 1.26's claim of "humanity made in God's image" invites a far more comprehensive and satisfying perspective on the story of human creation, fallenness, salvation, and destiny. The supreme, loving, Creator God who restores his image to humanity is the God who brings the originally-intended full communion between the divine and human. In so doing, God overcomes every possible type of estrangement, including ignorance, sin and physical death. End has been joined to beginning in Christ.[110] The soul is not merely educated but re-breathed by the Spirit. The created body, though currently corruptible, is not abandoned but recapitulated by the Word. In effect, Genesis 1.26 is a hermeneutical tool that enables Irenaeus to relate human fallenness to creation, while maintaining a fundamental distinction between them as well. Evil is not a corollary of the diversity introduced with the act of creation. In fact, the ontological distinction between divinity and humanity points not to a problem but an opportunity, as is evidenced by Irenaeus' third usage of this flexible tool.

---

[107] It may be noteworthy that, in Irenaeus' account at least, the Valentinians find little significance in the *narrative* of Genesis 3. *Gospel of Truth* does appropriate the language, but not the substance of the story.
[108] Douglas Farrow, "St. Irenaeus of Lyons: The Church and the World," *Pro Eccl.* 4 (1995): 336. Emphasis is original.
[109] *Gos. Truth* 30.34-31.1.
[110] *Haer.* iv.20.4.

Using Genesis 1.26: Human eschatological destiny

As contended above, Irenaeus employs Genesis 1.26 to describe human creation as God's gift of direct connection. Humanity's sin and Christ's recapitulation entails the loss and restoration of this unique relation. Finally, we turn to Irenaeus' use of the image and likeness motif as a means for articulating human eschatological destiny. The image and likeness of God, he says, is a "prize" to be pursued, received, and in such a manner fully realized.[111] In *Haer.* iv.37-39 (centered on iv.38.3), humanity is vividly depicted as ripening fruit (iv.37.7). Humans mature by growing into an adult-like relationship with God wherein one's created-ness is not bypassed, but transformed and enveloped by the glory of the immortal God (iv.38.3). For Irenaeus, then, Genesis 1.26 illumines God's purposes at every stage in the divine economy: beginning, middle, and end.

Haer. iv.37-39 contains some of Irenaeus' most quotable and provocative lines. For example, "How, then, shall he be a God who has not as yet been made a man?" (iv.39.2). To some, this section is refreshing and innovative. By accentuating the dynamic and linear features of human development, Irenaeus' words could comfortably resonate with certain humanist and modernist sensitivities in western culture.[112] Others, though, are uneasy with Irenaeus' portrayal of an upward human trajectory, insofar as it is seen as dissonant with the more mainstream Augustinian view of creation and fall. As recognized by the Lutheran Centuriators of Magdeburg who censured Irenaeus in the sixteenth century, the claim that humanity was not created "perfect" openly challenged what had become the dominant tradition in the western Church. Instead of underscoring possible discontinuities between creation and redemption, Irenaeus was concerned to portray God's oikonomia as a seamless unity. At first glance, it may seem difficult to reconcile Irenaeus' depiction of the divine image and likeness motif in iv.37-39 with those found in other contexts. Here, image is not so much something given at creation or lost and restored, but something progressively realized in time. Additionally, human volition, as well as divine action, plays a strategic role. Christ's incarnation is described as a step in the arrangement and sequence of God's plan whereby humanity is prepared to bear his image (iv.38.2-3). Though human fallenness may be a minor theme in this section, however, Irenaeus has not completely forgotten about it.[113] When

---

[111] *Haer.* iv.37.6.
[112] See, for example, John Hick, *Evil and the God of Love* (London: Macmillan, 1966).
[113] It is possible to place too much emphasis on the widely-held view (repeated by Demetrios Constantelos) that Irenaeus is "less concerned with sin and guilt and more and more with victory, transformation [and] eternal life" ("Irenaeos of Lyons and His Central Views on Human Nature," *SVTQ* 33 [1989]: 355-56).

Irenaeus uses Genesis 1.26 to speak of human growth toward an intended perfection, it is explicitly a human *moral* growth: "Or how can he be perfect who was but lately created? How, again, can he be immortal, who in his mortal nature did not obey his Maker?" (iv.38.2). In the sequence of human development commenced by the Son and Spirit, after creation but before glorification there is need for "recovery." This term ἐνισχύω (*convalescere*) implies that a temporary injury or loss – here, from sin – has been both incurred and reversed (iv.38.3). Yet what of evidence that not all people manifest such recovery and progressive resemblance to a good God? Is this God incapable of achieving his will? Answering these apparent charges from his opponents, Irenaeus provides a theodicy of sorts. "The skill of God, therefore, is not defective, for he has power of the stones to raise up children to Abraham; but the man who does not obtain it is the cause to himself of his own imperfections" (iv.39.3). Persons who shun the "hand" of the Maker, which "creates everything in due time," will not realize the moral growth of being "made" after this God's divine image. Humanity, now having "received the knowledge of good and evil," has the capacity to grow (iv.39.1). But if this knowledge is refused, one "unawares divests himself of the very character of a human being."[114]

As in previous sections, we shall propose that Irenaeus recognized in this distinctive theological context (eschatology) an opportunity to put Genesis 1.26 to a corresponding hermeneutical use. Perhaps the concerns occasionally expressed over how to reconcile Irenaeus' evolutionary picture of image and likeness in *Haer.* iv.38 with that found in other passages are unnecessary. One common approach is to treat these two terms separately: image refers to human original constitution and likeness refers to human eschatological destiny.[115] However, another possibility is that Irenaeus had no such technical distinction in mind, but simply adapted this compound Genesis motif as a tool to construct or reinforce a specific theological argument. Here Irenaeus uses Scripture to set forth a catholic-Christian view of human eschatological destiny. At the same time, he offers general suggestions as to how a requisite Christian theodicy may be articulated.

CONTEXT OF *ADVERSUS HAERESES* IV.38: ANTHROPOLOGY

Irenaeus' specific concern in *Haer.* iv.37-39 is to confront Valentinian anthropology, specifically the doctrine that human beings are simply good, potentially good, or evil by *nature* rather than by will (iv.37.2). Insofar as

---

[114] Literally: *latenter semetipsum occidit hominem* (*Haer.* iv.39.1; SC 100 [964.32]).
[115] On this issue, see David Cairns' seminal discussion (*The Image of God in Man*, 74-83).

Irenaeus twice in this context mentions Jesus' lament over Jerusalem,[116] he apparently sees this passage as strategically important in rebutting his opponents' position. Standing as the quintessential prophet, perhaps Jesus points to prophecy's intended – but resisted – purpose in the divine oikonomia:

> The expression [of our Lord], "How often would I have gathered your children together, and you would not," set forth the ancient law of human liberty, because God made man a free [agent] from the beginning, possessing his own power, even as he does his own soul, to obey the behests of God voluntarily, and not by compulsion from God (iv.37.1).

If, however, a Valentinian tripartite anthropology is adopted, what sense can be made of Christ's frustration and lament? It would seem that the logic of prophecy assumes that human response to God is not predetermined by human nature, but rather may be freely given. Indeed God has created human beings with this very capacity and therefore is just in holding humanity accountable for its exercise of freedom.

> If then it were not in our power to do or not to do these things, what reason had the apostle, and much more the Lord himself, to give us counsel to do some things, and to abstain from others? But because man is possessed of free will from the beginning (*Sed quoniam liberae sententiae ab initio est homo*), and God is possessed of free will, in whose *likeness* man was created, advice is always given to him to keep fast the good, which thing is done by means of obedience to God. And not merely in works, but also in faith, has God preserved the will of man free and under his control... (iv.37.4-5).

Freedom of will, then, is at least associated with humanity's creation after the likeness of God.[117] Yet the implications of this particular view on anthropology require a move to address theological concerns. If humans do not always use their freedom to choose rightly, do they not then infringe on God's will and sovereign power? "Could not God have exhibited man as perfect [that is, always choosing rightly] from the beginning?" (iv.38.1). Irenaeus must argue why his anthropology does not insinuate that God is deficient or impotent.[118] God *could* have created humanity perfect, but humanity, being then "like a

---

[116] *Haer.* iv.36.8 and 37.5; cf. Luke 13.34-35; Matthew 23.37-39.
[117] Cf. the emphasis on human response in the scriptural pericopes supplied by Irenaeus in *Haer.* iv.36.1-8.
[118] Cf. *Haer.* iv.37.6; 38.1.

child" (νήπιος), was not capable of "receiving," "containing," and "retaining" such perfection.[119] The incarnate yet perfect Word of God, through his recapitulation of humanity (iv.38.2), enabled us to finally "contain in ourselves the Bread of immortality, which is the Spirit of the Father" (iv.38.1). Denis Minns helpfully proposes to clarify the logic of Irenaeus' attempt to reconcile divine power with human nature.

> To understand Irenaeus' point we need to remember that the idea of "process" is embedded in the very word he uses to differentiate God and his creation. God is not in a state of Becoming, he is unoriginated, uncreated. Creatures, by definition, are in a state of Becoming. They cannot be said to be perfect (i.e. finished; fully made) until that process of Becoming ceases... God intends that humankind should also be infinite; not in Being, which is logically impossible, but in Becoming, which is its natural state.[120]

Yet Minns does not discuss a crucial implication from Irenaeus' argument – a point that would not have been missed by Irenaeus' opponents. As we shall see, Irenaeus uses Genesis 1.26 to assert that the *created time* in which humanity lives is the sphere of operation for the divine economy. Humanity is being made in time after God's image and likeness.

SELECTED TEXT AND COMMENTS FROM *ADVERSUS HAERESES* IV.38

In *Haer.* iv.37-39, three references to Genesis 1.26 lie at the heart of Irenaeus' argument about human eschatological destiny. In the first (iv.37.7) Irenaeus claims that God is:

> ...determining all things beforehand for the bringing of man to perfection, for his edification, and for the revelation of his dispensations, that goodness may both be made apparent, and righteousness perfected, and that the Church may be *fashioned after the image of his Son* [*ad figuram imaginis Filii ejus coaptetur*[121]], and that man may finally be made mature at some future time [*et tandem aliquando maturus fiat homo*], becoming ripe thorough such privileges to see and comprehend God [*in tantis maturescens ad videndum et capiendum Deum*].[122]

---

[119] *Haer.* iv.38.1-2.
[120] Minns, *Irenaeus*, 74.
[121] *Coaptare* denotes a fitting, joining or adjusting together with something.
[122] SC 100 (942.175-177).

Here Irenaeus uses Genesis 1.26 as a tool by which to speak about human eschatological destiny, placing alongside a colorful metaphor of fulfillment. As the Church is adapted to the image of the Son, so also humanity (*homo* in a collective sense) finally (*aliquando*) is made (*fiat*) mature, just as fruit becomes ripe for its harvest.[123] Such is the full manifestation of God's *dispositio* with respect to his creation.

At the end of iv.38.4, Irenaeus again draws on Genesis 1.26 (and Genesis 3) to describe human destiny in concert with its original creation.

> For it was necessary, at first, that nature should be exhibited (*apparere*); then, after that, that which was mortal should be conquered and swallowed up by immortality, and the corruptible by incorruptibility (*post deinde vinci, et absorbi mortale ab immortalitate et corruptibile ab incorruptibilitate*), and that man *should be made after the image and likeness of God*, having received the knowledge of good and evil *(et fieri hominem secundum imaginem et similitudinem Dei, agnitione accepta boni et mali).*[124]

Irenaeus stresses again that the divine economy has a necessary progression and sequential continuity. Human immaturity and frailty must come first. But after a time, this weakness is to be overcome and replaced with power. What was improper for Adam and Eve to seek when they were immature, the knowledge of good and evil, is now permissible and in fact granted since humanity has been re-made to have the requisite capacity.[125] In between these

---

[123] Cf. the repetition of *maturus* (adjective) and *maturescere* (verb).

[124] *SC* 100 (960.110-114).

[125] Irenaeus' contemporary, Theophilus of Antioch, similarly linked Adam's child-like condition with an inability "to acquire knowledge properly" (*Autol.* 2.25 [OECT, *Theophilus of Antioch*, 67]). Whether Theophilus served as a source for Irenaeus, however, has not been convincingly demonstrated despite the efforts of F. Loofs. Hermann Gunkel, when commenting on Genesis 2.25 ("And the man and his wife were both naked, and were not ashamed"), speaks of "Der Urstand" in a way that bears affinities with Irenaeus' description. To lack "knowledge of good and evil" (cf. Genesis 2.17) is emblematic of the state of childhood: The narrator "versteht also unter der 'Erkenntnis' das, was die Erwachsenen mehr haben als die Kinder, die Einsicht, die Vernunft, zu der auch das Wissen um den Unterschied der Geschlechter gehört" (*Genesis* [Göttingen: Vandenhoeck & Ruprecht, 1964], 14). For Irenaeus, the original state of humanity was necessarily one of immaturity (including sexual immaturity). He argues that this condition follows the fact that humanity was only "recently made" (*quae nuper facta sunt* [iv.38.1; cf. iii.22.4]). Gunkel points to Scripture references, such as Deuteronomy 1.39 (cf. 1 Kings 3.9; 2 Samuel 14.17), that correlate a lack of the knowledge of good and evil to a state of immaturity. Furthermore Isaiah 7.15-16 and 2 Samuel 19.35 specifically describe human immaturity / maturity in association with eating, and could be taken to inform the "eating" in Genesis 3.5-6. Immature persons

two references is a keystone passage (iv.38.3) in that Irenaeus grounds eschatological destiny in Genesis 1.26, and locates the fixed path to this destination (God's oikonomia) as being coterminous with God's created, temporal order. According to Irenaeus, God's wisdom is shown

> ...in those created things which he made with *harmony* (εὐρυθμία), unity (ἐμμελής), and craftsmanship (ἐνκατάσκευος) – things which through his super-abundant goodness receive growth and which, upon tarrying, will reflect the glory of the uncreated one... For from the very fact of these things having been created, [it follows] that they are not uncreated; but by their continuing in being throughout a long course of ages, they shall receive (προσλήψεται) a faculty (δύναμιν / *virtutem*) of the uncreated through the gratuitous bestowal of eternal existence upon them by God.... By this arrangement, therefore, and these *harmonies*, and this guidance (Διὰ ταύτης τῆς τάξεως καὶ τῶν τοιούτων ῥυθμῶν καὶ τῆς τοιαύτης ἀγωγῆς), the created and formed (πεπλασμένος) man is rendered (γίνεσθαι) *after the image and likeness of the uncreated God*....[126]

Much could be said by way of commentary on this theologically dense passage. Yet for our purposes, it is noteworthy that Irenaeus again insists that human eschatological destiny, as expressed in Genesis 1.26, develops within the "harmonies" and "guidance" of God's "arrangement." This is growth inside the framework of God's unified, created order. Irenaeus' repeated use of forms of ῥυθμός (εὔρυθμα, ῥυθμῶν) in this context may elicit a sense of temporality.[127] Indeed, the text that immediately follows the citation above more explicitly relates Irenaeus' view that the divine oikonomia, from a human standpoint, is a dynamic experienced within time. After his reference to humanity's destiny as

---

make decisions about food that shows lack of discernment. Although Irenaeus does not cite any of these scriptural passages in this connection, it is not unreasonable to think that he was aware of them. In fact, given his acute interest in the text of Isaiah 7.10-17 (cf. *Haer.* iii.19.3-21.6; iv.33.11), it seems highly likely that Irenaeus was familiar with this biblical motif. *Haer.* iv.38, then, may seem theologically innovative, but it very likely manifests Irenaeus' reflection on Scripture (akin to Gunkel's observations). Just as when the child Immanuel was too young to choose to eat "curds and honey" and too young to "know how to refuse the evil and choose the good," so also (says Irenaeus), "recently created" humanity lacked the capacity for "more substantial nourishment," that is, perfection (cf. Isaiah 7.15; *Haer.* iv.38.1; iii.18.3).

[126] *Haer.* iv.38.3; *SC* 100 (953.51-955.66). We cite the Greek instead of the Latin wherever extant.

[127] The semantic range of ῥυθμός includes measured motion or time; proportion or symmetry of parts; and arrangement or order.

its being made (γίνομαι) after the image and likeness of God, Irenaeus distinguishes the roles of Father, Son, Spirit, and humanity in this work of "making." Then, of the intended human recipient, he avers:

> ... man [is] making progress (προκόπτειν) *day by day* (ἡμέρα), and *ascending* (ἀνέρχεσθαι) towards the perfect (τὸ τέλειον), that is, approximating (πλησίος) to the uncreated one (iv.38.3).[128]

Three crucial points about Irenaeus' view of human τέλος can be drawn from *Haer.* iv.38.3. First, Genesis 1.26 – humanity being made after the image and likeness of God – supplies the means for speaking of human destiny as a progression or ascension toward the perfect. These are simply two alternative ways of saying the same thing. In effect, Irenaeus deploys Genesis language as a hermeneutical tool. By placing these two pictures of the one human destiny in side-by-side context, Irenaeus invites the reader to view them as parallels. Whereas the former depiction uses strictly biblical imagery, the latter (ascension to the divine) suggests Platonic *exitus* and *reditus* tradition. Yet Irenaeus has no qualms about allowing each picture to inform the other, epexegetically as it were. Both describe human destiny by harking back to the divine-human interface at the point of human origination. Secondly, we note that the latter image speaks of a human ascent to God as a progressing (προκόπτειν) that is measured in time (ἡμέρα). As a brief survey of the vocabulary in iv.35-39 will attest, this reference to time is not merely incidental. In fact, Irenaeus' frequent usage suggests that he rarely talks about human origination and destination without speaking the language of temporality and sequence. The term *initio* (ἀρχή) occurs seven times in chapters 37-38.[129] Of the six total occurrences of *nuper* (ἄρτι) in *Adversus Haereses*, four are found in chapters 37-39.[130] Other time-related terms include *novissimus* or *novus* (six times in chapters 35-38);[131] *tempus augmenti* (iv.38.4); and *jam* (iv.38.4). Irenaeus' eschatological interpretation of Jesus' parable of the vineyard workers (iv.36.7) is brimming with such words: *tempor-* (four times), *statim, initio, jam, progressis,* and *fine*.[132] In our passage (iv.38.3), Irenaeus affirms the unity of God's created order and his salvific order by using the same term ῥυθμός to describe them both. Thus the same ῥυθμός that God embedded into all "created things" is also the ῥυθμός that constitutes the "arrangement" and "guidance" in which the created human is

---

[128] *Haer.* iv.38.3; *SC* 100 (955-957.68-70).
[129] *Haer.* iv.37.1; 37.4; 38.1 (three times); 38.2; 38.4.
[130] *Haer.* iv.38.1; 38.2 (two times); 39.2. See especially iv.38.2 (*SC* 100 [950.45-53]).
[131] *Haer.* iv.35.4; 36.2; 36.3; 36.7 (2 times); 38.1.
[132] *SC* 100 (910.272-912.279).

rendered after the divine image (iv.38.3).¹³³ This is the harmony underlying the "daily progress of man." God's oikonomia for humanity (creation, restoration, and destination) is inseparably built into the structure of God's created temporal system. This claim is not unexpected, given the prominence that the Genesis account ascribes to humanity among the *facta sunt*. Third, if we grant that the "ascent" and the "making" are equivalent descriptions of one phenomenon, and that the former is described as a temporal journey, then we may naturally infer that the latter making of humanity after God's image is also seen as a dynamic work in time. Indeed, the context of iv.38 readily supports such a conclusion.

Why might Irenaeus have reasoned that Genesis 1.26 was indispensable for explaining human eschatological destiny? Why does he make reference to it three times in this short section? Certainly he recognized, as did the Gnostics, that speaking of human τέλος begs a backward reference to human ἀρχή. According to Irenaeus, however, Genesis 1.26 crucially demonstrates that (and how) the one God's one oikonomia joins human ἀρχή to its τέλος, and τέλος to ἀρχή. This continuous work cannot be abstracted from temporal creation, that is, the embedded rhythms and sequences fittingly arranged by the Creator. Genesis 1.26, then, accounts for God's identity as Initiator of created time and substance for the purpose of humankind's benefit.[134] Accordingly, Genesis 1.26 allows Irenaeus emphatically to link human destiny to significant divine and human actions in time. God initiates; humanity has been given the capacity to respond freely. In the creature's own habitat, gift and growth combine to yield a harvest of maturity and fruitfulness. According to the guidance (ἀγωγή) of its Maker, the "created and formed man" is made "after the image and likeness of the uncreated God" (iv.38.3).

CHALLENGING THE OPPOSITION: HUMAN DESTINY

When Irenaeus spoke of human eschatological destiny, he believed that Genesis 1.26 presented itself as a powerful and precise instrument for attacking Gnostic anthropological doctrines at their points of greatest vulnerability. Yet insofar as his opponents were serious interpreters of Scripture and would have also accorded significant hermeneutical weight to this text, Genesis 1.26 also served as a common starting point in the debate.

---

[133] *SC* 100 (953.49-955.66); cf. the terminology (*bene aptata, consonantia*) and theme in Irenaeus' hermeneutical discussion in *Haer*. ii.25.1-2.

[134] In light of modern scientific evidence, the vast expanse of geological or cosmic time seemingly renders humanity's time span inconsequential. Yet Irenaeus' expressly theological view of time (i.e., a purposeful creation for humankind) would resist such a conclusion.

Human destiny, according to the Ophites, is the eschatological ascent of the "holy souls" who know Christ.[135] Before being joined to Christ, however, these souls must "lay aside their mundane flesh" (*depositionem mundialis carnis*).[136] Christ then "possesses" these souls and is "enriched" by them. In the process, creator Ialdabaoth is emptied of *virtus*. The whole *humectatio spiritus luminis* is subsequently gathered together and carried off (*abripio*) into an *Aeonem incorruptibilitatis*.[137] However, souls which are "only of [Ialdabaoth's] substance, that is, those into which he has breathed" (cf. Genesis 2.7) cannot rise to the heights above.

For the Valentinians, the situation is a bit more nuanced. The destinies of the πνευματικοί and ὑλικοί depend not upon divine or human actions in time, but rather are fixed in pre-time eternity and realized in post-time eternity according to their compositional substance. The πνευματικοί are predisposed to be formed (μορφωθῇ) and perfected (τελειωθῇ) by γνῶσις.[138] It is the ψυχικοί who require a world for "training by perceptible things."[139] They are to be instructed (ἐπαιδεύθησαν) in ψυχικὰ, and thus "established (βεβαιούμενοι) through works and mere faith" to address their lack of "perfect knowledge."[140]

Christian readings of Genesis, as appropriated in gospel and Pauline writings, permitted Irenaeus to speak of human destiny using similar language as had his Gnostic opponents. Human beginning, as testified in Genesis 1.26, is marked by the close connection between divinity and humanity.[141] Human salvation leading to eschatological destiny is a return or ascent to God – the restoration of the quality of fellowship originally enjoyed. It is possible to think of the image of God as a divine *virtus* that could only be fully seen and realized in humanity when human corruptibility and death were vanquished. The journey back to God is a progression which, from the human side, involved both faith and works as one is led (ἄγειν) and educated by God.[142] Yet Genesis 1.26 provided Irenaeus with the means to undermine Valentinian anthropology and eschatology in fundamental ways.

First, Genesis 1.26 (and its context) enabled him to claim that the making of humanity after the image and likeness of God is truly *comprehensive*. This

---

[135] Citations in this paragraph are all taken from *Haer.* i.30.14.
[136] *SC* 264 (384.266).
[137] *SC* 264 (384.265-276).
[138] *Haer.* i.6.1; *SC* 264 (92.607-608).
[139] αἰσθητῶν παιδευμάτων / *sensibilibus disciplinis* (*Haer.* i.6.1; *SC* 264 [91.595-596]).
[140] *Haer.* i.6.2; *SC* 264 (93.612-614).
[141] Though for Irenaeus, of course, the crucial distinction to be made is that this divinity is the Creator of the natural order rather than an entity too lofty to be involved in such mundane matters.
[142] "And not merely in works, but also in faith, has God preserved the will of man free and under his own control…" (*Haer.* iv.37.5).

applies to human composition. Since both body and soul were made after the divine image,[143] humanity could not be said to reach its destiny until both are restored and transformed. Contrary to Gnostic teaching, "humanity" could not be abstracted on the basis of isolating sub-components of body and soul. Necessarily, then, this destiny is also comprehensive in regard to the corporate scope of humanity. Christ recapitulated Adam (the original composite human being), not the purely spiritual Seth as the Valentinians taught.[144] Therefore, to all the descendants of Adam, God has given the capacity for responsiveness toward God's gift of the divine image.[145]

Second, in that Genesis 1.26 asserts that humanity was made by God to be in and part of God's own created order, the path of human eschatological development (ἀγωγή) takes place in created time and space. When coupled with the belief that God has invested in humanity a capacity for free decision-making (as far as concerns the reception of the image of God), *then human decisions and actions in this world are eschatologically significant.* Salvation – being made after the image of the Creator – can never involve a mere escape from created time and nature. Genesis shows this belief to be both contrary to the will of God and impossible by virtue of the ontological distinction between the uncreated and the created. Being made after God's image means being made "approximate" (πλησίος) to the uncreated, not identical with or integrated into the uncreated.[146] Among creatures, we are meant to be nearest to God in sharing God's incorruptibility and immortality.[147] At the same time, however, we forever remain "created" and in "subjection" (ὑποταγή) to God.[148] Christ's recapitulation of humanity reveals that the *substantiam factae naturae* is not to be bypassed, but overcome (*vincere*) and brought to fulfillment (iv.38.4). To "escape" (*fugiere*) from creation would be to escape from the very loci of God's rhythmic oikonomia for humanity. Such an aspiration is, at any rate, futile since no one can actually escape the hands of the God who contains all things.[149]

---

[143] Cf. *Epid.* 11.

[144] As noted, the Valentinians identified Seth as the human archetype of the πνευματικοί, rather than tracing further back to Adam who was deemed of mixed composition.

[145] See, for example, *Haer.* iv.37.5.

[146] *Haer.* iv.38.3. "As 'creature,' the world of human experience is intrinsically finite. Its finitude, however, does not consist in an incapacity, a mere inferiority to the 'higher' world... [but rather] a potentiality: an openness to the purpose of the Creator" (Norris, "The Transcendence and Freedom of God," 100).

[147] Cf. Irenaeus' quotation of Wisdom 6.19: "but immortality renders one nigh unto God" (*Haer.* iv.38.3).

[148] *Haer.* iv.38.3; *SC* 100 (955. 61-62); cf. iv.39.4. In other words, "Being" and "becoming" always remain distinct (cf. Minns, *Irenaeus*, 33-34).

[149] Cf. *Haer.* v.1.3.

However, human rejection of God's eschatological plan does carry ramifications:

> For as in the case of this *temporal light* (*temporali lumine*), those who shun (*fugere*) it do deliver themselves over to darkness… so those who fly (*fugere*) from the eternal light of God, which contains in itself all good things, are themselves the cause to themselves of their inhabiting eternal darkness….[150]

This daily ascent (ἡμέρα ἀνέρχομαι) requires a human willingness to be "led," so that the divine image may be received, contained, and retained (iv.38.2). Being made after the image of God obliges human beings to "obey" God, "believe" in him and "keep his commandment" (iv.39.1). This, says Irenaeus, "is the life of man" (iv.39.1).[151] Yet with all his recognition of the role of human response, Irenaeus never permits an encroachment on the primacy of divine action. It is God, in the arranged work of the Spirit in time, who actually brings human persons to their destinies by enabling them to bear his image. In the final analysis, Genesis 1.26 shows that to be "human" in the fullest sense is nothing more nor less than "being made" (*fieri*) by the uncreated Creator God after his image and likeness.

Conclusion

As we have argued, taking seriously Irenaeus' theological claims related to the image and likeness of God does not necessarily entail a primary obligation to identify and harmonize the possible referents behind these terms across varied contexts. It is possible that Irenaeus intended to communicate a technical distinction between image and likeness. However, a survey of the themes and organization in *Adversus Haereses* suggests that a more fruitful approach is to assess the way in which Irenaeus puts this motif, *in toto*, to work in circumscribed theological tasks. By distinguishing Irenaeus' hermeneutical uses of Genesis 1.26 and noting their distinct contributions to advancing certain arguments, we gain a greater sensitivity to Irenaeus' vivacity as a practicing biblical theologian. Thus, the ramifications of Irenaeus' work appear to extend not only to the meanings that he gives to a given term or text but also to the manner in which he applies scriptural texts to address pertinent questions. In this respect, Genesis 1.26 constitutes a crucial test case. No less than the Gnostics,

---

[150] *Haer.* iv.39.4; *SC* 100 (972.88-95).
[151] This follows, insofar as the reception of God's image equals the reception of the knowledge of good and evil – knowledge involving a recognition that for one of God's creatures, the supreme good is to obey God.

Irenaeus discerned Genesis 1.26 to be perfectly suited as a hermeneutical tool insofar as it was densely packed and practically bursting with semantic potential. Despite theological differences between Irenaeus and Augustine, it is also clear that they shared hermeneutical similarities in their approaches to the opening sections of Genesis. Whereas Irenaeus exploits the flexibility of the image and likeness motif, Augustine makes a virtue of the diversity of possible orthodox interpretations of Genesis 1.1-2. Just as Irenaeus does not show an overt concern to maintain consistent, stable referents for image and likeness, Augustine claims that the "heaven and earth" made by God could mean "the entire visible world," "formless and chaotic matter," or "invisible and visible nature."[152] The basis for this, asserts Augustine, is that "through [Moses] the one God has tempered the sacred books to the interpretations of many, who could come to see a diversity of truths."[153] In the very characteristic of Genesis 1 to express "truths" through "terse words,"[154] Augustine discerns the author's invitation for later flexible interpretation:

> A spring confined in a small space rises with more power and distributes its flow through more channels over a wider expanse than a single stream rising from the same spring even if it flows down over many places. So also the account given by your minister [Moses], which was to benefit many expositions, uses a small measure of words to pour out a spate of clear truth. From this each commentator... may draw (*trahere*) what is true, one this way, another that, *using longer and more complex channels of discourse.*[155]

Whereas Augustine sensed the need to provide theoretical justification for pluriform interpretations of Genesis 1, Irenaeus' work apparently assumes this and proceeds to model pluriform *uses* of the text. To counteract Valentinian epistemology, particularly as concerns knowledge of the Creator and Supreme Father, Irenaeus uses Genesis 1.26 to assert that the one God was directly involved in the origination of the human being – a creation composed of soul and body. Highlighting humanity's loss of direct communion with its Creator, Irenaeus' Christology adapts the image and likeness motif to portray vividly the incarnate Word's work as a comprehensive recapitulation of humanity. When Genesis 1.26 is employed to speak of humanity's ultimate destination, the result is an anthropological sketch aimed at undercutting the Valentinian alternative.

---

[152] *Conf.*, 12.17.24-25 (Citations are from the Oxford World Classics edition: [trans. Henry Chadwick; Oxford: Oxford University Press, 1991], 258).
[153] Ibid., 12.31.42 (Chadwick, 271). According to Augustine, the only limit to a text's meaning is the truth itself (12.18.27).
[154] Ibid., 12.26.36 (Chadwick, 266).
[155] Ibid., 12.27.37 (Chadwick, 266). Emphasis is added. Cf. CCSL 27:236-37.

God's salvific plan does not require an escape from temporal and bodily existence, but is progressively fulfilled in even these created dimensions.

Although recapitulation is most often associated with Genesis 2.7, it is occasionally linked with Genesis 1.26.[156] However, the suggestion that Irenaeus used the image and likeness motif as a "medium" for expressing his biblical "doctrine" of recapitulation (i.e., the means of "translating" it into Greek terms),[157] risks underestimating the text's constitutive theological role. For Irenaeus, the flexibility of Genesis 1.26 did indeed make it an ideal hermeneutical vehicle, although it was employed in more tasks than is often recognized. Yet Genesis 1.26 cannot be separated from Irenaeus' theological content or doctrine. Seizing upon this text, Irenaeus is emboldened to summarize a Christian vision of divine activity and human teleology in a *single narrative*. Such a view is echoed by a recent theologian who is known to have admired Irenaeus' work: "To be in the image of God is not, therefore, to have some timeless quality like reason, or anything else, but to exist in a directedness, between our coming from nothing and our being brought through Christ before the throne of the Father."[158]

---

[156] Besides *Haer.* iii.18.1 (see above), cf. *Haer.* iii.23.1; v.12.4; *Epid.* 32.
[157] Lawson, *Biblical Theology*, 155.
[158] Colin E. Gunton, *Christ and Creation* (Carlisle: Paternoster, 1992), 102.

4. GENESIS 2.7 AND THE *HOMO VIVENS*

Introduction

Along with the Genesis couplet "image and likeness," the "breath of life" also appears on a recent list of "Irenaeus' four untidy problems."[1] Eric Osborn suggests that it "presents a puzzle which, like that of image and likeness, can only be solved by the concept of different levels of participation."[2] Without wishing to undervalue in the least Osborn's insightful analysis of Irenaeus' argument in light of the Middle-Platonist concept of participation, it seems advantageous to supplement Osborn's approach with one that directs greater attention to the hermeneutical function of Genesis 2.7 in Irenaeus' proposals. Whereas Osborn attends to possible philosophical lenses through which Irenaeus *read* texts such as Genesis 2.7, this chapter will focus on Irenaeus' theological *uses* of Genesis 2.7. In Irenaeus' formulation of Christian anthropology, designed as it were to counteract the competition, this one meager text carries an inordinate amount of theological freight. Indeed, in *Haer.* v.1-16 Irenaeus rarely speaks about God, humanity, and the arena of their interrelations without mentioning Genesis 2.7 in proximate context. By the light cast by this text, Irenaeus reads diverse scriptural materials (especially Pauline and gospel but also those of the prophets and the law) to craft a unique theological foundation to ground his anthropology: God, attested in Scripture as Father, Spirit and Son, is engaged in one harmonious "work" of "fashioning" humanity.[3] Fleshly bodies, not merely immaterial souls, are intrinsic to this humanity, made and addressed (as they are) by God. The Valentinians were notably enthusiastic about anthropology, as their attraction to 1 Corinthians 15 attests. Yet Irenaeus

---

[1] Osborn, *Irenaeus of Lyons*, 230.
[2] Ibid., 222.
[3] Cf. *Haer.* v.15.2: "Now the work of God is the fashioning of man."

was concerned first that the *sententia de Deo*, furnished by the apostles in Scripture,[4] provide the foundation for any derivative conclusions about humanity. With both sides ascribing priority to the New Testament witness of Christ, Irenaeus' interpretation and use of Genesis 2.7 would prove hermeneutically significant in separating their respective readings of Scripture.

This feature, however, invites greater attention than it often receives. For example, Osborn's well-reasoned study of Irenaeus' breath of life imagery might have also investigated how Irenaeus relates this motif to self-consciously Christian ways of speaking about the Father, Spirit, and (climactically) Christ.[5] John Behr points in the right direction when claiming that

> Irenaeus' reading of the verses in Genesis relating to the creation of man... is Christocentric... Furthermore, the text... [*Adversus Haereses*] is also *exegetical* rather than analytical: it demonstrates, from Scripture, that there is but one God, one Christ, one Spirit, and one human race in which the one economy is enacted, as unfolded in Scripture, rather than analysing the human constitution in static, philosophical terms.[6]

In our previous chapter, we examined excerpts from *Adversus Haereses* to show Irenaeus' remarkably flexible use of Genesis 1.26 in elaborating three crucial points along the sequence of God's economy. Assessing Irenaeus' use of Genesis 2.7, however, calls for a slightly different approach. In *Haer.* v.1-16, Irenaeus repeatedly turns to the text and imagery of Genesis 2.7 to make a variety of claims with a cumulative theological effect. This extended unit of material, constituting an integrated argument on the proper interpretation of 1 Corinthians 15.50, is our central focus.[7] Here we find Irenaeus, the biblical

---

[4] Cf. *Haer.* iii.5.1.

[5] Osborn cites G. Joppich (*Salus carnis. Eine Untersuchung in der Theologie des hl. Irenäus von Lyon* [Münsterschwarzach: Vier-Türme-Verlag, 1965], 68-69) in identifying "five main proofs for the salvation of the flesh" (Osborn, *Irenaeus of Lyons*, 228). However, he does not connect these to Irenaeus' crucial christological claims, such as recapitulation.

[6] *Asceticism and Anthropology*, 86; emphasis is added.

[7] Discerning literary features that might suggest boundaries between major units of material in *Adversus Haereses* book five is no straightforward task. The *Sources Chrétiennes* edition finds three primary sections, dividing between chapters 14 and 15 and between chapters 25 and 26. However, early readers of Irenaeus (let alone the author) have provided us with virtually no guidance. Unlike the first four books of *Adversus Haereses*, the fifth did not receive chapter headings before its translation into Latin and Armenian (Unger, *St. Irenaeus*, 18). The editorial decisions reflected in the *SC* edition are defensible, yet certainly not the last word. Chapters 1-14 encompass discussions of the roles of Father and Spirit in vivifying the human body. In chapters 15-24, Irenaeus'

exegete and theologian, reading the Scriptural texts in a way that, very possibly, was every bit as innovative in its time as the biblical hermeneutics of second-century Gnostic Christians.

Irenaeus' "roadmap" for Christian anthropology

In *Haer.* v.1-16, the primary subject is God in his triunity (the Father and his two hands), with humanity (particularly bodily "flesh and blood") as object. The divine economy is that sphere of God's interaction with humanity wherein his purpose is revealed as the presentation of the *homo vivens*. Genesis 2.7, when brought to bear on readings of Christ in the apostolic texts, illumines where and why the divine hands are at work in humanity.

Although Irenaeus' subsidiary arguments occasionally diverge as well as converge, it is possible to discern topical subdivisions in *Haer.* v.1-16 by distinguishing the different *purposes* for which Irenaeus uses Genesis 2.7. In so doing, three main sections emerge in (albeit fuzzy) relief. Irenaeus' striking introduction (preface through chapter 2) provides an overview of the divine work in humanity and introduces the three divine standpoints from which it will be surveyed: Father, Spirit, and Son. In chapters 3-8 he utilizes Genesis 2.7 to address requisite preliminary questions: Who is the God who purposes human vivification and what are the most basic grounds that establish its possibility? To explain this, Irenaeus concentrates on God the Father, who, as originator and ultimate destination of humankind, suffers no limits to his power. The second and third sections (comprising chapters 9-16) are counterparts to each other. Irenaeus describes the two active agents in the Father's economy in order to explain human vivification *in se*. First (chapters 9-13), he finds Genesis 2.7 needful when describing the Spirit's role in the composition and vivification of the created human being – soul and body. While 1 Corinthians 15 is his

---

attention is centered on the Son. Christ's healing ministry, death and resurrection achieves comprehensive victory for humanity. (To be more precise, the gradual shift from the Spirit to Christ begins earlier in *Haer.* v.12.6, with minor hints even before that.) However, the decision by the *SC* editors to locate a major disjunction between chapters 14 and 15 artificially distorts Irenaeus' naturally fluid argument. His ongoing concern is to speak of the triunity of God and the economic continuity that is the telltale mark of God's outworking toward humanity. In the transition of v.12-15 Irenaeus simply changes hands (so to speak), from Spirit to Christ, while continuing to discern in Scripture (particularly by means of Genesis 2.7) God's program for fashioning a "living man." Chapters 15 and 16 are thus securely bound to the previous context conceptually as well as methodologically, in part due to Irenaeus' theological uses of Genesis 2.7. Before shifting the discussion to Christ's passion and temptation (*Haer.* v.16.3-24.4), Irenaeus returns to Genesis 1.26, in combination with Genesis 2.7, to summarize neatly the anthropological significance of Christ's advent within God's economy (v.15.4-16.2).

principal resource, Irenaeus (following Paul) recognizes that Genesis 2.7 vitally informs not only a Christian view of creation but also of salvation. It clarifies how human bodiliness relates to each. Next (chapters 14-16), Irenaeus employs Genesis 2.7 to interpret the advent and ministry of the other divine hand, the Word. Christ's recapitulation of human flesh and blood secures it for God. His healing of a man born blind constitutes revelation of God and, derivatively, of humanity. In these "last times"[8] Christ clearly manifests the ongoing extension of God's purpose held since the beginning: to fashion the *homo vivens*. In following Irenaeus' untraditional thematic sequence of Father, Spirit, Son, our chapter will attempt to trace the logic of his interpretation of Scripture. Perhaps given the crucial hermeneutical and theological roles filled by Irenaeus' notion of recapitulation, Irenaeus' ordering enables him to bring the argument to an appropriate climax with the person and work of Christ. Although his reading of Genesis 1-2 impels him to critique his opponents' doctrines about the supreme Father and the divine Spirit, it is with respect to Christology that Irenaeus ascribes particular significance to Genesis 2.7. Generally speaking, then, this verse contributes materials for constructing three relatively discrete components: theological arguments concerning the Father, Spirit, and Son. Yet it also provides a stock of imagery and language to serve as thread for weaving these three discourses together into one grand story. It should be acknowledged that if he so chose, Irenaeus could have used abstract words and concepts to speak about God's economy. Instead, as we shall see, Irenaeus habitually calls on a dramatic picture evoked by Genesis 2.7, rich with visual and tactile connotations: God's gracious interaction with humanity is the intimate, fashioning work of his two hands. Through visualizing the presence and ministry of these two hands, the distinctive relation between God and humanity is lucidly revealed.

Because Irenaeus' introductory statement in *Haer.* v.1.3 is programmatic – preparing the reader to recognize the direction of Irenaeus' upcoming argument and disclosing the means by which he will argue it – this passage deserves close attention. In this roadmap (of sorts) to Irenaeus' Christian anthropology, Irenaeus hints at the vital tactical roles that will be filled by Genesis 2.7. The Ebionites, whom Irenaeus had accused of denying Christ's true "union of God and man," were

> ... not considering that just <u>as</u> (*quemadmodum*) in the beginning (*ab initio*) of our formation (*plasmatio*) in Adam, that *breath of life* which was from God, having been united to what had been fashioned (*unita plasmati*), enlivened the man and manifested him as a rational living being; <u>so also</u> (*sic*) in the end (*in fine*), the Word of the Father and the

---

[8] Cf. *Haer.* v.15.4, et al.: *in novissimis temporibus*.

Spirit of God, having become united with the ancient substance of Adam's formation (*plasmatio*), rendered man *living* (*vivere*) and perfect, [capable of] receiving (*capere*) the perfect Father, in order that <u>as</u> in the soulish (*animali*, i.e., Adam) we all were dead, <u>so</u> in the spiritual we may all be *made alive* (*vivificare*).[9] For never at any time did Adam escape the hands of God.... And for this reason in these last times, not by the will of the flesh, nor by the will of man, but by the good pleasure of the Father his hands formed a *living man* in order that Adam might be created after the image and likeness of God (*sed ex placito Patris manus ejus <u>vivum</u> perfecerunt <u>hominem</u>, uti fiat Adam secundum imaginem et similitudinem Dei*).[10]

Our first general observation concerns Irenaeus' references to God's hands. Used here, as elsewhere, Irenaeus is not merely concerned to embellish his rhetoric with a colorful expression. Rather, for Irenaeus, to speak of God's "hands" is to convey something of theological substance from Scripture.

DIVINE HANDS: GENESIS 2.7 AND ECONOMIC CONTINUITY

The divine economy as described by Irenaeus is where the Father's purpose and power are made present and effective to humanity through the activity of his own hands – hands that have held "Adam" continuously. Genesis 2.7 offers two powerfully emotive images. First, God forms the man from earth. This term πλάσσειν, for which Irenaeus has great affection, clearly serves to "evoke the particular tenderness of God for the man that he created in this way."[11] Second, God breathes (ἐμφύσαν) upon his face the "breath of life." Although Genesis 2.7 does not contain the term "hands" (nor is the phrase "hands of God" found in Genesis), Irenaeus' penchant for describing God's interaction with humanity as the activity of his hands has plentiful biblical precedent. In the wisdom tradition God's creation is depicted as the formative work of his hands. God's hands (χεῖρες), for example, form (πλάσσειν) the human being (Psalm 118.73[12]; Psalm 138.5; Job 10.8) and the dry land (Psalm 94.5). Given that πλάσσειν is

---

[9] Irenaeus adopts 1 Corinthians 15.22 here, with his own modifications.
[10] *Haer.* v.1.3; *SC* 153 (26.75-28.89). Emphasis is added. One might have expected *plasmare* rather than *perfecere* at the end, yet the link to Genesis 2.7 is evident in the reference to *vivum hominem*.
[11] Sesboüé, *Tout récapituler dans le Christ*, 185. In *Haer.* iv.19.2-3, Irenaeus also recounts biblical references to God's hand(s) that denote his power and greatness.
[12] ... αἱ χεῖρές σου ἐποίησάν με καὶ ἔπλασάν με... (All references are from LXX).

the verb used in Genesis 2.7a, it would be quite reasonable[13] for Irenaeus to draw from scriptural associations to make explicit what is perceived implicitly. In some way Genesis 2.7 affirms the activity and presence of God's hands.[14] Presumably, it would not be lost on Irenaeus that the gospels and apostolic writings use divine hand(s) language in a manner similar to that of Old Testament texts.[15] In boldly arguing that humans[16] have never "escaped the hands of God," Irenaeus appropriates Genesis 2.7 while probably having other scriptural references in mind as well. Using the anthropomorphism *manus* with God as subject *sixteen* times in the contexts of *Haer.* v.1-16, Irenaeus is clearly keen to underscore that one manifestly conspicuous feature of God's dealings with humanity is *continuity*. Humanity is held in the hands of God from beginning to end. The God to whom these hands belong ought to be recognized as one and the same throughout the extension of human history and the progression of God's economy. Accordingly, insofar as the ongoing work of these hands is connected and related in a perception of continuity, the divine activities in the "end" and in the "beginning" are mutually informative. Yet ought this relationship to be perceived as one of simple interchangeability (i.e., Adam and Christ are placed on equal footing and "located on the same horizontal plane")?[17] Irenaeus does maintain that an accurate interpretation of the activity at the "end" requires an accurate (and suitably catholic-Christian) interpretation of the activity at the "beginning." His *regula veritatis* makes this clear: a proper doctrine of creation and of Creator (as derived from Genesis 1-2)

---

[13] I.e., insofar as the action of forming implies the presence of hands. Cf. Isaiah 64.8 (and Jeremiah 18.6): "...we are the clay, and you are our potter; we are all the work of your hand."

[14] 2 Maccabees 7.23 provides a noteworthy example of the use of Genesis 2.7 *circa* 100 B.C.E. to 50 C.E.: "Therefore the Creator of the world, who shaped (πλάσσειν) the beginning of humankind and devised the origin of all things, will in his mercy give life and breath back to you again, since you now forget yourselves for the sake of his laws."

[15] Though Irenaeus does not cite these, examples are seen (amongst other places) in Luke 1.66; Acts 11.21; 1 Peter 5.6; Hebrews 10.31 (In the OT, see Deuteronomy 32.39; 2 Chronicles 6.4; Isaiah 41.20; Daniel 5.23). De Andía provides a helpful overview of Irenaeus' references to the co-ministry of the divine hands in the creation of humanity (cf. *Homo vivens*, 64-67).

[16] Irenaeus' term "Adam" at the end of *Haer.* v.1.3 clearly implies the human race in general.

[17] Cf. Francis Watson "Is there a Story in These Texts?" in *Narrative Dynamics in Paul: A Critical Assessment* (ed. Bruce W. Longenecker; Louisville: Westminster John Knox, 2002), 231-39. Watson argues against the view (proposed by Edward Adams in this same volume) that Paul in Romans 1-8 locates Adam and Christ "on the same horizontal plane, as 'fate-determining individuals'" (235). According to Watson, Paul introduces qualifiers elsewhere in his writings (especially seen in Romans 5.14) that preclude seeing "equivalence" between the actions of Adam and Christ (237).

is an obligatory theological and hermeneutical starting point. However, Irenaeus' central concern as a Christian theologian is to use Scripture and apostolic tradition to set forth a satisfying doctrine of *Christ* to compete with that offered by the Gnostics.[18] In this reading engagement, Genesis 2.7 is invited to inform and interpret the life of Christ and the work of the Spirit in these times at the "end." Insofar as Christian anthropology looks to a prerequisite theology (more specifically, Christology), the question at hand then is: *what kind* of continuity of relation is to be found between Adam and Christ, between beginning and end? *How* is a Christian reading of Genesis 2.7 crucial to a proper reading of Christ? The reverse also holds. How is a Christian reading of "Christ" crucial to a proper understanding of Genesis 2.7? To broaden this query a bit, if it is shown *that* Genesis 2.7 is crucial for Irenaeus' argument, how is this so? How does this passage function as Christian Scripture for this early church theologian? While our forthcoming comments on *Haer.* v.1-16 attempt to draw attention to the way Irenaeus models a distinct, self-consciously Christian hermeneutic of Genesis 2.7, his opening summary statement in *Haer.* v.1.3 provides a vital hint: the "as / so" construction. When we compare Irenaeus' "as / so" statements with Paul's (as far as Christian readings of Genesis 2.7 are concerned), Irenaeus emerges as a true pioneer.

"AS... SO": GENESIS 2.7 AND TYPOLOGY

In *Haer.* v.1.3, Irenaeus uses the Pauline "as / so" (*quemadmodum... sic*)[19] pattern twice. The second time, he loosely mimics Paul's wording in 1 Corinthians 15.22 by stating "... *ut, quemadmodum in animali omnes mortui sumus, sic in spiritali omnes vivificemur....*"[20] Here, as elsewhere, Irenaeus places the figures of Adam and Christ in an analogical relationship. In 1 Corinthians 15.22 and its context, Paul's analogy using the "as / so" pattern

---

[18] This illustrates the well-known hermeneutical circle: It may be argued that Christ ought to be the methodological and theological starting point. However, in order to interpret Christ, one must read Genesis 1-2 through a christological lens and allow this reading to inform one's Christology, as attested by New Testament tradition. Irenaeus models this dynamic.

[19] While there is no extant Greek text, since the Latin translation uses *quemadmodum... sic* for both occurrences, and the latter one is Irenaeus' paraphrase of 1 Corinthians 15.22, which has the Greek ὥσπερ... οὕτως, it seems likely that Irenaeus used these words, or at least words very similar to them. Additionally, the usage of ὥσπερ... οὕτως in 1 Corinthians 15.22 can be informed by its use in Romans 5.12-21, given Irenaeus' familiarity with Romans.

[20] Whether intentionally or not, Irenaeus reads terms from 1 Corinthians 15.44 and 46 back into verse 22 by substituting *animali* (cf. ψυχικός) for "Adam" and *spiritali* (cf. πνευματικός) for "Christ." Cp. 1 Corinthians 15.22: ὥσπερ γὰρ ἐν τῷ Ἀδὰμ πάντες ἀποθνήσκουσιν, οὕτως καὶ ἐν τῷ Χριστῷ πάντες ζωοποιηθήσονται.

highlights both the similarity and dissimilarity between Adam and Christ. The former is seen insofar as both figures inaugurate activities whose effects impact humankind on a universal scale. More significantly for Paul in 1 Corinthians 15, though, is the antithetical nature of their respective legacies. He emphasizes the contrast between the death brought by the first figure, and the life brought by the last.[21] While in this case Irenaeus simply endorses and adapts Paul's use of Genesis 2.7 by reiterating the analogical relationship between these two crucial figures, Irenaeus' other "as / so" statement in *Haer.* v.1.3 displays a hermeneutic which puts Genesis 2.7 to a more radical Christian theological use:

> ...*quemadmodum ab initio plasmationis nostrae in Adam ea quae fuit a Deo aspiratio vitae unita plasmati animavit hominem et animal rationabile ostendit, sic in fine Verbum Patris et Spiritus Dei adunitus antiquae substantiae plasmationis Adae viventem et perfectum efficit hominem, capientem perfectum Patrem....*[22]

Here, Irenaeus' hermeneutical approach to Genesis 2.7, again structured by the "as / so" pattern, shows not mere analogy but typology. It is not that Irenaeus was the first to offer a typological reading of Genesis texts. In Romans 5.14, Paul qualifies the "as / so" relationship between Adam and Christ that he had asserted in Romans 5.12[23] by remarking that Adam is a "type (τύπος) of the one who was to come."[24] What makes Irenaeus' hermeneutic as introduced here so ambitious and innovative is the *scope* of the typology. Whereas Paul's Christian readings of Genesis texts discern a typological relationship between two figures, Irenaeus' reading of Genesis 2.7 propounds a typological relationship between two ages – beginning and end. In effect, Irenaeus claims that he can speak theologically about the *whole history of salvation* from this Genesis text.[25] Read with Irenaeus' catholic-Christian hermeneutic, Genesis 2.7 tells not merely of

---

[21] However, as Francis Watson rightly notes, a relationship of analogy does not in itself imply that the two entities are related in a narrative sequence wherein the second of the entities is "derived" from the first ("Is there a Story," 235-36). Our discussion of Irenaeus' use of the "as / so" pattern in *Haer.* v.1.3 depends heavily upon Watson's astute analysis of the Pauline "as / so" pattern and his observations about typology in 1 Corinthians 15 and Romans 5.

[22] Cf. the translation provided earlier in this chapter.

[23] "Therefore, just as sin came into the world through one man, and death came through sin, and so death spread to all because all have sinned..."

[24] Cf. Watson, "Is there a Story," 236.

[25] H. Verweyen suggests that Irenaeus, "more intensively than other theologians... tried to imagine (*hineinzuversetzen*) himself in that basic act" of God's formation of the human being from earth in the beginning. From this point, "Irenaeus envisaged the entire history of salvation in one glimpse" ("Frühchristliche Theologie in der Herausforderung durch die antike Welt," *ZKT* 109 [1987]: 397).

creation, but of re-creation. To be sure, Irenaeus interprets Genesis 2.7 literally, as evidenced by his refusal to downplay created human bodiliness in marked contrast to his opponents' interpretations.[26] Yet insofar as he reads Genesis 2.7 with reference to God's re-creation in Jesus Christ and to resurrection,[27] Irenaeus clearly reads this text typologically as well. Paul, with his typological readings of Genesis texts in 1 Corinthians 15 and Romans 5, may have given Irenaeus an interpretative key. But Irenaeus exploits this finding in his own unique way. An expansive reading of Genesis 2.7 could uncover critical deficiencies and hidden incongruities in certain doctrines of God and humanity seeking legitimization as Christian teaching. Moreover, looking at Scripture through the lens of Genesis 2.7 could reveal – in sharpened outline – the pattern of God's continuous, cohesive actions toward humanity.

THE *DONATIO INCORRUPTIBILITATIS* IN GENESIS 1-2 AND JOHN 1

Before moving on to Irenaeus' three-part use of Genesis 2.7 to describe God and God's activity (*Haer.* v.3-16), one additional feature of his introductory "roadmap" statement in *Haer.* v.1.3 deserves a bit more elaboration. In Genesis 2.7 (and in Paul's reflection in 1 Corinthians 15), Irenaeus discovers the divine purpose of the continuous labor of the two hands of God to be *human vivification*. Just as there is only one God, so also there is one divine design. Just as the divine hands imagery bespeaks the continuity of divine presence, so it also confirms the continuity of the divine intention that is discerned wherever these hands are present.

In *Haer.* v.1, Irenaeus had referred to a *donatio incorruptibilitatis* possessed by the Creator and being "given" (*donare*) to humanity.[28] Such a gift would, of course, be a tremendously important feature of Irenaeus' construal of humanity. Precisely what this gift is and how it is given are matters to which Irenaeus will attend in his ensuing discussion. Not unexpectedly, the most controversial and complex question concerns the physical human body. How could the body, so obviously prone to corruption and destined for death, possibly be envisioned – or even termed, in any honest sense – as alive? As his ongoing critique of Gnostic teaching shows, Irenaeus cannot reconcile himself to a doctrine that would relegate a component of created humanity to a place outside the scope of the Creator's good intention and unfettered power. Seen together, Genesis 2.7 and 1.26 illumine for him not only the human condition, but also the target

---

[26] Cf., in *Haer.*v.1.3, the terms *plasmati* and *antiquae substantiae plasmationis* in light of the Valentinian interpretation of 1 Corinthians 15.
[27] E.g., *vivificemur* in *Haer.* v.1.3 (*SC* 153 [26.83]).
[28] *Haer.* v.1.1 (*SC* 153 [18.13; 20.39]). The verb *donante* is a present active participle.

toward which the activity of God's hands is directed. Irenaeus identifies this purpose of the divine economy, now visible in the advent of Jesus Christ, in the sentence immediately following the line (discussed above) that asserts continuity in this economy:

> Non enim effugit aliquando Adam manus Dei, ad quas Pater loquens dicit: Faciamus hominem ad imaginem et similitudinem nostram. Et propter hoc in fine non ex voluntate carnis neque ex voluntate viri sed ex placito Patris manus ejus <u>vivum</u> perfecerunt[29] <u>hominem</u>, uti fiat Adam secundum imaginem et similitudinem Dei.[30]

Irenaeus' allusion to John 1.13 suggests that he finds the Johannine prologue to be just as fundamental as do his Gnostic-Christian opponents. The Valentinians, employing an esoteric (and starkly literal) hermeneutic when reading John 1, had discerned a theogonic schemata. Terms such as Ἀρχή, Λόγος, Ζωή, Ἄνθρωπος, Θέλημα, Χάρις, Ἀλήθεια, and Χριστός actually named the multiplicity of divine powers that constitute Pleroma.[31] Irenaeus, on the other hand, finds the opening section of John's gospel to be extremely useful for the opposite reason. The Johannine verses he most frequently cites (1.3, 13, 14)[32] underscore his insistence that God's activity be viewed as a continuous whole. The same Word through whom "all things came into being" is the Word who "became flesh." There is no disjunction between the Creator God and the Father of Jesus Christ.[33] When in *Haer.* v.1.3 Irenaeus speaks of Christ, he surmises that Genesis 2.7 (and Genesis 1.26) must be allowed to inform John 1.1-14 (and vice versa). Naturally, the divine Word in whom life resides (John 1.4) is one of God's hands that has "brought to completion" (*perfecere*) not just man *qua* man but a "living man." Insofar as the man is made a *vivum hominem* (cf. ψυχὴν ζῶσαν in Genesis 2.7), he is made after God's image and likeness. By reading Old Testament Scripture together with the gospels and apostolic writings, Irenaeus recognizes that human vivification is the unswerving aim of the divine economy. Indeed, the section that follows (chapters 3-16) can be

---

[29] One might have expected *plasmare* rather than *perfecere*, yet the link to Genesis 2.7 is evident in the reference to *vivum hominem*.

[30] See the translation offered earlier in this chapter.

[31] Cf. especially *Haer.* i.11-13: Ἀρχή (denoted by "others": i.11.5; cf. John 1.1, 2); Λόγος (i.11.1; cf. John 1.1); Ζωη (i.11.1; cf. John 1.4); Ἄνθρωπος (i.11.1; cf. John 1.6); Θέλημα (cp. Θέλητός: i.11.1; cf. John 1.13); Χάρις (denoted by Marcus: i.13.2-3; cf. John 1.14); Ἀλήθεια (i.11.1; cf. John 1.14); Χριστός (1.11.1; cf. John 1.17). Earlier in *Haer.* i.8.5, Irenaeus had recounted in some detail the Ptolemaean interpretation of the Johannine prologue which purported to illumine the production of these Aeons.

[32] six, four, and six times, respectively

[33] Interestingly, when Irenaeus quotes from John 1.13, he substitutes "Father" for "God." Whether modifying the text he knew or not, this identification is made explicit.

reckoned to be an extended discussion of how humanity can properly be said to be "living," given Genesis 2.7.[34] For example, when he challenges Valentinian interpretations of 1 Corinthians 15.50, Irenaeus not only acknowledges but intensifies the apostle's engagement with the Genesis 2.7 "living soul" statement. However, Irenaeus in *Haer.* v.1.3 has again specified that he relates Genesis 2.7 to New Testament materials typologically. He claims that "in the last times, not by the will of the flesh, nor by the will of man, but by the good pleasure of the Father, his hands brought to completion (*perfecere*) a living man, in order that Adam might be created after the image and likeness of God." Here Irenaeus appropriates most of the text of John 1.13. However, instead of following John where the children "being born" of God are the subjects of the verse (note that the pronoun referent for verse 13 must be supplied from verse 12, τέκνα), Irenaeus' subjects are the Father's hands that fashion the "living man." However, there is a further emendation. Irenaeus' reading of John 1.13 follows the western tradition[35] wherein the verb "born" is singular in tense (ἐγεννήθη) rather than plural (ἐγεννήθησαν) as is the case in all the Greek manuscripts.[36] Yet one must still look backwards to verse 12 to find the pronoun referent. Since it is singular, it could not then be τέκνα but must be the third person masculine pronoun in that verse, αὐτος. This pronoun's referent, of course, is the λόγος from John 1.1. This means that when Irenaeus speaks of God's bringing to completion the *vivum hominem*, the object is not Adam (or humanity) but Christ. A catholic-Christian reading of Genesis 2.7, insofar as it is *typological*, informs a Christian understanding of Christ. Yet even if Irenaeus interpreted John 1.13 to identify Christ as the "living man" that God renders, the purpose clause which follows (introduced by *uti*) denotes the goal of God's economic activity: "in order that Adam might be created after the image and likeness of God" (v.1.3). According to Irenaeus, Genesis 2.7 and 1.26 are both read typologically and each verse informs the interpretation of the other.

Previewing Irenaeus' anthropological debate

Given Irenaeus' choice of Genesis 2.7 imagery to introduce his forthcoming readings of Scripture, we may anticipate why his hermeneutical method will

---

[34] While "spirit" is a crucial theme in this section, "life" receives even more emphasis (cf. *Haer.* v.12.6; 15.3). Regarding *Haer.* v.6.1 and v.16.2, Behr is warranted in critiquing J. Fantino's suggestion that it was the spirit, rather than life, that Adam lost (Behr, *Asceticism and Anthropology*, 115; cf. Fantino, *L'Homme, image de Dieu chez saint Irénée de Lyon* [Paris: Cerf, 1984], 117-18).

[35] Cf. the manuscript D*. The later manuscript D (corrected) attests the plural.

[36] On this textual variant, see Bruce Metzger, *A Textual Commentary on the Greek New Testament* (London: United Bible Societies, 1971), 196-97.

eventually yield an anthropology that looks nothing like the one offered by the Valentinians. Simply put, Irenaeus' principal claim is this: Genesis 2.7 declares that to be fully human means to be fully alive. The eschatological destiny toward which we are drawn is that of the *homo vivens*. Yet Genesis 2.7 must do more than offer a bold vision of humankind, for even Irenaeus' opponents found an anthropological scheme of their own in Genesis 2.7, situated as it was in the context of Genesis 1-3. How should one adjudicate between two interpretations of Genesis that sustain diametrically opposing views of the body? For Irenaeus, Genesis 2.7 underscores that God's care for the one human race involves his commitment to the physical body that he had formed from the dust. A human being is not complete until the body, as well as the soul, is enabled to participate in the divine life. According to the Valentinian reading, the Genesis creation accounts depict three human species. Genesis 2.7 describes the ψυχικοί and Genesis 3.21 explains the origin of human bodiliness.[37] But while Necessity must be temporarily accommodated, the body is not finally essential to humanity. For the fortunate human species that can anticipate a destiny with the Father, the body has no intrinsic worth. We therefore see that not even an acknowledgement of Genesis 2.7's value as a window into divine activity *per se* is a hermeneutically-sufficient basis for discriminating between two readings. Where Irenaeus recognized in Genesis 2.7 the characteristic work of God's two hands bringing about the *homo vivens*, Gnostic-Christian readers saw quite a different operation. The crucial difference between Irenaeus and his opponents, then, must be *theological*. When proposing an alternative Christian anthropology in *Adversus Haereses* book five, Irenaeus' demonstrates that it is not what Genesis 2.7 is seen to reveal about humanity, but rather about *God* that is decisive. Thus the distinguishing hallmark of Irenaeus' hermeneutic of Scripture in *Haer.* v.1-16 is to argue for the indispensable, though indirect contribution of Genesis 2.7 to a Christian view of humanity. Only when at first God is properly understood as a triunity – and God's activities framed accordingly – will humankind then be properly understood. Valentinian anthropology was deemed deficient not because Genesis 2.7 was ignored, but because it was not interpreted by means of a christological hermeneutic. The revelation of Christ, as mediated through apostolic writings, constitutes the authoritative standpoint from which to speak of God, God's activities, and humanity. As we shall see, Genesis 2.7 could then be seen to supply unique theological and anthropological insight not found elsewhere in Scripture. These two images, "formed from dust" and "breath of life" held extraordinary meaning for Christian anthropology precisely because they are situated within a catholic-Christian doctrine of God.

---

[37] *Haer.* i.5.5.

The following summary of such revelatory claims serves to outline our current chapter: Genesis 2.7 enables Irenaeus to speak of the Christian God as a triunity. From beginning to end, the Father and his two hands, Son and Spirit, have been present and engaged with humanity in order to bring about the *homo vivens*. *First*, as testified by both his creation and resurrection of humanity, the Father's intention to fashion the *homo vivens* is never limited by lack of power or commitment. *Second*, even the molded physical body is neither superfluous nor inherently ruinous but is integral to humanity. As such it is the object of God's attention. In the progression of God's oikonomia, the Spirit works to overcome all limitations and hindrances (including sin and death), so as to make the flesh fruitful and capable of participating in divine life.[38] The "life-giving Spirit" brings the breath of life to its fullest extension. *Third*, the Son who originally formed humanity became human in order to recapitulate the wounded human frame and reveal the identity of God. At home in the capable, skilful hands from which Adam has "never escaped," humanity will be made *living*, according to plan.

The Father and the *Homo Vivens* (*Haer*. v.3-8)

The first of the three divine standpoints from which Irenaeus views God's oikonomia is, appropriately, that of the Father. According to Irenaeus' reading, *Genesis 2.7 identifies the Father as the one whose power and purpose guarantee the vivification of the body, from human origination to completion.*

In the introductory statement of *Haer*. v.1.3 that we have scrutinized above, Irenaeus claimed that when the Word and Spirit became "united with the ancient substance of Adam's formation," the result is that "man is rendered living and perfect, [capable of] receiving the perfect Father." Thus it is the Father who is humankind's ultimate destination. Christ "graciously poured himself out so that he might gather us into the bosom (*sinus*) of the Father" (v.2.1).[39] It is also the Father who is the originator of the plan to make living human beings, for it is according to the *praescientia Patris* that humanity has even "come into being"

---

[38] On the centrality of the salvation of the flesh in Irenaeus' depiction of the divine economy, see, amongst others, Godehard Joppich's *Salus Carnis*, especially part two (beginning with page 79). Joppich also devotes attention, as will we, to the respective activities of Son and Spirit in the vivification of the human body. However, unlike Joppich's general assessment of this topic throughout Irenaeus' writings, our study focuses on a single unit of material, *Haer*. v.1-16 and moreover is concerned with Irenaeus' multifaceted appropriation of a single text, Genesis 2.7, in constructing an argument.

[39] On the Father as destiny, cf. *Haer*. v.14.3; 16.2.

(v.1.1).⁴⁰ On first glance, Irenaeus' doctrine may seem to correlate rather neatly with the *exitus* and *reditus* movement of Middle-Platonist metaphysics. Yet when he uses Genesis 2.7 to ascribe content and attributes to this divine "Father," the resulting mosaic looks rather different than the image arranged by the Valentinians. Irenaeus is well aware that any interpretation of the activities of God's two hands depends upon a given vision of the supreme Father. Indeed, as would be expected, each divine hand is defined not in relation to the other hand (or to anything else) but chiefly in relation to the Father.⁴¹ So Irenaeus' first intention, as seen in *Haer.* v.3-8, is to challenge Valentinian theology precisely as related to its depiction of this supreme being.⁴² Foundational to this task assumed by Irenaeus is a redefinition of the sense in which God, as Father, is said to be *powerful* in relation to humanity. It is in Genesis 2.7 that Irenaeus finds a strikingly clear revelation of the divine Father. Unfettered power must be ascribed to this Father because he is the one who creates and (eventually) resurrects the human body. As we progress through his argument in *Haer.* v.3-8, we will see that Irenaeus' literal reading of Genesis 2.7 allows him to recognize the Father's power in creating the physical human body. Irenaeus' typological reading of this verse elicits his affirmation of the Father's power to orient this physical body toward resurrection. In other words, given Irenaeus' Christian reading of Genesis 2.7, bodily resurrection is not merely a possible extrapolation from the text (in the manner of Paul's reading) but is actually affirmed by the text itself by virtue of the typology it represents. The contrast between Irenaeus and his opponents on this point could scarcely be greater. For the Gnostics whose teachings Irenaeus addresses, corporeality is a problem. The Demiurge's formation of human physical bodies reveals not a god of unchallenged power, but a god who is either feeble (cf. Ophites), or beholden to Necessity (cf. Valentinians).

Gnostic visions of creator in Genesis 2.7

As previously suggested, the Ophites read in Genesis 2.7 a gigantic blunder on the part of the creator god. By bestowing his breath of life (*virtus*) upon the man, he had fallen for Sophia's trap and had been "secretly emptied of his power" (i.30.6). Despite Moses' attempts to conceal it, Genesis 2.7 testifies to the creator's ignorance and impotence. The "dense, sluggish"⁴³ physical bodies

---

⁴⁰ *SC* 153 (18.16); cf. 1 Peter 1.2. On the Father as origin, cf. *Haer.* v.1.3; v.2.3.
⁴¹ Cf. *Haer.* v.1.1 (the Spirit is the "spirit of the Father" [cf. v.6.2; 9.2; 9.3; 9.4]); v.1.3 (the Son is the "son of the Most High God, the Father of all"); v.6.1 ("For by the hands of the Father, that is, by the Son and the Holy Spirit…").
⁴² The term "Father" is especially concentrated in *Haer.* v.1-8, occurring thirty times.
⁴³ *pinguius et pigrius* (*Haer.* i.30.9; *SC* 264 [374.151]).

with which the human creatures were cursed certainly were not part of an original intention, but rather were the by-products of Ialdabaoth's vengeance. After his purposes went awry, he cast the humans down to the "lower world" where they would languish in encasements of flesh. (cf. i.30.9). Only through a bit of hasty redaction work by Moses does the creator of Genesis 2.7 maintain some semblance of being powerful and intentional as far as human bodies are concerned.

Valentinian readings of Genesis 2.7, according to Irenaeus, discerned a circumscribed creator god simply giving what he was able to give.[44] He breathed into the man "the soulish part of his nature" (i.5.5). Yet, being a deity of psychic substance, the Demiurge was "incapable of recognizing any spiritual essences" (i.5.4), particularly the spiritual seed sown by Achamoth. The human fleshly bodies were almost an afterthought. The Demiurge had already created the "earthy man"[45] from an "invisible substance" which was emphatically "not... this dry earth" (i.5.5).[46] Then the breath of life had been given, that is, the substance associated with the divine image and likeness. Only afterwards does the Demiurge finally envelop the human being with "outward sensitive flesh" (i.5.5). Presumably, this last stage was not a showcase of the creator's might, but a concession to Necessity. During its temporary sojourn in the lower world, the invisible soul requires the sensitive flesh for self-training and education. Accordingly, for the Valentinians, Genesis 2.7 might provide indispensable insight into human beginnings, but it is a testament not to the creator's power but to his ignorance.[47] Only psychic substance can be reconciled with this deity in the end: "psychic souls of necessity rest forever with the Demiurge in the intermediate place" (i.7.5). The Valentinian Savior "came to the psychic substance... that he might secure for it salvation" (i.6.1). He did not come to save the material body, which is doomed to destruction. The Demiurge is incapable of unseating Necessity.

Irenaeus' vision of "Father" in Genesis 2.7

Irenaeus begins his main argument in book five by vehemently opposing implications about deity and humanity that his opponents drew from Genesis 2.7. Admittedly, human bodies enlivened by the Creator die. Yet, facile inferences about the characteristics of Creator and humanity on this basis alone may be downright erroneous, if made without the constitutive Genesis text

---

[44] Cf. our discussion in chapter two.
[45] ἄνθρωπον τὸν χοϊκόν.
[46] Cf. *Haer.* v.15.4: "a fluid and diffused substance."
[47] Of the Demiurge it was said καὶ ἄνθρωπον πεπλακέναι ἀγνοοῦντα τὸν Ἄνθρωπον (i.5.3).

(read, of course, through the lens of the rule of faith). Irenaeus suggests, "May it not be... that on this account God permitted our dissolution into the earth, so that we, being instructed (παιδεύειν) in every way (παντοίως), might be accurate (ἀκριβεῖς) in [our knowledge of] all things to come (ἐν πᾶσιν εἰς τὸ μέλλον), being ignorant (ἀγνοεῖν) neither of God nor of ourselves?"(v.2.3). Irenaeus' chief claim in chapters 3-8 is that a Christian reading of Genesis 2.7 ought to decisively banish our ignorance of God in one important respect. We ought no longer to doubt that God is *powerful*. This Father and Creator is not contained, nor can he be in any way hindered through lack of might. A selection from chapter three illustrates how Irenaeus uses Genesis 2.7 in this section to make this declaration:

> Those men, therefore, refute the power of God, and do not consider what is true when they dwell upon the infirmity of the flesh, but do not take into consideration the power (virtus) of him who raises it up from the dead. For if he does not make alive what is mortal... he is not a God of power. But that he is powerful in all these respects, we ought to perceive from our origin (ἐκ τῆς ἀρχῆς ἡμῶν συννοεῖν ὀφείλομεν), inasmuch as God, taking dust from the earth, formed man... (v.3.2).[48]

Projecting backwards and forwards, Irenaeus argues that God's power is unassailable given his involvement in the origin and eschatological destinies of our human bodies. A catholic-Christian reading of Genesis 2.7 discerns the interpenetration of creation and redemption. It is worth mentioning that we may distinguish Irenaeus' *theological* (or patrological) use of Genesis 2.7 here from his subsequent *pneumatological* and *christological* uses that we will investigate in parts two and three of our present chapter. When Irenaeus talks about resurrection here, he does not readily exploit the link between Christ's resurrection and the general resurrection, as did Paul (whose use may be termed christological). Instead, the theme of God raising the dead is relatively discrete from any christological or pneumatological elements. The Father's role in the divine economy *can* be identified.[49] This point, how the Father's power is to be defined and characterized, is particularly relevant for Irenaeus as he sets his theology in contrast to those of Gnostic teachers. Surely, continues Irenaeus in *Haer.* v.3.2, that σάρξ "shall also be found capable of receiving (δεκτικός) and containing (χωρητικός) the power (δύναμις) of God, which at the beginning received the skilful touches (τέχνη) of God." Ultimately, the Gnostic claim that human flesh is not fit to partake of life (cf. v.3.3) is less a judgment about

---

[48] *SC* 153 (45.33-34); emphasis is added.
[49] Cf. *Haer.* v.16.1.

human flesh and more a judgment about the Maker of that flesh. The necessary corrective, then, is a *theological* one.

Beginning in *Haer.* v.4.1, Irenaeus more explicitly focuses his discussion on this central issue of contention: What kind of supreme deity and creator does the Scripture and the apostolic tradition avow? Is he weak? Is he "envious" or anything less than "truly good"? Is he a "slave to necessity"?[50] Over and over, Irenaeus returns to the language of Genesis 2.7 in order to refute elements implicit in Gnostic theologies that he finds unpalatable. When concerns are raised over the capacity and destiny of the human as a created being, it is the power and purpose of the Creator that are to be reckoned as determinative. Stating the obvious (which he thinks his opponents have overlooked), Irenaeus notes: "For God is not subject to created things, but created things to God; and all things yield obedience to his will" (v.4.2).[51] The theological claims of Genesis 2.7 are deemed to constitute more decisive evidence, as it were, than the present human experience of temporal corruption and death:

> And therefore, since God has power to *infuse* life into what he has fashioned (ζωοποιεῖν τὸ πλάσμα), and since the flesh is capable of being *made alive* (τῆς σαρκὸς δυναμένης ζωοποιεῖσθαι), what remains to prevent its participating in incorruption, which is a long and never-ending life granted by God? (v.3.3).[52]

God's power in humanity is seen in the original giving of life and in its restoration. From Irenaeus' perspective, resurrection is just as much an accepted reality as is the first inbreathing of life. Indeed, Genesis 2.7 illumines resurrection's aim and place in the broader divine oikonomia. Since Genesis 2.7 avows that it was "by the hands of the Father, that is, by the Son and the Holy Spirit, [that] man [including the flesh], and not part of man, was made in the likeness of God,"[53] then human salvation, in effect, is defined as the power of God acting to unify the human constitution (cf. v.6.1). This unification requires the correlate "raising" of the flesh from death to life. In this section (as elsewhere), the label *substantia carnis* is interchangeable with the term *plasma* (v.6.1).[54] Drawing from the verb in Genesis 2.7a, Irenaeus frequently uses

---

[50] See the discussion in *Haer.* v.4.1-2.
[51] This confirms that for Irenaeus (unlike his opponents), the most important ontological distinction was defined in terms of *creation*: the uncreated and the created.
[52] *SC* 153 (55.84-85); emphasis is added.
[53] *Haer.* v.6.1.
[54] Of the fourteen times in which πλάσις / πλάσμα (*plasmatio*) is used with an active meaning (i.e., referring to God's activity), eight are in *Adversus Haereses* book five. There are seventy-five occasions where the terms carry a passive meaning (referring to the object that is formed). In analyzing Irenaeus' uses of these terms, Godehard Joppich

plasma to invoke richer theological connotations, for *plasma* speaks qualitatively not only of the object, but also of the subject (the Artificer) and of the quality of the action that produced the object. For humanity, the "reintegration and union of the *three*" – that is the in-breathed soul, the handcrafted body, and the divine Spirit – is plainly associated with the "*one* and the same salvation."[55] Commenting on 1 Thessalonians 5.23,[56] Irenaeus states: "But when this Spirit, mixed with the soul, is united (*unitur*) to handiwork (*plasmati*) on the basis of the effusion of the Spirit, man is made (*factus est*) spiritual and perfect, that is, made after the image and likeness of God" (v.6.1).[57] "Per-fection" and re-vivification, then, are simply the ongoing works of the Father's hands that made (*facere*) and vivified humanity in the first place. These are the hands from which "Adam" has never escaped – hands that are both powerful and purposeful.[58]

Irenaeus finds ample support for his hope-filled view of the human body by bringing Genesis 2.7 into conversation with apostolic writings. For example, *Unde et templum Dei plasma esse ait...* (v.6.2).[59] Shortly thereafter, he remarks that "... our bodies are raised (*suscitare*) not by reason of their own substance, but on account of the power (*virtus*) of God" (v.6.2). The God (i.e., the Father) who "raised the Lord will also raise us by his power."[60] Contrary to Valentinian belief, it is not the incorporeal soul that is raised, but "the mortal body... the

---

finds that although many contexts may suggest rather generic translations such as "individual" or "human being," the passive uses of *plasmatio* are "restricted" in *Adversus Haereses* book five to the specific meanings of "body" or "flesh," "almost without exception" (*Salus Carnis*, 31).

[55] *Haer.* v.6.1; *SC* 153 (78.46-50); emphasis is added.

[56] "May the God of peace himself sanctify you entirely; and may your spirit and soul and body be kept sound and blameless at the coming of our Lord Jesus Christ."

[57] This translation based on the *SC* text is preferable to the *ANF* translation. From a Valentinian standpoint, such a "mixture" is not the necessary condition for human perfection. For them, the human soul (of which Genesis 2.7 speaks) was not created by God *ex nihilo* but (being divine substance) was "living" by its very nature. H. Lassiat declares, "L'identification entre l'âme et son souffle de vie est la confusion gnostique par excellence, c'est à cette identification que l'on reconnaît si telle pensée est gnostique ou biblique" ("L'Anthropologie d' Irénée," *NRTh* 100 [1978], 405). If, however, the soul is "other" than God (as Irenaeus insists), then "en tant que nature, l'âme est essentiellement «capacité», puisqu'elle a été créée par Dieu pour «recevoir» l'existence et la vie" (404).

[58] For Irenaeus, Genesis 1.26 plainly declares the pleasure (cf. *placere*) and will (*voluntas*) of the Father as making humanity after his image and likeness (cf. *Haer.* v.1.3 and v.8.1).

[59] "Whence also [Paul] says that the handiwork is the 'temple of God'" (*SC* 153 [80.57]; cf. 1 Corinthians 3.16).

[60] 1 Corinthians 6:14: ὁ δὲ θεὸς καὶ τὸν κύριον ἤγειρεν καὶ ἡμᾶς ἐξεγερεῖ διὰ τῆς δυνάμεως αὐτοῦ.

thing that was molded... [which] God will vivify" by his power (v.7.1).⁶¹ Christian Scripture verifies that God's resurrection of the human body, inaugurated in Jesus, does not mark a radical discontinuity in the Father's dealings with humanity (the work of his hands), but authentically expresses the Father's will. Irenaeus points to the narratives of Enoch, Elijah, Jonah, and the three Hebrew men in the fiery furnace as affirming God's power to preserve *physical* life, according to his will. Significantly, he uses Genesis 2.7 motifs and "hands of God" language to speak not only of Adam, but also of Enoch and Elijah. Elijah, notes Irenaeus, was "taken up" when he was still ἐν τῃ τοῦ πλάσματος ὑποστάσει.⁶² Therefore,

> ... by means of the very same hands through which they were formed (ἐπλάσθησαν) at the beginning, they received this assumption and translation. For in Adam, the hands of God had become accustomed to arrange (ῥυθμίζειν⁶³), to possess (κρατεῖν), and to carry (βαστάζειν) his own workmanship (τὸ ἴδιον πλάσμα)....⁶⁴

Where these hands are present, whether in forming, sustaining, or resurrecting humanity, the Father's power is present and his purpose is manifest. As for Shadrach, Meshach, and Abednego, "the hand of God was present with them, working out marvelous things – [things] impossible by man's nature" (v.5.2). God's hand was "working to promote the will of the Father" (v.5.2).⁶⁵ Their bodies having been preserved, these men were "led forth" from the fiery furnace "by the hand of God, for the purpose of declaring his power" (v.5.2).

To summarize, Irenaeus uses Genesis 2.7 first in the section of v.1-16 primarily to make a *theological* claim directed at his opponents. That the Father is neither a "slave to necessity" nor limited in his power to accomplish his will for humanity (v.4.2) is deemed patently evident from this short verse. When supplemented with divine hands imagery, Genesis 2.7 asserts that God's actions reaching out to humanity throughout the entire course of human existence (not just at the beginning) is to be recognized as a manifestation of the Father's power enduring through time: "Never" (*non aliquando*) has Adam escaped God's hands (v.1.3). It is this divine power – in contrast to human weakness – that shows human vivification to be possible. In Genesis 2.7, it is possible to catch a glimpse of the divine economy. By his purpose and power manifest in the bodily resurrection of Jesus and outpouring of the Spirit, the Father inaugurates and secures a comprehensive human salvation.

---

⁶¹ Cf. Romans 8.11; 1 Corinthians 15.36-44.
⁶² *Haer.* v.5.1; *SC* 153 (63.9-10): "in the substance of the form[ed] [body]."
⁶³ On ῥυθμός in *Haer.* iv.38.3, cf. our chapter three above.
⁶⁴ *Haer.* v.5.1; *SC* 153 (63.12- 65.15).
⁶⁵ *SC* 153 (69.38): ὑπουργοῦσα τῷ θελήματι τοῦ Πατρός.

Given Aristotle's observation that a "well-constructed plot" has a beginning, middle and end,[66] we have seen in *Haer.* v.3-8 Irenaeus' use of Genesis 2.7 to describe the beginning and end of the divine oikonomia. Yet, as Irenaeus progresses in his argument, we find that he reads in Genesis 2.7 the *middle* of the story as well. This verse offers a revelation of the divine Spirit and Son by pointing to their economic activity in the human sphere. While not initiators, these two hands are the actors in this middle segment, bridging the gap between the origination of the Father's purpose and its realization. In our two subsequent chapter sections, we continue our sequential survey of *Haer.* v.1-16. When read through Irenaeus' hermeneutical lens, Genesis 2.7 casts illumination on the work of Spirit and Son as they actively fashion the *homo vivens*.

The Spirit and the *Homo Vivens* (*Haer.* v.9-12)

According to Irenaeus' catholic-Christian hermeneutic of Scripture, Genesis 2.7 provides crucial illumination to apostolic texts on human bodiliness, particularly 1 Corinthians 15, so as to reveal the *manner and scope* of human vivification. The Spirit of God works progressively to enable not just the soul but also the physical body to participate in the divine life.

At the beginning of chapter nine of *Adversus Haereses* book five, we may detect a thematic shift as well as the introduction of a new set of uses for the text of Genesis 2.7. In chapters 3-8, Irenaeus' primary concern has been God, rather than humanity. More precisely, Genesis 2.7 is found to inform Christian theology by its portrayal of God as Father. Irenaeus' implicit complaint is that when his opponents speak of anthropology or soteriology (here, the question of how a human may be said to be "living"), they tend to build their doctrines on either a faulty or a thin theological foundation. Yet the needful place to start is not with speculations about human composition, capacity, or strength, but with a fittingly Christian avowal of *God's* unhindered power, which ensures the success of his revealed plan (cf. v.2.3; v.3.1). Whereas "life" has been somewhat of a background issue in chapters 3-8, it is time for Irenaeus to define precisely what he means by the divine grant of life as received by the human creature. If the possibility of *homo vivens* has been established (and Irenaeus thinks it now is), this concept must be clarified. What, indeed, constitutes human living? Exactly how does divine life (cf. *virtus*) co-mingle with human substance?[67]

---

[66] Aristotle, *Poetics* (trans. Stephen Halliwell [LCL 199; Cambridge, Mass.: Harvard University Press, 1995]), 55.

[67] This is an underlying issue when Irenaeus begins to address Valentinian readings of 1 Corinthians 15 (cf. verse 35: Ἀλλὰ ἐρεῖ τις πῶς ἐγείρονται οἱ νεκροί; ποίῳ δὲ σώματι ἔρχονται;).

From a catholic-Christian standpoint, how do the key events attested in apostolic tradition – Christ's life, death, and resurrection, and the giving of the Spirit – inform a Christian understanding of God's broader plan for humanity? The immediate issue is whether it is valid (or at all meaningful) to describe human vivification in terms of bodily existence. Irenaeus is troubled, to say the least, by Valentinian interpretation of 1 Corinthians 15.50 ("Flesh and blood cannot inherit the kingdom of God"). In his response, Irenaeus offers a competing assessment of 1 Corinthians 15, and unsurprisingly, language and motifs from Genesis 2.7 feature prominently. Perhaps we might say that Irenaeus demonstrates how "Christ" compels a new hermeneutic of Genesis 2.7. Irenaeus employs Genesis 2.7 in ways that both mimic and broaden Paul's uses. In *Haer.* v.9.2, he anticipates and summarizes the way he will respond to this specific Valentinian challenge:

> For when the infirmity of the flesh is absorbed, it exhibits the Spirit as powerful; and again, when the Spirit absorbs the weakness [of the flesh], it possesses (*possedere*) the flesh as an inheritance in itself, and from both of these is formed (*factus est*) a living man (*homo vivens*) – living indeed because of the participation of the Spirit, but man because of the substance of the flesh (v.9.2).

Two initial points of orientation may be drawn from Irenaeus' statement. First, as already noted, any discussion of human composition and human living depends upon the validity of his preceding argument that God as Creator is supremely powerful. Secondly, as for the divine oikonomia, the presence of God's two hands manifests divine power, and the activity of God's hands in creating and sustaining human beings as "living" shows divine purpose. In another context, Irenaeus states this most succinctly: *[G]loria enim Dei vivens homo.*[68] The divine purpose for humanity as seen in the work of God's two hands in the one economy is the enabling of the *homo vivens* foreshadowed in Genesis 2.7. Before he considers the contribution of Christ's acts of recapitulation and revelation (chapters 13-16), Irenaeus assesses at length the Spirit's role in the divine economy of human vivification (chapters 9-12). In fact, as Irenaeus will argue from 1 Corinthians 15 and Genesis 2.7, any speech about the *homo vivens*, or of the relationship of the divine to the human requires reference to the Spirit. All discussion of the origination, potential, and limitation of human bodiliness requires recognition of the vital work of the Spirit. In the above citation from v.9.2, Irenaeus' position contrasts with that of his opponents. 1 Corinthians 15 and Genesis 2.7 insist that the terms "living" and "man" (including the physical body) can and indeed must be used conjunctively.

---

[68] *Haer.* iv.20.7.

Yet Irenaeus is not blind to the "infirmity of the flesh." The Valentinians had used 1 Corinthians 15.50 to substantiate their belief that the human body, being "flesh and blood," is not "saved" (9.1). From their perspective, the visible decay and death of the physical body is confirmation that such material is incapable of sharing in the divine life. However, in supplying a re-reading of 1 Corinthians 15 (and Genesis 2.7 standing behind it), Irenaeus defines *homo vivens* as the point of communion between human flesh and divine Spirit. Though there are hindrances to such participation, the mere physicality of a flesh and blood body is not one of them. Irenaeus claims that when the "flesh and blood" phrase of 1 Corinthians 15.50 is properly interpreted in its context, the very arrangement of human composition points to an endowed capacity to bear the divine life in accord with the order of God's oikonomia. Yet the implications of Adam's sin also must be taken into account. First, though, we turn to a more detailed look at how Irenaeus uses Genesis 2.7 to speak of human composition. His redefinition of "flesh and blood" depends upon a peculiar understanding of how body, soul, and Spirit relate.

The Spirit and human potential

In Irenaeus' estimation, the reason that the Valentinians misinterpret 1 Corinthians 15.50 is that they do not accurately discern (*conspicere*) the constitution of *perfectus homo*.[69] Both Irenaeus and his opponents propounded tripartite anthropologies. But the point of difference is where each ascribes "human" heterogeneity – whether at the corporate or individual levels. Whereas the Valentinians deemed *perfectus homo* to refer to an unadulterated "spiritual" person, Irenaeus argued that *perfectus homo* is necessarily a composite being. Insofar as the crux of the debate is a definition of human constitution, as far as divine Spirit and earthy bodies are concerned, Irenaeus quite naturally turns to the principal image found in Genesis 2.7, those famous words describing the interfacing of bestowed Spirit and formed-flesh. The first anthropological component is the divine Spirit which preserves (σῴζειν / *salvere*) and fashions (*figurare*) the flesh (*caro*); the second is the flesh that is actually preserved (*salvere*) and formed (*formare*); the third is the soul situated between the Spirit and the flesh (9.1). Since the Spirit alone is able to give life, human flesh must in some way be enabled to receive and bear the Spirit (cf. v.8.1). Irenaeus envisions this enabling, that is the flesh's assumption of the "quality of the Spirit," as the ongoing formative work of the divine hands depicted in Genesis 2.7. Yet this is not a mere "forming" but a "being made conformable to the

---

[69] *Haer.* v.9.1 (*SC* 153 [106.6-7]). This charge is ironic, given the Valentinians' preoccupation with human composition.

Word of God" (*conformis facta Verbo Dei*) (v.9.3). The end result is that the human "bears" "the image of him who is from heaven" (v.9.3).[70]

But while the divine work of the Spirit is necessary for human vivification, participation ought not to be seen to abrogate the ontological boundary between the divine and human. So while Irenaeus agrees with his opponents that human "life" is indeed spiritual in nature and origin, he finds inadmissible their notion of an intrinsically spiritual segment of humanity. The divine Spirit, and with it, life, are gifts imparted to the human substance from without. Since only the Spirit of God can properly be said to be "living," it follows that it is the Spirit who "rules and exercises power" over subjected human beings (v.9.4). Human beings ought not to presume that they have a claim on the Spirit. "Strictly speaking," then, the Spirit inherits the flesh, the flesh does not inherit the Spirit (v.9.4). In that it is the Spirit who completes and vivifies ($\zeta\omega\pi\text{οιεῖν}$) humanity,[71] Irenaeus is able to pronounce: *ubi autem Spiritus Patris, ibi homo vivens*.[72]

If God's glory and will is the *homo vivens*, that is, the unification and vivification of the human constitution including the body (cf. *Haer.* v.6-7), and if such life is communicated by the divine Spirit as an external agent rather than as a substance intrinsic to humanity, then the key issue is human *reception* of the Spirit. That such reception is not a matter of necessity is underscored by Irenaeus' discussion of human volition and action with respect to the proffered Spirit. Although the flesh can be made fit to be "transferred" ($\mu\text{εταφέρειν}$) into the kingdom of heaven (that realm of incorruptible life), transformation is not an inevitable function of necessity. Indeed, Irenaeus reads the $\delta\text{εῖ}$ in 1 Corinthians 15.53 not so much as a simple factual claim about necessary order, but as an admonition – a call to human action: "For this perishable [body] must ($\delta\text{εῖ}$) put on imperishability, and this mortal [body] must put on immortality" (v.10.2).

Building upon this assertion that, as far as reception of the Spirit is concerned, human will rather than nature is the decisive factor, Irenaeus deploys and extends Paul's olive tree graft analogy[73] to make the distinction between the flesh's substance and fruit. The olive tree, when engrafted so as to bear fruit, does not lose its substance of wood (v.10.2). Likewise, when the Spirit is received,[74] the fruit (i.e., works) of the flesh will change, but the substance of the

---

[70] 1 Corinthians 15.49.
[71] *Haer.* v.9.1; *SC* 153 (108.18; 109.19).
[72] *Haer.* v.9.3; *SC* 153 (112.44-45). Emphasis is added.
[73] Romans 11.17.
[74] Regarding human reception of the Spirit, the verb *adsumere* (to take to oneself, receive) is used frequently (*Haer.* v.10.1, 10.2, 10.2, 11.1, 12.2). The verb *accipere* is also used to describe reception of the Spirit in *Haer.* v.11.2 as well as reception of the Word in v.10.1.

flesh remains the same.[75] Thus 1 Corinthians 15.50 cannot be speaking merely of the substance of human flesh and blood in itself, but of that substance which, when estranged from the Spirit, produces *operas carnales* (v.11.1). Focusing on the term "inherit" (κληρονομεῖν), Irenaeus insists on reading 1 Corinthians 15.50 in light of 1 Corinthians 6.9.[76] Human volition and action, not human substance, are in view. One may live "in" the flesh without living "after" the flesh (cf. v.10.2). Indeed to be spiritual *is* to bear good fruits (cf. v.10.1). The apostle, says Irenaeus, describes "the spiritual actions which vivify a man, that is, the engrafting of the Spirit; thus saying, 'But the fruit of the Spirit is love...'" (v.11.1).[77] Therefore, Irenaeus interprets the Pauline phrase "living after the flesh" not as a statement disparaging human bodiliness, but as one disparaging human living apart from God, and apart from the divine life-giving Spirit. Such living in that sense is not true living. Irenaeus' more nuanced definition of the "flesh and blood" of 1 Corinthians 15.50 is a springboard toward substantiating his claim that human flesh is indeed capable of incorruption. But if Irenaeus' argument is to meet the challenge of his opponents, he must explain why this flesh, which he says is capable of bearing the divine life, clearly manifests the opposite – death and decay. If the problem is not solely a matter of the substance of the flesh, but rather its fruits, Irenaeus nonetheless recognizes that he must acknowledge and explain the *limitations* in the substance of the flesh that are undeniably real. For this task, Irenaeus relies upon Paul's use of Genesis 2.7 in the 1 Corinthians 15 passage, but he extends it significantly.

The Triumph of the Spirit

If Irenaeus' line of reasoning through chapter 11 envisages how the human frame was made capable of vivification, his pivotal text in v.12.1-3 reminds the reader of hindrances to its achievement. The *first limitation* of the substance of human bodiliness (the *plasma*) is seen as a matter of straightforward logic. The operative "fruits" of the flesh are mutually exclusive, so if the fruit of death is present, the fruit of life cannot at the same time be possessed.[78] However, the converse is true as well. If by some manner of events the human frame were to gain a state of perpetual life, obviously death would be robbed of the access it had heretofore enjoyed. Sounding much like Paul, Irenaeus remarks that if death's presence drove away life, "how much more will life, having gained

---

[75] Irenaeus uses Edenic language: the person receiving the Spirit "becomes a fruit-bearing olive, planted, as it were in a παράδεισον βασιλέως" (*Haer.* v.10.1). The phrase παράδεισον Θεοῦ is also used twice in this paragraph).
[76] "Do you not know that wrongdoers will not inherit the kingdom of God?"
[77] Cf. Galatians 5.22.
[78] *Haer.* v.12.1.

mastery of man, drive away death and re-present (ἀποκαταστήσει/ *restituet*) man living to God."⁷⁹ It is intriguing that Irenaeus then retrieves Isaiah 25.8 (LXX) to substantiate this point before employing Genesis 2.7:

> For if death brings mortality, why should not life, when it comes, vivify man? Just as Esaias the prophet says, "Death swallowed⁸⁰ [humanity] when it had prevailed, but on the other hand,⁸¹ God has wiped away every tear from every face." Thus that former life was expelled, because it was not given by the Spirit, but by the breath (*Expulsa est autem pristina vita, quoniam non per Spiritum sed per afflatum fuerat data*).⁸²

It is reasonable to ask why, in his discussion of life and death, Irenaeus takes an interest in Isaiah 25.8. Apparently, Paul draws attention to this text when he appropriates a piece of it (though following the Hebrew tradition reading) in 1 Corinthians 15.54 to speak of death being "swallowed up in victory." Irenaeus, however, uses the LXX text whose first clause makes a claim that is precisely opposite to that found in the Hebrew tradition text used by Paul. In the LXX rendering, death is the subject that "swallows." The second clause of the verse proclaims God's victory. Possibly, insofar as this text associates death with "prevail" (ἰσχύσας), it fits Irenaeus' concern to show that death and life are mutually exclusive entities (of sorts) in a given person. In the LXX (unlike the Hebrew tradition), these two clauses speak of a dramatic *contrast* between death's prevailing over humanity and God's sweeping act of restoration and salvation. To Irenaeus, Isaiah 25.8 illustrates this tension of contrasts, and thus introduces his explanation for how a body that is intentionally made capable of life (as he has argued) in fact manifests the very opposite.

Although human fallenness, the consequence of sin, is a limitation that Irenaeus will shortly comment upon, the *second limitation* to the *homo vivens*

---

⁷⁹ The Armenian text reads the equivalent of καταστήσει, thus without the connotation of repetition or reversal suggested by the prefix ἀπο. While this prefix has other possible meanings, the sense of "back again" (cf. ἀποδίδωμι) is supported by the Latin *restitere* (et passim). This issue relates to the question of Adam's original state, as compared to his condition when vivified by the Spirit (cf. *Haer.* v.12.3). Also, we note the temporal sequence seen in the verb tense shift from perfect / Aorist to future in the verbs *expulit* to *expellet* (ἐξέωσεν to the conjectured ἀπώσεται). On the contrast of life and death, Irenaeus may be influenced by Romans 6.11.
⁸⁰ καταπίνειν
⁸¹ Since Isaiah 25.8 contains καὶ πάλιν at just this place, we disagree with the *ANF* translation which places it outside the quotation. Rather than "and again," it serves within the verse to indicate contrast and suggest sequence, i.e., "but on the other hand..." (cf. *L&N*, 89.129 [πάλιν]).
⁸² *Haer.* v.12.1; *SC* 153 (142.13-14).

that he discerns is even more basic. It involves – or, possibly, implicates – the very order and arrangement of God's oikonomia itself. "That former life," reasons Irenaeus, "is expelled, because it was not given by the Spirit but by the breath" (v.12.1). In asserting that God intends and enacts a particular sequence for bringing humanity to fruition, Irenaeus depends on Paul's interpretative claim based on Genesis 2.7:

ἀλλ' οὐ πρῶτον τὸ πνευματικὸν ἀλλὰ τὸ ψυχικόν,
ἔπειτα τὸ πνευματικόν.[83]

The Valentinians may have been right to note the contrasts between the "spiritual" and the "physical" (or natural), and the parallel contrast between life and death (as attested in Isaiah 25.8). But in Irenaeus' estimation, not only are his opponents guilty of oversimplification by assuming that these two pairs of contrasts overlay directly, they also, indeed, *reverse* the divine order of the former. In fact, the spiritual comes after the physical (1 Corinthians 15.46). Paul's basis for making this claim was Genesis 2.7: "Thus it is written, 'The first man, Adam, became a living soul'; the last Adam became a life-giving spirit."[84] In recognizing the apostle's theological use of Genesis 2.7, Irenaeus then extends it further: "For the breath of life, which also rendered man an animated being, is one thing, and the vivifying Spirit another, which also caused him to become spiritual."[85] While the same Spirit is that hand of God who mediates both "breath" and his very self, Irenaeus is keen to emphasize (by the repetition of ἕτερον) a differentiation within the one, continuous divine economy. Though there is an overarching unity in terms of divine actor, intention, and power, there are different stages in the temporal sequence of the divine activity.[86] Genesis 2.7

---

[83] 1 Corinthians 15.46. In an influential monograph published in 1882, H. H. Wendt (whom Harnack had partly credited with the hypothesis of two distinct views of salvation in *Adversus Haereses*) claims that Irenaeus' uses of Genesis 2.7 and 1.26 in *Haer.* v.12.2 and v.6.1 (respectively) connect with Irenaeus' vision of human progression from infancy to perfection (*Haer.* iv.38). The distinctions between πνοή and πνεῦμα and between *Gottebenbildlichkeit* and *Gottähnlichkeit* correlate with the differences between these two human states (*Die christliche Lehre von des menschlichen Vollkommenheit* [Göttingen: Vandenhoeck & Ruprecht, 1882], 22).

[84] 1 Corinthians 15.45: οὕτως καὶ γέγραπται ἐγένετο ὁ πρῶτος ἄνθρωπος Ἀδὰμ εἰς ψυχὴν ζῶσαν, ὁ ἔσχατος Ἀδὰμ εἰς πνεῦμα ζωοποιοῦν.

[85] Ἕτερον ἐστι πνοὴ ζωῆς ἡ καὶ ψυχικὸν ἀπεργαζομένη τὸν ἄνθρωπον, καὶ ἕτερον Πνεῦμα ζωοποιοῦν τὸ καὶ πνευματικὸν αὐτὸν ἀποτελοῦν (*Haer.* v.12.2; SC 153 [143.14-16]). Whereas the Greek text uses two different verbs, ἀπεργάζεσθαι and ἀποτελεῖν, the Latin translates both as *efficere*. Whether these verbs were used synonymously or not, they carry a stronger connotation of "finishing" than ποιεῖν / *facere*. If the two verbs are used interchangeably, then this sentence asserts two distinct finished creations. Conversely, if ἀποτελεῖν holds a stronger nuance, then the finished work as a "spiritual" human being has a privileged status.

[86] Cf. *Haer.* iv.38 and our chapter three above.

then could be used not only to speak of continuity but of relative *discontinuity*. Following Paul's lead, Irenaeus highlights such distinctions: first and second Adam, "living soul" and "life-giving Spirit," the time of human origination and the *novissimis temporibus*,[87] and the temporality of breath and the eternity of Spirit.[88] Two additional passages from Isaiah (42.5 and 57.16) allow Irenaeus to further buttress this point. The giving of πνοή κοινῶς[89] to humanity is to be distinguished from the "outpouring" (ἐκχεῖν) of the Spirit. The former "proclaims" that humanity is created and, accordingly, "temporal" (v.12.2). The latter is "peculiar to God" (ἰδίως ἐπὶ τοῦ Θεοῦ), and accordingly eternal. By positing a reversed order in the divine economy for human development (spiritual then natural), the Valentinians in effect undermine the ontological distinction in that "what has been made is a different thing from him who makes it" (v.12.2). The underlying point is that the provisionality of human "breath" is not, in the end, attributable to the inferiority of human substance, or to some original human action or inaction. Instead, it expresses God's intention for humanity. Yet God's ultimate plan, as seen in the work of his two hands, is the progressive completion of the *homo vivens*, wherein humanity indeed "receive[s] the life-giving Spirit and find[s] [eternal] life" (v.12.2). With 1 Corinthians 15.45 in mind, Irenaeus again asserts that Genesis 2.7 informs our understanding of the basic *order* of the divine oikonomia, and therefore the role of the Spirit in human development toward the divine life:

> For it is *proper* (*oportere*) that in the first place, a human being should be fashioned (*plasmare*) and that what was fashioned should receive the soul, [and] in the same way, that afterwards (*deinde*) it should receive the communion of the Spirit.[90]

The tripartite nature of humanity refers, then, not just to three compositional elements, but to three corresponding developmental stages in the activity of God's hands to make the *homo vivens*.[91] By interpreting Genesis 2.7 within a broader Middle-Platonist narrative that begins rather than culminates with the life of the Spirit, the Valentinians (in Irenaeus' estimation) follow the erroneous

---

[87] *Haer.* v.12.2.
[88] On the contrast between the early times and the *novissimis temporibus*, and between the temporary and the eternal, perhaps Irenaeus recalls Romans 8.38-39 (cf. Irenaeus' citation of Romans 8 in v.10.2): Not even death causes the Spirit to separate from us (unlike "breath").
[89] "common breath"; cf. *Haer.* v.12.2.
[90] *Haer.* v.12.2; SC 153 (148.39-41). Emphasis is added.
[91] Cp. Paul's simple *two* part contrasts in 1 Corinthians 15 when talking about the divine order (i.e., ψυχικός / πνευματικός; χοϊκός / οὐρανός).

example of Adam.[92] Like Adam, they overreach – seeking the "spiritual" straightaway rather than waiting for God's hands to guide them through the preparatory steps of maturity.[93] Since the Valentinians misunderstand the proper order of God's economy, they also misunderstand the reason that human bodies universally decay and die. However, for Irenaeus, Genesis 2.7 enables one to speak of the order, and thus the purpose, of the activity of God's two hands. To understand the rationale of the third step, the giving of eternal vivification through the Spirit (cf. 1 Corinthians 15), one must revisit the rationale of the first two steps through a recapitulated catholic-Christian reading (of sorts). The Spirit intends to encompass and transform the molded human body and inbreathed soul. Yet any grasp of the Spirit's work is incomplete without considering a *third limitation* to the *homo vivens* that must be overcome: human fallenness.

Although the breath of life stage is meant to be transitory (its limit to be superseded when the Spirit is received), nevertheless in this early condition, humanity is particularly susceptible to death in a way that it will not be later. This crucial inference helps us to make sense of Irenaeus' depiction of the fall, wherein Adam is depicted simultaneously as both transgressor and victim. Certainly Adam is culpable for it was on account of his disobedience that he "lost" life.[94] Yet the serpent had taken advantage of Adam's then immature, vulnerable state when leading him into captivity: *Si enim qui factus fuerat a Deo homo ut uiueret, hic amittens uitam laesus a serpente qui deprauauerat eum....*"[95] Accordingly, "*odiuit Deus qui seduxit hominem, ei uero qui seductus est sensim paulatimque misertus est.*[96] Having the divine breath but not yet the Spirit himself, humanity was in a weak state when the Tempter seized the opportunity to introduce death into human flesh. Since life and death cannot be present in the same space at the same time, this unfortunate chain of obstacles blocked the realization of the *homo vivens*. Using imagery from Genesis 2.7, Irenaeus explains how death is to be displaced so that the divine life may ultimately prevail in the human body and soul. Just as Irenaeus describes human fallenness in terms of Genesis 1.26 (the "loss" of the image of God), in parallel fashion here he uses Genesis 2.7 to describe it as the "loss" of the breath of life:

---

[92] Cf. *Haer.* iv.39.2-4, et al.
[93] Denis Minns' discussion of Adam and Eve's sin is helpful in this regard (*Irenaeus*, 62-63). In addition, Irenaeus' citation of Isaiah 25.8 (in v.12.1) may show an awareness of broader context. Israel is warned against being impatient, that is, seeking an alliance with Egypt rather than waiting for God's salvation [cf. Isaiah 30; 31; 36]).
[94] Cf. *Haer.* iii.23.
[95] *Haer.* iii.23.1; *SC* 211 (444.10-12).
[96] *Haer.* iii.23.5; *SC* 211 (460.132-34).

Genesis 2.7 and the *Homo Vivens*

As, then, *he who was made a living soul utterly lost* (ἀπολλύειν / *perdere*) *life* when he turned aside to evil, so again the same individual, when he reverts to the good and receives the life-giving (ζωοποιοῦν) Spirit will find life. For it is not one thing which dies and another which is made alive, as neither is it one thing which is lost and another which is found (Οὐ γὰρ ἄλλο τὸ ἀποθνῆσκον καὶ ἄλλο το ζωοποιούμενον, ὡς οὐδε ἄλλο τὸ ἀπολωλὸς καὶ ἄλλο τὸ ἀνευρισκόμενον), but the Lord came seeking for that same sheep which had been lost. What was it, then, which was dead? Undoubtedly it was the substance (ὑπόστασις) of the flesh; the same, too, which had *lost* (ἀποβαλλειν / *amiserat*) *the breath of life*, and had become breathless and dead. This same, therefore, was what the Lord came to make alive (ζωοποιοῦν), that as in Adam we do all die, as being of a soulish nature, in Christ we may all live,[97] as being spiritual, not laying aside God's handiwork (πλάσμα) but the lusts of the flesh, and receiving the Holy Spirit.[98]

Furthermore, says Irenaeus a few sentences later, "The fruit of the work of the Spirit is the salvation (σωτηρία) of the flesh" (v.12.4).[99] Thus to his opponents, Irenaeus reiterates that what is overcome is not the substance of the flesh. Rather the same substance is made able to bear good, spiritual fruit. By recalling several of the similar terms and phrases he used in his contrast of the two olive trees (v.10.1), Irenaeus seems to invite a parallel reading wherein Adam was a "good olive tree," planted in God's paradise.[100] However, he lost life and the opportunity to grow in fruitfulness when he turned aside to evil. Thus humanity became a barren "wild olive tree." Yet now humanity has the opportunity to receive a new in-grafting of the Spirit. Those who accept it will find life and will bear spiritual fruit. The substance of the olive tree wood is not discarded, only its fruit changes. The substance of the flesh is not overcome, but rather "saved." Whereas Genesis 2.7 is used in v.12.2 to emphasize a

---

[97] Cf. 1 Corinthians 15.22.

[98] *Haer.* v.12.2-3; *SC* 153 (148.43-150.57). Emphasis is added. Cf. Tertullian, *Res.* 48.

[99] The *ANF* translation of "final result" rather than "fruit" for καρπός / *fructus* obscures the intentional way in which Irenaeus uses the term. The term fruit here ought to be interpreted in light of his use in preceding context (v.10.1) where he speaks of the olive tree bearing bad and good fruit.

[100] In the Latin (since the Greek is fragmentary), the similar phrases and terms include: *in melius recurrens* (*SC* 153 [150.45]), *profecerint in melius* [124.9]; *assumentes Spiritum sanctum* [150.56-57], *assumpserint Spiritum Dei* [124.10]; *fructus* [154.77], *fructifera* [122.8], *fructificans* [124.21], *recurrit fructificationem* [126.23-24], *fructificantes* [126.25], et al.

discontinuity between "breath" and "life-giving Spirit" (cf. ἕτερον... καὶ ἕτερον...), this same verse is used in v.12.3 to highlight the continuity of the physical body (cf. οὐ γὰρ ἄλλο... καὶ ἄλλο...). It is the object toward which the redemptive work of God's two hands is directed, from start to finish.

Christ and the *Homo Vivens* (*Haer*. v.13-16)

Our present chapter has looked at the constitutive role of Genesis 2.7 in Irenaeus' theological anthropology, as expressed in *Haer*. v.1-16. First, Genesis 2.7 establishes the Father as being the origin, destiny, and all-powerful guarantor of the *homo vivens* (*Haer*. v.3-8). Second, Genesis 2.7 informs an apostolic redefinition of humanity wherein the physical body is not opposed to but embraced by the divine Spirit (*Haer*. v.9-12). The Spirit's ongoing work endows the embodied human creature with the capacity to bear fruit and, eventually, to receive God – the one who is truly living. Finally, in *Haer*. v.13-16, Irenaeus employs Genesis 2.7 to provide a third viewpoint from which to describe the divine economy of human vivification, that of the Son. Insofar as the ministry of the Son is in some ways prerequisite of that of the Spirit, Irenaeus takes a step backward, of sorts, in the economic order. In his introduction to book five, he had declared that it is the Son who entrusts (*deponere*) God to humanity by pouring out God's Spirit; in addition, the Son introduces (*imponere*) humanity to God by means of his own incarnation (v.1.1).[101] Humanity receives the aforementioned *donatio incorruptibilitatis* as a result of the Son's work to achieve "communion" between humanity and God (cf. v.1.1). When Irenaeus later returns to describe at length the Son's pivotal and climactic work in God's economy, Genesis 2.7 again assumes an unparalleled role. It provides parameters for a "hermeneutic" of Christ, as he is read in the apostolic testimony. The exceptionally vivid motifs and powerful theological vocabulary of Genesis 2.7 and 1.26 are, for Irenaeus, perfectly suited for explaining the significance of the incarnation of the divine Word. In brief, according to Irenaeus' catholic-Christian reading, *Genesis 2.7 reveals two of the dominant features of Christ's work as recapitulation and revelation*. The incarnate Christ "sums up" embodied humanity, presenting it to God, its source and destiny. He also opens human eyes to see the identity and work of the God who is Creator. This unique Genesis text thus orients requisite Christian thought regarding

---

[101] ... *ad homines quidem deponente Deum per Spiritum, ad Deum autem rursus imponente hominem per suam incarnationem*... (*Haer*. v.1.1; *SC* 153 [20.37-39]). Noting the contrast implied by *deponere* / *imponere*, the *SC* edition retrojects terms with spatial connotations: καταγαγόντος / ἀναγαγόντος. The Son mediates downward, bringing God to humanity by means of the Spirit. The Son mediates upward, bringing humanity to God by means of his incarnation (cf. *Haer*. v.16.2).

Christ's relation to humanity and God, as well as enables one to interpret Christ's activity as advancing the Father's intention, the *homo vivens*.

Transition: From one divine hand to another

Irenaeus' ardent refutation of the Valentinians' understanding of 1 Corinthians 15.50 ("flesh and blood") continues to occupy center stage through *Haer.* v.15. However, in chapters 12 and 13 Irenaeus begins to shift his primary emphasis from speech about the Spirit's role in the divine economy to speech about the Son's. By changing "hands" (so to speak), Irenaeus brings his discussion of God's oikonomia to its climax in Christology.

As mentioned above, Irenaeus' reading of Genesis 2.7 portrays humanity as having "lost" life, and accordingly, the ability to bear fruit. Irenaeus' use of associated imagery in *Haer.* iii.16-18 is suggestive.[102] Adam's body, being mere "dust," could not "bring forth fruit unto life" (iii.17.2) without the "water" of the Spirit. When this watering was lost, human barrenness ensued. Irenaeus agrees with Paul that it is precisely in the physical body ("in these same members") that God "wish[es] us to [be obedient] unto righteousness, that we may bring forth fruit unto life" (v.14.4).[103] Describing the condition of human fallenness in the language of Genesis 1.26, Irenaeus notes that when humanity bears death in the body, it cannot rightly be "seen" to bear the image of a God who is incorruptible. According to Irenaeus, the way of salvation, that is, the way to the completion of the *homo vivens*, is therefore necessarily a way of recapitulation. Before the water of the Spirit could once more make humanity fruitful toward God, Adam's original physical formation from dust and his inbreath of life must be "capitulated" once again. Irenaeus later summarizes this thought:

> For in times long past, it was *said* that man was created after the image of God, but it was not [actually] *shown*... wherefore also he did easily lose the similitude. When, however, the Word of God became flesh, he... both *showed* (δεικνύειν) the image truly... and he *re-established* (*restituere*) the similitude after a sure manner, by assimilating man to the invisible Father through means of the visible Word. (v.16.2).

In our section ahead on Irenaeus' use of Genesis 2.7 to speak about Christ, we will highlight the two predicates that he ascribes to Christ in this statement.

---

[102] Cf. our chapter three above.
[103] *ut fructificemus vitae* (*SC* 153 [194.90]). Here, Irenaeus draws from Paul's writings – particularly Romans 6.12.

Christ shows (i.e., *revelation*) and Christ re-establishes (cf. *recapitulation*).[104] Yet, as suggested by his less-than-systematic writing style, Irenaeus knew that any survey of God's economy could not rightly view these two functions in sheer isolation. In a real sense, Christ's decisive work of recapitulation *is* the decisive revelation of the triune God. That Irenaeus was no less interested in the revelatory nature of Christ's life than were the Gnostics is seen in his remark: *agnitio enim Dei renovat hominem* (v.12.4).[105] When the "visible Word" is manifest, we see the "invisible Father"; he is the origin of the Son's image and the God whose "hand" this is. When God's hand is shown at work in these "last times"[106] healing the human frame, our eyes are also directed backward to this hand's original work in fashioning humanity – a work that was not truly illumined until Christ's advent.

In *Haer.* v.12.3-4, Irenaeus had argued the illogicality of supposing that there could be one flesh "that is lost and another which is found" (v.12.3). Surely there is only one flesh that is not discarded but rather changed during conversion. Insofar as it is Paul's writings that are under contention, Irenaeus (somewhat abruptly) recalls that the apostle's own autobiography may serve as a clear example of this point. Although Paul claims to have undergone a genuine transformation, his physical body afterward remained the same it was before his conversion. Here Irenaeus appears to read Galatians 1.15-16 symbolically as well as literally: "But when God, who had set me apart from my mother's womb and called me through his grace, was pleased...."[107] The "womb" is a symbol for ignorance – the state of a person living after the "ancient substance of flesh" (v.12.5). We may compare this "ignorance" (v.12.5) with the "ignorance" Irenaeus discussed in v.12.4. It refers to the person of mere flesh who, in "times

---

[104] When, in a different context, Colin Gunton speaks of Christ's ascension, he emphatically asserts that it "is not merely revelation, but event." That is, the ascension is not just something "shown" but something "done." It is "something which brings about a new state of affairs" (*Christ and Creation*, 65-66). Similarly, a Gnostic-Christian tendency which Irenaeus will directly challenge by means of his notion of recapitulation is the ascription of Christ's salvific role only to what he shows (i.e., revelation) rather than also to what he *does*, whether in life or in death. For example, Pheme Perkins observes: "The usual Gnostic explanation of the crucifixion is to see it as a 'type' of the cosmic situation of humanity. Either it reveals the 'passion' of the fallen Sophia, which stands at the origin of the cosmos (*Haer.* i.8.2), or it reflects the consequences for humanity, its entrapment in 'smallness,' the body [cf. *Letter of Peter to Philip*]... In short, it demonstrates the reason for Gnostic redemption but is not itself a factor in that redemption" (*The Gnostic Dialogue: The Early Church and the Crisis of Gnosticism* [New York: Paulist Press, 1980], 187).

[105] *SC* 153 (156.91-92).

[106] Cf. *Haer.* v.15.2.

[107] Cf. Irenaeus' assertion, shortly thereafter, that Lazarus' death also ought to be understood symbolically (13.1).

past," is "ignorant of God." Acts 9.8 may be in mind in that Saul's condition of blindness represents a fleshly state of ignorance, akin to enclosure in a dark womb. The opening of his eyes by Ananias is emblematic of Christ's self-revelation to Paul wherein Paul is "birthed" from the womb into the light of God's calling to ministry. It is this story of Paul's being healed of blindness that, in turn, prompts Irenaeus to reflect on how Christ's healing blind men in the gospels granted revelation of God. This link is Irenaeus' entrée into a christological discussion, where he intimates a twin focus to Christ's work as recapitulation and revelation. The same one who "from the beginning form[ed] man" is now seen to be the one who "confers healing" and "life" to "his own handiwork" (v.12.6). Christ's actions show that humanity's "flesh and blood" is the continuous recipient of God's care and attention. The blind men "received vision in the very same (*isdem ipsis*) eyes with which they formerly did not see" (v.12.5). Irenaeus uses Genesis 2.7 language to summarize his claim about Christ (and, implicitly, about the substance of the human body). The gospel writings entrusted to the church teach that Christ does not remove the flesh tainted with death but rather renews it through the ministration of healing and life.

> The Maker of all things, the Word of God, who did also from the beginning form (*plasmare*) man, when he found his handiwork (*plasma*) impaired by wickedness, performed upon it all kinds of healing… [H]ow can they maintain that the flesh is incapable of receiving the life which flows from him, when it received healing from him? For life is brought about through healing, and incorruption through life. *He, therefore, who confers healing, the same* [also confers] *life; and he* [who gives] *life also surrounds his own handiwork* (*plasmare*) *with incorruption* (v.12.6).[108]

This last sentence aptly points to the direction of Irenaeus' forthcoming thesis concerning Christ. Humanity is destined to bear the incorruptible life of God and indeed bear God himself.[109] But before God's handiwork can receive the divine Spirit, it must first be healed. In the brief transition paragraph from which this selection is taken (*Haer.* v.12.6), the term *plasmare* / *plasma* occurs five times, *vita* occurs five times, *fabricator* occurs once, and *ab* / *in initio* occurs twice. This ample fund of language and motifs from Genesis 2.7 arranged at the beginning of his christological section further signals the vital hermeneutical role that Irenaeus attributes to this text when speaking about

---

[108] *SC* 153 (160.121-162.137); emphasis is added.
[109] Cf. *Haer.* v.8.1; et al.

Christ. The lens of Genesis 2.7 invites Irenaeus' perception of Christ as *recapitulator* of humanity and *revealer* of divinity.

Using Genesis 2.7: Recapitulation (Haer. v.14)

INTRODUCTION AND OVERVIEW

In chapter 13, Irenaeus continues to press his opponents over their reading of 1 Corinthians 15.50. Building on his theological point drawn from the healing of the blind (cf. v.12.5), Irenaeus summons additional miracle narratives from the gospels to bolster his contention that it is the very same "afflicted" or dead human flesh that Jesus either healed or raised to life. In connection with this, Irenaeus makes a remarkable statement that has bearing on his upcoming discussion of Christ's recapitulation (chapter 14) where Genesis 2.7 will play such an important role. Irenaeus asserts that the persons whom Christ healed had received in their bodies health and "life which was granted by the Lord, who prefigures eternal things through temporal things (*per temporalia praeformante aeterna*) and shows (*ostendere*) that it is he who is himself able to extend both healing and life to his handiwork (*plasmati suo*)...."[110] The theme of revelation is one that we shall find recurrently. Here Irenaeus claims that Christ's earthly, temporal acts of healing "show" both his divine ability and his divine identity. Christ extends life to the human handiwork that belongs to him. In *Haer.* v.15, the Genesis 2.7 motifs of human fashioning from dust and the breath of life will be used in a more substantive way to speak of revelation: It is Christ who reveals God and who reveals the intimate relation between humanity and himself, insofar as he is its Creator. However, the phrase *per temporalia praeformante aeterna* here in v.13.1 warrants special attention. 1 Corinthians 15 (the primary text under consideration) is replete with references to order and sequence.[111] Practically from the first verse to the last of this chapter, we note its presentation of the arranged oikonomia as a series of contrasts circumscribed within one underlying unified order. It is the Valentinians' selective misreading of 1 Corinthians 15 that concerns Irenaeus. They interpret "flesh and blood" in verse 50 in a strictly literal sense. However, given their protological system, it would seem that they had understood verse 46 ("But it is not the spiritual that is first, but the physical, and then the spiritual") in a less than literal manner.[112] The Valentinians, insists Irenaeus, presume the sequence of God's economy to be the very reverse of what Scripture actually contends. If Christ is the architect

---

[110] *Haer.* v.13.1; *SC* 153 (164.20-22).
[111] Cf. 1 Corinthians 15.15-20, 21-22, 23-26 ("each in its own order..."), 39-44, 45-49 (the "physical" then the "spiritual").
[112] Interestingly, Irenaeus' reading of these two verses is precisely the opposite.

of human formation, and if Paul asserts that the "physical" precedes the "spiritual" in God's order, then is it not the case that Christ "prefigures eternal things through temporal things"? Christ's restoration of physical life to the human frame is a "pre-formation" of his restoration of eternal life to humanity. Therefore, Christ's ministry in life (not merely that in death or resurrection) constitutes his recapitulation of bodily humanity. It points to and enables the realization of the *homo vivens* in the fullest, eternal sense. Perhaps Irenaeus' zeal to counter what he believes to be erroneous doctrines of human bodiliness emerges from his belief (which he grounds in Pauline and Genesis texts) that in God's economic order for humanity, physicality is the beginning point. It must therefore be understood, appreciated, and reconciled before any talk of the extra-bodily aspects of human living. Christ brings the requisite illumination to human origination before human destination can be properly envisaged.

However, in addition to reading Irenaeus' statement as a theological assertion, might we perceive hermeneutical implications as well? We have argued above that Irenaeus read Genesis 2.7 in a typological manner that was much more expansive than even Paul's readings. If Genesis 2.7 is seen to speak of physical, "temporal things" as far as humanity is concerned, is it not necessary to approach this text before approaching texts that bespeak "eternal things"? Irenaeus would seem to suggest that it is Christ who spans the distance between that which is temporal and "pre-formed" and that which is eternal and fully-realized, whether speaking theologically or hermeneutically. As for theology, Christ's healing of the physical body shows him to be its original Creator. As for hermeneutics, catholic-Christian readings of Scripture portray Christ as the object that is "pre-formed," the subject who does the "pre-forming," and indeed as the very lens through which these texts are to be read. Our tentative hypothesis is strengthened when other uses of *praeformare* in *Adversus Haereses* are weighed. Though *praeformare* can conceivably denote a literal shaping or fashioning beforehand, in *Haer.* iv.33.10 and iv.26.1 this word is used to connote the more figurative sense of "preparing" or "directing" beforehand, as in our text under discussion from v.13.1.[113] In a section on the proper interpretation of Scripture, Irenaeus states:

> For since they [the *prophets*] themselves were members of *Christ*, each one of them in his place as a member did, in accordance with this, set forth the prophecy [assigned him]; all of them, although many, *prefiguring* (*praeformare*) only *one*, and proclaiming the things which pertain to one."[114]

---

[113] Unfortunately no Greek manuscripts survive for the sections of *Haer.* v.13.1 and iv.33.10. *Haer.* iv.26.1 is preserved in Greek only partially.
[114] *Haer.* iv.33.10; emphasis is added.

In the paragraph from which this selection is taken, the term *praeformare* is used in tandem with the term *praefigurare*, which occurs a few lines before and after *praeformare*. In essence, the terms function synonymously. In *Haer.* iv.26.1, *praeformare* is clearly used in the context of hermeneutics. Irenaeus asserts that

> ...when at the present time the *law* is read to the Jews, it is like a story (μῦθος / *fabula*); for they do not possess the explanation of all things pertaining to the advent of the Son of God, which took place in human nature; but when it is read by the Christians, it is a treasure, hid indeed in a field, but brought to light by the cross of Christ and explained, [thus] enriching (*ditare*) human understanding, showing forth the wisdom of God, manifesting his economy (*dispositio*) regarding humanity, *prefiguring* (*praeformare*) the kingdom of *Christ*....[115]

When taken along with these two citations, the *praeformare* statement in v.13 suggests that the revelation of Christ's true identity is a matter of prefiguring that is textually mediated. The texts of the "law and prophets" (but particularly the law, of which Genesis 1-2 is currently most pertinent to Irenaeus' argument) point to and prefigure Christ's eternal identity just as does his temporal earthly ministry. Indeed his temporal form (as disclosed in the apostolic texts) is only truly understood in light of the texts of law and prophets which precede him and disclose his eternal form and the form of his kingdom. From Irenaeus' ecclesial perspective, it would seem that the primary purpose of reading the Scripture (including the gospels and Genesis) is to properly identify Christ.[116] Genesis is an indispensable source of the revelation of God through Christ. Of course, for interpreters in the second-century church (Gnostic or otherwise), the precise question "*How* should we understand this Christ?" was the pivotal concern held in common. Irenaeus' argument in v.13-16 seeks to provide a credible answer. In his view, by failing to see the divine revelation manifest in temporal, physical, and textual matters, the Valentinians were blind toward spiritual reality, and, more significantly, blind to the figure of Christ as revealed in the writings of the evangelists and apostles.

At the end of v.13.2, Irenaeus makes a rather severe judgment. The "heretics," he says, who hold on to the mere expression "flesh and blood cannot

---

[115] *Haer.* iv.26.1; *SC* 100 (714.18-716.27). Emphasis is added.
[116] "Christ stands in the middle, as the Center and the Climax of the history of revelation, prophets 'anticipate' and foreannounce, apostles extend him to subsequent ages. Both the prophets and apostles have no other function but that of transmitting the revelation of Christ (revelation *by* Christ and *about* Christ)" (D. Farkasfalvy, "Theology of Scripture in St. Irenaeus," *RevBen* 78 [1968]: 323; emphasis is original).

inherit the kingdom of God" without properly discerning Paul's meaning in fact "die" (ἀποθνῄσκειν) in relation to these words. This is so because they are "overturning" (ἀνατρέπειν) the words wherein *"lies the entire economy of God"* (τὴν πᾶσαν οἰκονομίαν... τοῦ Θεοῦ).[117] Ought we to dismiss Irenaeus' claim as mere hyperbole, or might he indeed have reckoned 1 Corinthians 15.50, when interpreted so as to *include* the physical body in the divine inheritance, to be a comprehensive statement of God's activity in humankind? The contours of Irenaeus' argument in *Haer.* v.1-16 (as well as the dynamism propelling it) point to the latter. The question of the fleshly human body – its origin, purpose, and destiny – was absolutely central to Irenaeus' understanding of the Christian tradition. The determinative feature of catholic-Christian interpretation, then, would be to describe how *Christ* relates to human physicality. This feature holds attendant implications for a Christian view of reality.[118] Framed thusly, we may deem the section of *Haer.* v.12-16 to bring Irenaeus' argument to a climax. Certainly commentators are right to identify bodily recapitulation as at the "heart" of Irenaeus' theology.[119] In v.13.2, Irenaeus argues that by their spiritualized reading of 1 Corinthians 15.50, which excludes the possibility and promise that human bodies will be resurrected from the dead, the Valentinians "shun" the very "light of truth" (v.13.2). Put another way, Irenaeus seems to think that the Valentinians are tugging on the one loose thread that if pulled, unravels the whole garment of Christian doctrine. *Homo vivens* cannot be described apart from reference to the physical body. This is apparent in Irenaeus' comments on 2 Corinthians 5.4. It is essential to God's order of "perfecting" (*perficere* / κατεργαζεσθαι) human beings so that the "mortal" (i.e., physical, corruptible flesh) is to be swallowed (καταπίνειν) up by life (ὑπὸ τῆς ζωῆς).[120] In this manner, the flesh "remains living and incorruptible and hymning the praises of God who has perfected us for this very thing" (v.13.3). In summary, for Irenaeus, salvation is nonsensical apart from the resurrection of the human body. Other Pauline passages such as 2 Corinthians 5.4 and 2 Corinthians 4.11,[121] which refer to the "body of flesh and to none

---

[117] *Haer.* v.13.2; *SC* 153 (169.43-44). Emphasis is added.

[118] Cf. among many other instances, Irenaeus' citation of Philippians 3.21 in *Haer.* v.13.3: It is Christ who is able (*posse*) to transfigure our humble human bodies into conformity with the body of his glory, according to the working of his own power (*virtus*).

[119] Quasten, *Patrology*, 1:295.

[120] On καταπίνειν, cf. Irenaeus' earlier reference to Isaiah 25.8 ("death swallowed"). The *ANF* edition inexplicably translates this as "swallowed up *of* life." Yet the syntax simply follows the pattern wherein ὑπὸ with the genitive and a passive verb expresses a genitive of agency (i.e., "swallowed up *by* life").

[121] "... so that the life of Jesus may be made visible in our mortal flesh."

other,"[122] must be allowed to inform the interpretation of 1 Corinthians 15.50. Ultimately, says Irenaeus, the Valentinians' false and "deadly" interpretation of 1 Corinthians 15.50 is the end result of a hermeneutic that embodies their *choosing* falsehood: *Cogentur itaque haec tanta male interpretari, qui unum nolunt bene intellegere.*[123] According to Irenaeus, the problem is not that the wrong texts are used, but rather that the right texts are used wrongly; in other words, it is a problem of hermeneutics. Certain corollaries are implicit in his statement. First, to some degree the interpreter's "hermeneutic" is an entity discrete and separable from the text. Additionally, there are multiple possible hermeneutics. Human decision establishes the one that is eventually applied. In the section that follows (*Haer.* v.14), Irenaeus sketches his alternative hermeneutic for "reading" Christ in the texts of Scripture. Here, recapitulation functions not only as a theological concept or doctrine. It is a crucial feature within Irenaeus' overall interpretative schema, which, in turn, is propelled and guided by a protological orientation.

GENESIS 2.7 AND *PAUL*:
THE RECAPITULATION OF "FLESH AND BLOOD" (*HAER.* V.14)

Irenaeus' sequence in v.14 has two components. First he offers an *explanation* of his alternative hermeneutic, namely that in order to interpret properly Paul's statement in 1 Corinthians 15.50, one must interpret Christ's advent as a "recapitulation" of bodily humanity (v.14.1-3). Genesis 2.7 is a monumentally important text in this regard. Second, Irenaeus briefly draws out *implications* that follow from this Genesis-informed reading (v.14.4). Irenaeus summarizes these two components in the first sentence of v.14.4 where he notes that "if, therefore, flesh and blood are the things which procure (*facere*) for us life," then the Valentinians' "literal" reading of 1 Corinthians 15.50 is unsustainable. Paul's intent is not to disparage physical "flesh and blood" in itself, but rather to urge that we not allow it to be overtaken by "fleshly deeds" that "pervert a person to sin" (v.14.4). Ultimately, then, 1 Corinthians 15.50 speaks not of necessity and substance, but of human choice and action.

In previous sections we have noted Irenaeus' extensive use of Genesis 2.7 when speaking of the divine economy – the fashioning of the *homo vivens*. Genesis 2.7 enables him to describe the Father as the one who *originates* this intention and the Spirit as the one who secures this particular *end*. Now Irenaeus uses Genesis 2.7 to speak of the Son as the *means* by which the *homo vivens* is effected. Clearly, "interpreting" Christ is the most crucial – and controversial –

---

[122] *Haer.* v.13.4.
[123] "And thus they will be compelled to interpret these things improperly who do not choose to understand one correctly" (*Haer.* v.13.5; *SC* 153 [182.128-29]).

task of Christian theology. When responding to the appealing teachings of the Valentinians, Irenaeus must have sensed the need to depict Christ's activity and identity in an even more substantial and persuasive manner. However, Irenaeus' christological foray in this section continues to serve the purpose of substantiating his reading of 1 Corinthians 15.50. We might term Irenaeus' immediate focus here as *sarkological*, given his concern to undermine thoroughly Valentinian interpretation and application of this text. It is with this in mind that Irenaeus relies on the Genesis creation narratives (particularly 2.7) to support and inform his Christology, specifically by asserting Christ's salvific work to be a "recapitulation" of humanity. In *Haer.* v.14, Irenaeus will make reference to this notion *four times*.

Irenaeus asserts that Paul "has everywhere adopted the term 'flesh and blood' with regard to the Lord Jesus Christ, partly indeed to establish his human nature... and partly that he might confirm the salvation of our flesh" (v.14.1). It would seem that these two functions are necessarily related. If the first claim is valid – that Christ's human nature is rightly characterized as "flesh and blood" – then the second claim surely must follow – the salvation of human "flesh and blood" is at least possible (even if not yet demonstrated).[124] It was one thing for Gnostic predecessors, such as those described as Ophites, to depict the body of "Jesus" as left behind when the spirit (Christ) ascended to Pleroma. Yet (Irenaeus seems to imply) the Valentinians cannot afford such an indulgence. If they sought to be identified and approved as properly *Christian* interpreters, they must grapple with the potentially awkward issue of Christ's bodiliness. Assuming, based on John 1.14, it was granted that Christ's constitution did include flesh, one could scarcely (as a Christian) suggest that such material was, out of necessity, excluded from participation in the divine. On the other hand, Irenaeus is convinced that the Valentinians' solution – the depiction of a docetic Christ – is not a satisfying option. Together, then, Irenaeus' two claims point to a reading of Christ as the one who "recapitulates" a human race that is embodied.

As evidenced in *Haer.* v.14.1, Irenaeus relies on Scripture to make such a christological argument. With 1 Corinthians 15.50 in mind, Irenaeus invokes the references to "blood" in Genesis 4.10; 9.5-6; and Luke 11.50-51. These passages, so Irenaeus asserts, imply that it is precisely because Christ was made flesh and blood that his life and death serves to undo what went wrong in humanity. The Lukan text, in which Christ "charges" "this generation" with the shed "blood of all the prophets,"[125] "thus points out the future *recapitulation* in

---

[124] Irenaeus states that "if the flesh were not able (*habere*) to be saved, the Word of God would certainly not be made flesh..." (14.1; cf. John 1.14).
[125] Luke 11.50 reads: "so that this generation may be charged with the blood of all the prophets shed since the foundation of the world, from the blood of Abel to the blood of

[Christ's] own person of the effusion of blood from the beginning (*ab initio*) of all the righteous men and of the prophets, and that by means of himself (*per semetipsum*) there should be a seeking after (*exquisitio*[126]) their blood" (v.14.1).[127] If, on the basis of a christological reading of these three texts, God is understood to "seek after" (*exquirere*) "blood" to redeem it, how, asks Irenaeus, can the Valentinians declare (based on 1 Corinthians 15.50) that this blood is incapable of being saved?[128] Besides this statement of the sweeping impact of Christ's recapitulation on humanity "from the beginning," Irenaeus makes two other similar references to human and temporal origin when explaining recapitulation. Abel, he notes, is one of those righteous persons whose blood "cries out from the beginning (*ab initio*)" (v.14.1; cf. Luke 11.50). Irenaeus also remarks that Christ "would not have *recapitulated* these things in himself unless he had himself been made flesh and blood after the way of the original formation (*secundum principalem plasmationem*), saving in his own person at the end (*in fine*) that which had in the beginning (*in principio*) perished in Adam" (v.14.1).

Irenaeus had borrowed the term ἀνακεφαλαιώσασθαι (*recapitulare*) from its earlier semantic context in Hellenist rhetoric.[129] Now, in order to endow this term with precise theological meaning in reference to Christ's activity, Irenaeus must go back to Genesis 1-2 and the language descriptive of Adam and original formation. Situating the incarnate Word's work at the "end" of the divine economy invites a fresh understanding and evaluation of God's work at the beginning when he first fashioned an embodied humanity. Taken in an abstract

---

Zechariah, who perished between the altar and the sanctuary. Yes, I tell you, it will be charged against this generation" (cf. the parallel in Matthew 23.35).

[126] nominal form of the root *exquirere*.

[127] *Haer*. v.14.1; emphasis is added. Irenaeus describes Christ as "seeking after" the shed blood of Abel which "cries out from the beginning" (14.1). Genesis 9.5-6 reads: "For your own lifeblood I will surely require (ἐκζητεῖν) a reckoning: from every animal I will require (ἐκζητεῖν) it and from human beings, each one for the blood of another, I will require a reckoning (ἐκζητεῖν) for human life. Whoever sheds the blood of a human, by a human shall that person's blood be shed; for in his own image God made humankind." In Luke 11.50-51, which Irenaeus describes as Christ's words "to those who should afterwards shed *his* blood," the text similarly uses the Greek verb ἐκζητεῖν to speak of the blood from Abel and Zechariah that will be "sought" from "this generation" (*Haer.* v.14.1; emphasis is added).

[128] Cf. *Haer*. v.14.1.

[129] Grant cites a few uses of ἀνακεφαλαίωσις. "For Dionysius of Halicarnassus such an *anakephalaiôsis* is a 'concluding summary,' while in a rhetorical preface to his last book Theophilus says, 'I will not shrink from summing up for you... the antiquity of our writings.' For Clement of Alexandria (who knew Irenaeus' work), Christ's crown of thorns 'recapitulates' Moses' vision of the Logos in the burning (thorn) bush" (Grant, *Irenaeus of Lyons*, 50).

sense, "recapitulation" connotes not merely a new expression of some sort, but one that reflects and indeed asserts continuity (or identification) with what precedes it. The role of Genesis 2.7 in Irenaeus' christological vision will become clear in the next section of his argument, *Haer.* v.14.2.

Whereas *Haer.* v.14.1 emphasizes how Scripture (i.e., references to Abel, Noah, and Adam) points *forward* to recapitulation, *Haer.* v.14.2-3 places emphasis on how Christ (as interpreted by Paul) points *backward* to Genesis 2.7 to illumine and assert recapitulation. It is in this section that Irenaeus uses Genesis 2.7 to assist a right reading of 1 Corinthians 15.50 insofar as the text first helps to interpret Christ and his work as a recapitulation of flesh and blood, and subsequently invites the necessary conclusions about human "flesh and blood" itself (i.e., its relationship to the "kingdom of God"). Irenaeus' primary use of Genesis 2.7 is to assert that there is *only one human flesh*. It is the claim established by this most explicit use that contributes to two implicit, secondary uses of Genesis 2.7: to assert that there is only *one divine economy* for this flesh, and to assert that there is only *one God* (though triune) to which this flesh relates.

We will consider these three functions of Genesis 2.7 in order, teasing out the corresponding doctrinal claims that Irenaeus draws from each. First we look at his primary assertion, that is, concerning human flesh. Irenaeus remarks,

> But if the Lord became incarnate for any other order of things (*dispositio*), and took flesh of any other substance, he has not then <u>recapitulated</u> human nature in himself, nor in addition can he even be called flesh. For flesh has been truly made (*facere*) a succession (*successio*) of that which was originally formed (*plasmationis*) from dust (*e limo*) (v.14.2).[130]

Irenaeus uses Genesis 2.7 to make two claims about human bodiliness. First, human flesh is characterized by its temporal continuity. There is only *one* flesh, and its extension throughout the divine oikonomia is a "succession." What it was at the moment of its original molding by the hands of God, it is at the present time. Secondly, Genesis 2.7 identifies the substance of human flesh as dust. In other words, in order to speak intelligently (and "Christian-ly") about human "flesh and blood," one must go back to the texts in Genesis that tell of its origin. A straightforward reading of Genesis 2.7 discerns that human bodiliness, at its most basic level, is comprised of physical substance. The Valentinian inference that humanity was formed from an "invisible substance consisting of fusible and fluid matter"[131] is clearly antithetical to the sense of this text. All

---

[130] *SC* 153 (186.32-37); emphasis is added.
[131] *Haer.* i.5.5; v.15.4.

human beings participate in the physicality of the earthly body. Introducing his second reference to Genesis 2.7 in this paragraph, Irenaeus again speaks of Christ's "recapitulation" as a matter of stepping into the continuity of human bodiliness so as to "seek" the "salvation" of the very thing that had "perished."[132]

> For the Lord,[133] taking dust from the earth, molded (*plasmare*) man; and it was upon his behalf that all the economy (*dispositio*) of the Lord's advent took place. He had himself, therefore, flesh and blood, <u>recapitulating</u> in himself not a certain other, but that original handiwork of the Father (*principalem plasmationem Patris*), seeking out (*exquirere*) that thing which had perished (v.14.2).[134]

In *Haer.* v.14.2, Genesis 2.7's specific contribution to an understanding of Christ's work as recapitulation is now quite evident. According to the logic of recapitulation, it must be the very thing that had perished – flesh and blood – which is sought (*exquirere*) by Christ. Christ, now identified as the God who seeks,[135] must have (*habuit*) this same (*ipse*) flesh and blood that is the common heritage of all human beings molded by God. Being "righteous," Christ is able to "reconcile that flesh that was being kept under bondage in sin (*in peccato detinebatur*), and bring it into friendship with God (*in amicitiam adduxit Deo*)" (v.14.2).[136] Perhaps, in light of his discussion in *Haer.* v.14.1, Irenaeus' description evokes images of Abel's blood being detained in the earth (as in bondage to sin) and crying out to God. Christ, being truly innocent flesh and blood, redeems Abel's blood (as well as "all righteous blood") thus enabling final reconciliation to God.

If Irenaeus uses Genesis 2.7 to argue that there is only one human flesh fashioned by God, which the incarnate Word shares, then it is logical to presume that there is only one economic arrangement for that human flesh. The term *dispositio* (or more precisely, οἰκονομια, which stands behind it) was used by Irenaeus in a highly technical and theological sense. We would therefore expect his choice of this word to be not incidental but intentional. In the section v.14.2, Irenaeus speaks twice about God's *dispositio*. In the first (also cited above), he does indeed infer a connection between the one *substantia* and the one *dispositio* by setting these concepts in parallel to each other: *Si autem ob <u>alteram quandam</u>*

---

[132] *Haer.* v.14.2; *SC* 153 (186.42-43).
[133] The Latin reads *dominus* whereas the Armenian reads *deus*.
[134] *SC* 153 (188.44-48); emphasis is added.
[135] Cf. ζητεῖν in Luke 19.10: "For the Son of Man came to seek out and to save the lost."
[136] Irenaeus' flexible understanding of the notion of "flesh and blood" (following Paul's) is seen in that in *Haer.* v.14.3, Irenaeus describes the flesh not as lost or perished (cf. v.14.2), but as that which had "formerly been in enmity."

dispositionem Dominus incarnatus est *et ex altera substantia carnem attulit, non ergo in semetipsum recapitulatus est hominem: adhuc etiam nec caro quidem dici potest.*[137] The Valentinians, by assuming multiple *dispositiones* that corresponded to multiple *substantiae*, recognized this logical association. (Thus there was a fixed arrangement by which spiritual substance is restored to rest in Pleroma, and psychic and material substances are also sorted, like unto like.) Where they differed, of course, is in terms of number.[138] Both may have looked to the same sources, the Genesis creation accounts, but Irenaeus' interpretation of Genesis 2.7 recognized only one human substance (namely, physical) and one divine *dispositio* (namely, the Creator's). Irenaeus found the biblical interrelationship between a continuous (or unified) *substantia* and a continuous (or unified) *dispositio* as so close that that each term is, in effect, defined by means of reference to the other. God's economy is the arranged order that tells *how* God relates to the human physical body. As evidenced by his repeated association of *dispositio* and *exquisitio* in v.14.1-2, Irenaeus evidently views God's activity as principally his seeking after human flesh to redeem, restore, and enliven it. The Father is the flesh's point of origin and its destination. The Spirit and Son work to accomplish the flesh's perfection, which is essential to the *homo vivens*. So there is only one flesh; there is only one order. According to Irenaeus' statement above, these are the necessary preconditions for recapitulation. Of course if these preconditions are not accepted, then neither will be Irenaeus' interpretation of Christ's place in the single divine economy. But if, following Irenaeus' reading of Genesis 2.7, this correlated continuity of flesh and economy were affirmed, then (seemingly) one could not but reckon Christ's person and work as a recapitulation of bodily humanity. In his second reference to the term *dispositio* in this paragraph, Irenaeus reiterates that when Genesis 2.7 is allowed to inform one's Christology, Christ's work is recognized to be a recapitulation. It was, he says, on behalf of the man whom God molded (*plasmare*) from dust that "the whole economy (*omnis dispositio*) of the Lord's advent took place" (v.14.2). Irenaeus then specifies that insofar as he had "flesh and blood," Christ "recapitulated in himself" not "another certain economy" (*dispositio*), but "that original handiwork of the Father" (v.14.2). Genesis 2.7 contributes to Irenaeus' doctrine of recapitulation by asserting and explaining human origination as marked by one flesh and one economy of specified order. Its particular rendering of original "capitulation" and "de-capitulation" (the introduction of death into human flesh) points to an interpretation of Christ's

---

[137] "But if the Lord became incarnate for any other order of things, and took flesh of any other substance, he has not then recapitulated humanity in his own person, nor in that case can he be termed flesh" (*Haer.* v.14.2; *SC* 153 [186.32-35]; emphasis is added).

[138] Another difference, as we have noted elsewhere, is Irenaeus' unwillingness to use the Genesis texts as a basis or resource for doctrines of divine constitution.

salvific work as "re-capitulation." The story of Christ must fit in the larger story of God's consistent activity. His actions, like those of the other divine hand, must be in conformance with the Father's single intention. Consequently, as we turn to our last claim about Genesis 2.7's theological uses in *Haer.* v.14.2, it is only appropriate to note that if Genesis 2.7 affirms one flesh and one economy, it also affirms only one *God*.

If the Valentinians are right, namely that there are three basic human substances and thus three distinct divine orders for the origination and disposition of these substances, would it not follow that there are three distinct gods? Each substance corresponds with an order that is under the superintendence of a god. The πνευματικοί participate in the economy of Bythus (and Sophia); the ψυχικοί are situated in the world of the Demiurge (though some may possibly climb to the next level); and the χοϊκοί are trapped in the earthly realm of the Cosmocrator.[139] In fact, each human type is consubstantial with its god. While in *Haer.* v.14, Irenaeus does not specifically reiterate his argument for only one God, this is not strictly necessary for it has been an emphasis throughout his five-book treatise. It is the Christian doctrine of the unity of God that serves as Irenaeus' methodological starting point. His entire argument rests upon it. (We may recall that before Irenaeus engages in his detailed interpretation of Scripture in books three through five, he finds it needful in book two to rebut the Valentinian notion of divinity as a multiplicity.[140]) By underscoring that there is only *one* God, a catholic-Christian reading of Genesis 2.7 (and Genesis 1.26) serves to identify *who it is that relates* to the human physical body in his own divine arrangement. All that is known about God's oikonomia through nature[141] also points to the work of but one God. At the same time, the God whom Irenaeus reads in Genesis is a God whose unity is a triunity. It is possible to distinguish between the Father and his two hands. The actions of Spirit and Son address humanity in an inclusive scope.

---

[139] On Bythus and the Demiurge, as they relate to human beings of spiritual and psychic substance, cf. *Haer.* i.5.1-6.2; on the Cosmocrator, cf. *Haer.* i.5.4.

[140] Elaine Pagels takes issue with Irenaeus' characterization of Valentinian doctrine as denying the unity of God. In her view (as informed by *Excerpts from Theodotus*), Irenaeus' "polemical bias" led him to "change the meaning of specific terms and to omit crucial elements of Valentinian doctrine" ("Conflicting Versions of Valentinian Eschatology," *HTR* 67 [1974]: 51). The Valentinians, she says, actually did "profess belief in the ontological reality of *only one God* – the Father." It is only "existentially, then, throughout the *oikonomia* [that] there seem to be... 'two Gods'" (52-3; emphasis is original). However, even if Irenaeus were to acknowledge this concession, he surely would have found it theologically unacceptable nonetheless. In depicting divine economic activity as the work of God's "two hands," Irenaeus allows no room for God's unity to be doubted, even in the phenomenal realm of present human experience.

[141] See, for example, *Haer.* ii.25.

There are not multiple human substances but rather only one "flesh and blood." The Genesis texts contribute to Irenaeus' doctrine of recapitulation by identifying Christ as God the "seeker." Having "taken dust" to "mold man," God, or more specifically Christ, now takes on dust to "seek out" (*exquirere*) that very substance "that had perished" (v.14.2). That this one bodily substance will be quickened in accordance with God's plan, argues Irenaeus, is not contradicted but rather confirmed by the apostolic tradition. In *Haer.* v.14.2-3, Irenaeus is still using Genesis 2.7 (and related texts) chiefly in order to interpret Paul. Though the main text at hand is 1 Corinthians 15.50, its meaning must be reconciled with those of other Pauline texts, especially Colossians 1.21, Ephesians 1.7, and Ephesians 2.13-15. With a view toward this last citation, Irenaeus states that "now, by means of communion (*communicatio*) with himself, the Lord has reconciled man to God the Father, in reconciling us to himself by the body of his own flesh, and redeeming us by his own blood" (v.14.3). Irenaeus suggests that the contrast between his elaboration of Christian soteriology and that of his Valentinian opponents could not be greater. They assert salvation *from* human flesh; he asserts salvation *through* human flesh: "[I]n every epistle the apostle plainly testifies that through (*per*) the flesh of our Lord and through his blood, we have been saved" (v.14.3).[142] Irenaeus, like the Valentinians, explains human salvation and the body's relatedness to salvation by interpreting Christ through the textual mediation of the gospels and apostolic writings. Yet Irenaeus' robust Christology, distinguished as it is by his doctrine of recapitulation, bears little resemblance to that of his opponents' precisely because he insists that christological readings of key protological texts (here, Genesis 2.7) be allowed to inform and even constitute his portrait of Christ.[143]

Through recourse to Genesis 2.7, Irenaeus has attempted to offer a more attractive "reading" of Christ that is consistent with not only the gospels, but also with Pauline texts such as 1 Corinthians 15.50. Subsequently, in v.14.4 Irenaeus will briefly assess the *implications*. If Christ indeed procures life for humanity through the recapitulation of his own flesh and blood, then the Pauline attitude toward bodiliness is best seen in cohortative terms. Since it is not flesh and blood *per se* that "cannot inherit the kingdom of God," but rather flesh characterized by "carnal actions," then we ought not let sin "reign" in our mortal bodies, but rather "present" ourselves to God, "just as if being alive from the

---

[142] Cf. Ephesians 1.7.
[143] While the Valentinians did find relevance in Genesis texts, the fact that Genesis 3 was of more christological interest than the creation accounts (cf. *Gospel of Truth*) reflects their belief that the significance of Christ lay in his capacity as revealer of divinity, rather than as recapitulator of humanity. In contrast, we suggest that Irenaeus demonstrates how Genesis 2.7 enables both roles to be affirmed.

dead."[144] Thus we see that Irenaeus' underlying thesis is never far from the surface: the aim of God's redemptive work is to produce and exhibit the *homo vivens*. "Carnal actions" are a hindrance insofar as they "deprive (*privare*) humanity of life" (v.14.4). Appropriating language from Romans 6-7, Irenaeus claims that although our bodies would previously "bring forth fruit unto death,"[145] now God "wants us to [be obedient] unto righteousness, that we may bring forth fruit unto life (*ut fructificemus vitae*)."[146] A description of human activity in God's economy of redemption also suggests the grammar of recapitulation, as evidenced by Irenaeus' adaptive use of Colossians 2.19: "Remember, therefore, my most beloved, that by the flesh of our Lord you were redeemed (*redemptus es*),[147] and by his blood given back (*redhibitus*), and, '*holding the head* (*tenens caput*[148]) from whom the entire body of the church is fitted together and grows...'" (v.14.4). Irenaeus then elaborates. "Holding the head" means that "with respect to the fleshly coming of the Son of God," one "confesses him as God (*et Deum confitens*)," and "firmly receives his humanity (*et hominem ejus firmiter excipiens*)...."[149] By "making use (*uti*) of these proofs from Scripture," says Irenaeus, one will "easily overthrow" the opinions of the heretics.[150]

Although at the end of *Haer*. v.14.4, Irenaeus makes some rather general comments on his avowed goal to overturn his opponents' doctrines, these statements ought not be seen as signaling a conclusion of his discussion on the proper understanding of 1 Corinthians 15.50. Rather, as we shall see in our assessment of v.15, Irenaeus is about to enlarge and amplify his case that a scripturally-informed depiction of Christ offers the most determinative evidence of God's intent to bestow divine life upon the human bodies he has made. Before moving ahead, we shall briefly summarize the ground we have covered in our evaluation of the function of Genesis 2.7 in *Haer*. v.13-14. If the person and work of Christ is understood to be "prefigured" in the texts of law and prophets, then Genesis 2.7 may rightly be allowed to elicit and validate a particular christological view. Irenaeus' conclusion is that when Genesis texts and motifs are seen to point forward to Christ's activity (cf. Abel and Noah on

---

[144] *Haer.* v.14.4. Irenaeus here cites Romans 6.12-13. Tertullian (*Marc.* 5.10; 14; 48-51) and Clement of Alexandria (*Strom.* 2.20) refer to 1 Corinthians 15.50 in similar contexts (cp. Origen, *Cels.* 5.19).
[145] Cf. Romans 7.5.
[146] *Haer.* v.14.4; *SC* 153 (194.90). Along with Romans 7.4-5, Irenaeus also has Romans 6.16-23 clearly in view.
[147] The inflection is perfect passive.
[148] Colossians 2.19: κρατῶν τὴν κεφαλήν; cf. ἀνακεφαλαιώσασθαι
[149] Alternate renderings include "hold firmly to him as man" (Grant, *Irenaeus of Lyons*, 170), and "looking forward with constancy to his human nature" (*ANF* 1:542).
[150] *Haer.* v.14.4; *SC* 153 (194.94-95).

"blood"[151]), and Pauline texts about Christ are deemed to point backward to Genesis, what emerges is a Christology chiefly marked by a doctrine of bodily recapitulation. Irenaeus' *Recapitulationstheorie*, then, is best understood as an expression (or implication) of his distinctive theological hermeneutic – a hermeneutic that is orientated toward protological interests. In Christ's advent, the Creator brings salvation to the very "flesh and blood" that the Valentinians dismiss as expendable in the divine oikonomia. Accordingly, Genesis 2.7 insists that 1 Corinthians 15.50 be understood within the strictures required by such a recapitulation: the interrelation of only one human substance (physical flesh), only one divine economy (the vivification of this flesh) and only one God (the one who vivifies). In v.15, Irenaeus will suggest how Genesis 2.7 interprets Christ as disclosing the identity of this one God. His main point, that Christ reveals the Father to be the Creator of an embodied humanity, is by no means banal, given that Christian theology and (particularly) biblical hermeneutics in the second-century church was still in a nascent, malleable stage.

Using Genesis 2.7: Revelation (Haer. v.15.1-3)

INTRODUCTION AND OVERVIEW

Continuing into chapters 15 and 16 of book five, Irenaeus elaborates an understanding of Christ's earthly ministry which aligns with and demonstrates the divine intention to fashion a living humanity. Having argued that the human flesh and blood is able to partake of a divine inheritance by virtue of the incarnate Christ's *recapitulation* of the physical human frame, Irenaeus now looks at the very *revelation* of Christ as attested in the gospels. It is when Irenaeus "reads" Christ specifically in the light of Genesis 2.7 that he recognizes the identity of God. Here is the God who fashions, heals and completes the *homo vivens*. Though there is no evidence that Irenaeus made an intentional connection, his two christological concerns represented in v.14 and v.15 may be seen to correspond loosely to the two component parts of Genesis 2.7. In v.14, Irenaeus' focus aligns with the theme of Genesis 2.7a: "then the Lord God formed man from the dust of the ground...." Here Irenaeus asserts the significance of the bodily Christ for his affirmation that "flesh and blood" is indeed physical substance, yet is intimately related to the purposeful work of the eternal, incorruptible God. In v.15, Irenaeus reiterates and then advances the theme of Genesis 2.7a along the lines of Genesis 2.7b: "...and breathed into his nostrils the breath of life; and the man became a living being." Using this Genesis 2.7 imagery in connection with Ezekiel 37 and John 9, Irenaeus

---

[151] Cf. Jesus' pronouncement in Luke 11.50 about God seeking the blood of the righteous.

illumines the *purpose* of Christ's recapitulation of the human body and the *telos* to which his healing activities point. The God who fashioned the human frame now restores it, so as to present the completed *homo vivens*. Since his vision of this purpose emerges only in reference to God's linear economy, Irenaeus now speaks more specifically about the God who brings the body to this intended culmination. On four occasions, spaced evenly through this section of v.15-16, Irenaeus describes Christ as *God revealed to impart life to humanity*: Christ "confers" (*dare*) life;[152] he "restores" (*restituere*) the "lost sheep" to the "fold of life";[153] and he "prepares" (*coaptare*) us "for life."[154]

We continue to discover that when Irenaeus speaks of Christ in *Haer.* v.14-16, he has a penchant for speaking the language of Genesis 2.7. Although usage of the term *plasmare* is significant throughout *Adversus Haereses*, in this christological section of v.15-16 we find a dramatic concentration. Out of fifty-seven total occurrences of the verb *plasmare* in all five books of *Adversus Haereses*, eighteen are found in just these two short chapters. As for cognates, the noun *plasma* is used three times; the noun *plasmatio* is used six times, and the noun *plasmator* occurs three times.[155] It will become clear that Irenaeus' explanation of Christ's role in the resurrection (i.e., vivification) of the body depends on his understanding of the original formation of the body. The life given to the body in the "end" is viewed in light of the life given to the body in the "beginning." Previously, we have argued that Genesis 2.7 (along with other select texts) most likely underlies Irenaeus' depiction of the divine economy of Son and Spirit as the presence and activity of God's hands.[156] *Haer.* v.15-16 contains numerous references to God's "hand(s)." According to Irenaeus' reading of biblical texts which center here on Jesus' healing of the blind man in John 9, Christ's actions are purposeful: to "show forth the hand of God."[157] The hand that heals is revealed to be the very hand that "fashioned." God's presence has become visible and palpable in a new, unparalleled way. In light of this, avers Irenaeus, we ought not to "be seeking another hand by which man was fashioned, nor another Father."[158] Again Irenaeus uses "hand" language to

---

[152] *Haer.* v.15.1; v.15.3.

[153] *Haer.* v.15.2.

[154] *Haer.* v.16.1.

[155] Thus there are thirty total occurrences of the verb *plasmare* and cognates in v.15-16.

[156] Cf. for example, *Haer.* v.1.3. The "hands of God" which Adam has never escaped are the ones to whom "the Father" spoke, saying, "Let us make man in our image..." It is the "hands" of the Father that "formed a living man...."

[157] *Haer.* v.15.2. Irenaeus also had previously cited Isaiah 66.14: "the hand of the Lord shall be known to those who worship him" (15.1).

[158] *Haer.* v.15.2; v.16.1. Given his statement in v.15.2 ("...manifesting the hand of God to those who can understand by what [hand] man was formed out of the dust"), Irenaeus suggests that in the recognition of divine revelation, human will is a relevant factor. Only

emphasize the continuity of divine economy in which God works, as well as to assert the unity of God himself.

GENESIS 2.7 AND THE *PROPHETS*:
THE DIVINE PROMISE OF VIVIFICATION

So if it is granted that God is *able* to extend new life to human bodies since flesh and blood, strictly speaking, is not barred from inheriting God's kingdom, is God *willing* to do so? In *Haer.* v.15.1, Irenaeus bolsters his conviction that he, indeed, is by calling attention to the divine promise of resurrection found in Scripture, particularly in Ezekiel 37. In this text, it is the prophet himself who invokes the Genesis 2.7 imagery of fleshly bodies and breath of life when speaking of resurrection. However, as our brief survey of this section will suggest, Irenaeus not only found Ezekiel's echoes of Genesis 2.7 noteworthy in themselves; more crucially, he found the theological association between two distinct acts of divine life-giving to provide the requisite context for the interpretation of *Christ*.[159] Whereas previously (v.14 and earlier) Irenaeus had used Genesis 2.7 in connection with Christ to assert that God's intention to vivify extends to physical human flesh and blood, now Irenaeus looks at how

---

some people will see Christ as God's hand. This would fit Irenaeus' general accusation that the Valentinians, by virtue of their hermeneutical decisions, blind themselves.

[159] This interpretation follows in *Haer.* v.15.2-3. Irenaeus does not make explicit reference to Genesis 2.7 in his reading of Ezekiel 37 (in v.15.1) to the same extent that he does with John 9 (in v.15.2). Yet, given the allusions discussed in this section and the subsequent link between v.15.1 and v.15.2, it seems plausible – if not probable – that Genesis 2.7 informs and guides his readings of this prophetic material. Previously, Irenaeus claimed that though the prophets (including "Moses, Elijah and Ezekiel") "did not openly behold the actual face of God," they announced "the dispensations and the mysteries though which man should afterwards see God" (iv.20.10; cf. Simonetti, "Per typica ad vera," 360). Therefore, "it is manifest that the Father is indeed invisible... [b]ut his Word, as he himself willed it, and for the benefit of those who beheld, did show the Father's brightness..." (iv.20.11). Thus it is reasonable to presume that in Ezekiel's prophecy of the valley of dry bones, God's economy and indeed his Son are announced. For his part, Simonetti notes that Irenaeus opposes the "scriptural divisismo of the Gnostics" with a "concept of progressive revelation" deduced from a unitary view of Scripture ("Per typica ad vera," 363). However, Simonetti concludes that despite this achievement, Irenaeus "has not succeeded in also translating such a concept to the level of exegesis" (363). As we approach Irenaeus' readings of Ezekiel 37 and (especially) John 9, we shall propose that Irenaeus' predilection for a global christological hermeneutic is not necessarily at odds with the task of biblical "exegesis," if the latter is understood to be the close, careful reading of a given text in its own right within acknowledged historical, linguistic, and theological parameters. On this point, see Farkasfalvy, "Theology of Scripture in St. Irenaeus," *RevBen* 78 [1968]: 328.

this intention – or, better, "promise" – of God is fulfilled and *manifested* in Christ's advent.

Irenaeus begins by introducing the words of another prophet, Isaiah: "Seeing that he who in the beginning (*ab initio*) created (*condere*) man, after his resolution into the earth promised him a second birth (*secundam generationem*), Isaiah thus says "The dead shall rise again, and they who are in the tombs shall arise, and they who are in the earth shall rejoice...."[160] In Irenaeus' mind, then, speech about resurrection and "second birth" must start with creation and first birth. Coming on the heels of his re-interpretation of "flesh and blood" in 1 Corinthians 15.50, Irenaeus' main point is that God's promised gift of new life addresses the physical body. The prophet Isaiah could not have been referring to an immaterial soul, for he notes that what is raised is that dead human component located "in the tombs" and "in the earth." Irenaeus further reinforces the fact that the material body is in view by pointing to another rather unambiguous scriptural text: "your *bones* will rise like the grass" (Isaiah 66.13).[161] At this point, Irenaeus remembers Ezekiel's narrative of the dry bones. For Irenaeus, Ezekiel 37 serves as a bridge insofar as it connects Christ (through the text of John 9 [cf. v.15.2]) to the theology of Genesis 2.7. At the same time, Irenaeus will use Genesis 2.7 to inform his interpretation of Christ. Not only does Ezekiel 37 reiterate the sheer physicality of human vivification, it expands upon the Isaiah texts cited by Irenaeus. Rather than merely asserting *that* the dead bodies shall be made alive, Ezekiel actually envisions it in precise detail.[162] The text is jarring in its concrete depiction of the gritty, physical textures of human bodiliness. To some degree, Ezekiel 37 may be read as a re-envisioning or re-enactment of the creation story from Genesis 2.7. Here, the prophet more explicitly characterizes the giver of life, God, and outlines a familiar two-step creation sequence. First the bodies are assembled and their formation established. Dry bones are fastened together over which flesh and sinews

---

[160] *Haer.* v.15.1; *SC* 153 (196.1-5). See also Isaiah 26.19 (LXX). Note that the first passage cited (Isaiah 26.19) follows Isaiah 25.9 ("Death has swallowed... but God...") which Irenaeus had quoted previously in v.12.1 to speak of a contrast: both death and life vie for presence in flesh but only one can be present at any given time. Isaiah 26.19 is typically classified as a *Heilsorakel*, the "classic form of divine reassurance that salvation will come... [and] the literary vehicle for much of Second Isaiah's proclamation of God's purpose for the redemption of Israel and the world" (Brevard Childs, *Isaiah* [Louisville: Westminster John Knox, 2001], 191).

[161] *Haer.* v.15.1; emphasis is added.

[162] Joseph Ziegler lists some of the early Christian theologians who treated the *resurrectio mortuorum* from Ezekiel 37.1-14 as "evidence": Tertullian (*Res.* 29), Gregory of Elvira (*Tractatus in SS Scripturam*, 27), and Ambrose (*Exc.* 2.71, 72, 75). See Joseph Ziegler, ed., *Ezechiel* (Septuaginta: vetus testamentum Graecum 16.1; Göttingen: Vandenhoeck & Ruprecht, 1977), 22.

"grow" and skin is "stretched." Then the Spirit (or wind) is invoked to "breathe upon these dead that they may live."[163] "[B]reath entered them and they did live and stood upon their feet...."[164] Irenaeus appears to work with the interplay of resonant images between Ezekiel 37 and Genesis 2.7, as evidenced by his references in v.15.2 to God's "formation" of the human being from dust and his gift of the breath of life.[165]

Although Ezekiel's allusions to the Genesis creation narratives are numerous, Irenaeus is keen to accentuate and extend them even further. For example, when Irenaeus quotes Ezekiel 37.3, he adds a phrase to the end (underlined below) that is not found in the LXX nor known variants: *Et dixit ad me: Fili hominis, si vivent ossa haec? Et dixi: Domine tu scis, qui fecisti haec.*[166] Whether Irenaeus adds this phrase intentionally or renders this passage freely based on imperfect memory, it is clear that he is continually attentive to the theological importance of creation for construing redemption or resurrection. Another echo in Irenaeus' long citation from Ezekiel 37 may be discerned in verse five: "I will cause the spirit of life to come upon you." Although the Greek text of this section of *Adversus Haereses* is not extant, it would not be implausible to suspect that Irenaeus finds an allusion to Genesis 1.2. In Ezekiel 37.5, God promises to "bear" or "carry" (φέρειν) the πνεῦμα ζωῆς upon "you." In Genesis 1.2, the πνεῦμα Θεοῦ is "borne upon" (ἐπιφέρειν) the surface of the waters. Of course, the πνοήν ζωῆς of Genesis 2.7 is also clearly in view, though (as suggested above) Irenaeus shows an interest not only in comparing but also contrasting πνοή and πνεῦμα – the original breath of life and the end-time "life-giving Spirit." The last verse in Irenaeus' citation is Ezekiel 37.14: *et dabo Spiritum meum in vos, et vivetis, et ponam vos in terram vestram, et cognoscetis quoniam ego sum Dominus.*[167] We therefore see a further significant theological contribution of Ezekiel 37 in the inextricable link it asserts between resurrection and revelation. Indeed it may be reckoned that resurrection, thus described, has a revelatory purpose as intimated in verse 13: "… and you shall

---

[163] *Haer.* v.15.1; Ezekiel 37.9.
[164] *Haer.* v.15.1; Ezekiel 37.10.
[165] This may be compared with the Ophite reading of Genesis 2.7. Although the massive body was formed first, it was a sluggish, wriggling worm on the ground until the bestowal of heavenly *virtus* (cf. divine breath) from Ialdabaoth at which point it was able to stand erect and acknowledge the higher god.
[166] "And he said to me, "son of man, can these bones live?" And I said, "Lord, you *who made them* know" (*Haer.* v.15.1; *SC* 153 [198.14-16]). In their editions of *Adversus Haereses*, Grabe, Massuet, and Harvey suggest that either Irenaeus (or his translator) are responsible for adding this last phrase. The fact that the Göttingen LXX makes no reference to it, while noting other variants from Irenaeus, might reflect Ziegler's judgment that Irenaeus was only paraphrasing the text.
[167] *Haer.* v.15.1; *SC* 153 (200.37-39).

know that I am the Lord when I shall open your sepulchers...."[168] Immediately after his citation of Ezekiel 37.14, Irenaeus offers his interpretative comments.

> As we at once perceive that the Creator (*Demiurgos*) is in this passage represented as vivifying our dead bodies, and promising resurrection to them, and resuscitation from their sepulchres and tombs, conferring (*dare*) upon them immortality also – "for according to the tree of life," he says, "so shall their days be" – he is shown (*ostendere*) to be the only God who accomplishes (*facere*) these things, and as himself the good Father, benevolently conferring life to those who do not have life from themselves. And for this reason did the *Lord* (*Dominus*) most plainly manifest himself and the Father to his disciples....[169]

Ezekiel 37, says Irenaeus, reveals God. Contrary to Valentinian depiction, this *solus Deus* is both *Demiurgos* and *bonus Pater*. This God's consistent concern is to give life to human physical bodies. Incorruptible life is not intrinsic to the creature,[170] but has its source in God. Irenaeus uses the theme of "revelation by means of resurrection" in Ezekiel 37.13-14 to link the "God" in the texts of prophetic Scripture to the "Lord" revealed in the gospels. Christ is revealed in the light of the divine promise of Ezekiel 37, which in turn points backward to Genesis 2.7. As we shall see, Irenaeus then employs Genesis 2.7 much more directly and extensively in his interpretation of Christ, by means of the text of John 9. Before leaving the citation of Ezekiel 37, however, we may observe that Irenaeus has enclosed it between two "book-ends" of Genesis motifs. We have mentioned the creation language at the beginning of v.15.1.[171] Now we find his mention of Genesis language from Isaiah 65.22 *after* Ezekiel 37.14. In Isaiah's eschatological vision, Irenaeus finds the use of Genesis' "tree of life" language[172] to provide an apt description of the resurrection life promised by God in the end time: "For as the tree of life, so shall their days be."[173] A recollection of God's original gift of life provides the suitable standpoint from which to consider the ultimate resurrection of the physical body. Genesis 1-2 is crucial for discerning God's identity, and thus (as we shall see next) Christ's identity.

---

[168] *Haer.* v.15.1; cf. Ezekiel 37.13.
[169] *Haer.* v.15.1-2; *SC* 153 (200.41-202.49). Emphasis is added.
[170] Contrast with a Valentinian view of the πνευματικοί as composed of eternal spiritual substance.
[171] I.e., "...seeing that he who from the beginning created man, did promise him a second birth after his dissolution into earth" (v.15.1).
[172] Cf. Genesis 2.9; 3.22; 3.24.
[173] The MT of Isaiah 65.22 differs: "for as the days of the tree...."

GENESIS 2.7 AND THE *GOSPELS*:
THE REVELATION OF CHRIST AS GOD'S OWN HAND

In *Haer.* v.15.2-3, Irenaeus uses Genesis 2.7 to "interpret" Christ as the one who reveals God and publicly fulfils God's promise to enliven (resurrect) the human body. If the prophets, read through the lens of Genesis 2.7, reveal the Father and his concern for humanity, the next appropriate question then is, "Who exactly is this Christ?" The gospel text of John 9, Christ's healing blind eyes by the application of mud, had evidently made a strong impression upon Irenaeus. It is because he also reads this gospel account through the interpretative grid of Genesis 2.7 that he "reads" Christ to be the revelation of the very "hand of God." Irenaeus begins this section by claiming that

> ... for this reason did the Lord (*Dominus*) most plainly manifest (*manifestissime*) himself and the Father to his disciples, that they might not, by any means, seek after (*quaerere*) another God besides him who *formed* man (*plasmaverit hominem*) and who gave him the *breath of life* (*afflatum vitae donaverit ei*); and that they might not rise to such great insanity so as to falsely add (*adfingere*) another Father above the Creator (*Demiurgos*) (v.15.2).

After Irenaeus recounts the miracle story wherein Christ heals the blind man by "smearing his eyes with clay" and instructing him to wash, he summarizes its broader significance: "And for this reason when he was washed he came seeing, that he might both *know* him who had fashioned him (*ut et suum cognosceret Plasmatorem*), and that he might *learn* (*discere*) [to know] the Lord who has conferred upon him life."[174] Just as we saw in Irenaeus' citation of Ezekiel 37,[175] we see here reaffirmed that in the one divine economy, resurrection (the securing of the *homo vivens*) and revelation are tandem purposes. It is crucial that Christ's person and work be understood in light of these, and Genesis 2.7 crucially assists this recognition. In restoring life to the blind man's eyes, Christ provides knowledge of God, chiefly, that the highest Father is indeed the Creator. Certainly the central motif of the story Irenaeus chooses – Christ opens blind eyes – contributes significantly to this broader theme of revelation in the section *Haer.* v.15.2-3. Additionally, though, we note a cluster of "revelation" terminology.[176] As mentioned above, Irenaeus brings to fore one of his favorite

---

[174] *Haer.* v.15.3; emphasis is added.
[175] E.g., Ezekiel 37.13: "... and you shall know that I am the Lord when I shall open your sepulchers..."; cf. Ezekiel 37.14.
[176] In *Haer.* v.15.2-16.3, there are thirteen uses of the root *manifestare* (whether in verbal, adverbial or adjectival forms). Forms of the closely-related verb *ostendere* occur nine times.

metaphors when he speaks of divine revelation as attested in John 9. Christ shows forth the "hand of God." Such hand language is commonplace in Scripture's depiction of the powerful activity and presence of God. When speaking of the promised resurrection of the body in v.15.1, Irenaeus himself had cited Isaiah 66.14: "you shall see (*videbitis*)... and your bones shall flourish as the grass, and the *hand* of the Lord shall be known to those who worship him." Whereas in v.14.1, Irenaeus uses Genesis 2.7 to interpret Christ as the *active* hand of God (i.e., by taking on flesh and blood Christ recapitulates the human formation), now in v.15.2, Genesis 2.7 (and subsequently Genesis 1.26[177]) is used to interpret Christ as the *visible* hand of God (i.e., revelation). As suggested in his introductory section of *Haer.* v.1.3, when Irenaeus speaks of the hands of God, he means to call attention to God's economic work in the Spirit and Son. In v.15-16, Genesis 2.7 enables Irenaeus to identify Jesus Christ as the God who originally fashioned and now "restores" humanity "into the fold of life" (v.15.2). Though Christ may be differentiated from the Father (as hands from the rest of the body), this does not erode Irenaeus' claim that there is only *one* God. Irenaeus detects only one divine economy, stating that "the work of God is the fashioning of man" (v.15.2). There is only one divine will, and Christ, he asserts, "carries out the will of the Father" (v.15.3). Christ "gave sight" by an "outward action" to the man born blind "so that he might show forth the *hand* of God which had at the beginning molded man" (v.15.2). When God's hand is revealed, God is revealed. As now we look more closely at Irenaeus' interpretation of John 9, we will discover his prominent uses of Genesis 2.7 motifs and terms including *plasmare* and the gift or "breath" of life. More than a mere supplement, this text essentially functions as Irenaeus' interpretative key – the means by which he reads Christ, and thus "God" in the text of John 9.[178] In contrast with Valentinian attempts to disassociate Christ from a (lesser) Demiurge, Irenaeus here insists that Scripture only speaks of Christ and Creator *together*. Christ's self-revelation is the revelation of the God who creates and resurrects humanity comprehensively.

Irenaeus actually offers comments on two distinct healing miracles from John's gospel. The first is the story in John 5 of Christ's healing the lame man at the pool of Beth-zatha. Irenaeus claims this is an example of where Christ "healed by a *word*" all those persons upon whom "weakness" (*languor*) had

---

[177] Cf. *Haer.* v.15.4; 16.1-2.
[178] From Irenaeus' perspective, "[r]eference to the Old Testament makes the New both intelligible and authoritative, because the latter can then be seen as the expression of a continuous process" (J. Daniélou, *Gospel Message and Hellenistic Culture* [ed. and trans. John Austin Baker; London: Darton Longman and Todd, 1973], 229). Irenaeus' exegesis and application of Genesis 2.7 is a specific case illustrating this principle.

come "on account of sin" (*propter transgressionem*).[179] Following the gospel's lead, Irenaeus discerns the human problem and the revelatory significance of Christ's intervention here by recollecting the Genesis 3 account of human disobedience. In the second case, which Irenaeus contrasts with the first, Genesis 2.7 is the crucial hermeneutical text. "To that man, however, who had been blind from his birth, he gave sight not by means of a word, but by a *work* (*per operationem*), doing this not without a purpose, or because it so happened, but that he might show forth (*ostendere*) the hand of God which at the beginning had molded (*plasmare*) man."[180] Irenaeus is intrigued by Jesus' statement that the man's blindness is not due to his or his parents' sin, "but that the works of God (*opera Dei*) should be made manifest in him."[181] Continuing his Genesis-informed reading of Christ's words and deeds, Irenaeus quite matter-of-factly adds his own interpretation:

> Now the work (*opera*) of God is the fashioning (*plasmatio*) of man. For, as the Scripture says, he made [man] by a work (*per operationem*): "And the Lord took clay from the earth, and formed man." Wherefore also (*quapropter et*) the Lord spat on the ground and made clay, and smeared it upon the eyes, pointing out the original fashioning (*ostendens antiquam plasmationem*), how it was composed (*quemadmodum facta est*), and manifesting (*manifestans*) the hand of God to those who would be able to understand (*qui intellegere possint*)[182] by what (*per quam*) [hand] man was fashioned (*plasmare*) out of the dust. For that which the artificer, the Word, had omitted to form in the womb, he then finished (*adimplere*) in public "that the works of God might be manifested in him," in order that we might not be seeking out another hand by which man was fashioned, nor another Father; knowing that this hand of God which formed us at the beginning (*initio*), and which does form us in the womb has in the last times (*novissimis temporibus*) sought us out (*exquere*) who were lost (*perdere*), winning back (*lucrifacere*) his own, and taking up the lost sheep upon his shoulders, and with joy restoring it to the fold of life (*in cohortem restituens vitae*).[183]

---

[179] *Haer.* v.15.2; *SC* 153 (202.54-55). Emphasis is added.
[180] *Haer.* v.15.2; *SC* 153 (204.59-62). Emphasis is added.
[181] John 9.3.
[182] Our translation of this phrase (departing from the *ANF*) recognizes the use of the subjunctive (here, of *posse*) with a general antecedent to suggest a relative clause of characteristic.
[183] *Haer.* v.15.2; *SC* 153 (204.66-206.82).

As we analyze Irenaeus' innovative use of Genesis 2.7 to offer a sketch of Christ as the revelation of God, we shall make ongoing reference to this lengthy citation. These sentences merit close scrutiny for they express Irenaeus' theological reading of John 9 wherein Genesis 2.7 both contributes to Christology and is itself informed by a particular Christology. Read through the lens of Genesis 2.7, Christ, in John 9, exhibits the one work of God in humanity. At the same time, this revelation of the divine economy is a revelation of God himself for these two cannot be wholly separated or viewed in isolation from each other. The resultant portrait of God provided by Irenaeus is a strikingly different alternative to the one supplied by the Valentinians. As seen in the other sections of *Haer.* v.1-15 that we have examined thus far, Genesis 2.7 enables Irenaeus to speak of God's economic work as a unity, and God's identity as a unity, without reducing either to a uniformity. Before considering the question of divine identity, let us investigate the divine *work* in John 9 that Irenaeus so meticulously explores. Irenaeus' conviction that Christ's healing of the blind man is revelatory (according to the citation from v.15.2 provided above) yields three points for reflection. First, Irenaeus provocatively identifies "the work of God" as the "fashioning of man." Second, Irenaeus claims that Christ's action affirms the continuity of God's work. Third, he locates the purpose of this divine work as the "restoration" of the *antiquam plasmationem* – which includes the body – to the "fold of life." This purpose is what we have concisely labeled as the *homo vivens*.

We begin with the first point. If the *opera Dei* is the *plasmatio hominis*, then several conclusions may be drawn. First, Irenaeus speaks of the (one?) work of God. Since the Latin language lacks articles, translators must decide whether *opera* should be read as a definite or indefinite noun. Yet when the primary anthropological themes of *Adversus Haereses* book five are taken into account, the force of Irenaeus' sentence leaves little doubt that a definite article is implicit. Irenaeus is not intimating that the "fashioning" of humanity is but one work of God among many.[184] If this were so, this bold statement would make no sense insofar as Irenaeus' very purpose in joining the narratives of Genesis 2.7 and John 9 in this citation using *quapropter et* is to contend that Christ's healing activity should be understood as an extension that is continuous to his original activity of formation. Furthermore, a humanity that is uniquely designated as made "after the image and likeness" of God cannot fail to be the pinnacle and culmination of God's creation activity. The translation "Now *the* work of God is..." is therefore defensible. Irenaeus may use a variety of terms to describe God's work toward or in humanity – creating, healing, restoring, resurrecting – but these words are frequently used synonymously. Even when a

---

[184] The fact that *plasmatio* immediately precedes rather than follows the copula verb *est* (i.e., *Opera autem Dei plasmatio est hominis*) might suggest its emphasis.

distinction is implied, all the activities (of which these words are merely signifiers) may be plausibly subsumed under the category of God's one overarching, unified work of "fashioning" humanity. Next, Irenaeus' terse statement asserts that this *plasmatio* is a *divine* work. In Irenaeus' estimation, Scripture (especially Genesis 1-2) rules out anthropologies that describe the origination of humanity either as a necessity, a self-origination, or an origination confined entirely within the bounds of a natural order. This claim challenges a Gnostic anthropology that posits eternal souls and a human species that is spiritual by nature. Humanity's defining characteristic as *plasmatio* is not an inherent quality but one that is derived. It affirms humanity's most basic relation to its divine Fashioner. Finally, when passages such as *Haer.* iv.38 are allowed to inform Irenaeus' statement, it is clear that when Irenaeus speaks of the *opera Dei*, he speaks not of a static, punctuated event but a dynamic and progressive activity. The human race is perpetually held in the fashioning hands of its Creator. As cited in our third chapter, Irenaeus describes the "arrangement" of God's economy for humanity as an ongoing "sequence": "man [is] making progress day by day and ascending toward the perfect, that is, approximating to the uncreated one."[185] When Irenaeus reads that Jesus healed the blind man with dust, he is emboldened to claim that this instance summarizes God's activity. God's work of fashioning is revealed as *present* to humanity.

Secondly, in the larger citation Irenaeus reads Genesis 2.7 alongside John 9 so as to assert that God's work is *continuous*. He says, "...knowing that this hand of God which formed us at the beginning (*initio*), and which does form us in the womb has in the last times (*novissimis temporibus*) sought us out (*exquere*)... restoring [us] to the fold of life" (v.15.2). Such a strong claim may recall Irenaeus' programmatic statement in *Haer.* v.1.3 that "never at any time did Adam escape the hands of God." Insofar as *the* work of God's hand is a work of fashioning, whether active to "form" or "restore," this work is best characterized as a unity. As is evident, Irenaeus discerned a much wider significance in this story about Jesus healing the man born blind than that which could be limited to its original setting in first-century Palestine. Along with a plain sense reading, Irenaeus deploys a typological interpretation. As a recipient of God's work in Christ, this solitary blind man (in certain respects) represents all of humanity. In the citation from v.15.2 provided above, we note Irenaeus' seamless move from speaking about "him" to "we" or "us": The "works of God" were "manifested in *him*[186] in order that *we* might not be seeking out another hand... knowing that this hand which formed *us*... has in the last times sought

---

[185] *Haer.* iv.38.3.

[186] *uti manifestarentur opera Dei in ipso* (cf. John 9.3). Interestingly, in the Vulgate and in the Greek manuscript tradition (without variant), we do not find the demonstrative "intensive" pronoun (*ipso*) but rather the ordinary third person pronoun *illo* / αὐτῷ.

us who were lost...."[187] In *Haer.* v.16.2-3, Irenaeus will make more explicit his universal claim that Genesis 3 describes humanity as in a state of loss. Not all persons may need God's bodily re-fashioning as did the blind man, but according to Irenaeus' view of human fallenness,[188] all have become like "lost sheep" because of disobedience. Unless the Shepherd comes to restore us into the "fold of life," our prospects are limited to wandering and eventual death. So when John 9 is read through the spectacles of Genesis 2.7, we have a glimpse of God's economic activity writ large. The divine action seen in Jesus' healing is symbolic and representative of God's work humanity to fashion the *homo vivens*. Naturally, if Genesis and John attest to the continuity of the work, they also must attest the continuity and unity of the Worker. The God who restores life is none other than the God who gave life to begin with. Christ, the healer of the body of dust, must be the divine Word who first molded it. Irenaeus does not describe Christ's work in v.15 as *recapitulare*, as he had in v.14. Yet he certainly builds upon this previous theological claim. In v.14, Irenaeus describes Christ as recapitulating bodily humanity by virtue of his incarnation. Now in v.15, through an act of healing that symbolizes bodily recapitulation Christ reveals himself to be the very hand of God who both forms and re-forms humanity.

Although Christ manifests the continuity of God's economic work, its unity ought not to be confused with uniformity. Based on the citation from v.15.2, it is clear that Irenaeus takes seriously the perception (particularly championed by Gnostic-informed sects) that divine activities in creation and restoration are marked not only by continuity but also differentiation. The Word actively works in two distinct temporal locales: *in initio* and *in novissimis temporibus*. Furthermore, the former is divided into two spatial categories which are comparable. As for the first man, the Artificer formed him from dust and placed him in παράδεισος (as attested by Genesis 2). As for the rest, so Irenaeus observes in Jeremiah 1.5 and Galatians 1.15, "the Word of God forms us in the womb" (v.15.3).[189] Thus, the Word's healing activity – using dust to restore sight to the blind man's eyes which "the Artificer... had omitted to form in the womb" – is seen to be of a piece with the formative work of the divine Artificer who presides over human origination. The fact that this man had been blind from birth (*nativitate*) is not an incidental detail but is quite vital for Irenaeus' christological hermeneutic of John 9. When the content of the revelation is assessed and found to be in perfect harmony (despite possible objections), only one legitimate discontinuity then remains: *human access to this revelation*. This

---

[187] *Haer.* v.15.2; emphasis is added.
[188] Cf. our chapter three above.
[189] Tertullian also notes this parallel between the garden and the womb (cf. *An.* 26.5). In *Haer.* v.16.1, Irenaeus is keen to emphasize continuity between Adam and "us."

is the contrast that Irenaeus seizes upon. When the Word became incarnate and lived among us, he introduced a genuinely new and qualitatively different era of revelation in God's economy. In the citation from v.15.2 above, Irenaeus had highlighted this contrast: "what the Artificer, the Word, had omitted to form in the womb (*in ventre*), he then supplied in *public* (*in manifesto*) that the works of God might be manifested in him...." Now, Irenaeus will elaborate upon it:

> As, therefore, we are by the Word fashioned (*plasmare*) in the womb, this very same Word formed the faculty of sight in him who had been blind from his birth; showing *openly* (*manifesto ostendens*) *who* is our Fashioner (*Plasmator*) in *secret* (*in abscondito*), since the Word himself had been made manifest to men; and declaring the original formation of Adam (*et antiquam plasmationem Adae disserens*), and the manner in which he was created (*et quomodo factus est*), and by what hand he was fashioned (*et per quam plasmatus est manum*), indicating the whole from a part. For the Lord who formed the faculty of sight, this is he who fashioned (*plasmare*) the whole man (*universum hominem*), carrying out the will of the Father.[190]

Christ's act of applying dust to the eyes of the blind man to restore his sight *openly* reveals Christ's identity as the hand of God and it reveals God's identity as, simultaneously, Father of Jesus Christ and Creator of humanity. So although in Irenaeus' view, God is present and active in our original formation, his activity is hidden and his presence is shrouded. We are fashioned *in abscondito*. Accordingly, before the revelation of the divine Word in Christ, the body's purpose in God's economy could not be clearly discerned. Perhaps human beings could be excused for not knowing how this God related to human bodiliness, or, indeed, who this creator God was at all. But now "in these last times," the public ministry of Christ manifests both the identity of the God who fashions the human body, and God's purpose for that body in his oikonomia. Now that the visible Word has given access to qualitatively superior knowledge of God, the differentiated sequence of God's economy ought to be recognized as an intrinsic unity. Christ's public "recapitulation" of the body (of sorts) in turn casts light *backward* upon his original "capitulation" of the body in secret. This Word therefore "declares the original formation of Adam" (v.15.3).

Not surprisingly, then, we see that Irenaeus' intertextual reading moves in both directions. Just as Genesis 2.7 gives insight into the *work* (i.e., *why* Christ healed with dust), John 9 illumines the *Work-er*, the "God" of Genesis 2.7. Genesis 2.7 enables Irenaeus' typological, christocentric reading of John 9 so that Christ is located with respect to Scripture, here, to the creation narrative.

---

[190] *Haer.* v.15.3; *SC* 153 (208.88-97); emphasis is added.

John 9 brings crucial new illumination to that narrative, dispelling the fog that would obscure humanity's (bodily) origin from God and thus conceal its intended destiny with God. Irenaeus' appeal is that his opponents would come and "see" just as had the blind man.[191] Sight is restored so that (*ut*) one might come to know (*cognoscere*) the "Fashioner" (*Plasmatorem*) and become acquainted with (*discere*) the Lord who "confers" life.[192] To summarize this second point, Genesis 2.7 enables Irenaeus to read the John 9 account of Christ's healing as revealing the essential continuity of God's activity toward humankind. This revelation reflects, or possibly expresses God's own self-unity. Insofar as the Word's healing ministry opens blind eyes to the knowledge of God, it also procures for them *life*.

We have already made reference to this our third observation from Irenaeus' text in v.15.2 as cited above. God's work of fashioning humanity is oriented toward the goal of making it truly alive, as much in body as in soul. This *homo vivens* is God's purpose and humanity's intended destiny. Irenaeus tenderly imagines the Word as God's hand who "sought us out (*exquere*) who were lost (*perdere*), winning back (*lucrifacere*) his own, and taking up the lost sheep upon his shoulders, and with joy restoring it to the fold of *life* (*in cohortem restituens vitae*).[193] Throughout v.15.1-3, Irenaeus reiterates this depiction of God's eschatological gift of life to humanity, making mention of it at the end of each of the three paragraph divisions. Besides the "fold of life" metaphor at the end of v.15.2, at the end of v.15.1 Irenaeus speaks of the "good Father" as "benevolently conferring (*dare*) this *life* upon those who have not life from themselves." At the end of v.15.3, he describes the goal of Christ's healing as granting acquaintance with the one who fashions and confers (*dare*) life. Later, at the end of v.16.1, Irenaeus claims that the "Lord" is the "hand of God" who, "from the beginning even to the end, forms us and prepares (*coaptare*) us *for life*."

Having looked at three aspects of *work* of Christ (its content, process, and purpose) given Irenaeus' placement of John 9 in conversation with Genesis 2.7, we now turn to the question of *identity*. Christ is the very revelation of God. In the passage from v.15.2 which we have cited as paradigmatic of Irenaeus' intertextual reading, Irenaeus claims that Christ was

> ... manifesting (*manifestans*) the hand of God to the sort of people who would be able to understand (*qui intellegere possint*) by what (*per quam*) [hand] man was fashioned (*plasmare*) out of the dust... [The Word publicly "finished" the eyes that had originally been "omitted"] so that (*uti*) the

---

[191] *Haer.* v.15.3.
[192] *Haer.* v.15.3; *SC* 153 (210.103-105).
[193] *Haer.* v.15.2; *SC* 153 (206.80-82); emphasis is added.

works of God might be manifested in him, in order that we might not be seeking out another hand by which man was fashioned, nor another Father... (v.15.2).[194]

Regarding his hermeneutic, Irenaeus' reasoning, as informed by John 9.3, shows sequential order. God's work in Christ is manifest *so that* we might not "seek" another. Genesis 2.7 is not merely repeated but reinterpreted and relocated within the newly expanded vista of God's economy. To Irenaeus, Genesis 2.7 provides the requisite insight for perceiving the work of Christ as recapitulation. On the basis of this knowledge, Genesis 2.7 points to an interpretation of Christ himself as the tangible, public revelation of God the Father. As we have previously stressed, the revelation of God's work necessarily contributes to a revelation of God. In John 9, Irenaeus thinks he has uncovered compelling christological evidence with which to confront the amalgam of Valentinian theology. In order for Irenaeus' intended audience to be swayed by his "rule of truth" (i.e., only one God), they must be convinced by his distinctive answer to the question, "Who exactly is this Jesus of the gospels?"

Although Irenaeus' direct commentary is limited to John 9.1-7, he is plainly aware that the central question in the broader gospel context is that of Jesus' identity (cf. John 8.25: "Who are you?"). In John 9.5, just before applying the moistened dust to the blind man's eyes and healing him, Jesus says "While I am in the world, I am the light of the world" (cf. John 8.12). Indeed, through the careful arrangement of the words and actions of Jesus, John's gospel clearly highlights revelation as the central issue. This theme is particularly emphasized at the end of John 9. In the controversy that ensues after Jesus heals the man born blind, Jesus translates the concrete concepts of blindness and sight into *figurative* ones. When the healed man, prompted by Jesus, asks "who is the Son of Man," Jesus replies, "you have seen (ὁρᾶν) him and the one speaking to you is he."[195] Subsequently Jesus says within earshot of the Pharisees, "I came into this world for judgment so that those who do not see (βλέπειν) may see, and those who do see may become blind."[196] They correctly understand Jesus to imply that they, by claiming to have sight, are actually "blind." Proffering an entirely different perspective on the connection between sin and blindness than had been applied to the man born blind, Jesus remarks, "If you were blind, you would not have sin. But now that you say, 'we see,' your sin remains."[197] Evidently, not all persons will be able to see the revelation of God in Christ.

---

[194] *SC* 153 (206.72-78).
[195] John 9.37.
[196] John 9.39.
[197] John 9.41. Thus although the connection between sin and blindness is not as the Pharisees had presumed (cf. John 9.2-3, 34), Jesus insinuates that there *is* such a link, as evidenced by the Pharisees themselves.

Yet it is one thing for Irenaeus to recognize the Johannine textual concern with sight and to reflect theologically about Jesus as revealing God. It is quite another for him to hang the full weight of his argument on the merits of one very specific, bold claim that the word "dust" here conveys paramount *theological* significance. Because "dust" is found in both John 9 and Genesis 2, Irenaeus is confident that Scripture identifies Jesus as the cosmic Creator. At first glance, this interpretation of John seems either clumsily forced or distressingly naïve. Is it possible to defend a hermeneutic that shamelessly depends on one tenuous word association? Does not Irenaeus' early "canonical" reading show indifference to the textual integrity of both Genesis and John? Is this not rudimentary eisegesis rather than exegesis? When assessing early Christian interpretation of another Genesis text, the account in chapter 22 of Abraham's narrowly averted sacrifice of Isaac, Brevard Childs remarks: "One of the major problems of the typological interpretation of Genesis 22 was caused by an uncritical Christian tendency to fasten on to an external similarity between such features as Isaac's carrying the wood and Jesus' carrying the cross which obscured the *true witness of the text* itself."[198] If we, for the moment at least, accept Childs' interpretative standard, we may ask whether Irenaeus' reading of John 9.6 in light of Genesis 2.7 is hermeneutically defensible, or whether it instead "obscures the true witness" of John and Genesis. Is Irenaeus warranted in seizing upon this "external similarity" of dust? An assessment of this instance of Irenaeus' exegesis will offer particular insight toward a broader understanding of his anthropology and also his hermeneutical stance toward Scripture, derived, as it is, from certain christological commitments.

First, Irenaeus' specific interpretation of John 9.6 and indeed of the entire healing account in chapter 9 is not a crude example of proof-texting, but rather reflects his attempt to understand John first in light of *John* (not of Genesis). It is not surprising that we find a preponderance of Johannine themes in *Haer.* v.14-15, given that Irenaeus sees himself as standing in the tradition of Polycarp, whom he believed to have known "John, the disciple of the Lord."[199] "Shepherd" / "sheepfold" / "life" (v.15.2; cf. John 10.1-16) and fruit-bearing (v.14.4; cf. John 15.1-6) are simply two of the more obvious examples. Other than John 9 itself, though, the co-text most significant for Irenaeus' exegesis of John 9 is John 5. As we have seen, Irenaeus' exegesis of the text wherein Jesus heals the blind man makes backward reference to Jesus' healing of the lame man at Beth-zatha in order to draw a comparison and contrast of Jesus' methods. However, if we reasonably assume that Irenaeus found not only Jesus' actions in the first healing to have bearing on his second healing but also his associated

---

[198] Brevard Childs, *Biblical Theology of the Old and New Testaments* (Minneapolis: Fortress, 1993), 335-36; emphasis is added.
[199] Cf. *Haer.* iii.3.4; Eusebius, *Hist. eccl.* 5.20.5-6.

words (i.e., the Johannine Jesus' own interpretation of this healing), a fuller picture emerges. Jesus' response to the "Jews" who were "persecuting" him for healing on the Sabbath is to assist their interpretation of him. Explains Jesus, "Indeed, just as the Father raises the dead and gives them life, so also the Son gives life to whomever he wishes."[200] Yet Jesus acknowledges that his opponents do not accept this self-interpretation just provided, just as they will not accept the testimony of John the Baptist, or of Jesus' works, or of the Father himself (cf. John 5.31-38). In a move that simultaneously appeals to common ground and raises the stakes, Jesus climactically declares that even "Moses" testifies to his identity. There is in fact *textual* evidence to substantiate Jesus' claim to be the "giver of life" along with the Father.

> Do not think that I will accuse you before the Father; your accuser is Moses, on whom you have set your hope. If you believed Moses, you would believe me, *for he wrote about me*. But if you do not believe what he wrote, how will you believe what I say?[201]

Irenaeus himself cites this Johannine text in *Haer.* iv.2.3 as demonstrating that "the writings (*litterae*) of Moses are the words (*verba*) of Christ." Another text earlier in John's gospel is similar. When Philip came upon Nathanael he said to him, "We have found him about whom Moses in the law and also the prophets wrote, Jesus son of Joseph from Nazareth."[202] As Irenaeus interprets John 5 in connection with John 9 in order to challenge his own critics, one could envision that he might strive to emulate Jesus' strategy. To make his specific interpretation of Jesus as convincing as possible, he would seek to press forward the most conclusive – and convicting – evidence available. Of course the Pharisees acknowledged the pre-eminence of Moses, but even the Valentinians could not afford to ignore "Moses" and, therefore, Genesis 2.7. Their strategy was not to dismiss but rather co-opt these texts by providing a more persuasive re-interpretation. Presumably, Irenaeus would have been well aware that when in John 9 the Pharisees debated over how to "interpret" this Jesus who has just – allegedly – performed another healing (as in John 5), the text suggests the same hermeneutical point as before. The Pharisees admit "We know that God has spoken to Moses, but as for this man, we do not know where he comes from" (John 9.29). In John 5, Irenaeus sees that Jesus concurs with the Pharisees that the "Mosaic" texts are crucial, relevant, and authoritative when discerning and interpreting the revelation of God – even when the locus of such a disclosure is

---

[200] John 5.21.

[201] John 5.45-47; emphasis is added.

[202] John 1.45. Irenaeus does not cite verse 45, but his familiarity with this text is seen by his reference to John 1.47 in *Haer.* iii.11.6.

purported to be embodied in a person. But, argues Irenaeus following Jesus' pattern, although God has indeed spoken to Moses, this revelation is not to be seen in contradistinction to the revelation given by Christ. Moses' revelation (Genesis) is itself illumined by Christ, just as John's portrait of Christ is rightly understood in light of God's revelation through Moses. Both texts attest one and the same God.

In addition to the aforementioned contribution of the John 5 healing account, we discover additional reasons in the text of John 9 itself for sympathizing with Irenaeus' hermeneutical move. His explanation that Christ's action – using dust to heal a blind man – identifies him as Fashioner is perhaps simply Irenaeus' *answer* to the two questions that the Pharisees raise in John's narrative. (It would seem that Irenaeus takes seriously the questions raised by Jesus' opponents just as he takes seriously those of his own.) The first question raised of Jesus is this: *How* did Jesus heal these blind eyes? First the "neighbors" "kept saying" to the man who was healed, "then how were your eyes opened?"[203] Afterward, the Pharisees "also began to ask him how he had received his sight. He said to them, "He put mud on my eyes. Then I washed, and now I see."[204] This "how" question is the one they then ask amongst themselves (verse 16) and the one they ask of the man's parents (verse 19). Finally they return to question the man again: "What did he do to you? How did he open your eyes?"[205] The second question is closely related to the first: *Where* does Jesus come from? In verse 29 (mentioned above), the critics declare, "we know that God has spoken to Moses, but as for this man, we do not know where he comes from." The man replies by offering an answer of his own, "Here is an astonishing thing! You do not know where he comes from, and yet he opened my eyes... If this man were not from God, he could do nothing."[206] Irenaeus' glimpse of Genesis 2.7 in John 9.6 depends on the fact that this man's ailment was blindness *from birth*. The restored man himself highlights the significance of this factor: "Never since the world began (ἐκ τοῦ αἰῶνος) has it been heard that anyone opened the eyes of a person born blind."[207] When Irenaeus addresses these two questions together, the *how* and the *whence*, he asserts that the means by which Jesus healed (the moistened dust) actually points to Jesus' identity. He is the one who has come from the Father. As Jesus describes in John 5.36, "the very works that I am doing testify on my behalf that the Father has sent me." If the man's blindness is associated with his point of origination, the womb before birth, the only one who can conceivably reverse it is one who is present at this

---

[203] John 9.10.
[204] John 9.15.
[205] John 9.26.
[206] John 9.30, 33.
[207] John 9.32.

beginning and who is the Fashioner of the body. As we have noted above, Irenaeus locates the workspace of the Word who fashions as being both womb and garden. Insofar as Moses provides the only account of the God who formed the first man from dust and gave him the breath of life in the garden, Moses also speaks of the God who creates human life in the womb and who restores it to life by means of dust. A catholic-Christian hermeneutic insists that the gospel account of God's revelation in Christ is set in the context of God's other self-revelation. The resulting interpretation manifests and clarifies the theological basis for Christian speech of humanity: one God (Father and two hands), one harmonious economy, and one embodied human race. Perhaps Irenaeus' ascription of theological significance to "dust" in John 9.6 does not necessarily flout modern exegetical standards, such as fidelity to the "true witness of the text itself."[208] The Johannine text may not insist on Irenaeus' reading, yet it remains open and perhaps hospitable toward it.

As cited above, Irenaeus interpreted Christ's healing act as, in effect, "declaring the original formation of Adam, and the manner in which he was created, and by what hand he was fashioned, *indicating the whole from a part* (*ex parte totum ostendens*). For the Lord who formed the faculty of sight, this is he who fashioned (*plasmare*) the whole man (*universum hominem*), carrying out the will of the Father."[209] Certainly, Irenaeus means that Christ's healing of the eyes, the "part," shows him to be the one who fashioned the "whole," that is the entire physical body. But on the basis of how Irenaeus uses the Genesis and John texts theologically, we may find Irenaeus' words suggestive, and indeed emblematic of the wider hermeneutical judgment he makes: *The manifestation of the Word in the flesh is the "part" that indicates the "whole," that is, the whole revelation of God and of God's* oikonomia. Irenaeus' hermeneutic of Scripture is avowedly christocentric. However, the critical distinguishing feature of his christological method is its reliance upon Genesis 1-2 to provide the parameters within which this "part" (Christ) is to be construed in the apostolic texts.[210] When this part is applied, it functions as the hermeneutical tool that enables Christian readings of the *whole* of Scripture and indeed of the whole sphere of creation. If human access to knowledge of God's oikonomia and God himself is textually mediated, and if Christ is to be recognized and received as the hermeneutic by which to read this text, then a revelation of Christ is somehow a revelation of God, humanity and, in fact, of all reality without remainder.

---

[208] Cf. Childs, *Biblical Theology*, 336.

[209] *Haer.* v.15.3; emphasis is added.

[210] At the same time, we may be reminded that it is not Genesis 1-2 in itself that serves as the key part but rather Christ as read through the lens of Genesis.

Christ-speech summarized (Haer. v.15.4-16.2)

When the Valentinians read Scripture, the characterizations of God and of humanity they found in Genesis 2.7 may have seemed at best irrelevant and at worst irreconcilable to those offered in the gospel of John. Viewed through the lenses of their tradition, Genesis depicted a Demiurge who had encased humanity in a sensate fleshly substance only as a concession to Necessity.[211] The physical body was neither the intention nor the work of Bythus. It was a stopgap in that it provided a useful – albeit temporary – service to the ψυχικοί. Once successfully trained and educated, these people would be promoted, finally able to dispose of the body. John's gospel, beginning as it does, would appear to offer a view of deity and human bodiliness to contrast with Genesis. One can easily suspect that for Gnostic theologians eagerly searching sacred texts for hints of an unseen spiritual realm, the cryptic words ἐν ἀρχῇ ἦν ὁ λόγος proved more arresting than ἐν ἀρχῇ ἐποίησεν ὁ θεὸς τὸν οὐρανὸν καὶ τὴν γῆν. John furthermore describes this divine λόγος as the true light coming from outside the "world" into a world that "did not know him."[212] Only to a select group of people, those who "receive" him, is it granted to become "children of God."[213] However else these elect may be described, the gospel later plainly asserts that "God is *spirit* and those who worship him must worship in spirit and truth."[214] When Christ, the divine emissary, spoke of life he typically spoke of "eternal" life. Clearly, given Christ's frequent entreaties, the living, breathing, embodied persons to whom Christ spoke did not yet possess this divine quality of *eternal* life.[215]

Irenaeus, however, is quite unwilling to surrender any ground to these competing interpreters of John. Having responded with a christological reading of John 9 that is thoroughly invested in the text of Genesis 2.7, Irenaeus exclaims in summary:

> All the followers of Valentinus, therefore, lose their case when they say that man was not fashioned out of this earth (*non ex hac terra plasmatum esse hominem*), but from a fluid and diffused substance (*sed a fluida materia et effusa*). For from the earth (*terra*) out of which the Lord formed eyes for that man, *from the same earth* it is evident that man was also fashioned at the beginning (*ab initio*).

---

[211] Cf. *Haer.* i.5.5.
[212] John 1.10.
[213] John 1.12.
[214] John 4.24.
[215] Cf. John 3.15; 3.16; 3.36; 4.14; 4.36; 5.24; 5.39; 6.27; 6.40; 6.47; 6.54; 6.68; 10.28; 12.50; 17.2; 17.3.

> For it would be inconsistent (*non enim consequens erat*) that the eyes be formed from one source and the rest of the body from another; as neither would it be compatible that one [being] fashioned the body and another the eyes. But he, the very same who fashioned (*plasmare*) Adam at the beginning, with whom also the Father spoke, "Let us make man after our image and likeness," revealing (*manifestare*) himself in these last times (*in novissimis temporibus*) to humanity, formed the faculty of sight for him who had been blind from Adam (*qui ab Adam caecus erat*) (v.15.4).

Both of the key texts which have been our focus, Genesis 1.26 and 2.7, are here conjoined by Irenaeus to demonstrate how the Johannine portrait of Christ refutes Valentinian anthropology. The very criticism of incompatibility that the Valentinians had pinned on non-Gnostic Christian interpreters (i.e., the cobbling together of two disparate textual portraits of God), Irenaeus levels back at them. Given a protological orientation upon which both sides could agree, is not the gospel depiction of Christ incompatible with a depiction of two separate human substances superintended by two separate gods? Both Irenaeus' use of Genesis 2.7 to explain Christ's recapitulation of humanity (cf. our earlier study of *Haer.* v.14.2) and his use of Genesis 2.7 here to portray Christ's revelation of divinity, yield the same implication. The affirmation of "one human *substance*" must be added to Irenaeus' credo of unity (one God, one church, one economy). As the one who healed the blind man with dust is now "revealing himself in these last times to humanity" (v.15.4), it is apparent that he is the eternal Word. This is the one who formed Adam in the beginning with the intent that he be made after the divine image and likeness (v.15.4). Thus the Genesis creation texts enable the telling of a clear, coherent Christian narrative: God – Father, Spirit and now Son – is purposefully and steadily working to fashion the *homo vivens*.

In addition to drawing the narratives of John 9 and Genesis 2 together on the basis of the common term "dust," Irenaeus continues to find theological significance in the juxtaposition of their themes. As with his ambitious "as / so" statements in *Haer.* v.1.3,[216] Irenaeus uses this same construction in v.15.4 when offering an expansive typological reading of Genesis 3.8-9. More specifically, Irenaeus interprets these verses prophetically and *christologically*: they speak of Christ's advent to earth.[217]

---

[216] Cf. our discussion earlier in this chapter.

[217] Simonetti remarks that although Irenaeus primarily follows a "literal interpretation" of Genesis 1-3 in contrast to Gnostic approaches, this example shows that he nevertheless considers himself authorized to "overlap" this with "spiritual interpretation" where opportune ("Per typica ad vera," 379).

> Wherefore also the Scripture, pointing out what should come to pass,[218] says that when Adam had hid himself because of his disobedience, the Lord came to him at eventide and called him forth and said, "Where are you?" That means that in the last times, the very same Word of God came to call man, reminding him of his doings, living in which he had been hidden from God. For *just as* (*quemadmodum*) at that time God spoke to Adam in the evening, seeking him out, *so also* (*sic*) in the last times (*in novissimis temporibus*), by means of the same voice (*per eandem vocem*), he has visited, seeking out [Adam's] posterity (*visitavit exquirens genus ejus*).[219]

There is only one humanity, Adam's "race," just as there is only one God. Just as he did to Adam, God now calls to humanity "in the evening." Following Adam's disobedience and its bearing upon all of his descendants, humanity has sought to hide from God. The man from John 9, whom Irenaeus describes as *qui ab Adam caecus erat*, represents a humanity bereft of sight "from Adam."[220] That is, he stands not just for post-formation but post-transgression humanity.[221] If humanity has sought to hide from God, so also – to a limited degree – has God chosen to remain hidden. But now Irenaeus sees that Christ (in John's gospel) both illumines and completes the story of how an embodied humanity is related to its Creator God in the continuum of the divine economy. Irenaeus' Genesis hermeneutic manifests Christ as the maker and the seeker. He recapitulates humanity even as he reveals God. In *Haer.* v.16.1-2, Irenaeus reflects upon Christ's illumination and completion in summary form. Now that God's hand has been made known, we have no warrant for seeking "another Father" nor "another substance from which we have been formed." The Word is that "hand of God" who "from the beginning even to the end *forms us and prepares us for life*,[222] and is present with his handiwork, and perfects (*perficere*) it *after the*

---

[218] *Et propter hoc Scriptura significans quod futurum erat ait...*(SC 153 [212.119-120]).

[219] *Haer.* v.15.4; *SC* 153 (212.127-128). Emphasis is added.

[220] The *ANF* translation supplies additional words: "blind [in that body which he had derived] from Adam." But this gloss is possibly reductionist in this context, given Irenaeus' propensity to read John 9.6-7 symbolically and theologically.

[221] Cp. Origen, *Cels.* 4.40. Whereas "Adam" may be invoked as a figure epitomizing human excellence in the beginning of the story (cf. Tertullian), or at its end (cf. Clement of Alexandria), Irenaeus finds his "true excellence" "in the middle where he is perfected and restored" (Eric Osborn, "The Excellence of Adam in Second Century Christian Thought," *Cahiers de Biblia Patristica* 2 [1989]: 52).

[222] *ab initio usque ad finem format nos et* coaptat in vitam.... The Latin in plus the accusative, when speaking about time, may connote the sense of "for" This identifies the purpose of the Word's activities: "for life."

image and likeness of God" (v.16.1).[223] For Irenaeus, then, Genesis 2.7 and 1.26 illumine the intention, goal, actors, activities, and substance which characterize the divine economy. These texts supply an interpretative grid with which to read the rest of Scripture. In our third chapter, we suggested that Irenaeus utilized Genesis 1.26 as a flexible hermeneutical tool to speak of humanity's relation to God. Now, having used Genesis 2.7 to supply a scripturally-informed, Trinitarian[224] theological basis for Christian anthropology, Irenaeus returns to Genesis 1.26. This text facilitates an apt summary of the significance of Christ's advent.

> When the Word of God was made man, he assimilated himself to man and man to himself,[225] so that by means of his resemblance to the Son, man might be precious to the Father. For in times before (πρόσθεν χρόνοις), it was *said* (*dicere*) that man was made after the image of God, but it was not *shown* (δεικνύειν / *ostendere*), for the Word was invisible (ἀόρατος) after whose image man was made (γίνομαι). On account of this he easily lost (ῥαδίως ἀπέβαλεν) the likeness (ὁμοίωσις).[226]

Frequently, this passage has been cited by curious scholars as evidence of Irenaeus' technical understanding of the terms "image" and "likeness."[227] Drawing from the Middle-Platonist thought of his day as well as the New Testament, Irenaeus recognizes the divine Word (*Logos*) as the true image of God, and humanity as made in the image of this Word (that is, an image of an image).[228] Be this as it may, we should also note that Irenaeus' statement is situated in the context of his interpretation and theological use of diverse texts (John and Genesis) as Christian Scripture to locate humanity in relation to God's economic work. As mentioned above in our third chapter, while Irenaeus' reading of Genesis 3 did not permit him to absolve human responsibility for disobeying God, he does use Genesis 1.26 language to claim that mitigating circumstances attended this tragedy. In the infancy period of his fashioning,

---

[223] Emphasis is added.

[224] Irenaeus' depiction of God is at best "proto-Trinitarian" insofar as no reference is made to God's immanent relations. It is clear, though, that for Irenaeus, God is revealed as economically triune.

[225] ... *quando homo Verbum Dei factum est, semetipsum homini et hominem sibimetipsi assimilans*....

[226] *Haer.* v.16.2; *SC* 153 (216.21-29). Emphasis is added.

[227] For example, Sesboüé associates "image" with the work of the Word and "likeness" with that of the Spirit (*Tout récapituler dans le Christ*, 188-89). De Andía explains that these terms, as used here, identify a "double relation between man and the Word" (*Homo vivens*, 69).

[228] Cf. 2 Cor 4.4; cp. Plato, *Timaeus* 28a-29c; Philo, *Opif.* 30; *Confusion* 142; et al.

Adam's capabilities were limited and his judgment uninformed. Subsequent human generations also "saw" their divine Fashioner only but dimly. But, says Irenaeus, the Word's advent in the flesh "confirmed" (ἐπικυροῦν) humanity's image and likeness after God in both these ways: "he showed (δεικνύειν[229]) the image truly, since he became himself what was his image, and he securely re-established (*restituere*) the likeness [by] assimilating (συνεξομοιοῦν) man to the invisible Father by means of the visible Word" (v.16.2).

"Summing up": Irenaeus' Exploits with Genesis 2.7 and 1.26

In this chapter, we have drawn attention to Irenaeus' multifaceted deployment of Genesis 2.7 in response to the Valentinians' application of 1 Corinthians 15.50 to anthropology. In the process of supplying what he believes to be a superior interpretation of this Pauline text, Irenaeus appropriates the theological riches of Genesis 2.7 (i.e., imagery of God's formation of the human body from dust and his inbreathing the breath of life) to interpret a broader range of texts: prophetic, apostolic, and gospel. The results are two-fold. First, Irenaeus models an innovative hermeneutic of Scripture that is painstakingly christocentric, while showing remarkable flexibility and interpretative freedom. Second, Irenaeus employs this hermeneutic to cast an expansive, unique vision of God that prepares the way for an anti-Platonist Christian anthropology.

As for the first point on hermeneutics, a detailed rehearsal is not needed. Suffice to say, Irenaeus' uses of Genesis 2.7 and 1.26 suggest that his biblical interpretation was christological both in aim and means. Because the Word has recapitulated humanity and revealed divinity, to read Christ in Scripture is to discover that these texts all attest one God and one triune economy. Yet one further hermeneutical point remains to be made. Irenaeus, as an "exegete," was not amiss in exercising substantial interpretative freedom. His theological reading of John 9.6 by means of Genesis 2.7 has provided us the opportunity to examine this freedom in some detail. Previously, we offered reasons why it would be hasty to dismiss Irenaeus' christological association of these two texts bound by their common reference to "dust." Rather than exemplifying primitive and desperate proof-texting, Irenaeus shows a sensitivity to local textual integrity – albeit not in competition with *canonical* integrity – that is characteristic of sound exegesis. Unlike other seemingly unfettered allegorical readings, Irenaeus' interpretation draws on literary features and invitations expressed by the Johannine text itself.

---

[229] Aorist tense

Yet it is fair to challenge the interpretative standard to which we alluded earlier, namely Childs' claim that a given reading of Scripture ought never to "obscure the true witness of the text itself."[230] Presumably to clarify what he means by the (rather ambiguous) phrase "true witness of the text itself," Childs avers that a reading which "relate[s] each biblical witness mimetically badly blurs the radical discontinuities of the text."[231] Instead, "the basic theological task [is] to pursue exegetically how the *uniqueness of each text* is preserved along with a frequently broadened theological application for ongoing Christian faith."[232] Although Childs wishes to champion a canonical hermeneutic that provides the conditions for "broadening" the theological readings of texts as Scripture, his predilection for caution and textual segregation works against this objective. If, as Childs argues, "exegetical rigor"[233] is the safeguard against derivations of meaning based on the "mimetic" convergence of two texts, it is difficult to see how the "broadening" of "theological application" is even possible. In practice, Childs' proscription encourages the setting up of unwarranted and perhaps undesirable barriers to patently christological readings of the Old Testament. Each text may indeed express a certain exegetical "uniqueness," that is, a voice of its own. At the same time, it would be unwise to discount or deny the role of the theological interpreter. Irenaeus' initiative and freedom as a theologian is defensible. When he locates John 9 and Genesis 2 together in a canonical relationship, the theological meaning he ascribes to this conversation is one that emerges in the *conjunction* of these texts, not in their self-isolation.[234] What results is something that is genuinely new – a radically *christocentric* reading that breaches Childs' restrictive criteria.[235] At the same time, although Irenaeus' theological hermeneutic may be more daring than

---

[230] Childs, *Biblical Theology*, 336.
[231] Ibid.
[232] Ibid.; emphasis is added.
[233] Ibid.
[234] In his book *Agape, Eros and Gender* (Cambridge: Cambridge University Press, 2000), Francis Watson offers a paraphrase of Augustine's conjunctive reading of Romans 7 and Genesis 3. The powerful "desire" of which Paul laments is interpreted by Augustine as "pre-eminently sexual desire" (104; cf. 102-107). The narrative of Adam and Eve's use of fig leaves to hide their genitals, according to Augustine, makes this clear. The result of Augustine's hermeneutic is that theological meaning is attributed to neither text in itself, but emerges in the confluence of the two. Not only the texts, but the interpreter has played a significant role in this reading. Of course, all such interpretations should be subsequently evaluated on the basis of available evidence.
[235] On this general point, cf. Armstrong: "Als Geschichte sind die alttestamentlichen Ereignisse als solche für Irenaeus weniger bedeutsam; denn nur in ihrer Christusbezogenheit sind sie wirklich verständlich, Wenn man sie außerhalb ihrer gemeinsamen Beziehung zu Christus betrachten wollte, würden sie kaum einen Zusammenhang miteinander behalten" (*Die Genesis in der Alten Kirche*, 61).

Childs', he does not advocate an unregulated interpretative playing field. Whereas Childs is more concerned to set exegetical constraints determined by the "uniqueness" of individual texts, Irenaeus' avowed interest is with *theological* rules. In this respect, his reading of John 9.6 by means of Genesis 2.7 contributes to and reflects his *regula veritatis*. This template restricts as well as frees his activities as an interpreter of biblical texts. It is the standard by which he holds Valentinian readers accountable.

We now move to our second point, that Irenaeus' christological, Genesis-informed hermeneutic of Scripture is essential to his task of elaborating a satisfying non-Platonist anthropology. As we have argued above, to trace Irenaeus' argument in *Haer.* v.1-16 is to notice his concern to set anthropology on a firm theological foundation. Genesis 2.7 provides the means for Irenaeus to speak authoritatively about God as a triunity and about God's economy as his purposeful work in the human sphere. The Father and his two hands, Spirit and Son, provide humanity not a means of escape from their physical bodies, but a manner of bodily transformation so that human persons *as created* are enabled to have fellowship with God and participate in God's life. Genesis 2.7, in Irenaeus' eyes, identifies the Father as the origin and destiny of humanity. It furthermore outlines the Father's intention to vivify human bodies and affirms his power to accomplish this. Resurrection, not just creation, is in view at the beginning of Scripture's story of God's oikonomia. Using Genesis 2.7, Irenaeus can explain how the incorporeal divine Spirit relates to corporeal human bodies. Not only does this text reorient the question of human composition to focus instead on humanity's potential when engaged by the Spirit, it also depicts how the Spirit overcomes every obstacle that would hinder the fulfillment of God's plan to fashion the *homo vivens*. When Irenaeus finally comes to Christ and how a catholic-Christian interpretation of Christ bears upon both theology and anthropology, Genesis 2.7 is Irenaeus' preferred vantage point for rereading Paul, the prophets, and the gospels. 1 Corinthians 15.50 cannot be properly understood unless Christ's incarnation is first recognized as the activity of the one God to recapitulate the one human substance he has made. When Christ uses dust to heal a man blind from birth, Irenaeus sees, by way of Genesis 2.7, that he is the very revelation of this Creator God. No longer are the hands by which humanity was formed "in the beginning" hidden. No longer can the work of this God to restore comprehensive, divine life to an embodied humankind be declared obscure. Now as Irenaeus sums up his assessment of Christ's advent and ministry in *Haer.* v.16 before moving on to speak of his passion,[236] we note

---

[236] Cf. *Haer.* v.16.3: "And not by the aforesaid things alone has the Lord manifested himself, but also by his own passion." The passion of Christ and the temptation of Christ will occupy Irenaeus' attention from *Haer.* v.16.3-24.4. Despite occasional references to

his recourse to the other Genesis focal text that we have examined. Genesis 1.26, alongside Genesis 2.7, reinforces and delineates a christocentric anthropology to counter the one offered by the Valentinians. In God's continuous work of "fashioning humanity" his hands are present and active to "prepare us for life" and "perfect" us "after the image and likeness of God" (16.1). In the sequence of Irenaeus' argument in *Adversus Haereses* book five, Christ's work is portrayed as climactic and decisive within the divine economy. Therefore, as we have noted, Genesis 2.7 was a key contributor to Irenaeus' overall catholic-Christian hermeneutic of Scripture. By means of this verse, Irenaeus presumed the ability to read Scripture in harmony with itself. Scripture offers the completed picture of the triune God's activity – Father, Spirit and Son – to fashion and present the *homo vivens*.

In the end, then, our assessment of Irenaeus' multifaceted use of Genesis 2.7 in *Haer.* v.1-16 suggests that what we discover here is not so much a philosophical problem to solve (as Osborn suggests) but an opportunity to investigate, and perhaps critically appreciate the greater magnitude of Irenaeus' contribution to early Christian thought. Though well-known for his doctrinal proposals, this theologian's model of engagement with Scripture could ultimately prove to be of no less consequence.

---

the creation accounts, Genesis 3 unsurprisingly plays a more primary role in Irenaeus' interpretation of Christ in this section.

CONCLUSION

In 1986, Pope John-Paul II visited Lyons, the seat of Irenaeus' episcopacy, and volunteered to explain why the voice of this second-century bishop continues to speak with vigor and relevance to the generation of our time. "Because Irenaeus knew how to ally fidelity to the tradition to a creative ingenuity [une inventivité créatrice], he was at the same time a theologian of God and of man: of a God who puts his glory in the living man, of a man whose life consists in the vision of God."[1] Our study has suggested that Irenaeus' vibrant and enduring contribution to Christian thought depends in no small part on his outlook toward the textual accounts of creation. For some theologians,[2] creation functions almost as a neutral backdrop or stage for the main drama: Christ's procurement of salvation for humankind. By contrast, this "theologian of God and of man" achieves a remarkably coherent synthesis of Christian doctrine largely because he returns to Genesis to shed light on what is happening in Christ. By virtue of his close attentiveness to the theological significance and implications of a Christian view of creation, it would seem that Irenaeus is better equipped than many to engage the prominent concerns not only of his age, but also of ours.

If one acknowledges the drawbacks of isolating and inflating Irenaeus' view of recapitulation as a controlling doctrinal concept, a more productive approach would note its role within Irenaeus' broader interpretative method – a method conspicuously attuned to his protological interests. Thus, we have argued, although there are reasons for subjecting this bishop's work to a variety of different perspectives, most typically along doctrinal, ideological, rhetorical, and philosophical lines, these viewpoints are incomplete without a hermeneutical assessment. Recognizing that his struggle with new Gnostic-Christian competitors was chiefly a matter of textual interpretation, Irenaeus was

---

[1] Pope John Paul II from a speech quoted by Bernard Sesboüé, *Tout récapituler dans le Christ*, 201-202.
[2] It may be argued, for instance, that Anselm shows such a tendency.

particularly attentive to how the Genesis creation texts (especially Genesis 1.26 and 2.7) may be read and used for the construction of Christian theology. As a result, Irenaeus was able to offer a non-Platonic Christian anthropology grounded in a theological vision of the triune God and his economy. The Father, with his own two hands, fashions a living humanity.

As we conclude, it is appropriate that we offer a few final comments on Irenaeus' contribution as a biblical interpreter by focusing on the three points that were the primary concerns of our chapters one, two, and three through four (respectively): methodology, protological orientation, and anthropology.

Methodology

First, our study of Irenaeus suggests that conventional studies of the history of dogma (or doctrine) have often systematically undervalued the role of exegesis in theological construction. Many of the rather extreme conclusions put forward by Harnack have been discredited. Yet a train of academic scholarship over the last hundred years – including the recent flourish – typically segregates the study of Irenaeus for theological doctrine from the study of his work for other reasons, including exegesis. An alternative test-case, here examining how Irenaeus' exegesis of Genesis 1-2 is instrumental in his formulation of theology, can point out limitations in non-integrated approaches. If in the patristic era, biblical exegesis functioned more as the language of theology rather than as its acknowledged source, the case of competing Irenaean and Gnostic readings of Genesis should be a reminder that such language was not always deployed in a straightforward, unsophisticated manner. Theology was shaped not only by affirming a particular biblical text but also by creatively interpreting and using it for particular purposes, albeit within the bounds of a set of doctrinal parameters. Contemporary interest in philosophical hermeneutics, following a trajectory from Schleiermacher to Gadamer, points to the value of reflecting *critically* on the process of interpretation. Such a trend need not supplant but may actually encourage reflecting *theologically* on such a process of reading as well. If, as a general rule, a lesser degree of segregation between the modern categories of biblical studies and systematic theology is desirable, the area of theological hermeneutics provides some common ground for relating these two lines of enquiry and proclamation. Inevitably, even if one adopts a catholic-Christian paradigm that is more generous than Irenaeus', some theologies and certain biblical interpretations will be judged less acceptable or helpful than others. As a locus of study, then, theological hermeneutics provides a means of analysis and evaluation in a manner reminiscent of Irenaeus' strategy for refuting Valentinian uses of biblical texts. Likewise, in his own landmark, pace-setting work, Irenaeus' theological conclusions or conceptualizations (e.g., recapitulation, divine image, et al.) ought not to be viewed in abstraction from the manner in which he reaches them (i.e., exegesis). Part of the reason for this is that ultimately the conflict was over Scripture. Irenaeus does not tender theological reflections without provocation. He feels compelled to do theology in direct response to what he deems are faulty exegetical construals. To the degree that many contemporary theological projects are also viewed as, at heart, engagements with Scripture (even if only indirectly), Irenaeus' writings might be more self-evidently apropos today than they were during the heydays of biblical criticism or dogmatic theology. Hermeneutical mechanics become increasingly noticeable when one supposes that Scripture attests not only divine propositions but also, in some way, a divine narrative. At the same time, narrative theologies are found wanting if they lack an ontological anchor in dogma. Given Irenaeus' hermeneutic, Scripture attests a divine *economy* that encompasses both dimensions. Truth claims (e.g., the doctrine of God as a triunity) are related within a narratival world and thus found meaningful for Christian living.

We may discern possible lines of contemporary application when more specifically examining Irenaeus' methodology. Genesis 1.26 offers an example. Traditional Old Testament studies seek to identify the referent of the first common plural of "us" in "Let us make humankind in our image" on the basis of historical, cultural, or linguistic enquiry. Accordingly, it is asserted, "us" clearly does not *mean* the Trinity. Yet more recent approaches to texts in general call into question the modern impetus to assume an equivalency between meaning and (historical) referent.[3] Irenaeus, on the basis of an apostolic rule of truth coupled with an economic view of God's relation to humanity, interprets this text as attesting God's address to his Word and Wisdom. From a post-critical (rather than pre-critical) perspective, we might prefer to say at most that Genesis 1.26 is *open* to a christological reading (given suitable characteristics) without requiring it. At the same time, it would be misleading to assume that Irenaeus was unconcerned to read Genesis 1-2 in its own right. The radical contrast between his approach to the text and that of his competitors suggests otherwise. Using a hermeneutic of deconstruction, the Ophites had undermined the credibility of the creation narratives as a reliable story of human beginnings. For their part, the Valentinians had either viewed Genesis as a text needing the supplementation of Middle-Platonic metaphysics and a prequel narrative, or else as a store of symbolism for elaborating the Christ event (cf. *Gospel of Truth*). Irenaeus, however, read Genesis as a true testament to God's initiation of human beginning. One should not jump directly to restoration and re-creation without carefully considering original creation and its theological basis. Accordingly, it

---

[3] Whether or not Irenaeus himself conceptualized a formal distinction between such notions is immaterial.

is important to see that the biggest difference between an Irenaean-informed hermeneutic and a historical-critical hermeneutic is not where it starts but where it ends. Christology was the underlying doctrinal issue at hand in the Irenaean / Valentinian clash. The exegetical focus was not so much "how do we now read Scripture in light of Christ?" but rather "how do we now read Christ (vis-à-vis the apostolic texts) in light of Scripture"? Accordingly, from a confessional Christian standpoint, the exegetical focus ought to remain the same. The methodology starts with an enquiry: "How do we read this text in its own right (i.e., giving a meticulous account of the surrounding co-text and broader historico-cultural context)?" But the enquiry does not stop here but continues: "How do we read this text in light of Christ?" Yet even this is only a penultimate question. One ought then to ask: "How do we read Christ in light of this text?" By moving from the second to the third question, one acknowledges that just as the "critical" paradigm (first enquiry) is insufficient without the "narrative" paradigm (second enquiry), so also the narrative must prepare the way for the "economic" paradigm (third enquiry). This is true insofar as the latter is concerned not just with textual reality, but with reality that transcends (while still inhabiting) the texts.[4] Such a hermeneutic is exemplified by Irenaeus' wide typological interpretation of Genesis 2.7. This text, he argues, points out the identity of the Eternal Word who both forms and restores humanity according to the Father's will. In summary, by refusing to treat the exegetical features of an exposition as ornamental, one gains a greater awareness that texts are not only cited, but, in essence, used. Conversely, biblical exegesis is freed for the pursuit of enquiries not only into a text's referential "meaning" or even its narrative contribution, but also its function in constructive theology.

At the same time, if indeed the role of theological hermeneutics warrants its place at the table, Irenaeus' example is a reminder that theological hermeneuts ought to resist two temptations. First, they should be on guard against the appeal of theoretical digressions. Though a predominant focus on methodology, for example, may promise great explanatory power, Irenaeus' model insinuates that the interpreter's primary attention ought never to be diverted from the biblical texts themselves. It is Scripture, so the church has claimed, that offers the clearest, most decisive speech about the divine economy. Second, theological hermeneuts ought to beware the temptation to ground their work in anthropology rather than in a doctrine of God. For Irenaeus, an apostolic "rule of truth" provided the means by which he could read Scripture from a proto-Trinitarian perspective, and accordingly, interpret Old and New Testament texts as constituting a single witness to the divine economy. From a critical and post-

---

[4] On the preference of "economic" to "narrative," we are indebted to Colin Gunton, "A Rose by Any Other Name? From 'Christian Doctrine' to 'Systematic Theology,'" *IJST* 1 (1999): 18-19.

critical standpoint, we find greater diversity in the texts of Scripture than Irenaeus would have admitted. Yet efforts to locate the unity of Scripture in constructs such as "covenant," "kingdom of God," or even narrative will never be as satisfying as the simple assertion that Scripture's unity is a matter of theology, strictly-speaking. As interpreted in the church, this corpus of writings attests one God: Father, Son, and Spirit. A corollary to this fundamental point is that the relationship *between* the two testaments is also defined and regulated by a doctrine of God, specifically Christology. By his efforts to read Genesis 1.26 and 2.7 christologically and thus provide a basis for relating Old and New Testament texts, Irenaeus offers a model to be reckoned with today – despite the many developments of the past eighteen centuries. In Christian biblical interpretation, the Christ-event must be regarded as hermeneutically central. In a sense, then, recapitulation may be reconceived not merely as Irenaeus' contribution to a doctrine of atonement or a doctrine of Christ. As a manner of reading protological and christological texts together, recapitulation is a hermeneutical tool by which Irenaeus relates the unity of God to the unity of Scripture.

Protological Orientation

If it is granted that the Christ-event is hermeneutically central for reading a body of texts as Christian Scripture, our study has suggested that Irenaeus' protological orientation addresses the question of *which* texts in the canonical witness are particularly crucial to interpreting Christ. While we do not wish to ignore the fact that Irenaeus made use of a wide range of biblical texts, it would seem that he found characteristics in the Genesis creation narratives that warranted their treatment as focal texts. Especially amenable to flexible uses and wide typological readings, these texts seem to invite the ongoing process of theological interpretation. If the creation narratives are ascribed some sort of privileged status as a crucial resource for theology, we find a broader significance in Irenaeus' work in several respects.

First, when approaching the biblical canon from the theological assumption that it expresses a coherent, cohesive message, one need not choose between two methodological points of entry, that is, Christology *or* narrative chronology (beginning with Genesis 1). When reading a variety of biblical texts (law, prophets, gospels, and epistles), Irenaeus often starts with both. He read Genesis with Christ in mind – and, indeed, in sight. Although our study was limited to two primary motifs from Genesis, divine image and breath of life, an expanded evaluation would note Irenaeus' christological appropriation of additional images: virgin soil (cf. Mary),[5] the trees in the garden (cf. the cross),[6] the temptation of Adam and Eve (cf. Jesus' temptation),[7] and the "protoevangelion" of Genesis 3.15.[8] Theological hermeneutics must at least bring together (though not necessarily fuse) the points of departure in Old and New Testaments in order to demonstrate that together they articulate a single economy which may be termed a "Christian" depiction of reality. Dating back to Paul, Christian tradition has looked to Genesis for its ability to cast illumination on events from creation to the eschaton and to explain their interconnectedness *within* this one economy.

Secondly, Irenaeus' protological orientation, as expressed in his hermeneutical uses of Genesis 1.26 and 2.7, is significant because it provides guidance for negotiating (or addressing) the *boundaries* of the biblical narrative itself, and for navigating interactions *between* it and other external "narratives." The Valentinians were not exceptional in their curiosity about philosophical issues. The catholic-Christian creeds composed in the centuries following Irenaeus represented efforts to ask fundamental questions about extra-economic, non-contingent reality not directly addressed in Scripture. Yet the path that was eventually chosen owes much to Irenaeus. Unlike the Valentinians, who presumed to add a prologue and epilogue to the story of divinity attested by Scripture, Irenaeus insisted that God's economy has bounds to be acknowledged – boundaries that are ontological (i.e., Creator / creation) as well as epistemological (i.e., limits of human knowing). The language of narrative befits the proclamation of God's interaction with humanity, but God himself is neither circumscribed nor constituted by a story. The reason that Irenaeus attributed a special role to the Genesis creation narratives was not merely because he was convinced that elusive, ultimate truth was more accessible the further one went back in the story (cf., the return *ad fontes*). (This, he would have reckoned, was more indicative of Gnostic interest in Genesis.) Instead, Irenaeus continually returned to these focal texts primarily because of the unique *theological perspective* they afforded. In an act of imagination governed by ruled readings of Scripture, Irenaeus sees in Genesis a picture of the divine arrangements and harmonies that order human existence. God, by his two hands, is fashioning the *homo vivens* along a planned trajectory from origination, through restoration, to a final destination. When read in light of God's revelation in Christ, Genesis tells the whole story in rough outline and opens up the possibility of experiencing the world differently. If what is sought in a christological reading of Genesis is theological perspective and orientation (i.e., a glimpse of the divine economy) rather than fixed, self-sufficient knowledge about beginnings,

---

[5] *Haer.* v.19.1-2.
[6] *Haer.* v.16.1-3.
[7] *Haer.* v.21.1-3.
[8] *Haer.* iii.23.7.

then drawing on the Genesis narrative to engage extra-textual lines of enquiry (such as modern science) can be a productive enterprise. It is when these texts are *used* for constructive theology (in fidelity to the rule of faith), rather than simply parroted or plundered as a fund-bank, that effective response may be made to two characteristically modern attacks on Genesis.

One "in-house" extra-textual narrative, so to speak, emerges from a stream of interpreters from Spinoza through Wellhausen which challenges the historical reliability of the biblical narratives. Such a tradition generally relies on two assumptions. First, meaning is tightly bound to static, original-context referents and / or intentionality. Second, confidence is expressed that these elements may be sufficiently uncovered through analytical historical-critical research methods. Irenaeus' interpretations and flexible deployments of Genesis, however, invite post-critical interpreters to see the rationale for adopting a broader understanding of meaning which also accounts for a text's function or theological use. For example, the meaning of Genesis 1.26 is not exhausted by references to the presumed polemical intentions of a Priestly writer. Although historical and grammatical features associated with a text warrant close scrutiny and are always relevant to the interpretative process, Irenaeus demonstrates that the most important hermeneutical constraints for readers inside the church are theological. Even when it is granted that traditional dogmas (such as the rule of faith or the classic creeds) delineate an authorized space within which catholic-Christian readings may be proposed and used, there is still room for a significantly more flexible hermeneutic than has typically been welcomed under the auspices of modern exegesis.

An extra-textual narrative which has frequently sought an identity extricated from faith commitments is modern science. Indirectly, at least, scientific disciplines such as geology, astrophysics, or evolutionary biology are protological quests that reflect on humanity's place in the cosmos. Yet if theological discourse is disallowed, these uncover few compelling reasons to lead to the conclusion that human time and human personhood, as experienced, are ontologically significant. To the degree that knowledge of the cosmic expanses of space and time grows, the perceived status of humanity shrinks. Irenaeus' flexible, yet focused approach to the Genesis creation narratives provides guidance for facilitating explicitly Christian interactions with this tradition of enquiry. One practical arena of particularly fervent dialogue addresses the new ethical questions arising from the interface between technology and human biology. Uncomfortable dilemmas over such issues as genetic engineering, stem cell research, and health-care rationing push societies to try to mark out compromises where "what can be done" and "what ought to be done" enforce limits upon each other. In view of the recent hegemony of *technological* and *biological* perspectives on human life in the western world, the Christian community may increasingly recognize its role as offering, with integrity, a distinctively *theological* perspective on human life so as to inform ethics. Genesis 1-2 does provide a theological witness about the beginning of human life. But here Irenaeus saw more: divine purpose amidst tragedy, divine activities to redeem and nurture, and divine hands ushering humanity toward a time of eschatological destiny. Humanity has a place in an economy that is more beautiful and more enriching than the marketplace of the world, which, despite the furious pace of globalization, inevitably falls short of making good on all its promises. The world's marketplace can offer a place for human beings to exchange goods, services, experiences, and ideas. It cannot painstakingly "fashion" a human being or engender new life where there is none. This competing economy founders in its efforts to supply a universal template (or "image") in which humanity can see its fulfillment.

As Irenaeus set about to cast an alternative vision to counter the Valentinian story he deemed deficient (and dangerous), so also many will find similar contemporary opportunities for undertaking constructive theology. Assuming that its christological center is not compromised, a theological hermeneutic guided by a protological orientation reads Scripture from a standpoint that offers potentially long-range views of the human condition. The opening chapters in Genesis have attracted a certain fascination amongst Christian interpreters from Paul and Irenaeus onward. It is for *theological* reasons that their ongoing allure to current and future generations of readers is both merited and assured.

Anthropology

Finally, Irenaeus' contribution to a doctrine of humanity should be weighed. If he set out from a protological starting point (shared with his opponents) and subsequently applied a hermeneutical methodology dependent upon adaptive and typological readings of Genesis 1-2, the end result of Irenaeus' work was a non-Platonic Christian anthropology that could compete favorably with the elaborate Valentinian system. Whether in the second or twenty-first centuries, the tensions and ethical questions emergent in contexts of rapid social and cultural transformation invite fresh reconsideration of the human condition.[9] To name but a few popular options, human identity may be grounded in cosmology (non-theistic evolution), aesthetics, or even in itself. In self-grounding anthropologies, the significance of human existence is often portrayed in terms of pragmatism, ideology, politics (Nietzsche), or even random chance. Richard

---

[9] "[I]t is becoming clearer that we cannot give the right answer to the question about where we should be. 'What can we do?' will be false and pernicious while we refrain from asking, 'Who are we?' The question of being and the question of [human] hopes are inseparable" (Joseph Ratzinger, *In the Beginning: A Catholic Understanding of the Story of Creation and the Fall* [trans. Boniface Ramsey; Edinburgh: T&T Clark, 1995], 82).

Dawkins, the Oxford scientist and well-known critic of religion, perhaps epitomizes such anthropological reductionism. Dawkins summons us to celebrate our existence not because we are related to a larger purpose or plan but because we have, by chance, been found winners in the "lottery" that is life.[10] "We are going to die, and that makes us the lucky ones. Most people are never going to die because they are never going to be born... [T]he set of possible people allowed by our DNA so massively exceeds the set of actual people. In the teeth of these stupefying odds it is you and I, in our ordinariness, that are here."[11] Even if religion does serve as the point of departure for anthropology, it remains possible for a doctrine of God and a doctrine of humanity to be developed, *de facto*, in isolation from each other. Thus in contrast to many approaches, Irenaeus' answer to the question "who / what is humanity?" is (as we have endeavored to show in our last two chapters) far more *comprehensive*. Given its solid foundation in theology, his anthropology is able to serve as a nexus point at which a variety of doctrines are interrelated. Christology is foremost among these, though cosmology, hamartiology, soteriology, and eschatology are also integrated. Irenaeus' notion of humanity as situated in a divine economy for the purpose of being fashioned into a *homo vivens* (body and soul) relied on his creative interpretation and use of the Genesis creation narratives. Among the broader implications of Irenaeus' approach to anthropology suggested by our study, two are particularly worth reiterating. The first involves Irenaeus' epistemology; the second is his affirmation that to be human is to be embodied.

First, Genesis 1.26 and 2.7 help to guide Irenaeus' epistemological sequence in which theological enquiry is acknowledged as the *prerequisite* to and *basis* for anthropological enquiry. It may seem ironic that Irenaeus' thoughts about God begin with anthropogony and no earlier.[12] Yet this merely expresses his interest to confine himself to an economic interpretation of Scripture. As he does so, he avoids two extremes. Irenaeus does not assume that protology, in itself, is a sufficient basis for understanding humanity. The Genesis texts must be read in light of Christ's revelation of God as triune. The Father, through his two hands, is in remarkably close relation to humanity – actively present in the beginning, middle, and end of human time – though the ontological distinction between creation and Creator is never blurred. Likewise, naturalistic depictions of human progress (as have sometimes been adopted from selective readings of *Haer.* iv.38) can cast no great illumination on the question of human identity. It is God's identity and activities, as made known, which are the most crucial determinants. On the other hand, if anthropological enquiry does look to

---

[10] Cf. Richard Dawkins, *Unweaving the Rainbow* (London: Penguin, 1998), 2.
[11] Ibid, 1.
[12] Cf. our chapter three, footnote 26 referring to the later example of Genesis Rabba.

theology for its epistemological starting point, Irenaeus (unlike the Gnostic interpreters) recognized that Genesis 1-2 helps to tell the story of *humanity* and its perfection, not of God's perfection. From this economic vantage point, Scripture may be read inclusively as the story of God's completion of creation, rather than that of his self-completion by means of creation. Consequently, interpreters of any era whose primary interests lie in how Genesis relates humanity to cosmic substance (cf. Valentinian Platonist metaphysics) or to cosmic history (cf. forms of modern fundamentalist creationism) are vastly underestimating these texts' value for understanding humankind. When read theologically in sympathy with Irenaeus' approach, Genesis most importantly speaks of humanity and *teleology*, doing so in such a way so as to spur further reflection and imagination. The reason that Irenaeus' anthropology avoids both the extreme of anthropocentrism and that of cosmocentrism (or theo-monism) is that he finds the Genesis creation narratives to be of utmost significance for Christology. In some contrast to the later doctrines of Christ proposed in the fourth and fifth centuries, Irenaeus makes significant recourse to anthropology in his depictions of Christ. This move, in fact, correlates with his uses of Genesis 1.26 and 2.7 to construct theology and read Scripture as a whole. To a large extent, Genesis is reckoned to speak *both* about humanity and God because it speaks about Christ. Such a claim might sound strange to those whose ears have been trained in exegetical methods and who strive to keep each text free from the contamination of presuppositions or other texts. Yet a strong case may be made that Genesis 1-2 is only relevant for Christian anthropology insofar as it *is* read in light of Jesus Christ. In summary, then, the Genesis creation narratives constitute a sizable resource for Christian anthropology when they are read in an order conducive to Christian epistemology: first theologically, then economically, and finally anthropologically.

Second, we note that Irenaeus' argument shows that his debate with Gnostic opponents is not just a debate about Scripture in the abstract, but about readings of Scripture that devalue the human body, that is, those that express Platonist tendencies. Whereas some interpreters had gravitated toward biblical passages more amenable to the Middle-Platonist thought of the day, Irenaeus is an example of someone noticing and exploiting the anti-Platonizing potential of Scripture texts. His proposition is simple: *to be human is to be embodied.* Therefore, a disembodied humanity is inconceivable whether located at the beginning, in the middle, or at the end of God's economy. On the basis of the triune God's activity, human bodiliness is claimed to be a feature of theological and soteriological relevance in an inclusive sense. Less encumbered by the dualistic presuppositions of Platonic metaphysics, Irenaeus' readings of Scripture that highlight the ministries of God's two hands propose a vision wherein a genuine interface between divine and human, and between spiritual and material substance is not only possible but realized. Before moving on to a possible implication, a caveat is in order: To affirm that humanity's identity is inextricably linked to its embodied condition does not warrant the reduction of "embodiment" to sexuality. In our contemporary culture, which arguably reflects the ongoing tension between Gnostic and anti-Gnostic attitudes toward the human body, we see such a tendency on both extremes. For example, a growing number of theologians are making such assertions as: "The sexual is the very mark of embodiment itself"[13] or "The gospel has always been a story of carnal desire and erotic encounter, and only the Gnostic who fears and hates the material world would deny this."[14] Irenaeus, however, would likely dispute this perspective for many reasons – chief amongst them being that this is far too narrow a view of God's purpose and work to thoroughly enliven humanity. The texts of Genesis 1-2 provide an essential protological and theological basis from which to address the question of the body and its worth. The relation of creation to Creator, substance to Spirit, is far more relevant than a single characteristic of creaturely life (vital though it is). In view of this qualification, then, we suggest a further implication of Irenaeus' anthropology: Irenaeus affirms and anticipates the current proclivity for "relational" lines of anthropological enquiry[15] without abandoning traditional interests in "substance." While his theological interpretations of the Genesis creation narratives certainly gave Irenaeus warrant for defining human identity in terms of its relatedness to God, they also insist that it is not outmoded to speak of human identity as expressed in terms of old-fashioned flesh and blood. This double-sided emphasis in Irenaeus' anthropology provides a paradigm that is at least recognizable to non-Christian anthropologies in the world today. At the same time that, for example, philosophy, literary studies, and social anthropology highlight the ways that the humanity of an individual is constituted in relation to an "other," studies in neurobiology, genetics, and evolutionary biology point in the opposite direction toward the irreducible physicality of the human animal. Inevitably, approaches that are born out of a single perspective or sub-discipline suffer limitation. Despite the voices of objectors, both ancient and modern, Irenaeus shows that a Christian anthropology can indeed be unreservedly grounded in theology while still being fully comprehensive. The Valentinians were not faulted for their fascination with substance, but rather for their inadequate doctrine of God which

---

[13] Graham Ward, "On the Politics of Embodiment and the Mystery of All Flesh," in *The Sexual Theologian: Essays on Sex, God and Politics* (ed. Marcella Althaus-Reid and Lisa Isherwood; London: T&T Clark, 2004), 72.

[14] Gerard Loughlin, *Alien Sex: The Body and Desire in Cinema and Theology* (Oxford: Blackwell, 2004), 12.

[15] See, for example, the influence upon western theology of John Zizioulas' *Being As Communion* (Crestwood, N.Y.: St. Vladimir's Seminary Press, 1985) in light of post-modern critiques.

proscribed his involvement with or interest in physicality. Not only the *plasmare* language of Genesis 2.7, but also the "image of God" claim of Genesis 1.26 attest that relation *and* composition both feature in any Christian answer to the question, "Who / what is humanity?" Providing a biblical elaboration of this requires, as we have suggested, a rather flexible hermeneutic. By giving emphasis to mind, morality, and personality, the western tradition of Augustine, Kant, and Freud has tended to address humanity primarily as a psychological creature. While not overlooking this dimension, Irenaeus offers a more satisfying and thorough depiction by emphasizing that human beings are relational and physical creatures as well. Indeed, the culmination of God's salvific work in Christ, when read with an eye to protology, confirms this. Christ *revealed* God's relatedness to humankind as Creator while also *recapitulating* the very substance of Adam's formation.

With regard to all of Irenaeus' aforementioned contributions – whether in hermeneutics, theology, or anthropology – it is not granted that non-biblical or extra-biblical narratives (e.g., those from science, philosophy, or culture) ought necessarily to set the agenda for theological enquiry and Christian proclamation. Yet they should be ascribed no less careful study (and probably more) than Irenaeus gave to the investigation of his "opponents." New challenges afford stirring new opportunities. Certainly, Irenaeus did not bequeath to the church *the* definitive biblical narrative. Others have been skillfully elaborated and it is profitable that this process has continued. Yet there is reason to surmise that Irenaeus' ground-breaking theological hermeneutic, together with his venerable doctrines, represent resources of some value. We might be eager to retrieve Irenaeus because he is nearly as close to the genesis of a thoroughgoing biblical theology as we can get. He is an ancient figure whose influence on Christian thought has been vast. At the same time, considering our own age where the church (and academy) still debate over how the Old Testament is to be read and used as Christian Scripture, we might return to Irenaeus for another reason. The unique *perspective* on Christian theology and biblical interpretation he imparts, given his own cultural and religious setting, brings light to ours as well – or, at the least, it stimulates useful questions to be raised and reflected upon anew.

BIBLIOGRAPHY

1. Texts and Translations: Irenaeus

Texts

Grabe, Joannes Ernestus, ed. *Contra omnes haereses libri quinque.* Oxford: E. Theatro Sheldoniano, 1702.

Harvey, W. W., ed. *Sancti Irenaei Episcopi Lugdunensis.* 2 vols. Cambridge, 1857.

Massuet, R., ed. *Against Heresies.* Paris, 1710. Reprinted in *Patrologia latina* 7. Edited by J.-P. Migne. 217 vols. Paris, 1844-1864.

Rousseau, A., and L. Doutreleau, eds. *Contre les hérésies, Livre* I. Sources chrétiennes 263, 264. Paris: Cerf, 1979.

Rousseau, A., and L. Doutreleau, eds. *Contre les hérésies, Livre* II. Sources chrétiennes 293, 294. Paris: Cerf, 1982.

Rousseau, A., and L. Doutreleau, eds. *Contre les hérésies, Livre* III. Sources chrétiennes 210, 211. Paris: Cerf, 1974.

Rousseau, A., B. Hemmerdinger, L. Doutreleau, and C. Mercier, eds. *Contre les hérésies, Livre* IV. Sources chrétiennes 100; 2 vols. Paris: Cerf, 1965.

Rousseau, A., L. Doutreleau, and C. Mercier eds. *Contre les hérésies, Livre* V. Sources chrétiennes 152, 153. Paris: Cerf, 1969.

Translations

Grant, Robert M. *Irenaeus of Lyons.* London: Routledge, 1997.

MacKenzie, Iain M. *Irenaeus's Demonstration of the Apostolic Preaching: A theological commentary and translation.* Aldershot: Ashgate, 2002. Translation reprinted from J. Armitage Robinson, *The Demonstration of the Apostolic Preaching.* London: SPCK, 1920.

Roberts, Alexander and W. H. Rambaut. *Irenaeus*. Pages 1:315-567 in *The Ante- Nicene Fathers*. Edited by Alexander Roberts and James Donaldson. 10 vols. Grand Rapids: Eerdmans, 1986-1990. Reprint of *The Ante-Nicene Christian Library*. Edinburgh: T&T Clark, 1883-1884.

Smith, Joseph P. *Proof of the Apostolic Preaching*. Ancient Christian Writers 16. Westminster, Md.: Newman, 1952.

Unger, Dominic. *St. Irenaeus of Lyons: Against the Heresies*. Ancient Christian Writers 55. New York: Paulist Press, 1992.

2. Other Ancient Texts and Translations

Apocryphon of John (NHC II/1)
   Text and Translation: Waldstein, Michael and Frederik Wisse, eds. *The Apocryphon of John*. Nag Hammadi and Manichaean Studies 33. Leiden: Brill, 1995.

Aristotle, *Poetics*
   Text and Translation: Halliwell, Stephen, ed. Loeb Classical Library 199. Cambridge, Mass.: Harvard University Press, 1995.

Augustine, *Confessions*
   Text: Verheijen, Lucas, ed. *Sancti Augustini Opera: Confessionum Libri XIII*. Corpus Christianorum Series latina 27. Turnhout: Brepols, 1981.
   Translation: Chadwick, Henry. Oxford World Classics. Oxford: Oxford University Press, 1991.

Gospel of Philip (NHC II/3)
   Text and Translation: Layton, Bentley, ed. *The Gospel According to Philip*. Nag Hammadi Studies 20. Leiden: Brill, 1989.

Gospel of Truth (NHC I/3)
   Text: Attridge, H. W., ed. *The Gospel of Truth*. Nag Hammadi Studies 22. Leiden: Brill, 1985.
   Translation: MacRae, George W. Pages 37-49 in *The Nag Hammadi Library in English*. Edited by James M. Robinson. Leiden: Brill, 1977.

Justin, *Dialogue with Trypho*
  Text: Marani. D., ed. *Dialogue with Trypho*. Reprinted in *Patrologia graeca* 6. Edited by J.-P. Migne. 162 vols. Paris, 1857-1886.
  Translation: Roberts, Alexander and James Donaldson, eds. Pages 1:194-270 in *The Ante-Nicene Fathers*. 10 vols. Grand Rapids: Eerdmans, 1986-1990.

Origen, *Against Celsus*
  Text: Borret, M., ed. *Contre Celse, Livres* 3-4. Sources chrétiennes 136. Paris: Cerf, 1968.
  Translation: Crombie, Frederick. Pages 4:395-669 in *The Ante-Nicene Fathers*. Edited by Alexander Roberts and James Donaldson. 10 vols. Grand Rapids: Eerdmans, 1986-1990.

Philo, *On the Creation of the World*
  Text: Colson, F. H and G. H. Whitaker, eds. *Philo: Volume 1*. Loeb Classical Library 226. Cambridge: Mass.: Harvard University Press, 1929.
  Translation: Runia, David T. Philo of Alexandria: *On the Creation of the Cosmos According to Moses*. Leiden: Brill, 2001.

Philo, *Questions and Answers on Genesis*
  Translation: Marcus, Ralph. *Philo: Supplement 1*. Loeb Classical Library 380. Cambridge, Mass.: Harvard University Press, 1953.

Plato, *Timaeus*
  Text and Translation: Bury, R. G., ed. *Plato: Volume 9*. Loeb Classical Library 7. Cambridge, Mass.: Harvard University Press, 1942.
  Translation: Zeyl, Donald J. *Timaeus*. Indianapolis: Hackett, 2000.

Ptolemy, *Letter to Flora*
  Text: Quispel, Gilles, ed. *Ptolémée: Lettre à Flora*. 2d ed. Sources chrétiennes 24. Paris: Cerf, 1966.
  Translation: Layton, Bentley. Pages 306-15 in *The Gnostic Scriptures*. Garden City, NY: Doubleday, 1987.

Tertullian. *Against the Valentinians*
  Text: Fredouille, Jean-Claude, ed. *Tertullien: Contre les Valentiniens*. Sources chrétiennes 280. Paris: Cerf, 1980.
  Translations:
  Foerster, Werner. *Gnosis: A Selection of Gnostic Texts*. Edited and Translated by R. McL. Wilson. 2 vols. Oxford: Oxford University Press, 1972.
  Roberts, Alexander. Pages 3:503-520 in *The Ante-Nicene Fathers*. Edited by Alexander Roberts and James Donaldson. 10 vols. Grand Rapids: Eerdmans, 1986-1990.

Theophilus. *To Autolycus*
  Text and Translation: Grant, Robert M., ed. *Theophilus of Antioch: Ad Autolycum*. Oxford: Clarendon, 1970.

3. General Bibliography

Alexander, Philip. "Pre-Emptive Exegesis: Genesis Rabba's Reading of the Story of Creation." *Journal of Jewish Studies* 43 (1992): 230-45.

Altermath, F. "The Purpose of the Incarnation According to Irenaeus." *Studia Patristica* 13 (1975): 63-68.

Andía, Ysabel de. *Homo vivens: incorruptibilité et divinisation selon Irénée de Lyon*. Paris: Études Augustiniennes, 1986.

Armstrong, Gregory T. *Die Genesis in der Alten Kirche: die drei Kirchenväter*. Tübingen: Mohr, 1962.

Attridge, Harold W. "Valentinian and Sethian Apocalyptic Traditions." *Journal of Early Christian Studies* 8 (2000): 173-211.

Aulén, Gustaf. *Christus Victor: An Historical Study of the Three Main Types of the Idea of the Atonement*. Translated by A. G. Hebert. London: S.P.C.K., 1970.

Bacq, Philippe. *De l'ancienne à la nouvelle alliance selon S. Irénée: unité du livre IV de l'Adversus Haereses*. Paris: Lethielleux, 1978.

Balthasar, Hans Urs von. *The Scandal of the Incarnation: Irenaeus Against the Heresies*. Trans. John Saward. San Francisco: Ignatius Press, 1988.

Barr, James. *The Semantics of Biblical Language*. London: Oxford University Press, 1961.

Barth, Karl. *Church Dogmatics* III/1. Edited by G. W. Bromiley and T. F. Torrance. Edinburgh: T&T Clark, 1958.

Behr, John. *Asceticism and Anthropology in Irenaeus and Clement*. Oxford: Oxford University Press, 2000.

Bethune-Baker, J. F., *An Introduction to the Early History of Christian Doctrine*. 3d ed. London: Methuen, 1923.

Blumenberg, Hans. *Work on Myth*. Translated by Robert M. Wallace. Cambridge, Mass.: MIT Press, 1985.

Boersma, Hans. *Violence, Hospitality, and the Cross*. Grand Rapids: Baker Academic, 2004.

Bousset, Wilhelm. *Kyrios Christos*. Translated by John E. Steely. Nashville: Abingdon, 1970.

Bouteneff, Peter C. *Beginnings*. Grand Rapids: Baker Academic, 2008.

Brox, N. "Die biblische Hermeneutik des Irenaeus." *Zeitschrift für Antike und Christentum* 2 (1998): 26-48.

Brunner, Emil. *Man in Revolt: A Christian Anthropology*. Translated by Olive Wyon. London: Lutterworth Press, 1939.

Brunner, Emil. *The Mediator: A Study of the Central Doctrine of the Christian Faith*. Translated by Olive Wyon. London: Lutterworth Press, 1934.

Cairns, David. *The Image of God in Man*. London: SCM, 1953.

Campenhausen, Hans von. *The Fathers of the Greek Church*. Translated by Stanley Godman, revised by L. A. Garrard. London: A&C Black, 1963.

Campenhausen, Hans von. *The Formation of the Christian Bible*. Translated by John Austin Baker. London: A&C Black, 1972.

Childs, Brevard S. *Biblical Theology of the Old and New Testaments*. Minneapolis: Fortress, 1993.

Childs, Brevard S. *Isaiah*. Louisville: Westminster John Knox, 2001.

Constantelos, Demetrios J. "Irenaeos of Lyons and His Central Views on Human Nature." *St. Vladimir's Theological Quarterly* 33 (1989): 351-63.

Daniélou, Jean. *Gospel Message and Hellenistic Culture*. Edited and Translated by John Austin Baker. London: Darton Longman and Todd, 1973.

Dawkins, Richard. *Unweaving the Rainbow*. London: Penguin, 1998.

Dillon, John M. *The Middle Platonists: A Study of Platonism, 80 B.C. to A.D. 200*. London: Duckworth, 1977.

Donovan, Mary Ann. "Irenaeus in Recent Scholarship." *Second Century* 4 (1984): 219-41.

Dunderberg, Ismo. "The School of Valentinus." Pages 64-99 in *A Companion to Second-Century Christian 'Heretics.'* Edited by Antti Marjanen and Petri Luomanen. Leiden: Brill, 2005.

Erasmus, Desiderius. *The Correspondence of Erasmus, Letters 1658 to 1801: January 1526-March 1527*. Vol. 12 of *The Collected Works of Erasmus*. Translated by Alexander Dalzell. Toronto: University of Toronto Press, 2003.

Fallon, Francis T. "The Prophets of the OT and the Gnostics: A Note on Irenaeus, Adversus Haereses, 1.30.10-11." *Vigiliae Christianae* 32 (1978): 191-94.

Farkasfalvy, D. "Theology of Scripture in St. Irenaeus." *Revue Bénédictine* 78 (1968): 319-333.

Farrow, Douglas. *Ascension and Ecclesia*. Edinburgh: T&T Clark, 1999.

Farrow, Douglas. "St. Irenaeus of Lyons: The Church and the World." *Pro Ecclesia* 4 (1995): 333-55.

Ferguson, Thomas C. K. "The Rule of Truth and Irenaean Rhetoric in Book 1 of Against Heresies." *Vigiliae Christianae* 55 (2001): 356-75.

Filoramo, Giovanni. *A History of Gnosticism*. Oxford: Basil Blackwell, 1990.

Foerster, Werner. *Gnosis: A Selection of Gnostic Texts.* Translated and edited by R. McL. Wilson. 2 vols. Oxford: Oxford University Press, 1972.

Fredriksen, P. "Hysteria and the Gnostic Myth of Creation." *Vigiliae Christianae* 33 (1979): 287-90.

Grant, Robert M. "Irenaeus and Hellenistic Culture." *Harvard Theological Review* 42 (1949): 41-51.

Grant, Robert M. *Gnosticism and Early Christianity*. New York: Columbia University Press, 1959.

Grau, Marion. *Of Divine Economy*. London: T&T Clark, 2004.

Greer, Rowan, "The Dog and the Mushrooms: Irenaeus's View of the Valentinians Assessed." Pages 1:146-75 in *The Rediscovery of Gnosticism: Proceedings of the International Conference on Gnosticism at Yale*. Edited and Translated by Bentley Layton. 2 vols. Leiden: Brill, 1980-81.

Grobel, K. *The Gospel of Truth*. New York: Abingdon, 1960.

Gunkel, Hermann. *Genesis*. Göttingen: Vandenhoeck & Ruprecht, 1964.

Gunton, Colin E. "A Rose by Any Other Name? From 'Christian Doctrine' to 'Systematic Theology.'" *International Journal of Systematic Theology* 1 (1999): 4-24.

Gunton, Colin E. *Christ and Creation.* Carlisle: Paternoster, 1992.

Harnack, Adolf von. *History of Dogma*. Translated from the 3d German ed. by Neil Buchanan. 7 vols. London: Williams & Norgate, 1894-99.

Harnack, Adolf von. *Lehrbuch der Dogmengeschichte*. 3d ed. 3 vols. Freiburg I. B.: J.C.B. Mohr, 1894.

Hart, Trevor. "Irenaeus, Recapitulation and Physical Redemption." Pages 152-81 in *Christ in our Place: The Humanity of God in Christ for the Reconciliation of the World*. Edited by Trevor A. Hart and Daniel P. Thimell. Exeter: Paternoster, 1989.

Hoh, Josef. Die Lehre des Hl. Irenäus über das Neue Testament. Münster i. W.: Aschendorff, 1919.

Jonsson, Gunnlaugur A. *The Image of God: Genesis 1.26-28 in a Century of Old Testament Research*. Stockholm: Almqvist & Wiksell, 1988.

Joppich, Godehard. *Salus Carnis: Eine Untersuchung in der Theologie des hl. Irenäus von Lyon*. Münsterschwarzach: Vier-Türme-Verlag, 1965.

Kannengiesser, C. "The 'Speaking' God and Irenaeus's Interpretive Pattern: The Reception of Genesis." *Annali di storia dell' esegesi* 15 (1998): 337-52.

Keller, Catherine. *Face of the Deep: A Theology of Becoming*. London: Routledge, 2003.

Kelly, J. N. D. *Early Christian Doctrine*. 5th ed. London: A&C Black, 1985.

Lassiat, H. "L'Anthropologie d' Irénée." *La nouvelle revue théologique* 100 (1978): 399-417.

Lawson, John. *The Biblical Theology of St. Irenaeus*. London: Epworth, 1948.

Layton, Bentley. *The Gnostic Scriptures*. Garden City, NY: Doubleday, 1987.

Layton, Bentley. "Hypostasis of the Archons." *Harvard Theological Review* 67 (1974): 351-425.

Lerch, David. *Isaaks Opferung christlich gedeutet*. Tübingen: Mohr, 1950.

Loewe, William P. "Irenaeus' Soteriology: Christus Victor Revisited." *Anglican Theological Review* 67 (1985): 1-15.

Logan, Alastair H. B. *Gnostic Truth and Christian Heresy: A Study in the History of Gnosticism*. Edinburgh: T&T Clark, 1996.

Loofs, F. "Theophilus von Antiochien Adversus Marcionem, und die anderen theologischen Quellen bei Irenaeus." *Texte und Untersuchungen* 46, 2. Leipzig: Hinrich, 1930.

Loughlin, Gerard. *Alien Sex: The Body and Desire in Cinema and Theology*. Oxford: Blackwell, 2004.

Markschies, Christoph. *Gnosis. An Introduction*. Translated by John Bowden. London: T&T Clark, 2003.

McHugh, John. "A Reconsideration of Ephesians 1.10b in the Light of Irenaeus." Pages 302-309 in *Paul and Paulinism: Essays in Honour of C.K. Barrett*. Edited by M. D. Hooker and S. G. Wilson. London: SPCK, 1982.

Metzger, Bruce M. *A Textual Commentary on the Greek New Testament*. London: United Bible Societies, 1971.

Minns, Denis. *Irenaeus*. London: Geoffrey Chapman, 1994.

Nielsen, J. T. *Adam and Christ in the Theology of Irenaeus of Lyons*. Assen, The Netherlands: Koninklijke Van Gorcum, 1968.

Norris, Richard. "The Transcendence and Freedom of God: Irenaeus, the Greek Tradition, and Gnosticism." Pages 87-100 in *Early Christian Literature and the Classical Tradition, In Honorem Robert M. Grant*. Théologie historique 53. Edited by W. R. Schoedel and R. L. Wilkens. Paris: Beauchesne, 1979.

Nygren, Anders. *Agape and Eros: Part II The History of the Christian Idea of Love*. Translated by Philip S. Watson. 2 vols. London: SPCK, 1938.

O'Keefe, John J. and R. R. Reno. *Sanctified Vision: An Introduction to Early Christian Interpretation of the Bible*. Baltimore: Johns Hopkins University Press, 2005.

Olson, Mark Jeffrey. *Irenaeus, the Valentinian Gnostics, and the Kingdom of God*. Lewiston, NY: Edwin Mellen Press, 1992.

O'Regan, Cyril. *Gnostic Return in Modernity*. Albany, NY: State University of New York Press, 2001.

Osborn, Eric. *The Emergence of Christian Theology*. Cambridge: Cambridge University Press, 1993.

Osborn, Eric. "The Excellence of Adam in Second Century Christian Thought." *Cahiers de Biblia Patristica* 2 (1989): 35-59.

Osborn, Eric. *Irenaeus of Lyons*. Cambridge: Cambridge University Press, 2001.

Pagels, Elaine H. *The Gnostic Gospels*. New York: Random House, 1978.

Pagels, Elaine H. "Conflicting Versions of Valentinian Eschatology." *Harvard Theological Review* 67 (1974): 35-53.

Pagels, Elaine H. "Exegesis and Exposition of the Genesis Creation Accounts in Selected Texts from Nag Hammadi." Pages 257-79 in *Nag Hammadi, Gnosticism & Early Christianity*. Edited by Charles W. Hedrick and Robert Hodgson, Jr. Peabody, Mass.: Hendrickson, 1986.

Pearson, Birger A. *Gnosticism and Christianity in Roman and Coptic Egypt*. London: T&T Clark, 2004.

Pearson, Birger A. *The Pneumatikos-Psychikos Terminology in 1 Corinthians: A Study in the Theology of the Corinthian Opponents of Paul and its Relation to Gnosticism*. Missoula, Mont.: Society of Biblical Literature, 1973.

Pelikan, Jaroslav. *The Christian Tradition: A History of the Development of Doctrine. Vol. 1: The Emergence of the Catholic Tradition (100-600)*. 5 vols. Chicago: University of Chicago Press, 1971.

Perkins, Pheme. *The Gnostic Dialogue: The Early Church and the Crisis of Gnosticism*. New York: Paulist Press, 1980.

Perkins, Pheme. "Gnosticism and the Christian Bible." Pages 355-71 in *The Canon Debate*. Edited by L. M. McDonald, and J. A. Sanders. Peabody, Mass.: Hendrickson, 2002.

Perkins, Pheme. "Ireneus and the Gnostics: Rhetoric and Composition in *Adversus Haereses* book one." *Vigiliae Christianae* 30 (1976): 193-200.

Pétrement, Simone. *A Separate God: The Christian Origins of Gnosticism*. Translated by C. Harrison. London: Darton, Longman & Todd, 1991.

Potter, R. "Irenaeus and Recapitulation." *Dominican Studies* 4 (1951): 192-200.

Quasten, Johannes. *Patrology, Volume 1: The Beginnings of Patristic Literature*. 4 vols. Westminster, Md.: Newman, 1950.

Ratzinger, Joseph. *In the Beginning: A Catholic Understanding of the Story of Creation and the Fall*. Translated by Boniface Ramsey. Edinburgh: T&T Clark, 1995.

Reynders, Bruno. *Lexique comparé du texte grec et des versions latine, Armenienne et syriaque de l'Adversus haereses de Saint Irénée*. Louvain: L. Durbecq, 1954.

Roukema, Riemer. *Gnosis and Faith in Early Christianity*. London: SCM, 1999.

Runia, David T. *Philo of Alexandria and the* Timaeus *of Plato*. Leiden: E. J. Brill, 1986.

Russell, Norman. *The Doctrine of Deification in the Greek Patristic Tradition*. Oxford: Oxford University Press, 2005.

Schenke, Hans-Martin. "The Phenomenon and Significance of Gnostic Sethianism." Pages 2:588-616 in *The Rediscovery of Gnosticism: Proceedings of the International Conference on Gnosticism at Yale*. Edited and Translated by Bentley Layton. 2 vols. Leiden: Brill, 1980-81.

Schenke, Hans-Martin. "Das sethianische System nach Nag-Hammadi-Handschriften." Pages 165-73 in *Studia Coptica* 45. Edited by Peter Nagel. Berlin: Akademie, 1974.

Schoedel, William. "Theological Method in Irenaeus (*Adversus Haereses* 2.25-28)." *Journal of Theological Studies* 35 (1984): 31-49.

Sesboüé, Bernard. *Tout récapituler dans le Christ*. Paris: Descléé, 2000.

Simonetti, Manlio. "Per typica ad vera." *Vetera christianorum* 18 (1981): 357-82.

Smith, Christopher R. "Chiliasm and Recapitulation in the Theology of Ireneus." *Vigiliae Christianae* 48 (1994): 313-31.

Stanton, Graham N. *Jesus and Gospel.* Cambridge: Cambridge University Press, 2004.

Torrance, Thomas F. *Divine Meaning: Studies in Patristic Hermeneutics.* Edinburgh: T&T Clark, 1994.

Turner, H. E. W. *The Patristic Doctrine of Redemption: A Study of the Development of Doctrine during the First Five Centuries.* London: Mowbray, 1952.

Turner, John. "Sethian Gnosticism: A Literary History." Pages 55-66 in *Nag Hammadi, Gnosticism, and Early Christianity.* Edited by Charles W. Hedrick and Robert Hodgson, Jr. Peabody, Mass.: Hendrickson, 1986.

Vallée, Gérard. *A Study in Anti-Gnostic Polemics.* Waterloo, Canada: Corporation Canadienne des Sciences Religieuses, 1981.

Verweyen, H. "Frühchristliche Theologie in der Herausforderung durch die antike Welt." *Zeitschrift für katholische Theologie* 109 (1987): 385-99.

Ward, Graham. "On the Politics of Embodiment and the Mystery of All Flesh," Pages 71-85 in *The Sexual Theologian: Essays on Sex, God and Politics.* Edited by Marcella Althaus-Reid and Lisa Isherwood. London: T&T Clark, 2004.

Watson, Francis. *Agape, Eros and Gender.* Cambridge: Cambridge University Press, 2000.

Watson, Francis. "Is There a Story in These Texts?" Pages 231-39 in *Narrative Dynamics in Paul: A Critical Assessment.* Edited by Bruce W. Longenecker. Louisville: Westminster John Knox, 2002.

Webber, Robert E. *Ancient-Future Faith: Rethinking Evangelicalism for a Postmodern World.* Grand Rapids: Baker, 1999.

Wendt, H. H. *Die christliche Lehre von des menschlichen Vollkommenheit.* Göttingen: Vandenhoeck & Ruprecht, 1882.

Werner, Martin. *The Formation of Christian Dogma: An Historical Study of its Problem*. Translated by S. G. F. Brandon. London: A&C Black, 1957.

Wilken, Robert Louis. *The Spirit of Early Christian Thought*. New Haven: Yale University Press, 2003.

Williams, Jacqueline A. *Biblical Interpretation in the Gnostic Gospel of Truth from Nag Hammadi*. SBL Dissertation Series 79. Atlanta: Scholars Press, 1988.

Williams, Michael Allen. *Rethinking "Gnosticism": An Argument for Dismantling a Dubious Category*. Princeton: Princeton University Press, 1996.

Winden, J. C. M. van. "Terra Autem Stupida Quadam Erat Admiratione: Reflexions on a remarkable translation of Genesis 1:2a." Pages 458-66 in *Studies in Gnosticism and Hellenistic Religions*. Edited by R. van den Broek and M. J. Vermaseren. Leiden: Brill, 1981.

Wingren, Gustaf. *Man and the Incarnation: A Study in the Biblical Theology of Irenaeus*. Translated by Ross MacKenzie. London: Oliver and Boyd, 1959.

Xintaras, Zachary C. "Man - The Image of God According to the Greek Fathers." *The Greek Orthodox Theological Review*, 1 (1954): 48-62.

Young, Frances. *The Art of Performance: Towards a Theology of Holy Scripture*. London: Darton, Longman & Todd, 1990.

Young, Frances. *Biblical Exegesis and the Formation of Christian Culture*. Cambridge: Cambridge University Press, 1997.

Ziegler, Joseph, ed. *Ezechiel*. Septuaginta: vetus testamentum Graecum 16.1. Göttingen: Vandenhoeck & Ruprecht, 1977.

AUTHOR INDEX

A

Albinus · 86
Alexander, Philip · 1, 23, 112, 231, 232, 233, 235
Altermath, F. · 128, 233
Ambrose of Milan · xii, 194
Andía, Ysabel de · 118, 150, 213, 233
Aristotle · 164, 231
Armstrong, Gregory T. · 4, 99, 106, 107, 108, 215, 233
Athanasius · xiii, 13, 44, 125
Attridge, Harold · 52, 102, 231, 233
Augustine · xii, 39, 120, 143, 215, 229, 231
Aulén, Gustaf · 8, 9, 10, 11, 13, 19, 233

B

Bacq, Philippe · 20, 47, 233
Balas, David · 106
Balthasar, Hans Urs von · ix, 234
Barr, James · 21, 22, 24, 25, 28, 234
Barth, Karl · 124, 234
Behr, John · 17, 20, 146, 155, 234
Bethune-Baker, J. F. · 25, 234
Bingham, D. Jeffrey · 106
Blumenberg, Hans · 60, 234
Boersma, Hans · 17, 20, 26, 28, 104, 234

Bousset, Wilhelm · 7, 8, 11, 15, 26, 234
Bouteneff, Peter C. · ix, 234
Brox, Norbert · 112, 234
Brunner, Emil · 8, 12, 19, 26, 110, 119, 124, 234
Burrus, Virginia · 45

C

Cairns, David · 110, 133, 234
Calcidius · 80
Campenhausen, Hans von · 4, 47
Childs, Brevard · 194, 206, 209, 215, 216, 235
Clement of Alexandria · xiii, 17, 113, 184, 190, 212
Constantelos, Demetrios · 132, 235

D

Daniélou, J. · 198, 235
Dawkins, Richard · 226, 235
Dillon, John · 84, 235
Donovan, Mary Ann · 19, 20, 30, 235

E

Epiphanius · xiii, 76
Erasmus, Desiderius · 1, 43, 44, 235
Eusebius · xii, 206

F

Fallon, F. T. · 73, 235
Fantino, J. · 155
Farkasfalvy, D. · 180, 193, 235
Farrow, Douglas · 13, 15, 28, 29, 32, 131, 235
Ferguson, Thomas C. K. · 47, 236
Filoramo, Giovanni · 65, 236
Foerster, Werner · 54, 102, 233, 236
Fredriksen, P. · 80, 81, 236

G

Galen · 118
Goulder, Michael · 117
Grant, Robert M. · 47, 48, 66, 73, 74, 75, 76, 77, 79, 93, 94, 95, 109, 125, 184, 190, 230, 233, 236, 238
Grau, Marion · 45, 236
Greer, Rowan · 36, 236
Gregory of Elvira · 194
Grobel, Kendrick · 77, 236
Gunkel, Hermann · 136, 137, 236
Gunton, Colin · 144, 176, 221, 236

H

Harnack, Adolf von · x, 1, 2, 3, 4, 5, 6, 7, 8, 9, 10, 11, 12, 14, 16, 17, 18, 19, 20, 21, 22, 24, 25, 27, 29, 32, 41, 105, 170, 219, 236
Hart, Trevor · 14, 15, 32, 237
Hick, John · 132
Hoh, Josef · 3, 4, 237

J

Jonsson, Gunnlaugur · 124, 237
Joppich, G. · 146, 157, 161, 237
Justin Martyr · xii, 1, 38, 45, 108, 111, 115, 232

K

Kannengiesser, Charles · 106, 107, 237
Keller, Catherine · 44, 45, 46, 50, 104, 237
Kelly, J. N. D. · 13, 14, 19, 26, 237
Kittel, Gerhard · 25
Klebba, Ernst · 110

L

Lassiat, H. · 162, 237
Lawson, John · 11, 12, 19, 20, 21, 23, 24, 26, 29, 31, 32, 110, 144, 237
Layton, Bentley · 36, 53, 63, 76, 85, 231, 232, 236, 237, 240
Lerch, David · 108, 237
Logan, Alastair H. B. · 52, 54, 55, 237
Loofs, F. · 10, 14, 15, 19, 23, 32, 136, 238
Loughlin, Gerard · 228, 238
Luttikhuizen, Gerard · 57

M

MacKenzie, Iain M. · 10, 109, 110, 114, 230, 242

Marcion · 3, 23, 76, 99, 100
Markschies, Christoph · 34, 102, 238
May, Gerhard · 45, 160, 162
McHugh, John · 22, 238
Metzger, Bruce · 155, 238
Minns, Denis · 42, 105, 109, 116, 135, 141, 172, 238

N

Nielsen, J. T. · 99, 100, 128, 238
Noormann, Rolf · 106
Norris, Richard · 106, 108, 114, 141, 238
Nygren, Anders · 9, 19, 238

O

O'Keefe, John J. · ix, 42, 238
O'Regan, Cyril · x, 46, 100, 120, 238
Olson, Mark Jeffrey · 30, 31, 32, 238
Origen · 13, 15, 29, 43, 76, 80, 190, 212, 232
Osborn, Eric · ix, 15, 16, 19, 20, 24, 25, 26, 29, 31, 105, 109, 110, 145, 146, 212, 217, 239

P

Pagels, Elaine · 45, 64, 188, 239
Pearson, Birger · 50, 64, 239
Pelikan, Jaroslav · 14, 19, 239
Perkins, Pheme · 50, 53, 56, 57, 176, 239

Pétrement, Simone · 54, 55, 240
Philo · xii, xiii, 36, 64, 85, 86, 89, 117, 118, 213, 232, 240
Plato · 35, 62, 80, 83, 84, 85, 86, 87, 90, 91, 103, 117, 213, 232, 240
Potter, Roland · 12, 13, 19, 240
Ptolemy · xii, 44, 48, 51, 75, 76, 77, 78, 79, 93, 232

Q

Quasten, Johannes · 12, 26, 181, 240

R

Ratzinger, Joseph · 225, 240
Reno, R. R. · ix, 42, 238
Roukema, Riemer · 95, 240
Runia, David T. · 64, 85, 86, 232, 240
Russell, Norman · 126, 240

S

Sagnard, Francois · 77
Schenke, Hans Martin · 52, 53, 240
Schoedel, William · 109, 112, 118, 238, 240
Sesboüé, Bernard · 110, 149, 213, 218, 240
Simonetti, Manlio · 107, 193, 211, 240
Smith, Christopher · 28, 29, 30, 118, 231, 241
Stanton, Graham · 4, 241

Struker, Arnold · 110

T

Tertullian · xii, xiii, 1, 13, 44, 48, 49, 54, 80, 108, 173, 190, 194, 202, 212, 233
Theophilus of Antioch · xii, 23, 36, 113, 136, 184, 238
Torrance, T. F. · 15, 234, 241
Turner, H. E. W. · 13, 32, 52, 57, 241

U

Unger, Dominic · 73, 75, 92, 146, 231

V

Valentinus · 3, 6, 23, 45, 48, 49, 51, 53, 54, 55, 77, 94, 102, 210, 235
Vallée, Gérard · 50, 241
Verweyen, H. · 152, 241

W

Ward, Graham · 228, 241

Watson, Francis · 9, 150, 152, 215, 238, 241
Webber, Robert E. · xi, 241
Webster, John · 119
Wendt, H. H. · 6, 170, 241
Wilken, Robert Louis · ix, 242
Williams, Jacqueline A. · 94, 95, 96, 97, 98
Williams, Michael Allen · 43, 56, 101
Winden, J. C. M. van · 80
Wingren, Gustaf · 9, 10, 12, 19, 20, 21, 22, 23, 26, 27, 28, 104, 109, 111, 242

X

Xintaras, Xintaras · 110, 111, 242

Y

Young, Frances · 22, 36, 242

Z

Ziegler, Joseph · 194, 195, 242
Zizioulas, John · 228

SCRIPTURE INDEX

Gen 1 · x, 4, 15, 31, 36, 44, 58, 60, 61, 62, 63, 80, 81, 84, 87, 108, 111, 112, 115, 117, 143, 147, 219, 237, 242
  Gen 1.1 · 38, 58, 61, 62, 64, 81, 84, 143
Gen 1.2 · 44, 60, 61, 62, 80, 195
Gen 1.3-2.3 · 84
Gen 1.3-5 · 84
Gen 1.14-17 · 84
Gen 1.26 · x, 2, 19, 26, 27, 31, 33, 35, 38, 39, 40, 42, 58, 63, 64, 65, 88, 98, 104, 107, 108, 109, 110, 111, 112, 113, 114, 115, 116, 117, 118, 119, 120, 122, 123, 124, 126, 127, 129, 130, 131, 132, 133, 135, 136, 137, 138, 139, 140, 141, 142, 143, 144, 146, 147, 153, 154, 155, 162, 170, 172, 174, 175, 188, 198, 211, 213, 214, 217, 219, 220, 222, 223, 224, 226, 227, 229, 237
Gen 2.4 · 84
Gen 2.7 · x, 2, 19, 26, 27, 31, 33, 35, 38, 39, 40, 42, 63, 64, 65, 87, 88, 89, 95, 96, 98, 101, 102, 104, 107, 108, 109, 112, 115, 117, 118, 120, 126, 140, 144, 145, 146, 147, 148, 149, 150, 151, 152, 153, 154, 155, 156, 157, 158, 159, 160, 161, 162, 163, 164, 165, 166, 168, 169, 170, 171, 172, 173, 174, 175, 177, 178, 179, 182, 183, 185, 186, 187, 188, 189, 190, 191, 192, 193, 194, 195, 196, 197, 198, 199, 200, 201, 202, 203, 204, 205, 206, 207, 208, 210, 211, 213, 214, 216, 217, 219, 221, 222, 223, 226, 227, 229
Gen 2.8 · 64
Gen 2.16-17 · 69
Gen 2.17 · 97, 136
Gen 2.21 · 67
Gen 3 · 27, 31, 38, 39, 43, 66, 69, 70, 71, 88, 89, 98, 102, 117, 124, 127, 130, 131, 136, 156, 189, 199, 202, 211, 213, 215, 217
Gen 3.5 · 97
Gen 3.6-7 · 97
Gen 3.15 · 223
Gen 3.21 · 89
Gen 3.22 · 196
Gen 4.10 · 183
Gen 5 · 71, 89, 120
Gen 6.1-4 · 66, 67, 68
Gen 6.3 · 68
Gen 9.5-6 · 183, 184
Gen 12 · 73
Gen 22 · 74, 206
Gen 22.1 · 74
Deut 1.39 · 136
Deut 32.39 · 150
2 Sam 14.17 · 136
2 Sam 19.35 · 136
1 Kings 3.9 · 136
2 Chr 6.4 · 150
Job 10.8 · 149
Psa 19 · 73

Psa 94.5 · 149
Psa 118.73 · 149
Psa 138.5 · 149
Isa 7.10-17 · 137
Isa 7.15 · 136, 137
Isa 7.15-16 · 136
Isa 25.8 · 169, 170, 172, 181
Isa 25.9 · 194
Isa 26.19 · 194
Isa 40.12 · 119
Isa 42.5 · 171
Isa 45.5 · 57, 59, 82
Isa 57.16 · 171
Isa 64.8 · 150
Isa 65.22 · 196
Isa 66.13 · 194
Isa 66.14 · 192, 198
Jer 1.5 · 202
Jer 18.6 · 150
Eze 37 · 191, 193, 194, 195, 196, 197
Eze 37.3 · 195
Eze 37.14 · 195
Dan 5.23 · 150
2 Maccabees 7.23 · 150
Matt 8.9 · 92
Matt 22.20 · 122
Matt 23.35 · 184
Matt 23.37-39 · 134
Matt 27.46 · 75
Mark 12.16 · 122
Mark 15.34 · 75
Luke 1 · 74
Luke 1.66 · 150
Luke 7.8 · 92
Luke 10.29-37 · 122
Luke 11.50 · 183, 184, 191
Luke 11.50-51 · 183, 184

Luke 13.34-35 · 134
Luke 19.10 · 186
Luke 20.24 · 122
John 1 · 34, 37, 81, 82, 153, 154, 183
John 1.1-14 · 154
John 1.4 · 154
John 1.10 · 210
John 1.12 · 210
John 1.13 · 154, 155
John 1.14 · 154, 183
John 1.17 · 154
John 1.45 · 207
John 1.47 · 207
John 3.15-16 · 210
John 3.29 · 74
John 3.36 · 210
John 4.14 · 210
John 4.24 · 210
John 4.36 · 210
John 5 · 198, 206, 207, 208
John 5.21 · 207
John 5.24 · 210
John 5.31-38 · 207
John 5.36 · 208
John 5.39 · 210
John 5.45-47 · 207
John 6.27 · 210
John 6.40 · 210
John 6.47 · 210
John 6.54 · 210
John 6.68 · 210
John 8.12 · 205
John 8.25 · 205
John 9 · 101, 112, 191, 192, 193, 194, 196, 197, 198, 200, 201, 202, 203, 204, 205, 206, 207, 208, 210, 211, 212, 215

John 9.1-7 · 205
John 9.2-3 · 205
John 9.3 · 199
John 9.5 · 205
John 9.6 · 101, 112, 206, 208, 212, 214, 216
John 9.10 · 208
John 9.15 · 208
John 9.16 · 208
John 9.26 · 208
John 9.29 · 207, 208
John 9.30, 33 · 208
John 9.32 · 208
John 9.37 · 205
John 9.39 · 205
John 9.41 · 205
John 10.1-16 · 206
John 10.28 · 210
John 12.50 · 210
John 15.1-6 · 206
John 17.2 · 210
John 17.3 · 210
John 20.22 · 88
Acts 9.8 · 177
Acts 11.21 · 150
Rom 1.28 · 23
Rom 5 · 97, 126, 128, 152, 153
Rom 5.12 · 151, 152
Rom 5.12-21 · 151
Rom 5.14 · 150, 152
Rom 6.11 · 169
Rom 6.12 · 175, 190
Rom 6-7 · 190
Rom 7 · 190, 215
Rom 7.5 · 190
Rom 8 · 163, 171
Rom 8.11 · 163
Rom 11.17. · 167
Rom 11.36 · 35
Rom 13.9 · 126
Rom 14.9 · 121
1 Cor 2.14 · 90
1 Cor 3.16 · 162
1 Cor 6.9 · 168
1 Cor 15 · 8, 30, 31, 35, 39, 75, 88, 89, 90, 94, 97, 108, 145, 146, 147, 149, 151, 152, 153, 164, 165, 166, 168, 171, 172, 178, 190
1 Cor 15.20-23 · 97
1 Cor 15.22 · 89, 149, 151, 173
1 Cor 15.28 · 94
1 Cor 15.35 · 164
1 Cor 15.36-44 · 163
1 Cor 15.44 · 151
1 Cor 15.45 · 90, 170, 171
1 Cor 15.46 · 39, 170
1 Cor 15.47 · 88
1 Cor 15.49 · 167
1 Cor 15.50 · 8, 30, 31, 75, 108, 146, 155, 165, 166, 168, 175, 178, 181, 182, 183, 184, 185, 189, 190, 191, 194, 214, 216
1 Cor 15.53 · 167
1 Cor 15.54 · 169
2 Cor 4.4 · 213
2 Cor 4.11 · 181
2 Cor 5.4 · 181
Gal 1.15 · 176, 202
Gal 1.15-16 · 176
Gal 5.22 · 168
Eph 1.10 · 15, 22, 34, 35, 37, 38, 126
Eph 1.23 · 94
Col 1.15 · 78
Col 1.19 · 79

Col 2.9 · 35, 79, 93
Col 2.19 · 190
Col 3.11 · 35
1 Thess 5.23 · 162
Heb 10.31 · 150
1 Peter 1.2 · 158
1 Peter 5.6 · 150

www.ingramcontent.com/pod-product-compliance
Lightning Source LLC
Chambersburg PA
CBHW030515080526
44586CB00011B/192